From a turbulent and stormy personal life punctu-
ated by the crises of three unsuccessful marriages,
Sweden's greatest dramatist, August Strindberg,
forged a series of plays challenging the tone and
technique of contemporary dramatic literature.
Employing impressionistic scenery, pantomime,
symbolism, natural dialogue, and a modern theory
of tragedy, he molded a new drama based on the
naturalistic depiction of human conflicts.

Although a highly controversial figure in his own
day, Strindberg has since been universally
acclaimed for his dramatic power, depth of insight,
and technical brilliance. He has directly influenced
the works of Eugene O'Neill, Elmer Rice, Arthur
Miller, Jean Anouilh, and Sean O'Casey. Bernard
Shaw contributed his Nobel Prize money to have
the untranslated plays of Strindberg rendered into
English for the first time.

Ten of the thirteen plays in this volume of Strindberg's
complete one-act prose plays appear for the first time
in modern translation by Arvid Paulson. Mr. Paulson,
who has translated more works from the Scandinavian
languages than any other man, has been knighted by the
King of Sweden for his contribution to the cultural and
literary ties with the United States. He has been awarded
a gold medal by the Royal Swedish Academy of Letters,
the first time the award has been given for the translation of Swedish literature.

David Cirone
1995

Strindberg's
One-Act Plays

TRANSLATED
FROM THE SWEDISH BY

Arvid Paulson

INTRODUCTION BY
Barry Jacobs

WSP
WASHINGTON SQUARE PRESS · NEW YORK

STRINDBERG'S ONE-ACT PLAYS

A *Washington Square Press* edition

1st printing .... April, 1969

All rights of reproduction and of performance,
professional and amateur, are strictly reserved.
Inquiries should be addressed to Washington Square
Press, a division of Simon & Schuster, Inc., 630
Fifth Avenue, New York, N.Y. 10020.

L

Published by
Washington Square Press, a division of Simon & Schuster, Inc.,
630 Fifth Avenue, New York, N.Y.

WASHINGTON SQUARE PRESS editions are distributed in the
U.S. by Simon & Schuster, Inc., 630 Fifth Avenue, New
York, N.Y. 10020 and in Canada by Simon & Schuster
of Canada, Ltd., Richmond Hill, Ontario, Canada.

CONTENTS

INTRODUCTION

I

In the summer of 1908, two of the leading insurgents in the series of revolts that produced the modern theatre met in Stockholm under rather picturesque circumstances. The shock of recognition between August Strindberg and George Bernard Shaw was not very great. According to August Falck's version of the story, Shaw telephoned Strindberg one morning and suggested that they meet at two o'clock that afternoon. Strindberg is said to have replied (in German), "At —two—o'clock—I—am—going—to—be—sick!" and hung up.[1]

Shaw apparently liked this retort, for he made it the curtain line in each of his versions of their encounter. One of his primary reasons for visiting Strindberg was to encourage him to appoint William Archer as his English translator. In a postcard to Archer, Shaw quotes the line to signify that his mission had been a failure. Shaw writes that, as soon as he mentioned Archer's name, Strindberg terminated the discussion by objecting that Archer was not in sympathy with him. Shaw describes the ensuing awkwardness: "After some further conversation, consisting mainly of embarrassed silences and a pale smile or two by A. S., and floods of energetic eloquence in a fearful lingo, half-French, half-German, by G. B. S., Strindberg took out his watch and said in German, 'At two o'clock I am going to be sick.' The visitors accepted this delicate intimation and withdrew."[2]

Whatever the actual circumstances that provoked this ut-

---

[1] August Falck, *Fem år med Strindberg* (Stockholm, 1935), pp. 170ff.

[2] Cited by Hesketh Pearson, *G.B.S., A Full Length Portrait* (New York, 1942), p. 277.

terance may have been, Strindberg was aware that he had been rude to Shaw and hastened to make amends. Although the Intimate Theatre (established by August Falck the previous year for the purpose of performing Strindberg's plays) was closed for the summer, he sent for Falck and Manda Björling and asked them to arrange a special, private performance of *Miss Julie* in honor of Shaw. With considerable difficulty Falck reassembled a few stagehands and musicians, and, on July 15, Strindberg proudly showed Shaw around the small store-front theatre and then they watched a performance of the play. Whereas Strindberg, who had not seen *Miss Julie* since 1889, was deeply moved, Falck suspected that Shaw, who knew no Swedish, was both bored and a bit disappointed to find an old-fashioned piece of naturalism in what was then supposed to be the most advanced experimental theatre in the world.

Like all anecdotes, however, this one has another side. Shaw's arrival in Stockholm happened to coincide with the culmination of a very complex crisis in Strindberg's life, and the publication of part of his *Occult Diary* a few years ago enables us to imagine the meeting from Strindberg's point of view. Although he had been divorced from his third wife, Harriet Bosse, since 1904, Strindberg had been deeply distressed to learn on April 4, 1908, that she was engaged to be married to Axel Wingård, a prominent actor. Indeed, the announcement of her forthcoming marriage precipitated a mental crisis that bears many resemblances to the much more famous "Inferno crisis" that Strindberg underwent between 1894 and 1897. During the month of April, Harriet was constantly in his thoughts, and he began to imagine that she was visiting him "telepathically," that while the real Harriet was with Wingård her "double" was making erotic advances to Strindberg. Indeed, so vividly did he experience her presence that for a time he could no longer separate dream from reality. As her wedding day approached, his mental anguish was gradually translated into intense physical suffering. In May he began to be bothered by electrical currents and gastric attacks, which he at first attributed to the astral projections of the side of Harriet that—he was now convinced—hated him. He sensed that her erethic visits were pushing him toward suicide. On May 21 he purchased a revolver. Throughout this crisis he wrote passionate letters to Harriet, who was tormented by her inability to make him understand her side of the story. By the beginning of June he was hardly able to take any food, and on June 24 he made his last entry in the diary: "Dreadful days! So dreadful that I shall no longer describe them! I only pray to God to let me die, and thus escape from this terrible physical and spiritual agony." On the same day, he became aware of the real cause of his pain and wrote to his publisher, "I am sure that I have cancer of the stomach. I am in pain for twelve hours out of the twenty-four."[3]

This was Shaw's cue line. Juxtaposed to the grim reality behind it, this little anecdote becomes worthy of Pirandello. In search of an author, Shaw found instead a character. Shaw's pardonable ignorance of the man behind the character caused him—on that occasion—to be more impressed by Strindberg's apparent eccentricity than by Falck's production of *Miss Julie*. Unfortunately, a great many subsequent critics have either followed Shaw in this and concentrated upon the bizarrely comic aspects of his behavior or—what is perhaps even worse —they have been morbidly preoccupied with the pageant of Strindberg's bleeding heart. Or a combination of the two: the crazed Strindberg firing a pistol in a café to see which of the guests would be most frightened; the diabolical Strindberg among his crucibles and athanors seeking the formula for gold; the saintly Strindberg clasping the Bible and murmuring "All is atoned for" with his dying breath. In short, we have tended to be more interested in the legend of Strindberg than in his work.

Having already discovered the dramatist who was to dominate our dramatic tradition for half a century—Henrik Ibsen —Shaw did not immediately abandon his search for Strindberg. He wrote to him twice in March, 1910, begging him to have his early fairy-tale play, *Lucky Per's Journey*, translated into English. This Christmas fantasy had been Strindberg's most popular play in Sweden, and Shaw apparently felt that in England it might enjoy the same seasonal success as Barrie's *Peter Pan* and Maeterlinck's *The Blue Bird*. Anticipating an objection on Strindberg's part, he intimated that the production of Strindberg's *A Midsummer Night's Dream* would make

---

[3] August Strindberg, *Ur Ockulta Dagboken*, ed. T. Eklund (Stockholm, 1963), p. 176 (trans. Barry Jacobs).

the London public intensely eager to see his *Hamlet*. But was
the London public really ready for Strindberg's *Hamlet*?

Probably not. As Shaw no doubt realized, it would have
been considerably more difficult to create a taste for Strindberg in London than it had been to introduce Ibsen. Whereas
Ibsen wrote for the existing theatre of illusion and—after
they had recovered from their initial shock—for existing
theatre audiences, Strindberg is the first great dramatist whose
reputation now rests primarily on plays that were unplay-
able in the theatre of his time: they were either intense one-
act plays that were a bit shocking even to select audiences of
"advanced" theatre-goers (and unthinkable in commercial
playhouses), or else they were visionary pilgrimages like *To
Damascus* or *A Dream Play* that no theatre was then equipped
to produce.

Stage history is illuminating in this connection. Ibsen's
plays are full of rewarding parts, especially for actresses, and
many an actress became famous playing them. But although
Strindberg created most of the demanding female roles in his
plays specifically for his actress-wives, Siri von Essen and
Harriet Bosse, he really wrote for directors: Max Reinhardt,
Olof Molander, Ingmar Bergman—even Antonin Artaud—
owe more to Strindberg than any actress does. Ibsen's modern plays were eagerly awaited and—except for *Ghosts*—immediately put into production all over Europe. *Miss Julie*, on
the other hand, was not produced in Sweden until nearly
twenty years after it was written; before that it had one private production in Copenhagen in 1889, one performance at
the *Freie Bühne* in 1892, and one at the *Théâtre libre* in 1893.
By the time that Swedish audiences were hearty enough to
take *Miss Julie* in their stride—it was performed 134 times at
the Intimate Theatre—Strindberg was shocking and outraging
them with his "chamber plays." Thus *The Pelican*, which
Falck used to open the Intimate Theatre in 1907, was a total
failure and remained so until Max Reinhardt emphasized its
surrealistic qualities in his stunning production of it in 1920.

Audiences, however, were generally quicker to adapt to the
demands that Strindberg placed on them than theatres were.
The Royal Theatre was not technically equipped to produce
A Dream Play properly until nearly thirty-five years after it
was written. Max Reinhardt's production of it in 1921 was
more interesting than successful, and Artaud's eccentric stag-

ing of the play in 1928 ended in a riot. Indeed, *A Dream Play* did not come into its own until 1935 when, by using all the resources of the modern theatre to superimpose a dream landscape on a realistic set, Olof Molander mounted it brilliantly. Ibsen made theatre history; before he could do the same, Strindberg had to make a new theatre. He did not, of course, remake the theatre single-handedly; but he did play a decisive part in the destruction of old theatrical conventions and in the development of a new kind of drama.

Although the number of theatres increased and the theatre audiences continued to swell throughout the nineteenth century, the drama steadily declined. Whereas one of the leaders of the Romantics, Victor Hugo, proclaimed in 1827 that the *drame* is the goal toward which everything in modern poetry leads, one of the pioneers of literary naturalism, Edmond de Goncourt, confidently predicted in 1879 that in fifty years the novel would have killed the drama. Goncourt saw nothing in the cheerful banality of the well-made play or in the moralistic rhetoric of the thesis play—the two forms that dominated the theatre at the time—to suggest that the theatre of illusion could satisfy his novelistic demand for subtle psychological dissection. But other Naturalists, like Zola, Desprez, and Jullien, were attracted by the immediacy of theatrical presentation and hoped to bring all of life into the theatre, to use the stage as a means of popularizing their literary ideas. To this end they prescribed various formulas and excisions that they hoped would enable the drama to regain its lofty position in the hierarchy of the arts. Zola called for contemporary plays with realistic sets and even adapted several of his own novels for the stage, but no Naturalist seemed capable of capturing a theatre audience. By the end of the 1870s, the crisis of the drama had reached its peak; the question was no longer whether the theatre could carry naturalism, but whether naturalism could carry the theatre.

In formulating the law of the drama in 1893, Ferdinand Brunetière lent support to Goncourt's position by explaining why the drama had not been able to adapt to the positivistic assumptions of the age: whereas the central figure in a novel is constantly acted upon by outside forces, the dramatic hero must try to dominate circumstances in order to arrive at his goal. Although Brunetière reproves the French Naturalists for confusing motion with action, that is, for violating the conditions of the species by trying to dramatize the wrong subjects, he locates the ultimate source of their failure in the intellectual climate of the time. To write drama one must believe in free will; belief in determinism will quite obviously favor the progress of the novel. Between Goncourt's assertion and Brunetière's observation lies one of the most exciting decades in the history of the drama, the decade that saw the birth of the modern theatre in the controversial works of Ibsen and Strindberg.

Brunetière was not interested in practical solutions to the crisis that the drama was undergoing, and he failed to notice that it had, in fact, survived, that Goncourt's rejection of both the drama and the theatre was but the simplest of three obvious alternatives. Ibsen chose the most difficult of these: he left the theatre alone, but changed the drama. Perhaps it is because Ibsen did believe that man is, to a certain extent, the architect of his own destiny that he was able to transform the shallow well-made play into a dramatic form as powerful as the one Zola had envisioned. Indeed, in the very year that Goncourt turned his back on the hopeless artificiality of the stage, Ibsen created so perfect an illusion of reality in *A Doll's House* that audiences and critics immediately treated his heroine like a real person. Not only did Nora become the subject of endless drawing-room debates, but a German psychiatrist, Erich Wulffen, even devoted a whole book to a study of her "case." Heightened surface realism was one of the secrets of Ibsen's success. His characters are preoccupied with real things like macaroons, promissory notes, and Christmas trees. So skillfully did he exploit the relations between his characters and their environment that he was able to use sets and props to suggest a psychological complexity that Goncourt had considered beyond the scope of the theatre. Moreover, by dramatizing the aftermath of an action, that is, by linking the dramatic device of gradual revelation of the past with the "ghosts" in the past lives of his characters, Ibsen found a way to make psychological development his main subject. By means of these and other reforms of tired dramatic conventions, Ibsen remade the drama, but he did not resolve all the problems that the French Naturalists had uncovered in their considerations of the drama and the theatre.

By founding the *Théâtre libre* in 1887, André Antoine became the first man of the theatre to attempt the third alternative, to destroy "the theatre"—the established, popular, middle-class institution, which was the only theatre Goncourt had considered—in order to create an audience. Though he was only an amateur, a self-educated clerk in the Paris Gas Company, Antoine managed to transform a little band of deserters from the conventional theatre into an important avantgarde movement. His program was loosely based on Zola's formula for the modern drama—realistic sets and subject matter, simple and natural presentation—but he did not limit his repertory to naturalistic plays. During five successive seasons, he presented a select Parisian audience with a wide variety of plays, ranging from grim naturalistic tragedies like Tolstoi's *The Power of Darkness* to verse comedies like Theodore de Banville's *Le Baiser*. More important than any production he mounted, however, was the idea he launched, the idea of the experimental theatre that directly inspired others to follow his example. In 1889 Otto Brahm opened the *Freie Bühne* in Berlin, the theatre that was to establish the reputation of Gerhardt Hauptmann; in London two years later J. T. Grein founded the Independent Theatre, where G. B. S. got his start. The first playwright to see the possibilities in this fruitful idea was August Strindberg. Just a few days after Antoine's first successful performance, Strindberg, who had seen a newspaper account of the opening night, wrote to a friend suggesting that they found a small itinerant theatre: "Only do plays by August Strindberg and none of his earlier works. I shall write plays that will free us from the necessity of dragging costumes, decorations, and props along with us."[4]

Strindberg had very good reasons for making this proposal. Ever since 1879, when he created a sensation with the brilliant social satire in his first novel, *The Red Room*, his protest against all forms of established authority had become increasingly shrill. His antifeminism in particular had offended a great many people. Finding Sweden hopelessly stuffy and provincial, he had finally moved his family to Switzerland in 1883. The next year he had to return to Stockholm to face trial for blasphemy because of a slighting reference he had made to the Eucharist in one of his works. Although he was

---

[4] August Strindberg, *Samlade Brev,* ed. T. Eklund (Stockholm, 1948 to date), VI, p. 215 (trans. Barry Jacobs).

acquitted—and thereby became the hero of the younger generation—there was a strong reaction against him in conservative quarters. Swedish publishers were already wary of him when (in 1887) J. W. Personne attacked him in a famous pamphlet entitled "Strindberg Literature and Immorality among Schoolboys"; after that he often found it difficult even to publish in Sweden, and theatre directors would certainly not risk producing his new plays.

An author in search of an audience, Strindberg was quick to see the importance of Antoine's undertaking. Knowing that *The Father* (which he wrote in the spring of 1887) was hardly likely to succeed in Scandinavia, he immediately translated it into French and sent it to Zola and to Antoine. Perhaps now he could realize his recurring dream of literary conquest in France. But Zola damned the play with faint praise, and Antoine rejected it. Consequently, Strindberg's only hope of gaining a hearing was to start a theatre of his own, and he set about providing himself with a repertory of plays that could be produced on a shoestring by a tiny company. *Miss Julie*, which he wrote in the summer of 1888, was his first experiment with this concentrated form, and in the prefatory essay he outlines the principles that underlie this new genre and calls attention to his greatest innovation, "the characterless character."

Before the establishment of the avant-garde theatre, all the many forms of the one-act play constituted a miscellaneous minor genre, a collection of curtain-raisers. Following the example of Zola (and a number of minor French Naturalists), Strindberg, Hauptmann, and Maeterlinck exploited the *quart d'heure*—the short play with a single set—and transformed it into a major genre. As Strindberg indicated in the preface to *Miss Julie*, simplification and concentration of the drama is advantageous both to producers and to the public: the producer saves money and—by getting the kernel of the drama without having to bother with the husk of exposition, complication, and the like—the impatient modern audience saves time. But the greatest beneficiary of the new dramaturgy, as Strindberg shows in another important essay—"On Modern Drama and Modern Theatre" (1889)—is really the playwright. "Every play really seems to be written for the sake of one scene," he argues; therefore it is pointless for an author to waste his energies on the complicated superstructure of a full-length play.[5]

As this statement indicates, the new one-act form is not a whole action in miniature, but a part of a play—usually the penultimate moment—that can stand alone. Using this form, social determinists like Hauptmann and metaphysical determinists like Maeterlinck found a way around Brunetière's distinction between action and motion. For them, drama is neither action nor motion, but situation: nothing can happen that will change the course of events. In other words, they free the single scene from the larger structure by reducing volition to velleity. During the 1880s, Strindberg was as much under the shadow of Darwin as any literary Naturalist, but he differed from most of them in one very important respect. Because their interest in heredity and environment is almost exclusively centered on the past, many Naturalists tended to see life as a kind of trap, a view that Strindberg referred to as "little naturalism." But Strindberg, who felt that he represented "great naturalism," was interested in determinism as it manifests itself in the present, that is (in Darwinian terms), in the modification of living forms under the selective influence of environment. This difference in emphasis led him to a conception of drama as distinct from theirs as it is from Brunetière's. Indeed, his plays are about change.

Using a philological observation that he had borrowed from Nietzsche, Strindberg redefined drama in "On Modern Drama and Modern Theatre": "In archaic Greek, 'drama' apparently meant not 'action' (or what we call conscious intrigue), but 'occurrence.' As a matter of fact, life does not by any means fall into the neat patterns that one finds in a constructed drama, and so rarely do conscious intriguers have the opportunity to carry out their plans in detail that we have ceased to believe in those sly schemers who are given free rein to manage and arrange other human destinies."[6] Far from committing himself to a principle of fortuity here, Strindberg identifies action with contrivance merely in order to place human volition in the proper perspective. His plays "happen," and the conscious goals of his characters are con-

---

[5] August Strindberg, *Samlade Skrifter,* ed. J. Landquist (Stockholm, 1912–1922), XVII, p. 299 (trans. Barry Jacobs).

[6] *Ibid.,* p. 298.

stantly being modified by the changing situation. This theory of the drama complements his conception of the "character-less character" and allows him to create characters who continue to exercise free will—whose brains are capable of a multiplicity of choices, even though their psyches are as delicate and as volatile as cloud formations. Plot was precisely what Strindberg had to destroy in order to put his conception of the one-act psychodrama into effect. In doing so, he created a kind of theatre that still has much to teach us about dramatic art.

II

The biblical allusion in the title of Strindberg's famous auto-biography, *The Son of a Servant* (1886), calls attention to his bitter conception of the artistic outsider: Ishmael, the outcast. Whether he appeared as reformer or renegade, as anarchist or advocate of mankind, throughout his career Strindberg cast himself in a series of thankless pariah roles that all betray the same deep nostalgia for the values of the bourgeois society with which he was generally at odds. From time to time he dreamed of being reconciled with hostile authority by a woman's "pure" love, and like the Captain in *The Dance of Death*, each time his hope was disappointed he "crossed out and went on."

The initial cause for Strindberg's ambiguous attitude toward middle-class society was no doubt the social gap between his parents and his family's precarious economic situation during his childhood and youth. Whereas his father was the son of a successful and respected Stockholm businessman, his mother (the daughter of a poor tailor) really had been a servant. Moreover, they already had three illegitimate children at the time of their marriage in 1847. Johan August Strindberg, born in 1849, was the fourth of eleven children in a family whose fortunes vacillated between relative poverty and modest prosperity, depending on the father's success in business. In 1862 his mother died and his father soon remarried. Although the actual circumstances of his childhood were somewhat less wretched than he has painted them, he was a neurotic child full of anxiety and guilt feelings that made his psychological experience of childhood a nightmare.

Parallel to the conditions that produced Strindberg's feelings of social inferiority was a set of conflicting intellectual and emotional patterns that hindered his psychological development. His father was cold and reserved, quick to punish his children and slow to forgive them. Although Strindberg feared his father, he nevertheless admired his self-reliance. Opposed to his father's forbidding "Icelandic nature" and his rational theism was his mother's anti-intellectual and lachrymose pietism with its emphasis on self-abnegation. Shortly after her death, Strindberg became a pietist, and for nearly two years he vainly sought comfort and peace in a religion that stressed sin and guilt. Liberation from his growing melancholy and remorse—his "old self," as he called it—came from an unexpected quarter: in the optimistic unitarianism of "the Great American Preacher" and universal reformer, Theodore Parker, he found the vigorous denial of radical evil coupled with the inspiring, idealistic zeal for reform that laid the foundations of the whole first phase of his career. But his earlier religious attitudes led a subterranean life beneath his "new" Parkerian self and emerged whenever excessive strain precipitated a nervous crisis. By far the most famous and important of these breakdowns was the "Inferno crisis" (1894–1897), but he underwent similar upheavals in 1868, 1873, 1875, 1885–1886, 1904, 1907, and 1910. During each of these crises the conflicting "maternal" and "paternal" facets of his nature as well as his old and his new selves were caught for a time in an agonizing deadlock.

This aspect of Strindberg's psychological development not only helps explain his life-long vacillation between opposed points of view, it also suggests that we risk misunderstanding him if we attempt to use the old-fashioned psychobiographical division of his literary career into three periods: early-Romantic (1869–1879), middle-Naturalistic (1879–1892), and late-Expressionistic (1897–1909). These literary terms are confusing because Strindberg never belonged wholly to any of these traditions; consequently one can easily find "Expressionistic" elements in his "Naturalistic" works, "Naturalistic" elements in his "Expressionistic" works, and certain "Romantic" tendencies in nearly all his works. Therefore, it is perhaps better in dealing with his dramatic works to abandon the "isms" and to describe his development by isolating the five chronological periods during which he wrote plays: (1) 1869–1882, (2) 1886–1889, (3) 1892, (4) 1898–1903 (the only period not represented in this collection), and (5) 1907–1909. The inadequacy of the conventional description of his career is most evident if we try to apply a single label to the third period, which is the shortest, the least impressive, and yet the most typical of his productive periods. In 1892, Strindberg wrote seven plays: the first of these, *The Keys of Heaven*, is a spacious and somewhat sentimental *sagospel* (or fairy play) in five acts, so technically demanding that it has only been staged twice. The other six plays—all included in this volume —are cynical and concentrated "Naturalistic" dramas in one act. The generic principle behind Mr. Paulson's organization of this volume calls attention to a continuity in Strindberg's development as a dramatist that we obscure if we attempt to assign his productive periods to single stylistic categories.

First Period [1869–1882]

In 1867 Strindberg passed his matriculation examination and entered the University of Uppsala, but he was too impatient to concentrate on his studies for very long and too poor to taste many of the pleasures of student life. Between 1867 and 1872, he spent two full terms and parts of two academic years at the university, but since he received very little support from his father, he often had to interrupt his desultory studies in philosophy and modern languages to earn money first as a schoolteacher, then as a private tutor. Discontented with teaching, he became a medical student for a short time, but because he lacked the patience that scientific studies require he failed his examination in chemistry. In the autumn of 1869, he decided to prepare himself for an acting career. Although he dreamed of achieving stardom overnight by playing the leading role in Schiller's *Die Räuber*, he first appeared at the Royal Theatre as a messenger in Bjørnson's *Maria Stuart* with exactly eleven words to speak. When he did get a chance to try a longer part, he proved such a failure at the first rehearsal that he attempted to commit suicide by taking opium.

The morning after this melodramatic gesture, Strindberg became a playwright. As he lay in bed wondering how he could ever face his father and stepmother again, a dramatic scene began to form in his imagination. Four hours later he had completed a little play (now lost) entitled "A Name Day Gift," which depicted a young man's reconciliation with his stepmother. Such was the inauspicious beginning of an astonishingly rapid development that has few parallels in literary history: three years later, at the age of twenty-three, Strindberg wrote *Master Olof,* one of the undisputed masterpieces of nineteenth-century dramatic literature.

During his first year as a writer, Strindberg experimented with several dramatic forms. He wrote a full-length problem play, *The Freethinker,* about an implacable young teacher who loses his job, his family, and his fiancée because he will not renounce the teachings of Theodore Parker. A female variant of this protagonist next appeared in classical dress in *Hermione,* a five-act play in blank verse. An episode from the early life of the great sculptor Thorvaldsen—the young artist forced to choose between starving for his art or entering the business world—provided the subject for his first successful work, a one-act verse play entitled *In Rome.* In the autumn of 1870, Strindberg returned to Uppsala determined to comply with his father's wish that he take a degree, and to this end he began the study of Old Norse literature.

However they defined tragedy, Romantic aestheticians tended to agree that the greatest tragic subjects were to be found in periods of violent change, in the conflict of ideas or of religious ideologies. Adhering to this notion, many nineteenth-century Scandinavian writers found their two richest quarries in the confrontation of dying Hellenism with nascent Christianity and in the turbulent history of viking resistance to the spread of Christianity. Stimulated by the current popularity of Norse plays based on this aesthetic principle and inspired by his reading of the Sagas, Strindberg felt ready to try a full-scale tragedy and soon abandoned his studies to work on a play about Blotsven, a Swedish counterpart to Julian the Apostate. Had it been completed, *Blotsven* would have been a vast political tragedy with religious overtones, similar perhaps to *Emperor and Galilean,* which Ibsen was working on at the same time. With considerable anguish, however, Strindberg burned the play after it failed to win the approval of the members of a literary club to which he belonged. Out of the ashes, as he says in the preface to *Miss Julie,* arose *The Outlaw*.

The Outlaw is Strindberg's first important play. Though it did not win critical acclaim for its author, it did please one member of the audience, King Charles XV, who summoned Strindberg to the royal palace and rewarded him with a scholarship. Generically, it is the direct ancestor of all the plays in this collection, as Strindberg indicates in the preface to *Miss Julie,* where he refers to this work as his first experiment with a concentrated form of drama. Thematically, however, it looks forward to the great penitential dramas of his fourth period. Indeed, Strindberg's characterization of Thorfinn, the hero (in a letter to the actor who created the part of Orm in the first production), is equally applicable to the Stranger, the protagonist of *To Damascus:* "a self-sufficient person who is forced to acknowledge a higher being, a Titan, or Prometheus who fights against the gods."[7] Finally, it is the first of Strindberg's plays to exhibit his characteristically ambiguous use of symbols and thereby to present serious problems of interpretation.

Like Strindberg's comic oversight in letting Gunnar arrive in Iceland bearing fresh flowers from Sweden, many of the obvious faults in this play can be attributed to the fact that it is a conflation of a much larger work. For example, the characterization of Gunnar and Gunlöd was presumably not so fragmentary and inconsistent in the original tragedy. But the real difficulty in this little play resides in the central symbol, the silver falcon. Although Gunlöd has secretly become a Christian, she remains loyal to her pagan father and refuses to flee with Gunnar, who represents the Christian point of view in the play. Gunnar describes her internal conflict by referring to the heraldic device on his shield: ". . . and you will come, meek as the dove seeking shelter, even though now you—like the falcon—would fly beyond the clouds. . . . I still hold the leash in my hand—it is your love. It still ties you to me, and you cannot tear it away!"[8] These two sides of

[7] A. Strindberg, *Samlade Brev,* I, p. 80 (trans. Barry Jacobs).
[8] p. 11.

her nature—tender love and overweening pride—define the poles of Thorfinn's psychological development.

We gather from the exposition that Thorfinn's pride and his faith in his own strength have always isolated him from his family. At the time of his entrance, his self-sufficiency has also isolated him politically, for he learns that he has been declared an outlaw and that his enemies have already surrounded his house. At the height of the ensuing battle, which we only witness through the eyes of Gunlöd, the silver falcon reappears. This is the turning point in the play. Of course, Gunlöd sees and describes the falcon on Gunnar's shield, but she never reveals which side he and his men support. Taking the falcon to be a real bird, Valgerd reinterprets it symbolically; she thinks it must be an evil omen—as in fact it proves to be: Thorfinn is immediately wounded. But the fact that he enters the house a changed man suggests that the symbol has been expanded so that it now links the psychological poles of the action. Before he dies—apparently submitting to God—Thorfinn shows that his Viking spirit has been quelled, that he is finally ready to acknowledge the tender love of his wife and daughter. The intentional ambiguity in Strindberg's use of this symbol adumbrates the virtuosity of his later style. Indeed, this falcon foretokens the central symbol in the last play in this collection, *The Pelican*.

In the middle of his first period of dramaturgic activity, Strindberg became discouraged and—when his third reworking of *Master Olof* was rejected by the Royal Theatre in 1876—turned to other forms. At about the same time, he came under the influence of the great Danish critic Georg Brandes, who thought that literature should deal with contemporary issues. During the early 1880s, Strindberg directed his attention to problems resulting from the decadence of modern culture; in particular, he attacked outmoded forms of government and new-fangled ideas about women's rights. The title of one of his most important works from this period, *Utopias in Reality,* suggests that his reforming zeal was still very much alive. Inspired by the belated success of *Master Olof* in 1881 (and hoping to further the acting career of his first wife), he returned to the drama and wrote three long plays early in the 1880s, *Lucky Per's Journey, Sir Bengt's Wife,* and *The Secret of the Guild*.

This little burst of dramatic activity was short-lived, however, and he had little chance of succeeding in the popular theatre after 1884, when he was tried for blasphemy. Also, one notices many new elements in his work during the early 1880s. He gradually lost interest in social issues, and by 1886 he had renounced the social altruism of his early period in favor of ethical nihilism very much in the spirit of Schopenhauer and Hartmann. His former egalitarian principles were replaced with the idea of the intellectual superman that he found in Max Nordau's works. Finally, influenced by Naturalists like Paul Bourget and the Goncourt brothers, he turned from the problems of society to study the psychology of the individual. This transition was complete by the spring of 1887 when, besides writing *The Father,* he published a collection of short stories and essays entitled *Vivisections.* Vivisection (or psychological dissection) is the principal theme of most of the plays he wrote during his second and third periods of dramaturgic activity.

Second Period [1886–1889]

During the latter part of the 1880s, Strindberg absorbed from a number of different sources the ideas that eventually inspired him to return to the drama. He followed Max Nordau both in dividing humanity into two intellectual types, "the great" and "the small" (or the stronger and weaker brains), and in attributing all progress to the mental activity of a few superior individuals, who transmit the increased molecular activity of their brains to the less intelligent masses. Likening this process to mass hypnotism, Nordau called it "suggestion," which in a slightly different form was the aspect of mesmerism that had attracted Romantic writers like Poe and E. T. A. Hoffmann—two of Strindberg's favorite authors during these years. The demonstrable power of posthypnotic suggestion was also the point of departure for two direct extensions of mesmerism in the latter part of the nineteenth century: French psychology and German parapsychology. Whereas some French scientists—like Taine and Ribot—used the evidence of hypnosis to support and elaborate their study of the role of association in cognition, others—like Bernheim and the Nancy School of psychologists—studied hypnosis and suggestion in order to sound the depths of the human personality. Bernheim's investigations led him to reject the older notion that a high degree of suggestibility is a morbid symptom and to conclude that the malleability of the hypnotized subject is but an intensification of normal receptiveness—in short, that suggestion is possible in the waking state. Both Ibsen's *The Lady from the Sea* (1888) and Strindberg's *Miss Julie* (1888) are based on this fruitful idea.

By keeping abreast of new developments in clinical psychology Strindberg aligned himself with the naturalism of Paul Bourget and the Goncourt brothers. His deviation from their purely analytical approach to psychological problems is largely the result of the stimulus he received around the same time from a number of German spiritists. Extending mesmeristic notions of animal magnetism, German monists like du Prel and von Hellenbach speculated at length about mental telepathy and the properties of our "astral bodies." Although Strindberg remained skeptical about many of the findings of the occult sciences until he was liberated from determinism during his "Inferno crisis," he was immediately attracted by their belief in some sort of electrical nerve "fluidum," the medium through which spiritual emanations (or brain waves) travel. In combination with current theories of subliminal response, a belief in this mysterious substance provided the ideal culture in which Strindberg could grow his famous vampire theory of psychic assimilation.

In January 1887, Strindberg wrote to a friend that he had invented a new genre, "The Battle of the Brains," which is the title of one of the short stories in *Vivisections*. Had he simply wished to call attention to man's ever-diminishing dependence on brute strength in the struggle for survival, he might have chosen a Swedish equivalent of "battle of wits," but that phrase would have placed sharp restrictions on the biological basis of his whole conception of psychological conflict. For one thing, it might have suggested that mere intelligence is the best insurance against extinction and thereby obscured the central problem that he wished to treat: the paradoxical nature of strength. One cannot fail to notice that his intellectually fittest characters generally succumb to the animal cunning of the lower human forms, the vampires, against whom they are pitted.

The recurrent defeat of the superior individual in Strindberg's works is a function of his refusal to identify evolution with progress. Partly an extension of his earlier tendency to equate cultivation with decadence—his legacy from Rousseau—Strindberg's pessimism about human development was deepened by his reading of Schopenhauer and Hartmann. This outlook, in turn, made him very receptive to one of the amendments to the theory of natural selection, the so-called "law of the unspecialized." Thus distantly behind his choice of terms lies the observation of certain nineteenth-century paleontologists that the most highly organized and dominant forms in one geological era have usually evolved not from the master type of the preceding period, but from lower and less specialized forms that were capable of adapting to changes in their environment. One of the immediate sources for his paradox of the stronger and his vampire theory of human interaction was Lombroso's comprehensive study of the "criminal type," which seemed to many Naturalists to offer scientific proof that it is possible to isolate degenerate somatotypes and to reduce personalities to a formula.

"The battle of the brains" is Strindberg's name for hypnosis in the waking state, and it generally results in what he called "psychic murder," which is the subtitle of a famous essay on Ibsen's *Rosmersholm* that he included in *Vivisections*. By connecting the three points we have already located—the "characterless character," the vampire theory, and the paradox of the stronger—we can construct a figure that contains nearly the whole area of suggestibility that Strindberg mapped in the plays he wrote during this period. The "characterless character" is a dynamic conception of the *existing*, ever-changing personality that Strindberg generally reserved for superior individuals who continue to develop. Accretion, not development, is the process that nourishes the vampire, an inferior type—like Tekla in *Creditors*, who can only exist intellectually by draining words and ideas from her husbands. By combining these elements in different ways in each of the plays, Strindberg explores the complexity of the paradox of the stronger.

As a weapon, the power of suggestion is available to all of his characters. Its effectiveness depends entirely upon the receptivity and the resilience of the victim. In *Simoon*, the most straightforward (and by far the most technically demanding) application of these psychological ideas, we watch while Biskra "murders" Guimard in a desert shrine where he has sought refuge during a sandstorm. Capitalizing upon Guimard's heightened suggestibility and the suggestiveness of the milieu, she gradually brings him to the verge of hysteria by creating an atmosphere that coalesces with his emergent hallucination. Her triumph, however, depends upon his cooperation. She knows nothing about his past, but when his consciousness is sufficiently anesthetized, she follows him into his own imagination where she plants the seeds of despair by means of suggestions that galvanize his unconscious suspicions and fears. In the complex little play *Creditors*—Strindberg's favorite among these plays—Gustav (consciously) and Tekla (unconsciously) "murder" Adolph. Tekla is a parasite, a vampire whose flourishing state accounts for the deterioration of Adolph's health in the months just before the action begins. In his weakened condition, Adolph easily falls prey to Gustav's superior intelligence. But even Gustav is not a conscious intriguer of the sort that Strindberg deplored in most literary works. His plan cannot take definite shape until he has confirmed his suspicions that Adolph is a latent epileptic. He feels his way, working by suggestion and by deception until he has maneuvered Adolph into the adjoining room to overhear the shocking self-revelations he is able to elicit from Tekla. Adolph's horrified reaction to his wife's willingness to betray him completes the process that Gustav initiated by acting out the symptoms of epilepsy: he dies as the result of an actual epileptic attack.

Strindberg's use of suggestion is more subtle in *Miss Julie*. Jean first consciously facilitates his erotic conquest of Julie by verbal means: innuendo and suggestive images. Later he sows the idea of suicide in her mind, primarily by his use of objects (the razor and the ax). This is the kind of subliminal suggestion that Strindberg used much more extensively in the two plays that we have already considered. *Miss Julie* is unique, however, in that the heroine briefly enters a real hypnotic state. Finding that she lacks the courage to kill herself, she pleads with Jean to hypnotize her. In effect, she hypnotizes herself. When he obeys her and whispers a command in her ear, this delicate state of mind seems to spread to him. It works like a seesaw. As the effect of his command wears off, she becomes increasingly conscious and he becomes hysterical. Within a few seconds they have returned to their original roles so that when the Count rings, Jean is once more a cowardly menial and Julie a proud aristocrat. One may argue against this interpretation of the ending of the play— Jean does order her to go—but the symbolic sunrise and the stage direction *("Miss Julie . . . walks firmly out through the door")* imply that his command is now quite unnecessary, that she is finally prepared to answer the dictates of her aristocratic sense of honor.

The Stronger and *Pariah* are counterparts. Each deals with the cerebral conflict of two anonymous characters. Strindberg wrote them hastily—along with *Simoon*—in December-January 1888–1889, to add to the repertory for the experimental theatre he was then trying to establish in Copenhagen. He was very much under the spell of Nietzsche and Poe just at the time, and both influences are quite apparent in *Pariah,* which is a dramatization of a short story by a somewhat younger Swedish writer, Ola Hansson. In *The Stronger*—the direct ancestor of modern monodramas like O'Neill's *Before Breakfast* and *Krapp's Last Tape* by Beckett—Mrs. X talks herself into the discovery that she has been the victim of a "psychic murder," that the impulses her husband has transmitted from Miss Y have systematically undermined her taste and refurnished her entire personality. Miss Y's silence gradually makes Mrs. X aware of the irony of her opening speeches: her tastes and opinions, her son's baptismal name, the tulips she must embroider on her husband's slippers, the very chocolate she is drinking have all been imposed upon her by her more intelligent rival. Her retrospective analysis of her false position brings her to the verge of despair, but at the turning point in the play vampire and victim exchange roles. She discovers that it is not preservation of the self, but self-preservation that counts. Though less intelligent, she is stronger (in a Darwinian sense) because she can bend and adapt to her environment. This decision is reversed by a higher court in *Pariah,* where the more intelligent X emerges as the stronger—in a Nietzschean sense. Y is an outcast from the society whose norms he tries to use to blackmail X, but his ruse fails because X is beyond good and evil. Suggestion is subordinated to deduction in this play: Y has purloined the story of how he unconsciously became a forger. Since he is not strong enough either to accept the responsibility for his actions or to transcend his guilt, he is doomed to wander alone.

By the time that he wrote the plays in this group, Strindberg's marriage to Siri von Essen had dwindled into a business partnership. She became the director of the experimental theatre company that they finally managed to assemble in 1889. This period of his dramatic activity ended abruptly when the company closed after one private performance of *Miss Julie* and two public performances of the other plays. Strindberg's net loss came to thirty crowns, seventy-six öre, and what remained of his reputation: the Danish newspapers were demanding that he be deported at once.

Third Period [1892]

Shortly before the failure of the theatrical venture on which Strindberg had pinned his hopes, his friend Nietzsche collapsed on the street in Turin, overcome by a fit of insanity from which he never recovered. When Strindberg returned to Sweden in 1889, he had all but lost faith in the superman's power to control his environment. His family life was extremely unsettled, and he was beset by creditors. In 1891, he and Siri von Essen separated for good and began divorce proceedings. Even his literary future looked bleak, for naturalism, the literary movement with which his name had been connected for a decade, seemed to be dead. *Le Manifeste des Cinq contre La Terre* (1888)—the declaration of independence from Zolaism made by five young French writers—was echoed in Scandinavia by Verner von Heidenstam, who called for a poetic renaissance to replace the "shoemaker realism" that had dominated the 1880s. The cumulative effect of this series of defeats and disappointments in Strindberg's life is immediately evident in his writing. In 1890 he published *By the Open Sea*, a novel about the isolation and dissolution of a superman, who is "brainwashed" by his weaker opponents.

In the autumn of 1891, Strindberg dreamed once more of succeeding in the theatre and began to work on a new play, *The Keys of Heaven*. He obviously hoped to regain his former popularity by adapting the romantic form he had used to such advantage in *Lucky Per's Journey* a decade earlier. Although he was later to revolutionize the drama by twisting this form into *To Damascus* and *A Dream Play*, *The Keys of Heaven* is a diffuse and difficult work that was promptly rejected by several theatre directors. Strindberg then revived his old plan of creating an itinerant theatre, and in March 1892, he began writing a new set of plays. By September he had completed six one-act plays based on the formula he had used in 1888–1889: as few characters and as much tension as possible in the shortest possible time. In "The Author" (the last section of *The Son of a Servant*) he aptly referred to this group of plays as "Scenes from Cynical Life." Although they all fall within the general thematic area that we have already defined, one notices an important shift in emphasis in these plays: Strindberg is now dealing with the emotional rather than the intellectual side of the battle of the brains. Not only does his concentration on love and jealousy make these plays seem more cynical than clinical, it also brings them closer to a popular French form, the *proverbe*, which (in its simplest form) neatly sketches a situation that reaffirms the truth of some familiar proverbial saying.

More witty and playful than anything Strindberg wrote in the preceding period, *The First Warning* is a little play about jealousy, conceived as the invisible bond that holds people together. Because of jealousy, love is a long toothache—biologically bracketed here by two first warnings: just as Rosa's coming wisdom tooth signalizes the beginning of one passionate career, Olga's broken front tooth symbolizes the close of another. Discovering that his wife is now susceptible to jealousy, Brunner reverses his original decision to leave her. A decade later Strindberg wrote the sequel to this play, *The Dance of Death*, which is a kind of last warning.

The most neglected of these plays, *Debit and Credit*, seems to be an ironic self-portrait of Strindberg as he was in 1892. Axel, who is almost a caricature of the superman, is beset by a mob of "small" creditors. But since this battle of brains depends more on vulgar assertion than on subtle suggestion, he easily escapes from the responsibilities that they wish to force upon him. As the "stronger," he feels fully justified in canceling his debts by taking the easy way out—through the back door. But there is no easy way out for the hero of *In the Face of Death,* a modern Lear, who provides dowries for his daughters (there is no Cordelia among them) by committing suicide in his burning house so that they can collect the insurance. Whereas his role as the scapegoat for his wife and children links him with the dead father in *The Pelican,* the mother in that play is already sketched for us in *Motherlove,* where Hélène is shown to be the victim of a psychic murder. *Motherlove,* a bitter epilogue to *The Father,* also bears a certain similarity to *Mrs Warren's Profession* (1894) by Shaw. Hélène's mother is a former prostitute whose jealous "love" for her daughter has become an invisible wall that Hélène cannot break down, even after she learns the truth about her mother's sordid past.

In the first four plays in this group, Strindberg seems to be testing his new subject matter; the last two are masterful studies of love and jealousy. *Playing with Fire*—reminiscent at times of Sardou's *Divorçons*—is Strindberg's most successful comedy. The cliché in the title refers to the inchoate passions that flame up when Axel, a very Strindbergian young man, visits a young couple who live in a Chekhovian atmosphere of tedium and superfluity. In this updating of "The Damsel's Rash Promise," Strindberg poses and answers a modern *questione d'amore.* Moreover, the husband's ingenious resolution of the situation affirms the wisdom of the suppressed proverb on which his action is based: "Burnt child fire dreadeth." Knowing that Axel has just escaped from one wife and has no desire to take another, he graciously offers to step aside so that his wife will be free to marry her new lover. Faced with the consequences of his flirtation, Axel makes a hasty exit ("as though the seat of his pants had been on fire"), the wife collapses in hysterics, and the family sits down to breakfast with renewed appetite.

In *The Bond,* Strindberg examines the tragic nature of love, which he sees as a garment lined with hate. In this case, the invisible love-hate bond is connected with a real bond, the child. This powerful play is the summation of the themes Strindberg had been dealing with ever since he wrote *The Father* in 1887, and it contains echoes of nearly all the intervening works. Because it grows beyond the naturalistic framework of the courtroom situation and takes on allegorical overtones, it also looks forward to some of the masterpieces of his later production. For example, the Baron's conclusion that he and his wife are both to be pitied was to be echoed and applied to all mankind by Indra's Daughter in *A Dream Play*. Strindberg's use of the legal system—both in *A Dream Play* and in *The Pelican*—to symbolize the network of deceit in human life is already implicit in the Judge's mistrust of the imperfect laws he must apply in *The Bond*.

Fifth Period [1907–1909]

Strindberg's "Inferno crisis" was a turning point in his career. The lesson of *Inferno* was the message of *A Dream Play:* "Suffering is redemption." This theme dominates the plays that he wrote during his fourth period of dramaturgic activity, 1897–1903. Although he wrote twenty-six plays in these six years, only one of them—a curious little fantasy about marionettes entitled *Casper's Mardi-Gras* (1900)—bears any generic relation to the works in this collection. One reason for his neglect of the one-act play during this period was the fact that he had finally managed to succeed in Sweden's official and commercial playhouses. One after another, his new plays were being produced—at one time six of his works were playing simultaneously in Stockholm. When this popularity waned, he turned once again to other forms. By 1907, he was an Olympian figure living in semi-seclusion, but August Falck had little difficulty in resurrecting Strindberg's old dream of a Strindberg theatre. In the spring of 1907, he wrote four of his so-called "chamber plays," *Storm-clouds, The Burned Premise, The Ghost Sonata,* and *The Pelican,* for Falck's Intimate Theatre.

In returning to his old one-act form, Strindberg also revived some of his earlier thematic material, but now we witness the "battle of the brains"—the real world of deception, adultery, pretension, and lust for power—from afar. The main characters are all excluded from normal reality in some way; they are marked by death, dying, or already dead. They are sleepwalkers who gradually awaken to the fact that life is an illusion, a purgatory, a preparation for a better world. In fact, Strindberg first tried to deal with the material in *The Pelican* from the point of view of the dead father, who is the central figure in *Toten Insel,* which remains a fragment. Two of the rejected titles for *The Pelican*—"The Sleepwalkers" and "Purgatory"—draw attention to two different aspects of the negative conception of life that informs the play. The title that he finally chose is sufficiently ambiguous to allow him to show the relation between these two themes and to combine them with the idea of redemptive suffering. Since the pelican is emblematic of human self-sacrifice (as well as one of the traditional representations of Christ), the title seems at first to be crudely ironic. The mother, who thinks that she has sacrificed everything for her children, is one of the most vicious vampires that Strindberg ever created: she has "murdered" her husband and is slowly starving her children to death. By the middle of the second scene, however, it begins to become apparent that the symbol really applies to the father, who has done everything he can to provide for his family. As the purifying flames sweep through the house at the end of the play the ecstatic son exclaims: "I think it was *he* who was the pelican, for he did without things for our sake—his trousers were always baggy at the knees, and the velvet collar on his overcoat was threadbare, while we were dressed like children of the nobility." The pelican is an inverse vampire, but the symbol is ironic only so long as it is misunderstood. When the ambiguity is dispelled, Frederick and Gerda are liberated not only from their mother's power, but from their false view of life. Their death recalls not Durand's suicide at the end of *In the Face of Death,* but the ecstatic dematerialization of Indra's Daughter in *A Dream Play:* a journey back to innocence and unity.

Like many of Strindberg's symbols, the musical analogy in the generic title he gave to the plays he wrote in 1907—and later extended to *The Black Glove* (1909)—is sufficiently ambiguous to cause confusion. Throughout his career Strindberg used music (in early plays like *Miss Julie* and *Simoon* and to an even greater extent in his "post-Inferno" plays) to create a mood or suggest an idea. Also, he sometimes explained the apparent formlessness of his "dream plays" by referring to symphonies or fugues, to voice-leading or orchestration. Much more important than these quite normal literary uses of music, however, is the fact that in his later years he thought of music—especially Beethoven's quartets and sonatas—as being the purest expression of man's longing for liberation from life. Strindberg's tendency to identify this romantic view of music with the prevailing theme in nearly all his later plays has confused many critics. But we have more to learn from the obvious, practical reference to the "chamber" in "chamber play" than from his vaguer statements about music in general. In his *Memorandum to the Members of the Intimate Theatre,* he explicitly defines the concept of the "chamber play," which he had borrowed from Max Reinhardt: "If anyone should now ask what an Intimate Theatre has as its function and what is meant by the term *chamber play,* I shall answer as follows: In drama we are in search of the powerful, meaningful motif, but within bounds. In the treatment of it we wish to avoid everything touching on vanity, any calculated effects, scenes that beg for applause, *tour de force* rôles, monologues. The author must be constrained by no definite form, for the form is conditioned by the plot and the subject matter. Thus, [there must be] freedom of treatment, circumscribed only by the unity of conception and a feeling for style."[9] Much of this is a concise restatement of principles he enunciated in the late 1880s, especially in the Preface to *Miss Julie.* Indeed, it serves as the best summation of the important side of Strindberg's entire dramatic career that Arvid Paulson illuminates in this collection of brilliant new translations.

BARRY JACOBS

Harvard University

---

[9] August Strindberg, *Memorandum to the Members of the Intimate Theatre* (trans. Arvid Paulson), in *The Strindberg Reader* (New York: Phaedra, 1968).

To the memory of Vilhjalmur Stefansson*

The Outlaw

(1871)

A Tragedy in One Act

---

* The dedications are those of the translator.

CHARACTERS

VALGERD,
  wife of THORFINN

GUNLÖD,
  their daughter

GUNNAR,
  a Swedish crusader

A THRALL

ORM,
  foster-brother of THORFINN

THORFINN,
  the Jarl

A MESSENGER

SECOND MESSENGER

The action takes place in Iceland
in about the year 1100.

*A large room with a door, rear. In the
walls, loopholes with wooden shutters,
which are closed. Built-in benches, with
the high seat on the right. The posts for
this seat are embellished with carved
figures of Odin and Thor. A fire is burning in the open hearth in the center of
the room. Directly above the fire, a vent-
hole in the ceiling. From the wall beams
hang swords, battle-axes, and shields.
Beside the high seat stands a harp.*

Gunlöd *is standing by one of the loopholes, the shutter of which is open;
through it can be seen the open sea, illuminated by the northern lights.*

Valgerd *is seated near the open fire
center. She is spinning.*

Valgerd: Close the loophole.

(Gunlöd *remains silent.*)

  Gunlöd!

Gunlöd: Did you speak, Mother?

Valgerd: What are you doing?

Gunlöd: I am looking at the sea.

Valgerd: Will you ever learn to forget?

Gunlöd: You may take everything away from me—but let
me keep my memories.

Valgerd: Look to the future or you will perish.

Gunlöd: Does one find fault with the hardy viking if he
looks back at his homeland as he casts off from its shore?

3

VALGERD: You have had three winters to make your farewell.

GUNLÖD: There, Mother, you spoke the truth! Three winters—for there was no summer. . . .

VALGERD: When the pack ice melts we shall have spring.

GUNLÖD: The northern lights melt no ice!

VALGERD: Nor do your tears!

GUNLÖD: You never saw me weep.

VALGERD: I have *heard* you weep—and, since you do that, you are a child.

GUNLÖD: I am not a child.

VALGERD: If you would be a woman, you must suffer in silence.

GUNLÖD: I shall forget my sorrow, Mother.

VALGERD: No, no—bury it! Bury it as the most precious of all that you possess. The seed must not lie above ground if it is to grow and bear grain. You are carrying a deep sorrow. But your sorrow shall give birth to a great peace and a great happiness. . . .

GUNLÖD *(after a silence)*: I shall forget. . . .

VALGERD: Everything?

GUNLÖD: I shall try!

VALGERD: Will you forget your father's brutal behavior as well?

GUNLÖD: I have already done so.

VALGERD: Will you forget that your forefathers' home once stood on the shores of Bråviken—that the south wind sang its song in the oak forest when the ice belt broke up —that the spruce trees spread their fragrance, the finches twittered in the linden trees, and the scentless mayweed lulled you to sleep on the green meadows? Will you forget this when now you hear the merganser wailing upon the naked rocks, and the north wind with its sea storms whining among the gnarled dwarf birch?

GUNLÖD: Yes.

VALGERD: Will you forget that you once had a childhood friend from whom your father tore you away, to save you from the white Christ?

GUNLÖD *(in agony)*: Yes! Yes!

VALGERD: That brought the tears to your eyes!

GUNLÖD *(embarrassed)*: I hear footsteps outside. . . . Perhaps it is Father who has come back.

VALGERD: Will you now try to bear in mind—and without any tears—that we live in the land of ice, that we are fugitives from the land of the Swedes—and that in this land we are hated by the men of Christ? Yet we make no blood sacrifice. But we are hated because we refuse to be baptized and to kiss the bishop's hand. Have you spoken to any of the Christians since we came here?

GUNLÖD *(after a silence)*: No. . . . Tell me, Mother, is it true that Father is to be the Jarl of Iceland?

VALGERD: You must not worry yourself about that, my child. . . .

GUNLÖD: Alas, then I fear he will have trouble with the Christians!

VALGERD: You fear that he will?

GUNLÖD: I hear someone walking outside. . . .

VALGERD: Did you see the ship lying in the fjord this morning?

GUNLÖD: Yes, yes, I did! It made me so very, very glad!

VALGERD: Did the prow bear the figurehead of Thorfinn, your father?

GUNLÖD: I could not see it distinctly. . . .

VALGERD: Take care, child!

GUNLÖD: Is it tonight I may go out?

VALGERD: You know—it is tomorrow!

GUNLÖD: Mother!

VALGERD *(abruptly)*: Look after the fire!

(She goes out. GUNLÖD *stands gazing after her mother, then warily takes from her bosom a crucifix. She places it on the high seat and kneels before it.)*

GUNLÖD: Christ! Christ! Forgive me for speaking a lie! *(As her eyes fall on the images of the pagan gods Odin and Thor on the posts of the high seat, she springs up.)* No! I cannot pray with those ugly creatures gazing at me! *(She tries to find another place in which to pray.)* Hallowed Saint Olaf, and Holy . . . Oh, now I cannot remember what the bishop called her. . . . God! O God! Do not assign me to Purgatory for this my sin! I shall say every word of the long, difficult prayer as the monks say it. *Credo—credo—in patrem* . . . Oh, now I have forgotten that also. . . . I shall give five candles—five tall candles—for the altar of the Mother of God when next I go to the chapel. . . . *Credo in patrem omnipotentem. (She kisses the crucifix devoutly.)*

(Outside, a voice is suddenly heard singing to the accompaniment of a harp.)

VOICE: And the knight he fared to the eastern land
to pray for his dearest one:
O Christ, take the maiden's soul in Your hand,
let her enter Your heavenly realm.
Three summers he dwells in that land far away,
where the nightingale sings in the eve;
he has masses said throughout night and day
in the holy sepulcher shrine.
But I shall be back when the spruce stands in
[bloom. . . .
When the palm trees bud on the Jordan shore
he prays a prayer to his God,
beseeching that he may be home once more,
and there press his bride to his heart. . . .
And I shall be back when the spruce stands in
[bloom. . . .

(When GUNLÖD first hears the singing, she springs up and stands listening to it, perplexed. As the song comes to an end, she walks over to the door, intending to bolt it with the crossbar; but before she reaches the door, GUNNAR enters. He wears the attire of a crusader and has a harp slung across his shoulder.)

GUNNAR: Gunlöd!

(They embrace. GUNLÖD tears herself away and goes toward the door.)

You shrink from me, Gunlöd? Why do you . . . ?
GUNLÖD: You never embraced me like that before.
GUNNAR: We were children then!
GUNLÖD: You are right—then we were mere children. . . .
What does that falcon of silver I see on your shield mean?
I noticed this morning that you also had one on the prow
of your ship.
GUNNAR: You saw my ship, you recognized my singing—
and yet you tried to bar me from your door. . . . What am
I to think, Gunlöd?

GUNLÖD: Alas! Ask me no questions! My mind is so disturbed! But sit down, and let me talk with you. . . .

GUNNAR *(after seating himself)*: You do not say anything. . . .

GUNLÖD: Nor do you!

GUNNAR *(pressing her to him)*: Gunlöd! Gunlöd! Has the snow fallen so densely that it has frozen your memory? Even the crater on the mountain top over there can weep fire, but you—you are cold as a blizzard! But speak—speak! Why are you here in Iceland? What has happened?

GUNLÖD: Horrible things have happened—and still worse may come to pass if you remain here much longer! *(She springs to her feet.)* Go before my father comes!

GUNNAR: Do you think I would let go of you now—having sought after you these many years? . . . When I could not find any trace of you in our homeland, I went away to fight against Saracens and black men, hoping that I might meet you on the other side of the grave. . . . But my time had not yet come. And when summer drew near for the fourth time, I heard by chance through a viking mercenary that you were here in Iceland. Now I have you—and you want me to leave you here in this pagan darkness?

GUNLÖD: I am not alone!

GUNNAR: Your father does not love you, your mother does not understand you—and both are pagans!

GUNLÖD: I have friends who are Christians.

GUNNAR: Then the Holy Virgin has heard my prayer. You are a Christian, Gunlöd?

GUNLÖD: Yes, yes! Oh, let me kiss the cross you wear upon your shoulder! It is from the Holy Sepulcher—is it not?

GUNNAR: And now I give you the kiss of Christian brotherhood—the first kiss I have given you, Gunlöd. . . .

(They kiss.)

GUNLÖD: You must never kiss me again, Gunnar!

GUNNAR: But tell me—how did you become a Christian?

GUNLÖD: At first I put my faith in my father—he was so strong; then I put my faith in my mother—she was so good; and, lastly, I put my faith in you—you were both strong and good and so handsome as well. . . . And when you sailed away, I felt so alone, for I had no faith in myself; I was too weak. Then I called to mind your God,

Whom you had so often entreated me to love. . . . And I prayed to Him. . . .

GUNNAR: And the ancient gods?

GUNLÖD: I have never felt that I could believe in them, even though my father strictly bids me to do so. . . . They are abominable; they are evil.

GUNNAR: But who taught you the articles of faith and gave you the crucifix with the image of Christ?

GUNLÖD: The bishop did.

GUNNAR: And no one is aware that you are a Christian?

GUNLÖD: No, no one. I have had to lie to my mother—and that often gives me pangs of conscience.

GUNNAR: And your father hides you here so that you will not fall prey to Christianity. . . .

GUNLÖD: Yes. And now he is coming back from Norway, where he has been to gather partisans—for his desire is to be Jarl of Iceland.

GUNNAR: May God forbid!

GUNLÖD: Yes—yes. . . . But you must not linger here! He is expected home tonight!

GUNNAR: Very well. Over there, beyond Hjörleifsness, my ship is waiting. . . . Out to sea! A breeze is blowing from land—and before the cock crows we are beyond reach. . . .

GUNLÖD: Yes, yes!

GUNNAR: Soon we shall be in Östergötland—summer is still green there—and there you shall live in my stronghold, which I have built where your father's homestead once stood.

GUNLÖD: Is my father's homestead gone—no longer there?

GUNNAR: No. It was set on fire—burned down!

GUNLÖD: By the Christians?

GUNNAR: You are so agitated, Gunlöd!

GUNLÖD: Then I think I would rather be a pagan!

GUNNAR: What are you saying, Gunlöd?

GUNLÖD: Forgive me! Forgive me! I am in a savage mood. But when I hear of Christians—who should set a good example—committing such evil deeds . . .

GUNNAR: Put away such thoughts, Gunlöd, they are unholy!— Do you see this wreath?

GUNLÖD: Where did you get that?

GUNNAR (*handing her the wreath*): Do you recognize the flowers, Gunlöd?

GUNLÖD: They grew in my father's garden. . . . May I keep them?

GUNNAR: You may indeed. But since we are going to sail there, you will not need them, will you?

GUNLÖD: I shall feast my eyes on them during the long winter months. The spruce will be a reminder of the greening woods, and the anemones, of the blue sky. . . .

GUNNAR: And when they wither?

GUNLÖD: I did not think of that.

GUNNAR: And so you must come with me, away from this desolate land—come with me to our childhood home, where you can be as free as the birds, among flowers and sunlight and warmth. . . . There you shall have no need to steal your way to the house of the Lord when the bells are tolling the Sabbath hour. . . . Oh, there you shall see the new house of worship, with its vaulted ceiling and the lofty, soaring pillars lining the aisles, and hear the acolytes' singing when the bishop lights the incense on the high altar; there you shall take part in the divine service together with the Christians, and you shall have your heart cleansed of sin. . . .

GUNLÖD: You want me to leave my mother?

GUNNAR: She will forgive you—in time.

GUNLÖD: But my father will call me a coward. And I could not bear that!

GUNNAR: That you must suffer—for the sake of your faith!

GUNLÖD: The daughter of Thorfinn was never a craven!

GUNNAR: Your father has no love for you, and he will hate you when he learns of your conversion.

GUNLÖD: That he may do—but he shall never have disdain or contempt for me!

GUNNAR: Now you are lacking in valor, Gunlöd!

GUNLÖD: No! Is it not worthier to bear his hatred than to flee from his disdain?

GUNNAR: You are bargaining with your love, Gunlöd!

GUNLÖD: Love? . . . I remember—a maiden. . . . She had a lover who went away—and after that she never was happy again. All she did was sit, sewing upon cloth of gold and silks. What she was making, no one was allowed to see. And when anyone asked her, she wept; and when she was asked why she wept, she gave no answer: she merely wept. And she grew pale of cheek, and her mother made

ready her deathbed. . . . Then an old woman came, and
she said it was love, Gunnar. . . . I never wept when you
went away—for Father says it is shameful to cry. I never
sewed silk and cloth of gold, for Mother has never taught
me to. . . . Does that mean I was not in love, Gunnar?

GUNNAR: You have dreamt of me often during these long
years, Gunlöd?

GUNLÖD: I have dreamt of you so often, Gunnar—and this
morning, when I stood at the loophole, where I like to tarry,
and gazed out to sea and saw a ship come into view in
the east, I became anxious and uneasy—yet I did not
know that it was your ship.

GUNNAR: Why do you take joy in gazing out to sea?

GUNLÖD: You ask so many questions. . . .

GUNNAR: Why did you want to shut your door to me?

(GUNLÖD *is silent.*)

Why did you not bar me from coming in?

(*She remains silent.*)

Why are you silent?

(GUNLÖD *breaks into hysterical weeping.*)

You weep, Gunlöd, without knowing why. . . . I know—it
is the love within you. . . . (*He takes her in his arms and
kisses her.*)

GUNLÖD (*tearing herself free*): Do not kiss me! Go!

GUNNAR: Yes—but you are coming with me!

GUNLÖD: I refuse to let you dictate to me! I will not do your
bidding!

GUNNAR: The more fire the volcano spits, the quicker the
flame dies down.

GUNLÖD: You have destroyed my peace—for all time! Go,
and let me forget you!

GUNNAR: Would you like to know what the silver falcon
with the band stands for? It betokens the wild maiden I am
to tame.

GUNLÖD: You! Leave, before I hate you! No one has yet
bent me to his will!

GUNNAR: You have wild, seething blood in you! The fiery
blood of the vikings! But it will die down. . . . Gunlöd, I

shall wait for you for a day and a night—and you will come, meek as the dove seeking shelter, even though now you— like the falcon—would fly beyond the clouds. . . . I still hold the leash in my hand—it is your love. It still ties you to me, and you cannot tear it away. Tomorrow, when night has fallen, you will come. . . . Until then—farewell! *(He goes toward the door, where he stops.* GUNLÖD *is silent. As* GUNNAR *leaves, he says)* Farewell!

GUNLÖD: We shall see, proud knight, who comes first! When this wreath blooms—then I shall come! *(She throws the wreath into the fire. She stands pensive, watching it burn. When the wreath has turned to ashes, she bursts into hysterical weeping and falls on her knees.)* God! God! Curb my obstinate spirit! . . . Oh, why did he leave? *(She rushes toward the door.)*

> *(At that moment* VALGERD *comes in, going straight to the fireplace and passing by* GUNLÖD.*)*

VALGERD: Why did you not watch the fire?

> *(*GUNLÖD *is silent.* VALGERD *lays her hand on* GUNLÖD's *heart.)*

You have a secret.

GUNLÖD *(with suppressed emotion)*: Yes, Mother . . . yes.

VALGERD: Guard it well.

GUNLÖD: No—I must tell you. I cannot hold it back any longer.

VALGERD: Did you ever hear of a mother who did not know her daughter's hidden thoughts?

GUNLÖD: Who has told you mine?

VALGERD *(with primitive roughness)*: Dry your tears!

> *(There is a long silence.)*

GUNLÖD: Oh, let me out—up on the mountain—down to the shore. Here I am stifling!

VALGERD: Go up to the loft. There you can be alone.

> *(A* THRALL *enters.)*

What brings you here?

THE THRALL: The jarl is signaling with his horns from beyond the rocks, and the storm keeps growing.

VALGERD: Is it dark outside?

THE THRALL: Yes, there is a frightening dark.

(Silence.)

GUNLÖD: Put out a boat—two boats—as many as you can find!

THE THRALL: All the boats are out for the hunting.

GUNLÖD: Light some flares on the shore!

THE THRALL: The timber is too damp—we have not had so much as a twig for the hearth all through the evening.

VALGERD: Go!

THE THRALL: What will happen to the jarl, I wonder?

VALGERD: Do you care?

(THE THRALL leaves.)

GUNLÖD: You have not forgotten the wrong done you.

VALGERD: Nor my revenge! No man lays hand on the daughter of a jarl!

GUNLÖD: Well, then, your moment has come. Take your revenge—and I will show you how! *(She takes a torch and goes over to the mother.)* Place this torch in the loophole to the left—and you will wreck his ship. But if you place it in the right loophole, then you save his life. . . .

VALGERD: Give me the torch—and leave me!

(GUNLÖD hands her the torch.)

GUNLÖD: There is one sacrifice you can make that will appease your gods—offer up your revenge! *(She goes out.)*

(VALGERD goes quickly toward the right, where she opens a loophole. The sound of horns is heard from the sea.)

VALGERD: You struck me once, Thorfinn. I swore revenge. I shall now humiliate you—with a kind deed. . . .

GUNLÖD *(who has surreptitiously come back into the room, throws her arms around VALGERD's neck)*: Thank you, Mother!

VALGERD *(embarrassed)*: I thought you had gone.

GUNLÖD: Now I can go. *(She goes out.)*

VALGERD *(alone, by the loophole)*: You are pleading for help, you strong warrior, who always knew how to help yourself. . . .

(The blaring of a horn is heard again.)

Where is your great strength, your power, now—where is your kingdom?

(A gust of wind makes the shutter of the loophole flutter violently and extinguishes the torch. VALGERD, *shaken, lights the torch again.)*

Oh, he will perish! What am I to do? Pray? To whom? To Odin? . . . to Niord? To Ögir? For ten times four years I have beseeched their help, yet they have not given it! You, God—whatever your name may be— You mighty one, Who bid the sun rise and set— You great and powerful one, Who rule the sea and the winds, to You will I offer up my revenge, if You will only save him!

(Without being seen by her, ORM *enters.)*

ORM: A good evening to you, Valgerd! Cover yourself with your cloak—the air is biting. . . .

*(*VALGERD *is discomfited. She closes the shutter, after removing the torch from the loophole.)*

VALGERD: Welcome to you, Orm.

ORM: I thank you.

VALGERD: How goes it with you, Orm?

ORM: Sufferably well—when one can sit by the fire.

VALGERD *(impatiently)*: I asked how your voyage went.

ORM: That is a long saga.

VALGERD: Make it short.

ORM: Well—as you know, we were to sail to Norway to bring back men and timber.

VALGERD *(brusquely)*: Orm!

ORM: Valgerd!

VALGERD: You have not said a word about the jarl!

ORM: Did you ask me one word about your husband?

VALGERD: Where is he? Is he alive?

ORM: I do not know.

VALGERD: You do not know—you, his foster-brother? Where did you part from him? When?

ORM: Far out in the fjord. . . . It was lively out there, as you might well know. You should have seen him as he swam, holding my harp in one hand. He had vowed he would

guard it well for me. The seaweed was so tangled in hair
and beard that one might have thought he was the sea-god
himself. . . . And just then came a wave—the size of a
house. . . .

VALGERD: And—and then?

ORM: And then—I never saw my harp after that.

VALGERD: Orm! You are heartless enough to jest when your
master and foster-brother may be perishing out at sea! I
bid you go out at once and search for him! Do you hear
me?

ORM: What is ailing you, Valgerd? In years past you were not
so concerned about your husband and mate! You might at
least find time to give me a drink of mead before I go!

VALGERD: Warm yourself by the fire. . . . I shall go. I shall
dare the sea and the wind!

ORM (*taking hold of her hands*): Valgerd! Valgerd! You are a
woman, after all!

VALGERD (*with anger*): Let go of my hand!

ORM: The jarl is saved!

VALGERD: Saved?

ORM: Yes! *You* have been given back to him! And this was a
test he put you to! (*He goes out.*)

(*From outside can be heard the voices of* THORFINN *and*
ORM. THORFINN *is laughing boisterously.*)

VALGERD: The jarl is here—he is laughing—I have never
heard him laugh before. Oh, something dreadful is on the
way. . . . (*She wrings her hands.*)

(THORFINN *and* ORM *come inside.*)

THORFINN (*laughing*): That was a droll sight.

ORM: I promise it was!

VALGERD: Welcome home, my husband!

THORFINN: I thank you, wife! Have you been outside in the
rain? Your eyes are full of water.

VALGERD: You are in such a merry mood.

THORFINN: Merry . . . yes—yes. . . .

VALGERD: What happened to your ships?

ORM: They went to the bottom—all but one.

VALGERD (*to* THORFINN): And still you are in a happy mood!

THORFINN: Ho! Oh, well! There is no lack of timber up north
in the mountains. . . .

ORM: And now perhaps we may have something to put life in us again.

THORFINN: Well spoken! Bring us some mead, wife, and let us be merry!

ORM: And let us give thanks to the gods who brought us back safely!

THORFINN: When are you ever going to outgrow those old fairy tales, Orm?

ORM: Why do *you* force your wife and daughter to believe in them, Thorfinn?

THORFINN: Womenfolk should have gods.

ORM: Who do you think rescued you out there on the sea?

THORFINN: I did! I myself!

ORM: And nevertheless you called upon Åke-Thor at the top of your lungs when that monstrous wave swallowed you up!

THORFINN: That is a lie!

ORM: Orm does not lie!

THORFINN: Orm makes up ballads and tales.

ORM: Thorfinn must have swallowed too much sea water when he cried for help, since he is so salty in his tongue!

THORFINN: Hold your tongue in check, Orm!

VALGERD (*bringing the drinking horns*): Here, foster-brothers, I drink to your eternal friendship—and to more fortunate seafaring the next time!

THORFINN: I forbid you to speak of that again! (*They drink.* THORFINN *quickly removes the horn from his lips and inquires*): Where is the child?

VALGERD (*anxiously*): She is up in the loft.

THORFINN: Call her!

VALGERD: I think she is not feeling well.

THORFINN (*with a sharp look at* VALGERD): Tell her to come down!

VALGERD: You do not want her!

THORFINN: Did you hear what I said?

VALGERD: It is not your last word.

THORFINN: A man speaks but once, yet a woman must always have the last word.

VALGERD (*meekly*): You flout me!

THORFINN: I believe you are angry.

VALGERD: You laugh too much tonight. (*She goes out.*)

THORFINN: Orm—a thought strikes me. . . .

ORM: If it is a great thought, do not speak it. Keep it! There is a dearth of great thoughts these days.

THORFINN: Did you notice my wife?

ORM: I never notice other people's wives.

THORFINN: How friendly and gentle she was.

ORM: She had pity for you!

THORFINN: Pity?

ORM: Yes. For the sorrow that laughs is the sorrow of death—that is what she thought.

THORFINN: A woman cannot think.

ORM: Not with her head—but with her heart. That is why she has a smaller head but larger breast than we.

THORFINN: I am troubled by evil forebodings.

ORM: Poor Thorfinn!

THORFINN: My child! Orm—when she comes down I want you to bid her drink to Åsa-Odin from the horn.

ORM: The fox scents danger in the teeth of the wind. I understand.

THORFINN: Take care! They are coming. . . .

ORM: Do not treat the child harshly, Thorfinn. If you do, you will have to deal with me.

(VALGERD *and* GUNLÖD *come inside.* GUNLÖD *looks as if she were half asleep.*)

GUNLÖD: Welcome home, Father!

THORFINN: Do you mean it?

(GUNLÖD *is silent.*)

You are ill, are you not?

GUNLÖD: I am not feeling too well.

THORFINN: I fear you are not.

ORM: Gunlöd! Now you must empty this sacred horn to the glory of Odin, who rescued your father from distress at sea.

(*He takes the horn, moves it over the flames of the fire, and hands it to* GUNLÖD. *They all drink, except* GUNLÖD.)

THORFINN (*with fear and trembling*): Drink, Gunlöd!

(GUNLÖD *flings the horn to the ground, walks over to* THORFINN *and buries her head in his lcp.*)

GUNLÖD: Hear me, Father! I am a Christian! Do with me what you will—but my soul you cannot destroy! My soul is in the hands of God and all the saints!

(THORFINN, *beside himself with grief and anger, rises, pushes* GUNLÖD *away from him, and is about to speak. But he cannot find words and seats himself, speechless, in the high seat.* ORM *goes to the women, speaking to them in subdued tones. The two women walk toward the door, but* GUNLÖD *runs back into the room, where she faces* THORFINN.)

No! I will not go! I must speak so that you, my father, shall not go to your grave with a lie! For your whole life has been a lie! I shall forego my filial deference and respect for you—love is something I have never known—to show you what awesome guilt you have drawn down upon your head. . . . You have taught me to hate—for when did you ever give me love? You taught me to fear the great Thorfinn Jarl—and you have succeeded, for I tremble before your hardheartedness. . . . I honor and respect you for your many battle scars and your brave deeds, but you never taught me to love you as my father. . . . Whenever I wanted to come near to you, you thrust me from you—you poisoned my soul. . . . But now you can see God's punishment! You have made me into a criminal—for that is what I am at this moment—but I cannot help it! Why do you hate my faith? Why? . . . Because it is love—while yours is hate. Oh, my father! Father! I wanted to kiss the clouds from your brow, I wanted to caress your white hairlocks and make you forget the griefs that turned them into silver. I wanted to steady you and hold you up when your step began to falter. . . . Oh, forget what I have said—open your arms to me. . . . (*She kneels.*) And take me close to you. . . . Look at me with tenderness—look at me before it is too late. . . . One word from you . . . (*She gets up on her feet.*) Oh, I am cold—your glances are freezing me! You will not listen to me! You will not love me! I shall pray for strength to love you always! (*She bursts into tears and goes out, followed by* VALGERD.)

THORFINN: Sing a song, Orm!

ORM: I sing only lies!

THORFINN: Then lie!

ORM: Was the truth so bitter?

THORFINN: What is that you say?

ORM: Oh, well—you shall hear from me—later. . . . Now I
shall try to calm the beast in you with a beautiful lie! (ORM
*takes the harp and speaks the following verses, plucking the
strings with his fingers between each stanza.*)

> When May wind blew
> over billowing sea,
> and the shoots sprang up
> from the tawny soil,
> then the king pulled out
> his ship from the shed
> and sailed bravely off
> upon white-edged waves.

> Our ship we then steered
> toward Leiregård,
> where the king of the Danes
> gave us mead to drink.
> Then we sailed toward the east,
> where with dark-eyed maidens
> we drank of the wine
> in Micklagård.

> But when shield was hoisted
> to masthead high
> bucklers were shattered,
> and the coats of mail,
> while the arrows were singing:
> "It is spring it is spring";
> and like sap from the birch
> sprang blood from the wounds.

> No woman did dare to
> reject our embrace;
> from the tiller of soil
> we took what we wished,
> but if he were stubborn
> and hid his gold,
> we roasted his cattle
> in the flames of his farm.

How glorious the life
we lived those days! . . .
When the sea trolls pounded
'gainst ironclad prow,
then the viking's heart
felt joy in living
and, plucking the harp strings,
great songs were sung.

And praise of the vikings,
their manhood, their boldness,
was sung by troubadours
throughout the wide world. . . .
But now the swords rust,
and extolled is weakness. . . .
And sea-kings are sleeping
by grimy hearth.

What now can the bard praise,
with brave deeds gone?
Prattle and vanity
are not for harp strings. . . .
I shall put it away—
hang it on the wall—
having sung my farewell
to brawn and brave deeds.

THORFINN (*awakens, after having been lost in thought*): Is that the end of it?

ORM: Yes—that is how it usually ends.

THORFINN: Orm . . . you are my friend. . . .

ORM: H'm—I should think I am!

THORFINN (*timorously*): I can find no peace. . . .

ORM: There are two ways of finding peace. One is to do nothing that will cause regret; the other is never to regret what one has done.

THORFINN: But if one has already done something that one regrets?

ORM: Then you do feel sorry that you treated your child harshly, Thorfinn?

THORFINN (*angrily*): I never regret anything! And as for the child—hold your tongue!

ORM: Listen to me, Thorfinn! Have you never given a thought to what you have done with your life?

THORFINN: To think is something for old women to do when they sit by the fire. . . . My life has been a life of action.

ORM *(after a moment of silence)*: What do you mean to do now?

THORFINN *(hesitantly)*: What do I mean to do?

ORM: Yes.

(THORFINN *makes no answer. He is shaken.*)

You see how even that little thought struck home and confounded you! Then think what a great thought would do if it came to you! Why have you not the courage to look back upon your life? I shall tell you—because you are afraid that you would see a host of gruesome sights!

THORFINN: Let the past be buried!

ORM: No—I shall dig up the dead bodies from their burial mounds, and they shall stare at you with their empty sockets until you shrink in fear and turn away in horror. . . . And then you shall see that—despite all your brawn and bravery—you were not a man!

THORFINN *(in a rage)*: What is this twaddle you are prating, you harebrained fool!

ORM: Keep screaming—you are still a mere youth at heart! . . . Oh, yes—I have seen men—great, big men with thick beard and graying hair, and a crooked back besides—who were nothing but children. . . .

THORFINN *(with growing rage)*: Hold your tongue, Orm!

ORM: You may yell until the house falls down, but you cannot outscream the truth.

THORFINN: Keep silent—or I shall strike you!

ORM: Go ahead and strike—strike me to death—tear the tongue out of my mouth—but the truth shall nevertheless be blasted into your ears with brass horns: "Your life has been a lie!"

THORFINN *(curbing his anger somewhat; pained)*: Orm—I beg of you—say no more!

ORM: Oh, yes, Thorfinn, I have still more to say! Do you feel the earth quaking under you? That means an earthquake is coming! The whole world trembles today because it is in the throes of giving birth—giving birth with terrible pain and suffering—to a great and glorious man. Open your eyes and see—don't you see how the peoples of the east are in conflict with the peoples of the west? It is the beginning of the battle of love. . . . The new bride trembles under the embrace of the older mate. She struggles and suffers—but eventually she will rejoice, and torches by the thousands will be lighted; and the whole of the earth shall be illuminated by peace and joyfulness because He shall have been born— He, the young, the strong, the beautiful, radiant ruler who is to reign over all peoples. And his scepter bears the name of love, his crown is one of light—and He himself is the new era! Thorfinn—do you remember the saga about Thor and Loke of the Outlying Farmstead? He held the cat so high in the air that the trolls paled, and he took so deep a swallow of mead that they trembled! But when the old witch knocked him to his knees—then the trolls laughed! It was age that defeated him; and it is this age in which we live that you have been fighting against, and which has defeated you. . . . It is the lord and master of the ages—it is God—who has crushed and defeated you!

THORFINN: I have never known any other god than my own strength—and that is the god I put my faith in!

ORM: I have no faith in such a god! You have been feuding with that god of yours—with yourself—all through life! It was he who drove you from your homeland—and you thought you were then out of his reach! It was he who sank your ships and took away your kingdom! And then your power was ended! It was he who weaned your child from you! And you say that you cannot find peace of mind. . . . It was he who . . .

(*A* MESSENGER *enters.*)

THE MESSENGER (*to Thorfinn*): Are you Thorfinn the Jarl?

THORFINN: I am he.

THE MESSENGER: You made a descent upon the coast of Reydfjord last spring?

THORFINN (*without flinching*): I did.

THE MESSENGER: You raided the farmstead of Hallfred at Thorvalla, and plundered and burned it.

THORFINN: Yes.

THE MESSENGER: And then you sailed away. . . .

(THORFINN *is silent.*)

The Althing has now declared you an outlaw, and from now on you are branded with the name of nithing. You are an outcast among men. Your home is to be burned, and who so will may take your life. Your foes are stalking you; therefore flee while there is yet time—flee this very night! *(He leaves.)*

(There is a pause.)

ORM: Do you know who he was?

THORFINN: You may well ask.

ORM: He was a messenger of that old witch Time.

THORFINN: You talk like an old woman.

ORM: Our age will suffer no use of force! You committed an outrage against the age in which we live—therefore, it strikes back at you!

THORFINN: This day and age does not know what strength is— that is why it worships weakness!

ORM: Thorfinn! When you came to Iceland, you swore to keep the peace. . . . You have broken your oath—you have profaned your honor—and that it why you will die an outcast, a nithing!

THORFINN: You, too, call me a nithing!

ORM: Yes.

THORFINN: Are you being so bold as to break an oath of your own? Have you the courage to let yourself be called a nithing?

(ORM makes no response.)

You poor weak-kneed creature! It is you who hold me fettered when I want to take to flight—you coil yourself about my feet like a serpent. . . . Let go of me!

ORM: I have sworn the oath of foster-brother.

THORFINN: I break the oath.

ORM: You can not!

THORFINN: Then I shall kick you out of the way!

ORM: That will mean the death of us both!

THORFINN: Do you call yourself a man, Orm?

ORM: I grew to be only a bard!

THORFINN: That is why you are now nothing!

ORM: I knew what I wanted to be—but it was out of my reach. You knew everything—yet you did not know what you wanted.

THORFINN: I thank you for your verses. Farewell!

ORM: Who is to sing your death song?

THORFINN: No doubt the ravens.

ORM: Have you the courage to die, Thorfinn?

THORFINN: I dare more than dying. I dare to be forgotten!

ORM: You were ever the stronger of us two. Farewell! We shall meet again. . . . (*He goes out.*)

THORFINN: Alone . . . Alone . . . Alone!

(*There is a silence.*)

> I call to mind—it was in autumn. . . .
> The equinoctial gale raged furiously
> over England's sea. My ship was wrecked;
> and I alone was cast upon a rock. . . .
> Then calm set in, dead calm. What trying days!
> For all I saw was cloudless sky
> and endless, deep-blue sea about me!
> Not e'en a sound of living creatures;
> no sea gull waked me with its screeching;
> no breeze to cause the very lightest wave
> to plash against the rock. . . .
> It seemed to me as though I'd lost my life;
> I spoke aloud, I shouted, screamed—
> was frightened by my voice. . . .
> Then dryness tied my tongue—
> and all that made me know I lived
> was that my heart still beat. . . .
> However, after listening to its sound,
> I suddenly no longer heard it. . . .
> Then I sprang up in fear
> again and still again, until I swooned.
> When finally I wakened, I then heard,
> quite close to me, a sound as of a heartbeat;
> I heard a panting from a mouth that was not mine,
> and courage grew again within my soul. . . .
> I looked around.
> It was a seal which lingered to find rest. . . .
> It gazed at me with tearful eyes
> as though it felt compassion for me. . . .
> Now I no longer was alone!
> With outstretched hand I tried to stroke
> its shaggy body; then it fled—

and I was doubly lonesome. . . .
Again I stand upon a rock. . . .
What do I fear now? Aloneness!
Then—what is loneliness?
It is myself!
Who am I then that I should fear?
Am I not Thorfinn Jarl, the strong one,
who bends yet thousands to his mighty will—
who never asked for friendship or for love,
but kept unto himself his sorrows!
No! No, I am another—
and that's why I, Thorfinn the Strong,
now dread Thorfinn the Weak!
Who took away my strength? Who weakened me?
Was it the sea? Did I not conquer it
a score and ten times; yet it defeated me
but once—and then to death. . . .
The sea is stronger thus. It is a god. . . .
But who subdued the sea and pacified it
when raging? Who did it? Who? Who? Who?
It was the one still stronger!
Who are you, then, you who are the stronger?
Oh, answer, that I may believe in you! . . .
He does not answer! There is but silence! . . .
Now I can hear again my heartbeat!
Oh, help—oh, help! I am so cold—
I'm freezing. . . . (*He goes toward the door, call-
ing out*): Valgerd!

THE THRALL (*enters*): You called me, noble Jarl!

THORFINN (*quieting down*): Your ears deceived you!

THE THRALL: Then may I leave, master?

THORFINN (*placing his hand on* THE THRALL's *shoulder*): No—
torches—it is so dark here. . . . And put wood on the fire—
I am cold. . . .

(THE THRALL *puts logs on the fire and lights torches,
which he places around the room on the walls.*)

THE THRALL: Would you anything else, master?

THORFINN: I want you to carry out some errands.

THE THRALL: Yes, master.

THORFINN: How many men are we here?

THE THRALL: I venture . . . half three score—I think.

THORFINN: Are you afraid of death, thrall?

THE THRALL: I cannot be afraid, since I shall then find salvation. *(He makes the sign of the cross.)*

THORFINN: What meaning has that?

THE THRALL: We have been taught to do that by the bishop.

THORFINN: I forgot that you are a Christian.

THE THRALL: And do you still wish me to remain in your service although you are a pagan?

THORFINN: I will show you how little it matters to me what people believe. We must put double crossbars on the north gateway door!

THE THRALL: Yes, master! But faith is stronger than a hundred barriers!

THORFINN: Did I ask you? *(Silence.)* What did they do to you when you became Christians here in Iceland?

THE THRALL: Oh, it was much easier than you would think. They just scooped some water on us, and the bishop read from out of a big book—and then they gave each of us a white shirt.

THORFINN: Go tell the twelve strongest of the men to fetch their new broadaxes! Do you understand?

THE THRALL *(about to leave)*: Yes, master!

THORFINN: One moment—tarry! *(There is a pause.)* Do you remember what it said in the big book?

THE THRALL: I do not remember too much of it—but one thing I do remember, and that was when he spoke of two thieves who were hanged on a cross together with the son of God . . . and one of them went to heaven. . . .

THORFINN: Did they scoop water on him also?

THE THRALL: I do not know—the bishop did not say.

THORFINN: Do you know if there are any horses in the stable?

THE THRALL: I think they are out grazing. I shall go out and see.

THORFINN: No, stop! I do not want you to leave me! *(Pause.)* If you died tonight—could you die in peace?

THE THRALL: Yes, if I had time to say a prayer first.

THORFINN: Will that bring you peace? Will it?

THE THRALL: Oh yes, master! Yes!

THORFINN *(rises, then fetches a beaker)*: If you will pray for me, I shall give you this.

THE THRALL: It is not enough!

THORFINN: You shall have ten! But if you speak one word about it—I shall take your life!

THE THRALL: It will not help—not even if you gave me a hundred! You must pray yourself!

THORFINN: I can not! But I bid you do it for me!

THE THRALL: I shall do as you bid me. . . . (*The* THRALL *prays.*) Christ Jesus! Have compassion on this poor sinner, who pleads for your mercy. . . .

THORFINN: That is a lie! I never beg for anything!

THE THRALL: You see now—it is of no avail!

THORFINN: Bring me my coat of mail and help me with it!

(*The* THRALL *takes down the coat of mail and helps* THORFINN *buckle it on.*)

THE THRALL: You are not standing still, master—I cannot fasten the buckles. . . .

THORFINN: You are a poor creature!

THE THRALL: Your whole body is trembling. . . .

THORFINN: You are a liar!

(VALGERD *and* GUNLÖD *enter.*)

THE THRALL: May I go now?

THORFINN: Go!

(*The* THRALL *leaves.*)

VALGERD (*coming up to* THORFINN): You called me. . . .

THORFINN: I did not call you!

VALGERD: Your foes are upon you!

THORFINN: What is that to you?

VALGERD: Arm yourself! I have heard what has come to pass!

THORFINN: Then you and Gunlöd had best hide on the porch!

SECOND MESSENGER (*enters*): Thorfinn Jarl—we have come! Will you yield and give yourself up? We are here in numbers!

(THORFINN *does not reply.*)

You give no answer. Then let your women leave—for we are setting fire to your farmstead!

(THORFINN *remains silent.*)

Your answer!

(Gunlöd, who has tarried in the doorway, steps forward and takes a battle ax from the wall.)

GUNLÖD: I shall give you your answer! Ill would Thorfinn Jarl have reared his daughter, and little would his wife love him, if they were to desert him now. Here you have your answer! *(She throws the ax at his feet.)*

SECOND MESSENGER: You are stronger than I thought, Thorfinn! For your daughter's sake you shall be allowed to fall as a hero and not as an outlaw! Be ready for open combat—outside—on the field. . . . *(He goes out.)*

THORFINN *(to* VALGERD*)*: Shame to you—you faithless, cowardly woman, who guarded my treasured offspring so ill! You have made my child into my enemy!

GUNLÖD: Oh, Father—am I now your enemy?

THORFINN: You are a Christian. . . . Yet it is not too late—if you will disavow your white Christ!

GUNLÖD: No! Never! But I will follow you into death!

VALGERD: Thorfinn! You called me cowardly—and that I can suffer. . . . But faithless—no, there you wronged me! I may not have loved you as passionately as the women in the south are said to love—but I have been true to you all through our life together; and I have vowed—as is our ancient custom—to follow you in death. . . . *(She opens a trapdoor in the floor.)* Here you see my burial place—I have made it ready! Here is where I shall die—beneath these grimy beams that have witnessed my anguish and heartbreak—together with these gods of ours, who showed us the way here. I wish to be devoured by the flames, so that my spirit may rise to Gimli, and there be given light and peace!

GUNLÖD: Am I to be left alone, then? Oh, let me die with you!

VALGERD: No, my child. You are young—you can still be replanted under a gentler, more merciful sun—but the old fir tree dies where it is rooted.

GUNLÖD: Father! Father! You must not die! I shall save you!

THORFINN: You?

GUNLÖD: Your kinsman Gunnar has his ship lying on the other side of Hjörleifsness—he has his men there. Send one of your thralls by a roundabout way to him, and he will come.

THORFINN: So it was from that well you scooped your courage! Keep your counsel for yourself and go to him if you want to!

GUNLÖD: You are not to call me a craven! I shall die with you, Mother! You cannot keep me back!

(THORFINN *walks toward the door. He is noticeably moved.*)

VALGERD: No, Thorfinn, stay! And for once let me see your true soul, that I may read the faded runes there!

THORFINN: Do you think I should tell you how to read what is in my soul? If you have not learned to read it by this time—then what is written there may as well be erased by time when I have turned to stone and crumbled away!

VALGERD: You are not the flinty, hard-hearted rock you give yourself out to be! You have feelings. Show them—give vent to them—and then you shall find peace!

THORFINN: My feelings are my heart's blood—would you like to see it? (THORFINN *leaves.*)

(*From outside is now heard the clanging of swords and other warlike sounds and outcries, which continue until* THORFINN *re-enters. When* THORFINN *hears these sounds, he is about to go out again.*)

VALGERD: Oh, stay, Thorfinn, and speak a word of farewell. . . .

THORFINN: Woman, you take away my strength with your sentimental words! Let me go! The contest has begun!

VALGERD: Speak at least a word of farewell!

THORFINN (*with difficulty hiding his emotion*): Farewell, my child! (*He goes out.*)

VALGERD: Nothing will unbend that man!

GUNLÖD: Only God can bend him!

VALGERD: There is great loftiness in his hardness!

GUNLÖD: The mercy of God is still greater.

VALGERD: May you live happily!

GUNLÖD: Have you the courage to leave me behind?

VALGERD (*taking* GUNLÖD *in her arms*): Are you ready?

GUNLÖD: The Holy Virgin prays for me!

VALGERD: I put my trust in a god who is love. . . .

GUNLÖD: And in the Mother of God. . . .

VALGERD: I do not know her.

GUNLÖD: You must believe in her!

VALGERD: Your faith is not mine.

GUNLÖD: Forgive me!

(They embrace.)

VALGERD: Take your place now!

(GUNLÖD opens the shutter of one of the loopholes and scans the scene outside. VALGERD takes one of the torches from the wall and then places herself by the trapdoor.)

GUNLÖD: They are fighting fiercely, Mother!

VALGERD: Do you see the Jarl?

GUNLÖD: He is standing in the middle of the gateway.

VALGERD: How does he demean himself?

GUNLÖD: Everything gives way to him!

VALGERD: Does he show weariness?

GUNLÖD: He still stands erect. . . . Look! Do you see the awesome northern lights?

VALGERD: Have many been slain?

GUNLÖD: I cannot see too clearly—they are withdrawing from the picket fence. . . . Oh—the sky is red as blood!

(There is a silence.)

VALGERD: Speak—what do you see?

GUNLÖD *(with great animation)*: The silver falcon!

VALGERD: What is it you see?

GUNLÖD: I saw a falcon!

VALGERD: A falcon is a bad omen!

GUNLÖD: Now Father is coming here. . . .

VALGERD: Is he wounded?

GUNLÖD: Oh! He is falling. . . .

VALGERD: Fasten the door after him—and then—in the name of your God. . . .

GUNLÖD: No—not yet—a moment more . . .

VALGERD: Are you afraid?

GUNLÖD: No—no! *(She rushes toward the door.)*

(The sounds from outside gradually diminish. THORFINN enters. He is pale and bleeding. GUNLÖD is about to disappear outside, but THORFINN stops her.)

THORFINN: Stay inside!

(VALGERD *goes up to him. There is a silence.* THORFINN *walks to the high seat and sits down. He beckons to* GUNLÖD *and* VALGERD.)

Come here! *(They go to him. He strokes* GUNLÖD's *hair, presses a kiss on her forehead, then clasps* VALGERD *by the hand.)* You see my heart's blood now. . . . *(He kisses* VALGERD.)

VALGERD *(rises to fetch the torch)*: Now we have spoken our farewells!

THORFINN: You must tarry—must not take leave—you must remain with your child. . . .

VALGERD: I made a vow.

THORFINN: My whole life has been a broken oath—and still I hope. . . .

ORM *(enters. He is wounded and stops in the doorway)*: Will you let me come in?

THORFINN: Come in!

ORM: Have you found peace now?

THORFINN: Soon . . . soon . . . *(He caresses the two women.)*

ORM: Then we are ready for the journey?

THORFINN *(gazing at* VALGERD *and* GUNLÖD): Not yet!

ORM *(seating himself on a bench)*: Do not tarry—if you wish to have company. . . .

THORFINN: Orm—are you a Christian?

ORM: You have a right to ask.

THORFINN: What, then, are you? A riddle . . .

ORM: I was everything—and I was nothing. I was a bard—a rhymester. . . .

THORFINN: Do you believe in anything? Have you a faith?

ORM: I came to have a faith.

THORFINN: Who gave it to you?

ORM: Doubt—misfortune—grief.

THORFINN *(to* VALGERD): Valgerd—give me your hand. . . . There—hold me fast—harder— You must not let go before —before it is over. . . .

(GUNNAR *enters. He stops in the doorway.)*

Who is that?

GUNNAR: You know me.

THORFINN: I know your voice—but my eyes do not see you. . . .

GUNNAR: I am your kinsman—Gunnar.

THORFINN: Come inside.

> (GUNNAR *remains standing in the doorway, gazing at* GUNLÖD *with an inquiring look.*)

Is he here?

> (GUNLÖD *gets up and slowly, with head bowed, she comes over to* GUNNAR, *takes him by the hand, and leads him to* THORFINN. *They then kneel before him.* THORFINN *places a hand on the head of each.*)

God! (*He dies.*)

CURTAIN

To Lois Smith

Miss Julie

(1888)

A Naturalistic Tragedy in One Act

THE AUTHOR'S PREFACE

In common with art generally, the theatre has long seemed to me to be a *biblia pauperum*, i.e., a bible in pictures for those who cannot read the written or printed word. Similarly, the playwright has the semblance of being a lay preacher presenting the views and sentiments of his time in popular form—and in a form sufficiently popular so that the middle classes, from which theatre audiences are chiefly drawn, can understand what it is all about without racking their brains.

Thus the theatre has long been a public school for the young, for people not too well educated, and for women who still possess that primitive faculty of deceiving themselves and letting themselves be deceived; or, in brief, who are impressionable to illusion and susceptible to the suggestions of the author. For the self-same reason it has seemed to me as if, in our time—when the rudimentary, immature way of thinking (which is a process of the imagination) appears to be developing into reflection, inquiry and analysis—the theatre, like religion, is in the throes of being abandoned as a moribund form of art for which we lack the conditions requisite to enjoyment. The profound crisis now sweeping through the whole of Europe gives credence to this assumption, and not least the fact that in those countries of culture which have given us the greatest thinkers of the age, namely England and Germany, the drama, in common with most of the other fine arts, is dead.

In other countries, however, efforts have been made to create a new form of drama by employing elements reflecting the ideas of modern times within the framework of the old forms. But on the one hand, there has not been sufficient time for these new ideas to have been so generally accepted that the audiences can fathom their purport and implication; on the other hand, some of the audiences have been so impassioned by partisan polemics and propaganda that it has been impossible to enjoy the play in a purely objective manner while one's innermost feelings and convictions are being assailed, and when an applauding or hissing majority displays a tyranny so openly as only a theatre affords an opportunity for. And, furthermore, the new content has as yet been given no fresh form; as a result, the new wine has burst the old bottles.

In the present drama I have not attempted to create anything new (for that is an impossibility) but merely to modernize the form to meet the demands which, it occurs to me, people of our time are likely to make upon this art. To this end I have chosen (or rather, been captured by) a theme which may be said to lie outside the partisan and controversial issues of the day. The problem of social rise or downfall, of who is higher or lower, or who is better or worse, whether man or woman, is, has been and shall be of enduring interest. When I chose this theme from real life—as I heard it related a number of years ago, at which time I was greatly moved by the story—I saw in it the ingredients of a tragic drama. To see an individual on whom fortune has heaped an abundance of gifts go to her ruin and destruction, leaves us with a tragic feeling; to see a whole line die out is still more tragic. But perhaps there will come a time when we will be so enlightened that we will view with indifference the brutal, cynical and heartless spectacle that life has to offer—perhaps when we have done with our imperfect, unreliable thought mechanisms which we call feelings, and which may be superfluous when our reflective organs have developed.

The fact that the heroine in this play arouses our pity and compassion is due solely to our weakness and inability to resist such a feeling for fear that we ourselves may meet with the self-same fate. And the over-sensitive spectator may still not be content with feeling pity and compassion; the man with faith in the future may demand some sort of positive action or suggestion for doing away with the evil—in short, some stroke of policy. But, first of all, there is nothing absolutely evil; for the extinction of one family is nothing short of luck for another family that gets a chance to rise in the world. And the succession of rise and fall is one of life's greatest fascinations as luck is only relative. And to the man with a program who desires to rectify the unfortunate fact that the bird of prey devours the dove and that the lice eat the bird of prey, I wish to put this question: "Why should it be rectified?" Life is not so mathematically idiotic that it allows only the big to eat the small, for it happens just as often that the bee kills the lion or at least drives it mad.

That my tragedy has a depressing effect upon the many is the fault of these many. When we have grown as hardened as the first French revolutionaries were, then it will without question produce only a happy and wholesome impression to see the crown parks weeded out and ridded of rotting, super-annuated trees that too long have stood in the way of others, equally entitled to their day of vegetation—the kind of impression one experiences when one sees somebody with an incurable disease taken by death.

Not long ago I was upbraided by someone who thought my tragedy *The Father* was too sad. As if a tragedy were meant to be amusing! People are constantly clamoring pretentiously for the *joy of life,* and play producers keep demanding farces—as if the joy of life consisted in being ludicrous and in depicting all human beings as if they were suffering from St. Vitus' dance, or idiocy. For my part, I find the joy of life in the hard and cruel battles of life; and to be able to add to my store of knowledge, to learn something, is enjoyment to me. It is for that reason I have chosen an unusual situation—yet one that teaches a moral; an exception, in brief,—but a rare exception that proves the rule and that no doubt will make all those who love the commonplace, feel offended. The next thing that will offend the simple-minded is the fact that my motivation for the action is not a simple one and that the *raison d'être* is not a single one. A happening in life—and this is a fairly recent discovery!—is generally brought about by a whole series of more or less deeplying motives; but as a rule the spectator selects the one which in his opinion seems the easiest to understand or that is most flattering to his own best judgment. A suicide takes place. "Bad business!" says the burgher. "Unrequited love!" say the women. "Physical illness!" says the invalid. "Crushed hopes!" says the human derelict. But now it is possible that the motive may be all or none of these things, and that the

deceased may have concealed the actual motive by letting
another be known that would cast a more favorable light
over his memory!

The sad fate of Miss Julie I have motivated by a host of
circumstances: the mother's fundamental instincts, the father's wrong upbringing of the girl, her own strange nature,
and the suggestive influence of her fiancé upon an insipid,
vapid and degenerated mind. In addition, and more directly,
the festal mood of Midsummer Eve, the absence of her father, her monthly period, her preoccupancy with animals,
the excitement of the dance, the long twilight of the night, the
strongly aphrodisiac influence of the flowers, and lastly, the
chance bringing together of the two alone in a secluded
room—not to mention the aroused passion of a bold and
aggressive man. Consequently my mode of procedure has
been neither one-sidedly physiological nor psychological: I
have neither placed the blame exclusively on traits inherited
from the mother nor have I cast the blame on the girl's physical indisposition. By the same token, I have not put the
blame solely on "immorality," and I have not merely
preached a moral. For want of a priest, I have left this task
to the cook.

I commend myself for the introduction of this multiplicity of motives; they are in keeping with the times. And if
others have done the same thing before me, I will acknowledge with pride that I was not alone in my paradoxes—
as all discoveries are called.

With regard to the delineation of the characters, I have
made them somewhat lacking in character for the following
reasons:

In the course of time the word *character* has been given
many meanings. Originally it no doubt denoted the dominant trait in the soul-complex and was confused with temperament. With time it became the middle-class term for an
automaton, an individual who had become so fixed in his
nature—or who had adapted himself to a particular role in
life and who, in a word, had ceased to grow—that people
called him *a character*. On the other hand, a man who continued to develop, an able navigator on the river of life, who
sailed not with sheets set fast but who veered down the wind
to steer closer to the wind again—this man was called lacking in character. And this, of course, in a derogatory sense

—because he was so hard to capture, to categorize, to keep an eye on.

This bourgeois notion of the fixed state of the soul was transmitted to the stage, where the middle-class element has always been in dominance. There a character became synonymous with a man permanently settled and finished, one who at all times appeared as a drunkard, a jolly jester, or as a deplorable, miserable figure. And for the purpose of characterization nothing more was needed than some physical defect such as a clubfoot, a wooden leg, a red nose—or that the actor in the role be given some repetitious phrase such as: "That's splendid!" or "Barkis will be glad to do it!", and so forth.

This one-sided manner of looking at human beings still survives in the great Molière. Harpagon is a miser and nothing else, although he could have been both a miser and an excellent financier, a fine father, a good man in his community. And what is worse, his infirmity is precisely of utmost advantage to his son-in-law and daughter who are his heirs. For that reason they ought not to take him to task, even if they have to wait a little before they take to their nuptial bed. I do not believe, therefore, in simplified characters for the stage. An author's summary judgment upon men (this man is a fool; that one brutal; this one is jealous; that one stingy, etc.) ought to be challenged and rejected by the Naturalists who are aware of the richness of the human soul and who know that vice has another side to it that is very like virtue.

I have depicted my characters as modern characters, living in an age of transition at least more breathlessly hysterical than the period immediately preceding it. Thus I have made them more vacillating, disjointed: a blending of the old and the new. And it seems not improbable to me that modern ideas, absorbed through conversations and newspapers, could have filtered down to the domain of the domestics.

My souls (characters) are conglomerates of a past stage of civilization and our present one, scraps from books and newspapers, pieces of humanity, torn-off tatters of holiday clothes that have disintegrated and become rags—exactly as the soul is patched together. I have, besides, contributed a small fragment of evolutionary history by having the weaker character parrot words purloined from the stronger one, and by having the souls (the characters) borrow "ideas" (or suggestions, as they are called) from one another.

Miss Julie is a modern character. Not that the half-woman, the man-hater, has not existed since time immemorial but because she has now been discovered, has trod into the open and begun to create a stir. The half-woman of today is a type who pushes herself forward; today she is selling herself for power, decorations, aggrandizement, diplomas, as she did formerly for money; and the type is indicative of degeneration. It is not a wholesome type and it is not enduring, but unfortunately it can reproduce and transplant its misery in another generation. And degenerate men seem instinctively to choose their mates from among such women; and so they multiply and bring into the world progeny of indeterminate sex, to whom life becomes a torture. Fortunately, however, they come to an end, either from being unable to face and withstand life, or from the irresistible rebellion of their suppressed desires, or because their hope of coming up to men has been thwarted. It is a tragic type, revealing the spectacle of a desperate struggle against nature; tragic also as a Romantic inheritance now being put to flight by Naturalism, whose aim is only for happiness; for in order to achieve happiness, strong, virile and wholesome types are required.

But Miss Julie is also a remnant of the old war nobility, which is now giving way to the new aristocracy of the mind with its nervous driving force. She is a victim of the discord which a mother's "crime" produces in a family; a victim also of the delusions and deceptions of her time, of circumstances, of her own defective constitution—all of which adds up to the "fate" or "universal law" of days now past. The Naturalist has done away with the idea of guilt, as well as God; but the consequences of the act: punishment, imprisonment (or the fear of it)—*that* he cannot do away with for the simple reason that they are bound to remain. They will remain whether he (the Naturalist) lets the protagonists go free or not; for the injured parties are never so good-natured as outsiders (who have not been wronged) can be—at a price.

Even if the father for compelling reasons should take no vengeance, the daughter would avenge herself—as she does here—from that innate or acquired sense of honor which the upper classes have as their inheritance. From where? From the barbarian ages, from the original homeland of the Aryans, or from the chivalry of the Middle Ages? It is a beautiful thing, but these days it has become somewhat of a disadvantage to the preservation of the race. It is the noble-man's hara-kiri—which is the law of the Japanese, of his innermost conscience, that bids him cut open his own ab-domen after receiving an insult from another man. The cus-tom survives, in modified form, in the duel, also a privilege of the upper classes. And that is why Jean, the valet, re-mains alive; but Miss Julie cannot go on living once she has lost her honor. This is the advantage the serf has over the earl: that he is without this deadly superstition about honor. In all of us Aryans there is something of the nobleman, or Don Quixote, which makes us sympathize with the man who takes his own life after he has committed a dishonorable deed and so lost his honor. And we are noblemen enough to suffer when we see a person once considered great, suddenly topple and then be looked upon as dead and a nuisance. Yes —even if he should raise himself up again and make up for the past by performing an act of nobility. Jean, the valet, is a procreator, and he has acquired a distinct and separate character. He was born the son of a farmhand and has grad-ually taken on the characteristics of a gentleman. He finds it easy to learn, his senses are well developed (smell, taste, vi-sion), and he has a feeling for beauty. He has already come up in the world; and he is hard and unscrupulous enough not to allow sensitiveness to interfere when it comes to using others for his purposes. He is already a stranger to those around him (the servants and farmhands) whom he looks down upon, as he does upon the life he has turned his back on. He avoids the menials and fears them because they know his secrets, pry into his scheming, watch with envy as he betters himself, and anticipate his downfall with glee. This accounts for the duality of his indeterminate character, which vacillates between love of power and glory and hat-red against those who have it. He thinks of himself as an aristocrat. He has learned the secrets of good society. He is polished on the surface, but the inside is uncouth and vul-gar. He has learned to wear formal clothes with taste, but one cannot be so certain that his body is clean.

He has respect for Miss Julie but is timid and apprehensive about Kristin (the cook), for she knows his precarious secrets. He is also sufficiently callous not to let the night's happenings interfere with his plans for the future. With the brutality of the serf and the lack of squeamishness of the ruler he can see blood without losing consciousness, and he can throw off any hardship or adversity. Consequently he emerges from the battlefield unscarred, and no doubt he will end up as a hotelkeeper; and if he fails to become a Roumanian count, his son will probably attend a university and may end up as a petty official.

For the rest, Jean gives a rather enlightening insight into the lower classes' conception of life—of life as they see it —when he speaks the truth, which he infrequently does; for rather than adhere to the truth he asks what will do him most good. When Miss Julie suggests that the lower classes must feel oppressed by those above them, Jean naturally agrees with her because his aim is to gain sympathy. But when he realizes that it is to his advantage to place himself apart from the common herd, he quickly takes back his words.

Aside from the fact that Jean is well on his way up in the world, he possesses an advantage over Miss Julie because of being a man. Sexually he is the aristocrat because of his male strength, his more acutely developed senses, and his capacity for taking the initiative.

His feeling of inferiority can principally be ascribed to the temporary social environment in which he lives, and he can probably rid himself of it when he sheds his servant's livery.

The mental attitude of the slave manifests itself in his inordinate respect for the count (as exemplified in the scene with the boots), and in his religious superstition. But his respectfulness is chiefly inspired by the fact that the count occupies a position of rank which he himself would like to attain. And this deference remains with him after he has won the affections of the count's daughter and seen the emptiness within the shell.

I find it hard to believe that a relationship of love in a higher sense could exist between two souls so different in nature. For this reason I have made Miss Julie imagine that she is in love—to justify her behavior, to blot out her transgression; and I let Jean think that if social conditions were different, he might be able to love her. I imagine love is much like the hyacinth: it has to strike roots in darkness *before* it can produce a healthy, hardy flower. In this instance, it shoots up instantaneously—and therefore the plant withers and dies so soon.

Finally there is Kristin. She is a female slave, obsequious and dull (from standing at the hot stove) and laden with morality and religion that serve as a cloak for her own immorality, and as a scapegoat. Her church-going is a means of lightheartedly and glibly unloading on Jesus her household thieveries and taking on a new lease of guiltlessness. Otherwise she is a subordinate figure, and therefore intentionally sketched much in the manner of the Pastor and the Doctor in *The Father*—the reason for this being that I wanted to have precisely this type of ordinary human being (such as country clergymen and country doctors usually are). If these subordinate figures of mine have appeared as abstractions to some, it is because everyday people go about their work in a somewhat detached manner. By that I mean that they are impersonal and that they show only *one* side of their personality. And as long as the spectator feels no need of seeing the other sides of their personality, my abstract characterization of them is quite correct.

As far as the dialogue is concerned, I have, to a certain degree, broken with tradition by not making catechists out of my characters; that is, they do not keep asking silly questions merely for the sake of bringing forth a clever or jocular retort. I have avoided the symmetrical, mathematical construction commonly used by the French in their dialogue. Instead I have had my characters use their brains only intermittently as people do in real life where, during a conversation, one cog in a person's brain may find itself, more or less by chance, geared into another cog; and where no topic is completely exhausted. That is the very reason that the dialogue rambles. In the early scenes it piles up material which is later worked up, gone over, repeated, expanded, rearranged and developed much like the theme in a musical composition.

The plot is tolerable enough, and as it is really concerned with only two persons, I have concentrated my attention on them. I have added only one other character, a minor one: Kristin (the cook), and have kept the spirit of the unfortunate father hovering over and in the background of the entire action. I have done this because I seem to have observed that the psychological course of events is what interests the people of our time most. I have also noticed that our souls, so hungry for knowledge, find no satisfaction in merely seeing something done; we want to know *how* and *why* it is done! What we want to see are the wires—the machinery! We want to examine the box with the false bottom, take hold of and feel the magic ring in an attempt to find where it is joined together; we want to scrutinize the cards and try to discover how they are marked.

In this attempt of mine I have had in mind the brothers de Goncourt's monographic novels which, among all literature of modern times, have appealed to me most.

As far as the technical side is concerned, I have, as an experiment, done away with the division into acts. This I have done because I seem to have found that our decreasing capacity for illusion might be disturbed by intermissions, during which the theatregoer would have time to engage in reflection and thereby escape the author-mesmerizer's suggestive influence. The performance of *Miss Julie* will probably last one hour and a half. As people can listen to a lecture, a sermon, or a parliamentary proceeding lasting that length of time or longer, it has struck me that a theatrical piece ought not to fatigue an audience in a similar space of time. Already in 1872, in one of my earlier playwriting experiments, *The Outlaw*, I tried using this concentrated form, although without much success. The play was originally written in five acts, and when it was completed, I was cognizant of the chaotic and alarming effect it had upon me. I burned the manuscript and from out of the ashes rose a single, well-constructed act, fifty printed pages in length, that took one hour to perform. While the form of *Miss Julie* is not absolutely original, it nevertheless seems to be my own innovation; and as public taste appears to be changing, there may be prospects for its being accepted in our time.

My hope is that we may some day have audiences so educated that they will sit through a whole evening's performance of a play consisting only in one act. But to attain this, tests would have to be made.

In order, however, to provide momentary interludes (or rest stops) for the audience and the actors without allowing the spectators to lose the illusion that the play has created, I have included three art forms, all integral parts of the drama, namely: the monologue, the pantomime, and the ballet. Originally they were part of the tragedies of antiquity, the monologue having been derived from the monody and the ballet from the chorus.

The monologue has now been condemned by our realists as not being true to life; but if its motivation is sound, it can be made believable, and consequently it can be used to good advantage. It is, for instance, quite natural that an orator should walk up and down in his home practising aloud his speech by himself; not at all improbable that an actor should rehearse the lines of his role in a stage voice; that a servant girl should babble to her cat; that a mother should prattle to her little child; that an old spinster should chatter with her parrot; that anyone might talk in his sleep. And in order that the actor, for once, may have an opportunity to do some independent work, free from any interference, suggestions or directions from the author, it may be preferable that the monologue scenes not be written out (in so many words) but merely indicated. For it is of small importance what is being said by a person in his sleep, or to a parrot, or a cat—it has no influence on the action in the play. A gifted actor may, however, improvise such a scene better than the author can, because the actor has become part and parcel of the situation and is imbued with the mood of it. In short, the author has no way of determining in advance how much small talk may be used and how long it should last without having the audience awakened from the spell it is under.

It is general knowledge that certain theatres in Italy have gone back to the art of improvising—and as a result have produced some creative artists. They follow, however, the author's general outline and suggestions; and this may well prove to be a step forward, not to say a new art form which may truly be said to be *creative*.

Wherever the monologue, on the other hand, has made for improbability, I have resorted to the pantomime; and there I have given the actors still wider scope for creating imagery—and to win individual acclaim. To prevent the audience from being strained to the utmost, I have designated that the music—for which there is ample justification owing to the fact that it is Midsummer Eve, with its traditional dancing—exert its seductive influence while the pantomime is going on. And I address a plea to the musical director that he consider carefully his choice of music selections, lest he conjure forth an atmosphere foreign to the play and lest he induce remembrances of strains from current operettas, or reminders of popular dance music, or of primitive folk airs which are too pronouncedly ethnographic.

The ballet which I have introduced could not have been replaced by a so-called mob (or ensemble) scene. Such scenes are generally badly acted and afford a lot of grinning fools, bent on attracting attention to themselves, an opportunity to shatter the illusion. As rustics usually do not improvise into ditties their derision and jeers, but make use of already existing material (which frequently carries a double meaning) I have not composed their scurrilous innuendo but have chosen a little-known dance game, which I came across in the vicinity of Stockholm and wrote down. The words fit the actual happenings only to a degree and not entirely; but that is exactly my intention—for the wiliness and insidiousness in the slave makes him shrink from attacking in the open. Thus there must be no cackling buffoons in a serious drama such as this, no exhibition of coarse grinning in a situation which forever places the lid on the coffin of a family lineage.

With regard to the scenery, I have borrowed from impressionistic painting its asymmetry, its terse and pregnant concision, and in this way I think I have increased the possibilities for creating illusion. The very fact that the room is not seen in its entirety (nor all of its furnishings), gives us the incentive to conjecture. In brief, our imagination is set to work and fills in what is lacking before our eyes. I have also gained something by getting rid of the tiresome exits through doors, primarily because the doors in a stage set are made of canvas and move at the slightest touch. They can not even give expression to an angry father's temper when he, after an execrable dinner, gets up and leaves, slamming the door after him "so that the whole house shakes." On the stage "the whole house" (of canvas!) moves unsteadily from one side to the other. Similarly, I have used only one single setting, and this for two purposes: to blend the figures into the environment, and to break with the habit of using extravagant scenery. And with only one setting, one can expect it to be realistic in appearance. Yet there is nothing so hard to find on the stage as an interior set that comes close to looking as a room *should* look, no matter how convincingly the scenic artist otherwise can produce a volcano in eruption, or a waterfall. We may have to tolerate walls made of canvas, but it is about time that we stopped having shelves and kitchen utensils painted on it. There are so many other conventions on the stage that strain our imagination; certainly we might be freed from overexerting ourselves in an effort to believe that pots and pans painted on the scenery are real.

I have placed the rear wall and the table obliquely across the stage for the purpose of showing the actors full face and in half-profile while they face each other across the table. I once saw a setting in the opera *Aïda* that had a slanting backdrop, and it opened up to the eye unknown perspectives; and this arrangement did not have the look of having been made in a spirit of rebellion against the trying straight line.

Another innovation that is much needed is the removal of the footlights. The lighting is designed to make the actors appear plumper of face. But now let me ask: Why must all actors have plump faces? Does not the light from below tend to erase many of the sensitive, subtle character traits of the lower part of the face, and especially round the mouth? And does it not change the shape of the nose and cast a shadow effect above the eyes? Even if this were not so, there is one thing that is certain: that the eyes of the actors are suffering under a strain, making it difficult for them fully and effectively to project the varying expressions of the eyes across the footlights. For the light strikes the retina in places that under ordinary circumstances are protected (except in the case of sailors: they get the glare of the sun from the water), and consequently one seldom witnesses anything but a glare, a stare, or a crude rolling of the eyes—in the direction of the wings or upward toward the balconies—so that the whites of the eyes show. Very likely this also accounts for the tiresome habit of blinking with the eyelashes, especially by actresses. And whenever anyone on the stage has to speak with his eyes, there is only one way in which he can do it (and that a bad one): to gaze straight out into the audience, and so come in close contact with it from the stage apron outside the curtain line. Rightly or wrongly, this nuisance has been re-ferred to as: "Greeting one's acquaintances!"

Would not sufficiently powerful lighting from the sides (with parabolas or similar devices, for instance) be of help to the actor and enable him to project more completely the sensibility of expression and mobility of the eyes, which are the most important means of facial expression?

I have no illusions about being able to persuade the actors to play *for* the audience and not *to* it, although this would be highly desirable. Nor do I look forward with much hope to the day when I shall see an actor turn his back completely to the audience throughout an important scene; but I do wish that crucial scenes would not be given close to the prompter's box (in the center of the stage) as though the actors were performing a duet and expected it to be received by applause. I would like to have each scene played at the very place where the situation demands it to be played.

And so there must be no revolutionary changes, only minor modifications. To transform the stage into a room with the fourth wall removed, and to carry out the effect of realism by placing some pieces of furniture with their backs to the audience would, for the present, provoke an outcry.

And I would also like to say a word about the make-up, although I dare not hope that the actresses will pay much attention to me. They much prefer to look beautiful rather than look their part in the play. But it might be well to give a thought to whether it is expedient and becoming for the actor to smear his face with make-up until it becomes an abstraction and its character is obliterated by a mask. Let us imagine an actor who—in order to achieve an irascible, choleric look—applies a couple of bold, black lines between the eyes and that he, still looking wrathful with his in-eradicable expression, has to smile in response to somebody's remark! What a horrible grimace it will result in! And again, how can the old man possibly wrinkle the false forehead of his wig (which is smooth as a billiard ball!) when he flies into a rage?

Presented on a small stage, a modern psychological drama, in which the most subtle reactions of the soul must be reflected by facial expression rather than by gesture, shouting and meaningless sound, would be a most practi-cable testing ground for the use of powerful lighting from the sides, with the participating actors using no make-up, or at least very little.

If, in addition, the visible orchestra with the disturbing glare from the lamps (on the music stands), and with the faces of orchestra members turned toward the audience, could be made invisible; and if the parquet ("orchestra") could be elevated so that the eyes of the spectators focused on a level higher than the actors' knees; if the stage boxes, with their giggling, snickering late dinner and supper party arrivals, could be got rid of; and if, in addition, we could have absolute darkness in the auditorium while the play is in progress; and if we, first and foremost, could have an intimate stage and an intimate theatre—then we may see the inception of a new drama, and the theatre could again become an institution for the entertainment of the cultured.

While waiting for this kind of theatre to come into being, we may as well continue our writing and file it away in preparation for the repertory that is to come.

I have made an attempt! If I have not succeeded, there is time enough to make another!

CHARACTERS

MISS JULIE,
  25 years old

JEAN,
  butler and valet, 30 years old

KRISTIN,
  cook, 35 years old

*The action takes place in the Count's
kitchen on Midsummer Night's Eve.*

*A large kitchen the ceiling and side walls
of which are masked by borders and
draperies. The rear wall runs diagonally
across the stage, from the right of the
stage to the left, at a slight angle. On
the wall, to the right, are two shelves
with utensils of copper, iron, tin and
other metals. The shelves are trimmed
with fancy paper. Further over, on the
left, can be seen three-quarters of a
great arched doorway, which has two
glass doors; through these doors are
seen a fountain with a figure of Cupid,
lilac shrubs in bloom and the tops of
some Lombardy poplars. On the right,
the corner of a large stove, faced with
glazed bricks; a part of its hood is also
seen. On the left, one end of the servants' dining table of white pine; around
it are a few chairs. The stove is decorated with branches of birch, and twigs
of juniper are strewn on the floor. On
the table stands a large Japanese spice
jar, filled with lilac blossoms. An ice-
box, a kitchen table, and a sink. Above
the door, a big, old-fashioned bell; to
the right of the door, a speaking tube.
Downstage, left, there is a triangular
opening in the wall, inside which are
doors upstage and downstage leading to
JEAN's and KRISTIN's rooms. Only the
door leading to JEAN's room (upstage) is*

visible. KRISTIN *is standing at the stove. She is busy frying something. She wears a light-colored cotton dress and a kitchen apron.* JEAN *enters. He is wearing livery and carries a pair of large riding-boots with spurs which he puts down on the floor so that they are in full view of the audience.*

JEAN: Now Miss Julie's mad again—absolutely mad!

KRISTIN: So—you are back again, are you?

JEAN: I took the Count to the station, and when I came back and went by the barn, I stepped inside and had a dance. And there I saw Miss Julie leading the dance with the gamekeeper. But the instant she set eyes on me, she dashed straight over to me and asked me to dance the next waltz with her; and from that moment on she has been waltzing with me—and never in my life have I known anything like it! She is stark mad!

KRISTIN: She's always been crazy—but after the engagement was broken off two weeks ago, she is worse than ever.

JEAN: Just what was the trouble, I wonder? I thought he was a fine young man, even if he didn't have any money to speak of. . . . Oh, but they all have so many queer notions! (*He seats himself at one end of the table.*) Anyhow, don't you think it's strange that a lady like her—h'm—should want to stay at home with the help instead of going away with her father to visit some of their relatives?

KRISTIN: I suppose she is sort of embarrassed after the break-up with her fiancé—

JEAN: I shouldn't be surprised! But I must say, he was the sort who could stand up for himself. Did you hear, Kristin, how the whole thing happened? I watched it from beginning to end—although I never let on that I did.

KRISTIN: You don't mean it? You saw it—did you?

JEAN: I certainly did! They were together out in the stable-yard one evening—and Miss Julie was trying to "train" him, as she called it. What do you think she did? She had him jump over her riding crop—the way you train a dog to jump! And each time she gave him a whack with her riding crop. But the third time he snatched the whip from her hand and broke it into bits! And then he left.

KRISTIN: So that's what happened! Well, I never—

JEAN: Yes, that's the way it happened. . . . But now—what have you that's good to eat, Kristin?

KRISTIN (*dishes out from the pan and places a plate before Jean*): Oh, it's only a piece of kidney that I cut from the veal steak.

JEAN (*smells the food*): Splendid! That's my special *délice*. . . . (*He feels the plate.*) But you didn't heat the plate!

KRISTIN: I must say—you are more of a fuss-box than the Count himself when he wants to be particular. (*She runs her hand through his hair caressingly.*)

JEAN (*crossly*): Stop that—stop pulling my hair! You know how sensitive I am about that!

KRISTIN: Why, why—you know I only do it because I love you—don't you know that!

JEAN (*eats.* KRISTIN *uncorks a bottle of ale*): Beer on Midsummer Eve! No, thanks! I have something better than that. (*He pulls out a table drawer and produces a bottle of red wine with yellow seal.*) You see the yellow seal, don't you? Now bring me a glass! A glass with stem—*always*—when you drink it undiluted.

KRISTIN (*goes over to the stove and puts a small pan on the fire. Then she brings him a wine glass.*): God help the woman who gets you for a husband! I never knew anyone to fuss like you!

JEAN: Don't talk nonsense! You ought to be glad to get a fellow as fine as I! And I don't think it's hurt you any to have them call me your sweetheart! (*He tastes the wine.*) Good! Very good! Could be just a trifle warmer. (*He warms the glass with his hands.*) We bought this in Dijon. Four francs a liter from the cask—not counting the duty. What are you cooking over there that smells so horrible?

KRISTIN: Oh, it's some devilish mess that Miss Julie has me cook for Diana.

JEAN: You might be a little more careful with your expressions, Kristin!—But I don't see why you should stand and cook for that damned cur on Midsummer Eve! Is anything the matter with the bitch?

KRISTIN: Yes, she is sick. She has been sneaking out with the gatekeeper's pugdog, and now she's in trouble—and that's just what Miss Julie doesn't want, don't you see?

JEAN: The young lady is too haughty in some respects, and in others she has no pride at all—exactly like her mother, the countess, when she was alive. She was especially at home in the kitchen and in the stables, but she would never drive behind one horse only—she had to have at least two. She went around with dirty cuffs, but she had to have a crest on each button. And speaking of Miss Julie, she shows a lack of self-respect. She has no regard for her position. I could almost say she lacks refinement. Why, just now when she was dancing out there in the barn, she pulled the game-keeper away from Anna and started to dance with him, without any ado. Would we do anything like that? We would not!—But that's what happens when aristocrats try to act like the common people—they become common! But she is splendid to look at! Gorgeous! Ah, what shoulders! And what—etcetera—

KRISTIN: Oh, stop your ranting! Haven't I heard what Clara says about her?—and she dresses her.

JEAN: Oh! Clara! You women are always jealous of one another! But don't *I* go out riding with her? . . . And can she dance!

KRISTIN: Listen, Jean—how about a dance with me when I get through with my work here?

JEAN: Why, certainly—why not?

KRISTIN: Is that a promise?

JEAN: Do I have to take an oath? When I say I'll do a thing, I do it!—Well, thanks for the snack, anyhow . . . it tasted good! (*He corks the wine bottle with gusto.*)

MISS JULIE (*appears suddenly in the doorway. She speaks to someone outside*): I'll be back immediately—you just wait there . . .

> (JEAN *quickly slips the bottle into the table drawer; then he rises respectfully.* MISS JULIE *enters and goes over to* KRISTIN *by the mirror.*)

MISS JULIE: Well, Kristin, is it ready?

> (KRISTIN *indicates* JEAN's *presence.*)

JEAN (*with gallantry*): Do you ladies have secrets between you?

MISS JULIE (*with a flip of her handkerchief in his face*): No inquisitiveness!

JEAN: Ah—what lovely fragrance—the smell of violets—

MISS JULIE (*coquettishly*): So—you are impertinent, are you? Are you a connoisseur of scents, too? You are an expert at dancing. Now, now—no peeking! Go away!

JEAN (*impudently, yet with a semblance of politeness*): Is it some sort of witches' brew for Midsummer Night that you two ladies are concocting? Something to help you look into the future and see what your lucky star has in store for you —and get a glimpse of your intended?

MISS JULIE (*tartly*): You have to have good eyes for that! (*To* KRISTIN.) Pour it into a small bottle and put the cork in tight.—Now come and dance a schottische with me, Jean.

JEAN (*hesitantly*): I don't mean to be disrespectful, but I promised Kristin this dance . . .

MISS JULIE: Oh, she can dance the next one with you instead. How about it, Kristin? You'll loan me Jean, won't you?

KRISTIN: That's not for me to say. (*To* JEAN.) If Miss Julie condescends, it's not for you to say no. Go on, Jean, and be thankful to Miss Julie for the honor!

JEAN: If you will permit me to speak frankly, Miss Julie— and I hope you won't be offended—I wonder whether it's wise of you to dance more than one dance with the same partner . . . especially as people here are only too prone to misinterpret, to imagine things . . .

MISS JULIE (*flares up*): What do you mean? What kind of interpretations? Just what is it you mean?

JEAN (*servilely*): Since you refuse to understand, Miss Julie, I'll have to speak more plainly. It doesn't look good to single out one of your domestics in preference to some of the others, who would like to have the same honor paid to them . . .

MISS JULIE: Single out? Preference? What an idea! I am astonished! I—the mistress of the house—honor the people by attending their dance . . . and when I feel like dancing, I want to dance with someone who knows how to lead! I don't want to dance with someone who makes me look ridiculous!

JEAN: Just as you say, Miss Julie! I am at your service!

MISS JULIE (*in an appeasing tone of voice*): Don't take it as an order now! Tonight we are celebrating! We all want to enjoy the holiday. We are all happy—and all just plain human beings . . . and rank doesn't count! Come now, give

me your arm! You don't have to worry, Kristin—I am not
going to take your sweetheart away from you!

(JEAN *offers her his arm; she takes it, and they go out.*)

(*The following scene is entirely in pantomime. It is to be
played as if the actress were alone on the stage. Whenever necessary, she should turn her back to the audience and she should not look in the direction of the
audience. She must be in no hurry, as though afraid
that the audience might become impatient.* KRISTIN *is
alone. The faint sound of violin music in the distance,
played in schottische tempo, is heard. She hums the
tune while clearing* JEAN'S *place at the table, washes
the dishes and utensils in the sink, dries them and
puts them away in the cupboard. Then she removes
her apron, takes out a small mirror from a drawer and
places it on the table, supporting the mirror against
the jar of lilacs. She lights a candle and heats a hairpin,
with which she curls her forelock. This done, she goes
to the door and stands there listening. Then she goes
back to the table and discovers* MISS JULIE'S *forgotten
handkerchief. She sniffs of it; then she distractedly
smoothes it out and folds it carefully.*)

JEAN (*enters alone*): She is mad, really! Dancing the way she
does! The people are standing behind the doors, grinning at
her. . . . What do you think has got into her, Kristin?
KRISTIN: Oh, she's having her period—and then she is always
so peculiar.—Well, do you want to dance with me now?
JEAN: I hope you are not cross with me because I let you
down a moment ago, are you?
KRISTIN: Certainly not! Not for a little thing like that—you
ought to know that! And I know my place . . .
JEAN (*puts his arm round her waist*): You show good sense,
Kristin. You'll make a good wife. . . .
MISS JULIE (*enters. She is unpleasantly surprised. She speaks
with forced good humor*): Well—you are a fine young
swain—running away from your partner!
JEAN: On the contrary, Miss Julie, I just hastened back to the
one I deserted . . .
MISS JULIE (*changing tactics*): Do you know—you dance as

nobody else! But why do you wear your livery on a holiday like this? Take it off—this minute!

JEAN: Well—then I must ask you, Miss Julie, to step outside for a moment. . . . My black coat is hanging over there. . . . *(He points toward it and goes over to the left.)*

MISS JULIE: You are not embarrassed because of me, are you? Just to change your coat? —Go into your room, then, and come back when you have changed. . . . Or you can stay here, and I'll turn my back.

JEAN: If you'll excuse me, then, Miss Julie. *(He goes to his room, on the left. One sees the movement of his arm while he is changing coats.)*

MISS JULIE *(to* KRISTIN*):* Tell me, Kristin, is Jean your fiancé, is he? You seem to be so intimate.

KRISTIN: Fiancé? Well—yes, if you like! We call it being engaged.

MISS JULIE: Oh, you do?

KRISTIN: Well, you have been engaged yourself, Miss Julie, and . . .

MISS JULIE: Yes, but *we* were *properly* engaged.

KRISTIN: Just the same, nothing came of it.

> *(JEAN re-enters, now dressed in a black cutaway and carrying a black bowler.)*

MISS JULIE *(regards him admiringly): Très gentil, Monsieur Jean. Très gentil.*

JEAN: *Vous voulez plaisanter, madame!*

MISS JULIE: *Et vous voulez parlez français?* Where have you learned that?

JEAN: In Switzerland—when I was steward in one of the largest hotels in Lucerne.

MISS JULIE: Why, you look a real gentleman in that cutaway! *Charmant! (She seats herself at the table.)*

JEAN: Oh, you flatter me!

MISS JULIE *(offended):* Flatter you?

JEAN: My natural modesty forbids me to believe that you could honestly pay compliments to anyone like me—and that is why I had the audacity to assume that you were merely exaggerating—or, as it is called, engaging in flattery.

MISS JULIE: Where did you learn to phrase your words so nimbly? You must have visited the theatres a good deal?

JEAN: I've done that, too! Yes, I have been to many places.

MISS JULIE: But you were born here in the neighborhood, weren't you?

JEAN: My father was a farmhand on the county prosecutor's estate nearby. I remember seeing you when you were a child. But you never took any notice of me.

MISS JULIE: Oh, you do, really?

JEAN: Yes, and I especially remember one time . . . oh, but I can't tell you about that.

MISS JULIE: Oh, yes, do—go on—why not? This is just the time . . .

JEAN: No, really—I can't . . . not now! Some other time, perhaps . . .

MISS JULIE: Another time may be never. Is it anything so shocking?

JEAN: No, it isn't anything shocking at all—just the same I feel a little squeamish about it. Look at her there. (*He points to* KRISTIN *who has gone to sleep in a chair by the stove.*)

MISS JULIE: She'll make a delightful wife, won't she? Perhaps she snores, too?

JEAN: No—but she talks in her sleep.

MISS JULIE (*with sarcasm*): How do you know?

JEAN (*with bravado*): I have heard her. (*There is a silence. They eye each other.*)

MISS JULIE: Why don't you sit down?

JEAN: I couldn't—not in your presence!

MISS JULIE: And if I order you to?

JEAN: I would obey.

MISS JULIE: Sit down, then!—Oh, wait! Would you get me something to drink first . . .

JEAN: I don't know what there is in the ice-box here. I think there is only some beer.

MISS JULIE: That's not to be despised—and my tastes are so simple that I prefer it to wine.

JEAN (*takes out a bottle of ale from the ice-box, and opens it. Then he goes to the cupboard and brings out a glass and a plate, and serves her*): If you please!

MISS JULIE: Thank you! Wouldn't you like some yourself?

JEAN: I am not particularly fond of beer—but since you insist . . .

MISS JULIE: Insist? I should think ordinary good manners would prompt you to keep me company . . .

JEAN: You are quite right, Miss Julie! (*He uncorks a bot-*

tle of ale and brings out another glass from the cupboard; then pours himself a glass of ale.)

MISS JULIE: Now drink a toast to me! *(JEAN hesitates.)* Old as you are, I believe you are bashful.

JEAN *(kneeling, he raises his glass and jestingly parodies)*: To my sovereign and mistress!

MISS JULIE: Bravo! Now you must kiss my foot—as a crowning touch!

> *(JEAN hesitates, and then he boldly takes her foot and gives it a light kiss.)*

MISS JULIE: Superb! You should have been an actor!

JEAN *(rises)*: We must not go on like this, Miss Julie . . . someone might come in and catch us—

MISS JULIE: Why should that matter?

JEAN: Because people would start to gossip, that's the reason! You should have heard their tongues wagging out there just now . . .

MISS JULIE: What did they say? Go on, tell me! Sit down . . .

JEAN *(sits down)*: I don't wish to hurt your feelings, Miss Julie—but they used expressions . . . that . . . well, they blurted out suspicions of a kind that . . . well, you can well imagine what kind— You are not a child, Miss Julie, and if you see a lady drinking alone with a man—and especially a servant—and at night—why—

MISS JULIE: What then? And besides, we are not alone. . . . Kristin is here, isn't she?

JEAN: Yes—asleep!

MISS JULIE: I'll wake her up! *(She rises.)* Kristin, are you asleep?

KRISTIN *(in her sleep)*: Bla-bla-bla-bla . . .

MISS JULIE: Kristin!—She is sound asleep!

KRISTIN *(still in her sleep)*: The Count's boots are polished— put on the coffee—I'll do it this minute—this very minute —phew—pish—ho— *(She snores.)*

MISS JULIE *(twists her nose)*: Wake up, will you?

JEAN *(sternly)*: One should never disturb people when they are asleep!

MISS JULIE *(in a sharp tone of voice)*: What's that?

JEAN: Anyone who stands at the stove all day long has a right to be tired at the end of the day. And sleep should be respected.

MISS JULIE (*in a different tone*): It's considerate of you to think like that—it does you credit! Thank you! (*She extends her hand to him.*) Come outside with me and pick a few lilacs . . .

(KRISTIN *wakes, rises and goes sleepily to her bedroom, on the left.*)

JEAN: With you, Miss Julie?

MISS JULIE: Yes, with me!

JEAN: It would never do! Absolutely not!

MISS JULIE: I don't understand what you mean. . . . You couldn't possibly be imagining things, could you?

JEAN: No—not I . . . but the people.

MISS JULIE: What? That I am in love with a domestic?

JEAN: I am not conceited—but such things *have* happened. . . . And nothing is sacred to anybody.

MISS JULIE (*tartly*): You talk like an aristocrat!

JEAN: Yes—and I *am*!

MISS JULIE: And *I*—am I lowering myself?

JEAN: Take my advice, Miss Julie, do not lower yourself! No one will believe you did it innocently. People will always say that you fell!

MISS JULIE: I have a higher opinion of people than you have. Come and let us see if I am right—Come on! (*She gives him a challenging glance.*)

JEAN: You know, Miss Julie, you are a very strange young lady!

MISS JULIE: Perhaps I am—but so are you strange! For that matter, everything is strange! Life, human beings—everything is scum and slime that floats and drifts on the surface until it sinks—sinks to the bottom! It makes me think of a dream that comes back to me ever so often: I am perched on top of a tall column and can see no way of getting down. When I gaze below, I feel dizzy. Yet I must get down; but I haven't the courage to jump. There is nothing to hold on to, and I hope that I may fall—but I don't. . . . Nevertheless I feel I cannot be at peace until I am down, down on the ground. . . . And if I should once reach the ground, I would want to be buried in the earth. Have you ever had such a feeling?

JEAN: No! *I* usually dream that I am lying underneath a tall tree in a dark forest. I have a desire to get up high, to

the very top of the tree and look out over the bright landscape where the sun is shining—and to rob the bird's nest
up there of its golden eggs. And I climb and climb; but the
tree's trunk is so thick and so slippery, and the lowest
branches are so high up. But I know that if I can only reach
the first branch, I'll get to the top as easily as on a ladder.
So far I have never reached it, but I am going to—even
if it's only in my dreams.

MISS JULIE: Here I stand talking about dreams with you. . . .
Come now! Only into the garden! (*She offers him her arm
and they go out.*)

JEAN: We must sleep on nine midsummer blossoms tonight,
Miss Julie; then our dreams will come true.

(MISS JULIE *and* JEAN *turn at the door.* JEAN *suddenly
covers one eye with his hand.*)

MISS JULIE: Let me see what you have in your eye.

JEAN: Oh, it's nothing . . . just a speck of dust. It'll disappear
in a minute.

MISS JULIE: It was from my sleeve—it brushed against
your eye. Sit down and let me help you! (*She takes him by
the arm and leads him to a chair, takes hold of his head
and bends it backward, then tries to remove the speck from
his eye with the tip of her handkerchief.*) Sit still now, very
still! (*She slaps him on the hand.*) Will you do as I tell
you!—I believe the great, big, strong fellow is trembling!
(*She feels his biceps.*) With arms like yours!

JEAN (*tries to dissuade her*): Miss Julie!

MISS JULIE: Yes, Monsieur Jean!

JEAN: *Attention! Je ne suis qu'un homme!*

MISS JULIE: Will you sit still!—There now! I got it out!
Kiss my hand now and say "thank you"!

JEAN (*gets up from the chair*): Miss Julie, will you please
listen to me!—Kristin has gone to bed now.—Will you
listen to me!

MISS JULIE: Kiss my hand first!

JEAN: Very well—but the blame will be yours!

MISS JULIE: Blame for what?

JEAN: For what? You are twenty-five years old, aren't you,
and not a child? Don't you know it's dangerous to play
with fire?

MISS JULIE: Not for me. I'm insured.

JEAN (*boldly*): No, you are not! And if you are, you are not far from danger—you may trigger a combustion!

MISS JULIE: I presume you mean yourself!

JEAN: Yes. Not because it is I, but because I am a man, and young!

MISS JULIE: Of prepossessing appearance. . . . What incredible conceit! Another Don Juan, perhaps! Or a Joseph! Upon my soul, I believe you are another Joseph!

JEAN: You do, do you?

MISS JULIE: Yes, I almost think so . . .

(JEAN *boldly goes up to her and tries to embrace and kiss her.*)

MISS JULIE (*boxes his ears*): That'll teach you manners!

JEAN: Were you serious or were you jesting?

MISS JULIE: Serious.

JEAN: In that case, you were serious a moment ago also? You play much too seriously—and there is where the danger lies! Now I am tired of playing and beg to be excused so that I can go back to my work. The Count has to have his boots ready when he returns, and it's long past midnight. (*He picks up a pair of boots.*)

MISS JULIE: Put down those boots!

JEAN: No. This is my work which I am hired to do—but I was never hired to be your playmate, and that's something I can never be. . . . I consider myself above that!

MISS JULIE: You are proud.

JEAN: In certain ways, yes—not in others.

MISS JULIE: Have you ever been in love?

JEAN: We don't use that word; but I have been fond of many girls—and once I felt sick because I couldn't have the one I wanted: sick, you know, like the princes in *A Thousand and One Nights*—who could neither eat nor drink merely for love!

MISS JULIE: Who was the girl? (JEAN *does not answer.*) Who was she?

JEAN: That's something you couldn't force out of me.

MISS JULIE: If I ask you as an equal, ask you as a— friend. . . . Who was she?

JEAN: It was you!

MISS JULIE (*seats herself*): How priceless!

JEAN: Yes, you may call it that! It was preposterous!—You see—it was that incident I was loath to tell you about, a moment ago—but now I shall. . . . Do you know how your world looks from below? No, you don't. Like hawks and falcons—whose backs we rarely see because they are always soaring high up in the sky. . . . I lived in my father's little shack with seven brothers and sisters and one pig out in the gray, barren fields where not even a tree grew. But from the windows I could see the wall enclosing the Count's park, with the apple trees rising above it. That was to me the Garden of Eden; and it was protected by a multitude of fierce angels with flaming swords. In spite of their presence, I and some other boys found our way to the tree of life. . . . Now you despise me, don't you?

MISS JULIE: Heavens, no—all boys steal apples!

JEAN: You say so now, but you have contempt for me just the same. . . . Well—one time I went into the Garden of Paradise with my mother, to weed the onion beds. Near the vegetable garden there was a Turkish pavilion standing in the shade of jasmine, and overgrown with honeysuckle. I had no idea what it could be used for; but I had never seen such a beautiful building. . . . People went inside, then came out again; and one day the door was left open. I sneaked in and saw the walls were covered with pictures of emperors and kings; and hanging at the windows were red curtains with tassels. Now you understand where I was . . . I . . . (*He breaks off a spray of lilac and holds it close to her nostrils.*) I had never been inside the castle, and had never seen any place as grand as the church, but this was if anything more beautiful. . . . And no matter which way my thoughts went, they always returned to—to that backhouse. . . . And gradually it developed into a yearning to experience some day all of its splendor and charm.—*Enfin,* I stole inside, gazed and admired, but just then I heard someone coming! There was only one exit for cultivated people—but for me there was another; and I had no choice but to take it . . .

(MISS JULIE, *who meanwhile has accepted the lilac spray from* JEAN, *lets it drop on the table.*)

JEAN: . . . and then I took to my heels, plunged through a raspberry hedge, dashed across the strawberry patches and found myself on the rose terrace. There I gazed at a figure in pink dress and white stockings—it was you. I hid underneath a heap of weeds and lay there—lay there, imagine, with thistles pricking me and under dank, stinking earth. And as I watched you among the roses, I thought to myself: If it is true that a thief can get to heaven and be with the angels, why should it be impossible for a poor peasant child here on God's earth to get into the castle park and play with the Count's daughter . . .

MISS JULIE (*with an expression of pain*): Do you think all poor children have the same thoughts that you had?

JEAN (*at first hesitantly, then with conviction*): That all poor children . . . Yes—of course—of course . . .

MISS JULIE: It must be terrible to be poor!

JEAN: Oh, Miss Julie—oh! A dog may lie on the Countess's sofa—a horse have his nose stroked by a young lady—but a lackey . . . (*In a changed tone.*) Oh, of course, there are some who have the right stuff in them and who swing themselves up in the world—but that doesn't happen every day. Anyhow, do you know what I did? I ran down to the mill-pond and jumped in, with my clothes on. I was dragged out and given a thrashing. But the following Sunday when my father and the rest of the family had gone to visit my grandmother, I schemed to stay at home. I then washed myself with soap and warm water, put on my best clothes and went to church—where I knew I would see you! I saw you and went back home, determined to die. . . . But I wanted to die beautifully and comfortably, without pain. I suddenly remembered that it was dangerous to sleep beneath an alder bush. We had a large one that was just blooming. I stripped it of its flowers; then made a bed of them in the oats-bin. Did you ever notice how smooth and silken oats are? Soft to the touch as the human skin. Well, I closed the lid, shut my eyes, and fell asleep. And when I woke up, I was very, very sick! . . . But as you see, I didn't die. What was in my mind, I really don't know! . . . I had no hope of ever winning you, of course—but you represented to me the hopelessness of ever rising above the social level to which I was born.

MISS JULIE: You know, you express yourself charmingly! Did you ever go to school?

JEAN: Briefly. But I have read a great many novels. And I have gone to the theatre. Also I have listened to cultured people talking, and I've learned most from that.

MISS JULIE: You stand and listen to what we say?

JEAN: Certainly! And I have heard much—much—when I've been sitting on the carriage-box and when I've been at the oars in the rowboat. I once heard you, Miss Julie, and a girl friend of yours . . .

MISS JULIE: Oh!—What did you hear?

JEAN: Well, I don't know that I can tell you. . . . But I must say I was rather surprised; and I couldn't imagine where you had learned words like that. After all, perhaps there isn't such a great difference between people as one thinks—

MISS JULIE: Shame on you! We don't behave like you do when we are engaged!

JEAN (*with a penetrating look*): Are you so sure? There is no use making yourself out so innocent, Miss Julie . . .

MISS JULIE: The man I gave my love to turned out to be a blackguard!

JEAN: That's what you always say—when it's over.

MISS JULIE: Always?

JEAN: Yes, always—at least that's what I think, having heard the same expression before—under such circumstances.

MISS JULIE: What sort of circumstances?

JEAN: Such as this one! The last time—

MISS JULIE: Stop! I don't want to hear any more!

JEAN: Strange to say, that's exactly what *she* said!—Well, now I must ask you to let me go to bed . . .

MISS JULIE (*softly*): Go to bed at this hour—on Midsummer Eve?

JEAN: Yes—I don't care the least bit about dancing with that riff-raff out there . . .

MISS JULIE: Go and get the key to the boathouse and take me for a row on the lake! I want to see the sunrise!

JEAN: Would that be a wise thing to do?

MISS JULIE: It sounds as if you were afraid of your reputation!

JEAN: And why shouldn't I be? I don't want to be made to look ridiculous and I have no desire to be discharged without a reference just when I am hoping to start on my own. And besides, I feel I am under some obligation to Kristin . . .

MISS JULIE: Oh, so it's Kristin again?

JEAN: Yes—but it's you, too. Take my advice: go to bed!

MISS JULIE: Should I take orders from you?

JEAN: Yes, for once—I beg of you—for your own sake! It's long past midnight. Lack of sleep brings on feverish excitement; it intoxicates and makes one reckless. Go to bed! And besides, if I am not mistaken, I hear the people coming this way, and they will be looking for me. . . . If they find us here, you'll be under a cloud!

(*The crowd, approaching, is heard to sing:*)

> There came two wedded maids from the wood—
> Tridiridi-ralla tridiridi-ra.
> The one had wet her little foot
> Tridiridi-ralla-la.
>
> They kept talking of nothing but money—
> Tridiridi-ralla tridiridi-ra.
> Yet they scarcely owned a farthing
> Tridiridi-ralla-la.
>
> Your ring I now give back to you
> Tridiridi-ralla tridiridi-ra.
> For I've another man in view
> Tridiridi-ralla-la.

MISS JULIE: I know the people here, and I love them as they love me. Let them come and you'll see.

JEAN: No, Miss Julie, they don't love you. They accept your food, but spit at you behind your back! Believe me! Listen to them! Just listen to what they are singing. . . . No—don't listen!

MISS JULIE (*stands listening*): What is it they are singing?

JEAN: It's an indecent parody! About you and me!

MISS JULIE: It's disgraceful! Shameless! What deceit!

JEAN: People like them are always cowardly! All you can do when you fight with rabble is to flee!

MISS JULIE: Flee? But where? We can't get out, and we can't go into Kristin's room . . .

JEAN: Well—into mine, then? We have to—there is no other way—and you can trust me. I am your friend, truly and respectfully . . .

MISS JULIE: But suppose—suppose they should look for you in your room?

JEAN: I'll bolt the door—and if they try to break in, I'll shoot! Come! *(He pleads with her, on his knees.)* Come, please!

MISS JULIE *(significantly)*: Will you promise me . . .

JEAN: I swear!

(MISS JULIE goes quickly into his room, left. JEAN follows her excitedly.)

(Dressed in their holiday best and with flowers in their hats and caps, the farm people enter. Leading them is a fiddler. They place a keg of small beer and a firkin of corn brandy, both decorated with garlands of fresh green leaves, on the table; then they bring out glasses and start drinking, form a ring and begin to dance, singing to the tune of "There came two wedded maids from the wood." When they have finished the dance, they leave, singing.

MISS JULIE *comes from* JEAN's *room, alone. She sees the kitchen in a deplorable mess, and claps her hands together in dejection. Then she takes out her powder-puff and powders her face.)*

JEAN *(enters with bravado)*: Don't you see! Did you hear them? Do you think you can stay here after this?

MISS JULIE: No! I don't think I can! But what are we going to do?

JEAN: Get away from here—travel—go far away from here . . .

MISS JULIE: Go away—travel. Yes, but where?

JEAN: To Switzerland—to the Italian lakes. . . . You have never been there, have you?

MISS JULIE: No—is it beautiful there?

JEAN: Ah! Eternal summer—orange groves—laurel trees. . . . Ah!

MISS JULIE: And when we are there—what shall we do?

JEAN: I'll start a hotel business—everything first class, and for exclusive guests . . .

MISS JULIE: A hotel?

JEAN: That's a lively business, believe me! All the time new faces, new languages, you never have time to worry or to be bored. . . . You nerve yourself against anything—you never have to look for something to do, for there is never any let-up. Bells ring day and night—you hear the train whistles—buses and carriages come and go—and all the time the money keeps rolling in. That's the life, I tell you!

MISS JULIE: Yes—that's living. . . . And what about me?

JEAN: You'll be the mistress of the house—its chief attraction and ornament! With your looks, and your style and manner, why, our success is assured from the start! It'll be colossal! You'll be sitting like a queen in the office and you'll keep the slaves moving by pressing an electric button —the guests file past your throne and place their tribute timidly before you—you have no idea how nervous it makes people to have their bills presented to them. I'll salt the bills, and you'll sugar them with your sweetest smile. . . . Ah, please—let us get away from here! (*He takes out a timetable from his pocket.*) Without delay—by the next train! We'll be in Malmö at six-thirty—in Hamburg at eight-forty in the morning—in Frankfort and Basel within a day—and we'll get to Como, by way of St. Gothard, in— let me see—in three days. Three days!

MISS JULIE: That's all very well—but, Jean—you must give me courage. Tell me that you love me! Come and take me in your arms!

JEAN (*hesitates*): I want to—but I lack the courage . . . ever to do it in this house again. I love you—you know that— you can't doubt that, can you, Miss Julie?

MISS JULIE (*shyly, with true womanly feeling*): Miss Julie? Call me Julie! Between us there can no longer be any barriers! Call me Julie!

JEAN (*pathetically*): I can't! As long as we are in this house, there are barriers between us. There is tradition—and there is the Count. Never in my life have I met *anyone* who strikes such awe into me! I have only to see his gloves lying on a chair, and I feel servile. . . . I have only to hear him ring upstairs, and I cringe like a shying horse—and even now when I look at his boots standing there so stiff and cocky, I feel a chill down my spine. (*He kicks at the boots.*) Superstition, prejudice, convention—knocked into us from childhood—but that can easily be got rid of. . . . All you have to do is to go to another country, to a republic, and there you will see how they prostrate themselves before my porter's uniform. . . . Yes, they'll bow and scrape—but here is one who won't! I wasn't born to crawl before others—I have the right stuff in me—I have character . . . and if I only get to the first branch, you watch me climb to the top! Today I am a lackey—next year I'll be in business for myself—ten years from now I'll be rich and retire—and then I'll move to Roumania and get myself a decoration—and I may, mark my words, I may end up a count!

MISS JULIE: Very nice, very nice!

JEAN: Yes—for in Roumania you can buy yourself a title —and so you may, after all, be a countess, Miss Julie. . . . *My* countess!

MISS JULIE: All that doesn't interest me at all—I'm leaving all that behind me! Tell me only that you love me . . . for if you don't . . . well—then what would I be?

JEAN: I'll tell you—I'll tell you a thousand times—later on! But not now—not here! And above all, let's not be sentimental, or everything will go wrong! We must look at this matter calmly, soberly, like sensible people. (*Takes out a cigar, bites off the butt end and lights it.*) Now you sit down there, and I'll sit here; then we'll talk it over as if nothing had happened.

MISS JULIE (*desperately*): My God—haven't you any feelings?

JEAN: *If* I have feelings! There isn't a man with more feeling than I! But I know how to control myself!

MISS JULIE: A moment ago you kissed my slipper—and now . . .

JEAN (*brutally*): That was then—now we have other things to think of!

MISS JULIE: Don't speak to me so cruelly!

JEAN: I am speaking sensibly, that's all! One folly has been committed—don't commit any more! The Count may be here any moment now; and before he comes, we must settle our future. Now—what do you think of my plans, Miss Julie? Do you approve of them?

MISS JULIE: They seem likely enough—but let me ask one question: Have you sufficient capital to start such a large undertaking?

JEAN (*chewing his cigar*): Have I? Of course I have! I have my training in the business, my vast experience, my linguistic ability! That's a capital to be reckoned with, don't you think?

MISS JULIE: But you couldn't buy a railroad ticket with it, could you?

JEAN (*keeps chewing the cigar*): That's quite true—and that is why I am looking for a partner who can advance the necessary funds.

MISS JULIE: Where do you expect to find such a person in a hurry?

JEAN: That is where *you* come in—if you want to be my partner—

MISS JULIE: I couldn't . . . and I haven't any money of my own. (*There is a silence.*)

JEAN: Then we'll have to drop the whole thing . . .

MISS JULIE: And so . . .

JEAN: And so . . . things remain as they are . . .

MISS JULIE: Do you think I'll remain under this roof as your mistress? Do you think I will allow the people here to point a finger at me? Do you think I could face my father after this? Never! Take me away from here—from this humiliation and disgrace! Oh, my God, what have I done? My God! . . . (*She breaks into tears.*)

JEAN: So, that's the tune you are singing *now?* What you have done?—What many others have done before you . . .

MISS JULIE (*screaming hysterically*): And now you despise me! I'm falling—falling—

JEAN: Fall low enough—fall down to my level—then I'll raise you up again!

MISS JULIE: What dreadful power could have drawn me to you? The attraction of the weak to the strong, the ones on the decline to the ones rising? Or could it have been love? Is this what you call love? Do you know what love is?

JEAN: Do I? You may be sure I do! Do you think I never had an affair before?

MISS JULIE: What a way to speak? And such thoughts!

JEAN: That's the way I was brought up, and that's the way I am! Now don't get excited, and stop acting so prim and prudish! For now you are not a bit better than I am. . . Come here, my little girl, let me treat you to a glass of something very special! (*He opens the table drawer and brings out the wine bottle; then he fills the two glasses which were used previously.*)

MISS JULIE: Where did you get this wine?

JEAN: From the wine cellar.

MISS JULIE: My father's burgundy!

JEAN: Isn't it good enough for his son-in-law?

MISS JULIE: And I drink beer!

JEAN: That only shows your taste is not as good as mine!

MISS JULIE: Thief!

JEAN: You are not going to give me away, are you?

MISS JULIE: Oh, God! To be the accomplice of a thief—and in my own home! Have I been under the influence of some intoxication? Have I been dreaming this Midsummer Night? —This festival of frolic and innocent merriment?

JEAN (*sarcastically*): Innocent, h'm!

MISS JULIE (*paces back and forth*): Could there be anyone in this world more miserable than I am?

JEAN: Why be miserable—after a conquest like yours? Think of Kristin in there—don't you think that she, too, has feelings . . .

MISS JULIE: I used to think so, but I no longer do! No— once a servant, always a servant!

JEAN: And once a whore—always a whore!

MISS JULIE (*on her knees, her hands clasped*): Oh, God in heaven—put an end to my miserable life! Take me away from this filth—I am sinking down in it! Help me! Save me!

JEAN: I can't help feeling sorry for you. . . . When I lay in the onion bed and watched you in the rose garden, I—yes, I can tell you now—I had the same nasty thoughts that all boys have.

MISS JULIE: And you—you wanted to die for me!

JEAN: You mean in the oats-bin? I just made that up!

MISS JULIE: Just a lie, then!

JEAN (*he is beginning to be sleepy*): Not exactly! I think I once read somewhere in a newspaper about a chimney-sweep who went to sleep in a chest used for firewood. He had filled it with lilacs—because he was sued for non-support of his child . . .

MISS JULIE: So that's the kind of person you are . . .

JEAN: I had to make up something. Glitter and tinsel are what dazzle the women—and catch them.

MISS JULIE: Cad!

JEAN: Garbage!

MISS JULIE: And now you have seen the hawk's back!

JEAN: Not exactly its *back* . . .

MISS JULIE: And I was to be the first branch . . .

JEAN: But the branch was rotten . . .

MISS JULIE: I was to be the hotel sign . . .

JEAN: And I the hotel . . .

MISS JULIE: . . . Sitting behind the desk to attract and lure customers, falsify the bills and overcharge them . . .

JEAN: That would have been *my* business . . .

MISS JULIE: To think that the human soul can be so low, so rotten—

JEAN: Wash it clean, why don't you?

MISS JULIE: You lackey! You menial! Stand up when I speak to you!

JEAN: You—a menial's strumpet—whore to a lackey—keep your mouth shut and get out of here! Is it for you to rake me over the coals for being coarse and uncouth? Never have I seen any of our kind behave so vulgarly as you behaved tonight! Do you think a servant girl would accost a man the way you did? Did you ever see a girl of my class throw herself at a man as you did? That's something I have only seen done by animals and prostitutes!

MISS JULIE (*crushed*): That's right! Stone me—trample on me—I deserve it—all of it! I am a wretched woman! But help me—help me out of this—if there *is* a way out of it!

JEAN (*now in a milder tone of voice*): I would belittle myself if I denied having a share in the honor of seducing you; but do you really think that anyone of my class would have dared to cast a glance at you, if you yourself had not sent out the invitation? I still can't get over it—

MISS JULIE: And you take pride in it!

JEAN: Why not?—Although I must confess the victory was much too easy to give me any real intoxication!

MISS JULIE: Keep on being brutal!

JEAN (*rises*): No—on the contrary, I ask you to forgive me for the things I just said! I never strike a defenseless person —least of all a woman. I won't deny that it gives me a certain satisfaction to discover that what dazzled us down below was nothing but cheap tinsel; that the hawk's back was only gray, like the rest of his fine feathers; that the delicate complexion was mere powder; that the polished nails had dirty edges; that the handkerchief could be soiled, despite its perfumed scent. . . . But on the other hand, it hurts me to realize that what I was striving to reach was so unsubstantial and artificial . . . it pains me to see that you

have sunk so low that you are far beneath your own cook
. . . it saddens me as when I see the autumn leaves torn
into tatters by the rain and turned into mud.

MISS JULIE: You talk as if you already feel yourself above
me?

JEAN: Of course I am! You see, I might be able to make you
a countess—but you could never make me a count.

MISS JULIE: But you are a thief, and I am not!

JEAN: There are worse things than being a thief! Much worse!
Besides, when I am employed in a household, I consider
myself, in a way, a member of the family, related to it, so
to speak; and to pick a berry or two when the bushes are
full is not stealing. . . . (*His passion comes to life again.*)
Miss Julie—you are a glorious woman—far too good for
one like me! You are under the spell of some sort of
intoxication, and now you want to cover up your mistake
by deluding yourself that you love me! But you don't! You
may be attracted to me physically—and in that case your
love is no better than mine! But I am not content with
being just an animal, to you; and I can never kindle any
love in you for me—

MISS JULIE: Are you so sure of that?

JEAN: Do you mean to say that I could?—I could love you,
yes—no doubt of that! You are beautiful, you are refined—
(*He comes close to her and takes hold of her hand.*) . . .
cultivated, and charming—when you feel like it; and I don't
think that any man who has once fallen for you will ever
stop loving you. (*He puts his arm round her waist.*) You are
like mulled wine, strongly spiced—and a kiss from you. . . .
(*He tries to lead her out of the kitchen. She gently frees
herself from him.*)

MISS JULIE: Let me go! You will never win me that way . . .

JEAN: Then *how?* Not *that* way, you say. Not by caresses and
pretty words—not by thoughtfulness about the future—
trying to save you from disgrace! How then?

MISS JULIE: How? You ask how? I don't know . . . haven't
a thought! I loathe you as I loathe a rat—but I can't escape
you!

JEAN: Escape *with* me, then!

MISS JULIE (*straightens up*): Escape? Yes, we must get away
from here! But I am so tired!—Pour me a glass of wine!

(JEAN *serves her a glass.*)

MISS JULIE (*looking at her watch*): But first we must have a
   talk—we still have a little time left. (*She empties her glass
   and holds it out for another drink.*)
JEAN: You must drink moderately, or it'll go to your head.
MISS JULIE: What does it matter?
JEAN: What does it matter? To be intoxicated is a sign of
   vulgarity. . . . What was it you wanted to tell me?
MISS JULIE: We have to get away from here! But first we
   must have a talk—that is, I must do the talking—for so far
   it is you who have done it all. You have told me about
   your life; now I shall tell you about mine—then we shall
   really know each other, before we begin our journey
   together.
JEAN: Wait a second! If you'll pardon my suggestion—don't
   you think you may regret it afterwards, if you bare your
   life's secrets?
MISS JULIE: Are you not my friend?
JEAN: Yes—in a way. . . . But don't put too much confidence
   in me.
MISS JULIE: You don't mean what you say—and besides:
   everybody knows my secrets. You see, my mother was not
   an aristocrat by birth. She came of quite simple stock. She
   was brought up in conformity with the ideas of her generation: equality of the sexes—the emancipation of women—
   and all that sort of thing. She looked upon marriage with
   downright aversion. Therefore, when my father proposed
   marriage to her, she replied that she would never be his wife
   —but—she married him just the same. I came into the
   world—against my mother's wishes, as I have learned; and
   now I was to be reared by my mother as a child of nature
   and in addition was to be taught all the things a boy has to
   learn, all in order to prove that a woman is quite as good
   as any man. I had to wear boy's clothes, had to learn how
   to handle horses, but I was never allowed in the cattle barn.
   I had to groom, harness and saddle my horse and had to
   go hunting—yes, I even had to try my hand at farming!
   And the farmhands were given women's chores to do, and
   the women did the men's work—and the upshot of it was
   that the estate almost went to rack and ruin, and we became
   the laughingstock of the whole countryside. . . . At last

my father seems to have come out of his inertia, for he rebelled; and after that all went according to his will. My mother took sick—what the sickness was I never learned—but she frequently had spasms, shut herself up in the attic, or secluded herself in the garden—and sometimes she stayed out all night. Then came the great fire which you have heard about. The house, the stables, and the cattle barns burned down, and under suspicious circumstances that pointed to arson. The disaster happened, namely, the day after the quarterly insurance period had expired; and the insurance premium, that my father had forwarded by a messenger, had arrived too late because of the messenger's negligence or indifference. (*She fills up her glass, and drinks.*)

JEAN: You mustn't drink any more!

MISS JULIE: Ah, what do I care!—We were left with nothing, we had no place to sleep, except in the carriages. My father was desperate; he didn't know where to get money to build again. Then my mother suggested to him that he borrow from an old friend of hers—someone she had known in her youth, a brick manufacturer not far from here. Father got the loan, and without having to pay any interest—and this was a surprise to him. And the estate was rebuilt! (*She drinks again.*) Do you know who set the place on fire?

JEAN: The Countess, your mother . . .

MISS JULIE: Do you know who the brick manufacturer was?

JEAN: Your mother's lover?

MISS JULIE: Do you know whose money it was?

JEAN: Wait a second!—No—I don't—

MISS JULIE: It was my mother's.

JEAN: In other words, your father's—the Count's—unless they had made a marriage settlement.

MISS JULIE: No, there was none. My mother had a little money of her own. She didn't want my father to have charge of it, so she—entrusted it to her friend!

JEAN: And he helped himself to it!

MISS JULIE: Precisely! He appropriated the money. All this my father came to know. He couldn't bring action against him, couldn't repay his wife's lover, couldn't prove that the money was his wife's!—That was the revenge my mother took on him because he had made himself the master in his own house. He was on the verge of committing suicide when all this happened; as a matter of fact, there was a rumor that he tried to and didn't succeed. . . . However, he took a new lease of life, and my mother had to pay the penalty for her behavior! You can imagine what the next five years did to me! I felt sorry for my father, yet I took my mother's part because I didn't know the true circumstances. She had taught me to mistrust and hate men, for she herself hated men, as I told you before— and she made me swear never to become the slave of any man . . .

JEAN: And then you became engaged to the county prosecutor!

MISS JULIE: Yes—in order to make him my slave.

JEAN: And he refused?

MISS JULIE: He would have liked it, don't worry; but I didn't give him the chance. I became bored with him . . .

JEAN: I saw that you did—out in the stableyard.

MISS JULIE: What did you see?

JEAN: Exactly what happened—how he broke off the engagement.

MISS JULIE: That's a lie! It was I who broke the engagement! —Did he tell you he did? The scoundrel!

JEAN: I wouldn't call him a scoundrel. . . . You just hate men, Miss Julie.

MISS JULIE: Yes, I do! Most men! But occasionally—when my weakness comes over me—oh, the shame of it!

JEAN: You hate me, too, don't you?

MISS JULIE: I hate you no end! I should like to have you slaughtered like an animal!

JEAN: As one shoots a mad dog, eh?

MISS JULIE: Precisely!

JEAN: But as there is nothing here to shoot with, and no dog —what are we to do?

MISS JULIE: Get away from here!

JEAN: And then torture each other to death?

MISS JULIE: No—live life for a few brief days, for a week— for as long as we can—and then—die . . .

JEAN: Die? What nonsense! No—I think it would be far better to go into the hotel business.

MISS JULIE (*who, absorbed with her thoughts, has not heard what he said*): . . . by Lake Como, where the sun is always shining—where the laurel tree is still greening at Christmas —and the oranges are golden red—

JEAN: Lake Como is a hole where it rains all the time, and I never saw any oranges there except in the grocery shops. But it's a good place for foreigners—and there are plenty of villas to be rented to lovers—and that is a business that pays! And do you know why? I'll tell you why—because they have to sign a six months' lease, and they never stay longer than three weeks!

MISS JULIE (*naïvely*): Why only three weeks?

JEAN: Because they quarrel, of course. But the rent has to be paid in full just the same. And then the house is rented out again; and that's the way it goes—on and on—for people will always be in love, although their love doesn't last very long . . .

MISS JULIE: Then you don't care to die with me, do you?

JEAN: I don't care to die at all! Not only because I like to live, but because I consider suicide a sin against God, who gave us life.

MISS JULIE: You believe in God—*you?*

JEAN: Of course I do! I go to church every other Sunday. But now—quite frankly—now I am getting tired of all this talk, and I am going to bed.

MISS JULIE: Oh, you are, are you? And you think that will be a satisfactory ending? Do you know what a man owes to a woman he has taken advantage of?

JEAN (*takes out his purse and throws a coin on the table*): There you are! Now I owe you nothing!

MISS JULIE (*pretends to ignore the insult*): Are you aware of the legal consequences?

JEAN: It's too bad that the law provides no punishment for the woman who seduces a man!

MISS JULIE: Can you think of any way out of this—other than going abroad, getting married, and being divorced?

JEAN: Suppose I refuse to enter into such a degrading marriage?

MISS JULIE: Degrading?

JEAN: Yes—for me! For, mind you, my lineage is cleaner and more respectable than yours—I have no pyromaniac in my family—

MISS JULIE: How can you be so sure of that?

JEAN: And how can you prove the opposite? We have no register of our ancestors—except in the police records! But I have seen your genealogical chart in the book on your drawing-room table. Do you know who your first ancestor was? A miller who let his wife sleep with the king one night during the Danish War!—I haven't any ancestors like that! I have no ancestry of any kind—but I can start a family tree of my own!

MISS JULIE: This is what I get for opening my heart to one like you, to an inferior . . . for betraying the honor of my family . . .

JEAN: You mean *dishonor!* . . . Well, I warned you—and now you see— People shouldn't drink, for then they start talking—and people should never be garrulous.

MISS JULIE: Oh, how I regret what I have done! How I regret it! Oh, if—at least—you had loved me!

JEAN: For the last time—what is it you want me to do? Do you want me to burst into tears? Do you want me to jump over your riding whip? Do you want me to kiss you?—to elope with you to Lake Como for three weeks?—and then. . . . What do you want me to do? What is it you want? This is getting to be intolerable! But that's what one gets for sticking one's nose into a female's business! Miss Julie— I know you must be suffering—but I can't understand you. . . . We have no such strange notions as you have—we don't hate as you do! To us love is nothing but playfulness —we play when our work is done. We haven't the whole day and the whole night for it like you! I think you must be sick. . . . Yes, I am sure you are!

MISS JULIE: You must treat me with kindness—you must speak to me like a human being . . .

JEAN: Yes, if you'll behave like one! You spit on me—but when I spit back, you object!

MISS JULIE: Oh, help me—help me! Tell me what to do—and where to go!

JEAN: In the name of Christ, I wish I knew myself!

MISS JULIE: I have behaved like a madwoman . . . but is there no way out of this?

JEAN: Stay here—and stop worrying! Nobody knows a thing.

MISS JULIE: I can't! They all know—and Kristin knows. . . .

JEAN: They know nothing—and they wouldn't believe such a thing!

MISS JULIE (*after a moment's hesitation*): But—it might happen again!

JEAN: Yes—it might.

MISS JULIE: And have consequences? . . .

JEAN: Consequences? . . . What have I been thinking about? That never occurred to me!—Then there is only one thing to do. You must leave—and immediately! If I come with you, it would look suspicious—therefore you must go alone —go away—it doesn't matter where.

MISS JULIE: I—alone—but where? I couldn't do it!

JEAN: You must—and before the Count gets back! If you remain here, we both know what will happen. Having committed one mistake, it's easy to make another because the damage has already been done. . . . With time one gets more and more reckless—until finally one is caught! That's why I urge you to leave! Later on you can write to the Count and tell him everything—except that it was I!—He would never suspect, of course—and I don't think he would be eager to know!

MISS JULIE: I'll go, if you'll come with me . . .

JEAN: Are you stark staring mad, woman? Miss Julie eloping with her lackey! It would be in the newspapers before another day had passed. The Count would never get over it!

MISS JULIE: I can't go—and I can't stay here! Can't you help me! I am so tired, so dreadfully tired!—Order me to go! Make me move! I am no longer able to think—I can't bring myself to do anything!

JEAN: Now you see what sort of miserable creature you are, don't you? Why is your sort always so overbearing? Why do you strut with your noses in the air as if you were the lords of Creation?—Very well, then—I shall order you about! Go upstairs and get dressed, take enough money with you for traveling and then come down!

MISS JULIE (*almost in a whisper*): Come upstairs with me—

JEAN: To your room?—Now you are mad again! (*He hesitates a moment.*) No! Go immediately! (*He takes her by the hand and escorts her to the door.*)

MISS JULIE (*walking toward the door*): Why don't you speak gently to me, Jean?

JEAN: An order always sounds harsh.—Now you are beginning to find out how it feels . . .

(JULIE *leaves.* JEAN *is now alone. He gives a sigh of relief, seats himself at the table, takes out a pencil and a notebook, writes down some figures; now and then he counts aloud, all in pantomime, until* KRISTIN *enters. She is dressed for church-going; carries a white tie and a false shirt front with collar, for* JEAN.)

KRISTIN: In heaven's name—look at my kitchen! What's been going on here?

JEAN: Oh—it's Miss Julie—she brought them all inside. . . . Don't tell me you've been sleeping so soundly you didn't hear them?

KRISTIN: Yes, I slept like a log!

JEAN: And you are already dressed for church?

KRISTIN: Sure! You promised to come to communion with me today, didn't you?

JEAN: Why, of course—so I did, didn't I?—And I see you have my outfit there—let's get ready, then!

(JEAN *seats himself, and* KRISTIN *starts to put the dickey, collar and tie on him. There is a silence.*)

JEAN (*sleepily*): What is the text for today?

KRISTIN: Oh—I think it's about the beheading of John the Baptist.

JEAN: Then I imagine it's going to be a terribly long service! —Ouch, you are choking me!—Oh, I am so sleepy, so sleepy!

KRISTIN: Well, what have you been doing the whole night— you are all green in the face?

JEAN: I've been sitting here talking to Miss Julie. . . .

KRISTIN: She just has no decency, that one!

(*Silence.*)

JEAN: Tell me, Kristin, don't you think—

KRISTIN: What?

JEAN: Isn't it strange, after all, when you think about it— that she—

KRISTIN: What is it that's so strange?

JEAN: Everything!

(*There is a pause.*)

KRISTIN (*with a glance at the wine glasses that stand on the table, half-filled*): You haven't been drinking together, have you?

JEAN: Yes!

KRISTIN: You ought to be ashamed of yourself! Look me straight in the eye! (JEAN *affirms her suspicions.*) Can it be possible? Can it really be possible?

JEAN (*deliberates for a moment, then answers her*): Yes—that's what happened.

KRISTIN: Why! I would never have believed it! Never! Shame on you! Shame on you!

JEAN: You are not jealous of her, are you?

KRISTIN: No, not of her! If it had been Clara or Sophie—I would have scratched your eyes out! Yes—yes, that's the way I feel—and I can't tell you just why I feel that way! Oh, but this is disgusting—disgusting!

JEAN: Do you hate her for it?

KRISTIN: No—I am furious with you! It was a shameless thing to do—shameless! I pity the girl!—To tell the truth, I don't care to stay in this house any longer—I want to feel some respect for the people I work for . . .

JEAN: Why do we have to have respect for them?

KRISTIN: Well, you tell me—you who know everything! You don't want to work for people who don't behave decently, do you? Do you? . . . I think it's degrading, that's what I think . . .

JEAN: Yes—but it makes you feel good to know that they are not a bit better than we are!

KRISTIN: No—I don't look at it that way at all. If they are no better than we are—what's the use of trying to be like them—of becoming any better than we are? And think of the Count—think of him—who has had so much grief in his day! No—I won't stay here in this house any longer! . . . And with such as you!—Now—if it had been the county prosecutor—or someone who was a little bit better than you—

JEAN: What's that?

KRISTIN: That's just what I said! You may be good enough in your own way, but just the same there is a difference between high and low. . . . No—I'll never be able to get over this!—Miss Julie who was so proud—who acted so superior toward men. . . . You would never have thought that she would have let any man become intimate with her—and, least of all, a fellow like you! She—who was about to have her poor little Diana shot just because she was running after the gatekeeper's pugdog. . . . Can you imagine it! But I won't stay here any longer—the twenty-fourth of October I quit!

JEAN: And then?

KRISTIN: Well—since you bring the matter up—it's about time you looked around for something to do, for we are going to get married just the same.

JEAN: Yes—but what kind of place am I to look for? If I marry, I couldn't get a place like this.

KRISTIN: No, I know that. But you can get a job as a janitor or porter—or try to get a position in some government bureau. The government doesn't pay much, but it's security—and, besides, the wife and children get a pension.

JEAN (*with a grimace*): That's all very good, but it doesn't exactly fit in with my plans just now to be thinking about dying for the benefit of wife and children. I must confess that my aspirations are aimed at something a little bit higher.

KRISTIN: You and your ideas, yes! But you have responsibilities, too! Try to think of them!

JEAN: Don't make me lose my temper by talking about responsibilities! I know what I have to do! (*He suddenly listens to some sound from outside.*) Anyhow, we have plenty of time to decide just what to do. Go and get ready now so we can go to church.

KRISTIN: Who can that be I hear walking upstairs?

JEAN: I've no idea—unless it's Clara.

KRISTIN (*as she is leaving*): I don't suppose it could be the Count, could it? Could he have come home without anybody hearing him?

JEAN (*panic-stricken*): The Count? Why, no—I would never think so. . . . If he had, he would have rung . . .

KRISTIN: Well, God help us. . . . I've never heard of anything like this! (*She goes out.*)

(*The sun has now risen and casts its rays on the treetops in the park. The light beams keep moving until they fall obliquely through the windows. JEAN goes over to the door and gives a sign to JULIE outside.*)

MISS JULIE (*comes inside. She is dressed for travel and*

carries a small birdcage, covered with a towel. She places the cage on a chair): I am ready now.

JEAN: Ssh! Kristin is awake!

MISS JULIE *(from this moment on, she shows signs of extreme nervousness)*: Does she suspect anything?

JEAN: Not a thing! She knows nothing!—Lord in heaven—how you look!

MISS JULIE: Look? Why—what's the matter?

JEAN: Your face is livid! You look like a corpse . . . and if you'll pardon me, your face is not clean!

MISS JULIE: Then I must wash my face! *(She goes over to the sink and washes her face and hands.)* Would you give me a towel?—Oh . . . I see the sun is rising . . .

JEAN: . . . and now the spell will be broken!

MISS JULIE: Yes, the trolls have been out this night!—But now, Jean,—you can come with me, do you hear, for I have all the money we need.

JEAN *(with disbelief and hesitation)*: You have enough?

MISS JULIE: Enough to start with. . . . Please come with me! I can't travel alone now. . . . Imagine my sitting alone on a stuffy train, squeezed in among crowds of passengers gaping at me . . . and with long stops at the stations, when I would like to fly away on wings. . . . No—I can't do it—I just can't do it! And then I'll be thinking of the past—memories of the midsummer days of my childhood—the church, covered with wreaths and garlands, with leaves of birch and with lilac—the festive dinner table—relatives and friends—and the afternoon in the park, with music and dancing, games and flowers. . . . Oh—no matter how one tries to get away from the past, the memories are there, packed into one's baggage. . . . They pursue one, hitched onto the tail of the train . . . and then comes remorse—and the pangs of conscience—

JEAN: I'll come with you, but let's hurry—before it's too late! We haven't a second to lose!

MISS JULIE: Hurry up and dress! *(She picks up the birdcage.)*

JEAN: But no baggage! Then we would be found out immediately!

MISS JULIE: No, nothing . . . only what we can take with us in our compartment.

JEAN *(who has just reached for his hat, stares at the birdcage)*: What's that you have there? What is it?

MISS JULIE: It's only my green siskin . . . I couldn't go without her!

JEAN: Well, of all the— Are we going to take a birdcage with us now? You must be completely out of your mind! (*He tries to take the cage from her.*) Let go of the cage!

MISS JULIE: It's the one thing I am taking with me from my home—the only living thing that loves me since Diana was faithless to me. . . . Don't be cruel! Please let me take her with me!

JEAN: Put that cage down, I tell you—and don't talk so loud! Kristin can hear us!

MISS JULIE: No—I won't part with her to anyone else! I'd rather you killed her . . .

JEAN: Give me the little beast then—I'll chop its head off!

MISS JULIE: Oh—but—don't hurt her, please!—No—I can't let you . . .

JEAN: But I can—and I know how. . . . Give it to me!

MISS JULIE (*takes the bird out of the cage. She kisses it*): Oh, my poor little Sérine, must your mother lose you—must you die?

JEAN: Let's have no scenes—it's now a question of life and death—of your own future. . . . Quick, now! (*He snatches the bird from her, goes over to the chopping block, and picks up the ax lying on it. MISS JULIE turns away her face.*) You should have learned how to kill chickens instead of how to shoot . . . (*He lets the hatchet fall on the bird's neck.*) . . . then the sight of a little blood wouldn't make you faint!

MISS JULIE (*screams*): Let me die too! Kill me! You—who can take the life of an innocent little creature without even a tremble of the hand! Oh—how I hate you—how I loathe you! Now there is blood between us! I curse the day I was born, the day I was conceived!

JEAN: Stop cursing—it does you no good! Let's be off!

MISS JULIE (*approaches the chopping block, as if drawn to it against her will*): No—I am not ready to go yet—I can't go—I must first see . . . (*She suddenly stops. She stands listening; all the while her eyes are riveted on the chopping block and the ax.*) You think I can't stand the sight of blood! You think I am such a weakling, do you?—Oh, I should like to see *your* blood—*your* brain—on the chopping block. . . . I should like to see your whole sex bathing in its own blood, like my little bird! I even think I could drink out of your skull—I would revel in bathing my feet in your caved-in chest—and I could devour your heart roasted! You think I am a weakling—you think that I am in love with you because my womb felt a craving for your seed—you think that I yearn to carry your offspring under my heart, to nourish it with my blood—to bear your child and your name? Come to think of it, what is your name? I have never heard your last name—I guess you haven't any. . . . I was to be Mrs. Gatekeeper—or Mme. Refuseheap. . . . You dog who wear my collar—you lackey with my family crest on your buttons! I was to share you with my cook—a rival of my own servant! Oh, oh, oh!—You think I am a coward and that I am eager to flee! No—this time I am not leaving—come what may! When father returns he will find his chiffonier ransacked and the money gone! Immediately he will ring that bell—his usual two rings for you, Jean,—and he will send for the sheriff . . . and then—then I shall tell the whole story! The whole story! Oh, what a relief it will be to get it over with. . . . If only that moment were here! And father will have a stroke and die! . . . And that will be the end of our family. And then, at last, we shall be at rest—find peace—eternal peace! . . . And the family coat of arms will be broken against the coffin—the noble line will be extinct—but the lackey's line will go on in an orphanage—reaping laurels in the gutter, and ending in prison . . .

JEAN: There's your royal blood talking! Bravo, Miss Julie! And don't forget to stuff the miller's skeleton in your family closet!

(KRISTIN *enters. She is dressed for church and carries a prayer book.*)

MISS JULIE (*rushes toward her and flings herself into her arms, as if to plead for protection*): Help me, Kristin! Save me from this man!

KRISTIN (*stands cold and unmoved*): What kind of spectacle is this on the sabbath morning? (*She notices the dead bird and the blood on the chopping block.*) And what's this piggish mess you have made here?—What's the meaning of all this? And why are you screaming and making so much noise?

MISS JULIE: Kristin—you are a woman—and you are my friend! Look out for this man—he is a villain!

JEAN *(somewhat abashed and timid)*: While you ladies are conversing, I am going in to shave. *(He goes into his room left.)*

MISS JULIE: I want you to understand me—I want you to listen to me—

KRISTIN: No—I must say I can't understand all these goings on! Where are you planning to go—you are dressed for traveling—and Jean had his hat on. . . . Why?—What's going on?

MISS JULIE: Listen to me, Kristin! You must listen to me—and then I'll tell you everything . . .

KRISTIN: I don't care to—I don't want to know . . .

MISS JULIE: You must—you must hear . . .

KRISTIN: Just what is it—what's it all about? Is it about this foolishness with Jean, is it?—Well, I don't let that bother me a bit—it's none of my concern. . . . But if you are thinking of tricking him into running away with you—then I'll soon put a stop to that!

MISS JULIE *(with extreme nervousness)*: Try to be calm, Kristin, and please listen to me! I can't stay here—and Jean can't stay here—and that is why we must leave . . .

KRISTIN: H'm, h'm!

MISS JULIE *(brightening)*: Oh, I know—I have an idea! Suppose the three of us—if we should go abroad—we three together—to Switzerland—and start a hotel business—have the money, you see. . . . *(She dangles the handbag before KRISTIN.)* . . . and Jean and I would run the business—and I thought you could take charge of the kitchen. Don't you think that would be perfect?—Say that you will! Do come with us—then everything will be settled! Will you? Say yes! *(She puts her arms round KRISTIN and gives her a pat on the back.)*

KRISTIN *(coldly reflective)*: H'm, h'm!

MISS JULIE *(presto tempo)*: You have never been out in the world, Kristin,—you must travel and see things. You have no idea what fun it is to travel by train! Always new people, new countries! And in Hamburg we stop over and look at the Zoological Garden—you will like that . . . and when we arrive in Munich, we have the museums there—and there you'll see Rubens and Raphael and other great masters, you know. . . . You have heard of Munich, haven't you?—There is where King Ludwig lived—the king, you know, who lost his mind. . . . And then we'll visit his castles—his castles still are there; and they are beautiful like the castles in the fairy tales—and from there, you see, it is only a short distance to Switzerland—and the Alps! Think of it, they are covered with snow in the middle of the summer—and oranges grow there—and laurels that stay green the year round!

(JEAN *appears from the left. While he is sharpening his razor on a strop that he holds between his teeth and his left hand, he is listening with evident satisfaction to their conversation. Now and then he nods approvingly.*)

MISS JULIE *(tempo prestissimo):* And in Switzerland we'll buy a hotel—and I'll take care of the accounts while Jean looks after the guests—does the marketing—attends to the correspondence. . . . It'll be a hustle and bustle, believe me. . . . You hear the whistle of the train—the omnibus arrives—the bells ring, from the hotel rooms and the dining-room. —I make out the bills—and I know how to salt them, too. . . . You can't imagine how diffident tourists are when their bills are presented to them!—And you—you will preside in the kitchen! You won't have to stand at the stove yourself, of course,—and you will have to be dressed neatly and nicely so that you can show yourself among people . . . and with your looks—yes, I am not trying to flatter you—with your looks, you might very well get yourself a husband one fine day!—Some rich Englishman, why not? They are so easy to . . . *(in a slackened pace)* . . . to capture . . . and then we'll build ourselves a villa at the edge of Lake Como. . . . Of course, it rains there a little occasionally, but . . . *(Her voice fades a little.)* . . . the sun must be shining there some time—even though the gloom seems to persist—and—so—well, we can always return home—and then go back again . . . *(There is a pause.)* . . . here—or somewhere else . . .

KRISTIN: Miss Julie, do you really believe all this yourself?
MISS JULIE *(crushed):* . . . If I believe it—myself?
KRISTIN: Just that!
MISS JULIE: I don't know . . . I don't believe in anything any

more! (*She sinks down on the bench, puts her head between her hands and drops her head on the table.*) Not in anything! Not in anything!

KRISTIN (*turning toward the left where* JEAN *is standing*): So–o, you were going to run away, were you?

JEAN (*crestfallen and looking foolish, he lays the razor on the table*): Run away? Well—that's a strong word to use! Miss Julie told you about her project, didn't she? Well—she is tired now after being up all night . . . but her plan can very well be carried to success!

KRISTIN: Now you listen to me! Was it your intention that I was to be cook for that one—

JEAN (*sharply*): You will be good enough to speak of your mistress in a proper manner! You understand me, don't you?

KRISTIN: Mistress, yes!

JEAN: Yes, mistress!

KRISTIN: Ha, listen—listen to him!

JEAN: Yes, that's just what you *should* do—listen—and talk a little less! Miss Julie *is* your mistress—and the very same thing that you now look down upon her for should make you feel contempt for yourself!

KRISTIN: I always had so much respect for myself that . . .

JEAN: . . . that you felt you could show disrespect for others!

KRISTIN: . . . that I could never let myself sink beneath my level! Nobody can say that the Count's cook has had any goings-on with the stablehand, or the fellow who looks after the pigs! No—nobody can say that!

JEAN: Yes—you are lucky to have been able to catch a fine fellow like me, that's all I can say!

KRISTIN: A fine fellow, indeed,—selling the oats from the Count's stable . . .

JEAN: You should talk about that—you, who take a rake-off from the grocer and let the butcher bribe you!

KRISTIN: I don't know what you mean . . .

JEAN: And you—you can't have any respect for the family you are working for! You—you—you!

KRISTIN: Are you coming with me to church now? You could stand a good sermon after your great triumph!

JEAN: No, I am not going to church today. . . . You have to go alone and confess your *own* exploits!

KRISTIN: Yes—that's what I intend to do, and I'll come back with enough forgiveness for us both! The Saviour suffered and died on the Cross for all our sins; and if we come to Him with faith and repentance in our hearts He will take all our trespasses upon Himself.

JEAN: Including petty grocery frauds?

MISS JULIE (*who suddenly lifts her head*): Do you believe that, Kristin?

KRISTIN: That is my living faith, as sure as I stand here. It is the faith that was born in me as a child and that I have kept ever since, Miss Julie. . . . And where sin abounds, grace abounds much more . . .

MISS JULIE: Oh—if I only had your trusting faith! Oh, if I . . .

KRISTIN: Yes, but you see you can't have faith without God's special grace—and it is not given to all to receive that.

MISS JULIE: To whom is it given then?

KRISTIN: That, Miss Julie, is the great secret of the gift of grace . . . and God is no respecter of persons: in His Kingdom the last shall be first . . .

MISS JULIE: Well—but in that case He shows preference for the last, doesn't He?

KRISTIN (*continues*): . . . and it's easier for a camel to go through the eye of a needle than for a rich man to enter the Kingdom of Heaven. You see, Miss Julie, that is the way it is!—But now I am going—alone—and on my way I'll stop and tell the stableman not to let out any of the horses to anybody . . . just in case anybody'd like to get away before the Count returns!—Goodbye! (*She goes out.*)

JEAN: What a bitch!—And all this just because of a green siskin!

MISS JULIE (*apathetically*): Never mind the siskin!—Can you see any way out of this? Any way to end it?

JEAN (*thinking hard*): No—I can't.

MISS JULIE: If you were in my place—what would you do?

JEAN: In your place? Let me think!—As a woman—of noble birth—who has fallen . . . I don't know. . . . Yes—now I think I know— (*His glance falls upon the razor.*)

MISS JULIE (*picks up the razor and makes a telling gesture*): This, you mean?

JEAN: Yes . . . but *I* would never do it! Not I—for there is a difference between us two!

MISS JULIE: You mean—because you are a man and I a woman? What, then, is the difference?

JEAN: The same difference—as—between man and woman—

MISS JULIE (*with the razor in her hand*): I want to do it . . . but I can't!—My father couldn't either—that time when he ought to have done it . . .

JEAN: No—he ought not to have done it! He had to take his revenge first!

MISS JULIE: And now my mother gets her revenge once more—through me!

JEAN: Did you ever love your father, Miss Julie? Did you?

MISS JULIE: Yes, I did—immensely—but, at the same time, I think I must have hated him. . . . I must have done so without being conscious of it! It was he who brought me up to look with contempt upon my own sex—to be part woman and part man! Who is to be blamed for the consequences? My father, my mother, or myself? Myself? Am I then really myself? There is nothing I can call my own; I haven't a thought that wasn't instilled in me by my father —not a passion that I didn't inherit from my mother . . . and that last notion of mine—the idea that all people are equal—that came from him, my fiancé . . . and that is why I call him a mischief-maker, a scoundrel! How can *I* possibly be to blame? To put the burden of blame on Jesus Christ as Kristin did just now—for that I have too much pride and too much sense, thanks to what my father taught me. . . . And as for the idea that a rich man may not enter Heaven—that's a lie; and Kristin, who has put her savings in the bank, won't get there either, for that matter! Now—who is to blame?—What does it matter who is to blame? After all, it is I who have to bear the burden of guilt and suffer the consequences. . . .

JEAN: Yes—but . . . (*Two abrupt rings interrupt him.* MISS JULIE *jumps to her feet;* JEAN *quickly changes his coat.*) The Count is back! What if Kristin . . . (*He goes over to the speaking tube and listens.*)

MISS JULIE: Could he have been to the chiffonier already?

JEAN: Yes, sir—this is Jean. (*He listens. The Count's voice is not heard by the audience.*) Yes, sir.—Yes, sir. Immediately!—At once, sir!—Yes, sir. In half an hour!

MISS JULIE (*in extreme agitation*): What did he say? For God's sake—what did he say?

JEAN: He asked for his boots and his coffee in half an hour.

MISS JULIE: Half an hour, then! . . . Oh, I am so tired—I have no strength to do anything—not even to feel repentant —or to get away from here—or to stay here—to live—or to die! . . . Help me, please! Order me to do something— and I'll obey like a dog. . . . Do me this last service! Save my honor—save his good name! You know what I would like to have the will to do—yet don't like to do. . . . Use your willpower on me—and *make* me do it!

JEAN: I don't know why—but now *I* haven't any willpower either. I can't understand it. . . . It's just as if wearing this coat made it impossible for me to—to give orders to you; and now, after the Count spoke to me, I—well, I—I just can't explain it—but—oh, it's the damned menial in me . . . and if the Count should come in here this very minute, and he should order me to cut my throat, I believe I'd do it without the slightest hesitation!

MISS JULIE: Can't you make believe that you are he, and that I am you! You did a good piece of acting just now when you were on your knees—then you acted the nobleman—or, perhaps, you have seen a hypnotist when you've been to the theatre? (JEAN *gives an affirmative nod.*) He tells his subject: "Pick up that broom!"—and he picks it up; he tells him to sweep—and he starts to sweep . . .

JEAN: But he must put his subject to sleep first . . .

MISS JULIE (*ecstatically*): I am already asleep—the whole room is like a cloud of dust and smoke before me—and you look like a tall stove—and the stove looks like a man in black with a top hat—your eyes glow like embers in a fireplace—and your face is merely a patch of white ash . . . (*The sun's rays are now falling across the room and shine on* JEAN.) . . . It's so pleasantly warm . . . (*She rubs her hands together as if she were warming them by the fire.*) And how bright it is—and so peaceful!

JEAN (*takes the razor and places it in her hand*): Here is the broom! Walk outside now while it's still light—out into the barn—and . . . (*He whispers in her ear.*)

MISS JULIE (*awake*): Thank you! I'm going—to find rest. . . . But before I go, tell me—that even those who are among the first can receive the gift of grace. Please tell me that— even if you do not believe it!

JEAN: Among the first? No—that's something I cannot do. . . .

But wait, Miss Julie. . . . Now I know the answer! Since you no longer are one of the first—you must be—among the last!

MISS JULIE: You are right!—I am among the—very last—I am the last! Oh!—But something holds me back again. . . . Tell me once again to go!

JEAN: No—I can't tell you again—I can't—

MISS JULIE: And the first shall be the last . . .

JEAN: Stop thinking—stop thinking! You are robbing me of all my strength—you are making me a coward. . . . What's that? I thought I heard the bell! No—but let's stuff it with paper. . . . Imagine, to be so afraid of a bell! Yes—but it isn't merely a bell—there is someone behind it—a hand that sets it in motion—and something else sets the hand in motion—but you can stop your ears—stop your ears—and then—yes, but then it keeps ringing louder than ever—keeps ringing until you answer—and then—it's too late! And then the sheriff appears on the scene—and then . . .

(Two peremptory rings from the bell.)

JEAN *(quails; then he straightens himself)*: It's horrible! But it's the only way to end it!—Go!

(MISS JULIE, with the razor in her hand, walks firmly out through the door.)

CURTAIN

To Agnes and Gunnar Jarring

Creditors

(1888)

A Tragicomedy in One Act

CHARACTERS

TEKLA

ADOLF,
  her husband; a painter

GUSTAV,
  her divorced husband; a teacher. (He is
  traveling under an assumed name.)

TWO LADIES

A WAITER

*The action takes place at a Swedish seaside resort
in the late 1880s.*

A seaside resort. A drawing room with a view of the landscape and a door to a veranda in the rear. Toward the left, a table with newspapers on it; to the right of it, a chair; to the left of it, a chaise longue. There is a door to an adjoining room on the left.

ADOLF and GUSTAV are seated at the table, left. ADOLF is kneading a wax figure on a revolving base.

ADOLF (*with a pair of crutches beside him*): . . . and for all this I am indebted to you!

GUSTAV (*puffing at a cigar*): Nonsense.

ADOLF: Most decidedly! During the first few days after my wife had gone away, I lay on my sofa—my strength had left me. I missed her so desperately I could think of nothing but her. . . . It was as if she had taken my crutches with her so that I couldn't move from the spot. After having slept for a few days, my strength began to come back, and I tried to collect myself; my mind, which had been working feverishly, had a chance to rest a little; ideas I had been nourishing in the past came back to me; and the old joy in my work—the desire to do something creative —took hold of me again. And with it returned the capacity to see things as they are, to contemplate, to look at them boldly, and then—then you showed up on the scene. . . .

GUSTAV: I must say you were in rather a bad state when I first met you, having to rely on your crutches. But that doesn't mean that I had anything to do with the improvement in your health. What you were in need of was rest, and you were also in need of male companionship.

ADOLF: Yes, that is undoubtedly true—like everything else you say. Before I was married, I had men friends; but after being married, I found I did not need them any more. I was completely satisfied to have her as my sole companion. And then I was brought into different circles and made many new acquaintances. But my wife grew jealous of them. She wanted to have me to herself, and—what was worse—she wanted also to have my friends to herself! And so I was left alone with my jealousy.

GUSTAV: You have tendencies toward that malady, I'm afraid.

ADOLF: I had a fear of losing her—and tried to prevent it. Does that seem so strange to you? But I had not the least suspicion that she would ever be unfaithful to me. . . .

GUSTAV: Oh, no! That's something that never enters a married man's head!

ADOLF: No—isn't that curious? But what I did have a fear of was that our friends would have an influence over her and in that way indirectly exert an influence over me—and that was something I would not have been able to abide.

GUSTAV: In other words, you and your wife did not always think alike, did you?

ADOLF: Since I have already told you this much, I may as well tell you the whole story. My wife has an independent nature. . . . What are you laughing at?

GUSTAV: Go on. . . . You say she is of an independent nature. . . .

ADOLF: . . . and she refuses to listen to anything I suggest. . . .

GUSTAV: . . . but takes suggestions and ideas from everybody else.

ADOLF: Yes. And it seems to me as if she hates my opinions simply because they come from me, and not because she finds them unreasonable or lacking in sense. For on many occasions she has come forward with ideas that I had given to her some time in the past, presenting them as her own. Yes, and then there have been times when one of my friends has repeated some idea he had heard me expound— and then she would accept it ravenously. She would devour anything—anything except what she knew came from me.

GUSTAV: In short, you are not precisely happy, are you?

ADOLF: Oh, yes, I am. I have been given the one woman I wanted, and I have never wanted anybody else.

GUSTAV: And you have never felt a desire to be free of her?

ADOLF: No, I can't say that I have. There have been times, of course, when I have thought that—if I were free—I might get some peace and rest; but the moment she no longer is near me, I begin to yearn for her—I ache for her as I would for my arms and legs if I were to lose them. It's strange, but there are times when it seems to me as though she were nothing by herself, and yet an inseparable part of me—an alter ego that interferes with my mind and robs me of my will. It is as though I had relinquished to her the very spark of life, which science is so concerned with.

GUSTAV: When all is said and done, that may not be far from the truth.

ADOLF: But how could that possibly be? For she is an independent individual with a fertile mind of her own. And when I first met her, I amounted to nothing, frankly, a mere fledgling of an artist; and she gave me my education.

GUSTAV: But in time you developed *her* intellectual faculties and so, in turn, educated her, didn't you?

ADOLF: No—she stopped growing, while I continued to develop.

GUSTAV: Why, yes—it's singular how her writing degenerated after her first book; or, at any rate, that it did not amount to much afterward. But she had a grateful subject for her initial effort; they say she portrayed her own husband in it. You didn't know him, did you? He must have been an idiot.

ADOLF: No, I never did meet him. He had gone away somewhere on a six-month journey. But, judging by her description of him, he must have been a thorough imbecile.

(There is a silence.)

And you may be sure that her portrayal of him was not exaggerated.

GUSTAV: I am convinced of that. But why did she ever marry him?

ADOLF: For the simple reason that she didn't know him. And we never learn to know one another—until it's too late.

GUSTAV: That's the reason why we should never get married

until—afterward. And he—the husband—he was a tyrant, of course.

ADOLF: Why do you say *of course?*

GUSTAV: All husbands are tyrants. . . . *(Feeling his way.)* . . . and not least you.

ADOLF: I? I—who let my wife come and go as she pleases?

GUSTAV: Well, that's the least you can do. Would you want to lock her up? But do you like having her stay out nights?

ADOLF: No, I most certainly do not.

GUSTAV: You see! *(In a changed tone.)* Quite frankly—if you did, you would be a fool.

ADOLF: A fool? Would I be a fool if I showed that I trusted my wife?

GUSTAV: You certainly would. And you already are. You are thoroughly ridiculous.

ADOLF *(convulsively)*: I—ridiculous! That is the last thing I would want to be. And I'll soon change that!

GUSTAV: Don't take it so to heart or you'll be having another attack.

ADOLF: Then why isn't *she* ludicrous when I spend a night away from home?

GUSTAV: Why? Why, that's none of your concern—and that's the way it is. And while you are wondering why it is so, calamity strikes.

ADOLF: Which calamity?

GUSTAV: However—the husband was a tyrant, and she had married him in order to be free; for the only way a girl can get her freedom is by marrying a chaperon—in brief, getting a so-called husband.

ADOLF: Naturally.

GUSTAV: And now *you* are the chaperon.

ADOLF: I?

GUSTAV: Yes—now that you are her husband.

(ADOLF *seems confused.*)

Am I not right?

ADOLF *(showing uneasiness)*: I don't know. . . . You live together with a woman for years, and you never give her a thought or think about the relationship between you, until all of a sudden you begin to reflect—and after that you never stop thinking. . . . Gustav, you are my friend! You are the only man I have known whom I can call my friend!

You have given me fresh courage to live during these past eight days. I feel as if you have infused me with your magnetism—you have been like a watchmaker to me: you have repaired the mechanism in my head and wound up the spring. Don't you notice how much clearer I speak, how much saner and more rational my thoughts are—and it seems to me that I have even regained my own usual voice.

GUSTAV: Yes, I notice that, too. I wonder why?

ADOLF: I wonder whether we don't get the habit of talking in subdued tones when we are together with women? I know that Tekla would always reproach me for talking too loudly.

GUSTAV: And so you put a mute on your voice and allowed yourself to be henpecked and become a cipher in your own house.

ADOLF: Don't call me that! *(Reflecting.)* But now that I think of it, I'm afraid things are even worse. However, let us not talk about that now.—But what was it I was going to say? Oh, yes. You arrived here on the scene and you opened my eyes to the unrecognized possibilities of my art. To be sure, I had long felt my interest in painting gradually growing less. Color did not seem to offer sufficient scope for bringing out what I wanted to express. But it was not until you gave me your logical reasons for your conclusions and your theory and explained why painting could not remain the art form of today that a light went up for me—and it was then I realized that from that moment on I could never again create anything in color.

GUSTAV: And are you absolutely convinced that you can't continue with your painting any longer? I mean—so that you won't be having regrets afterwards and go back to it?

ADOLF: Absolutely! And I have proved it! After our talk that night, I thought over everything you had said, your arguments and reasoning, point by point, after I had gone to bed —and I was persuaded that you were right. But then—when I awakened after a sound night's sleep, and my head was perfectly clear—the thought suddenly gripped me that you might be wrong. I jumped out of bed, lined up my paints and brushes, to start painting. But I couldn't paint! My inspiration was gone—all I saw was daubs and splashes of paint; and it astounded me to think that I could ever have believed, and made others believe, that this painted canvas was anything but just that: a painted canvas. The veil had been removed from my eyes, and after that experience it would be as unthinkable for me to continue with my painting as it would be for me to be a child again.

GUSTAV: And that is how your eyes were opened to the fact that the naturalistic aspirations of our times, the insistence upon realism and believability, could only be given concrete form through sculpture—which gives you body in three dimensions.

ADOLF (*in an uncertain tone of voice*): Three dimensions . . . Yes, body, in short . . .

GUSTAV: And so you turned sculptor or, I should say, you already were a sculptor, but you had strayed from your proper domain, and all you needed was someone to guide you back onto the right path again. —Tell me, are you now fired by an indomitable inspiration when you are at work?

ADOLF: Today I am really living!

GUSTAV: Would you let me see what you are working on?

ADOLF: The figure of a woman. (*He uncovers a female figure on the base.*)

GUSTAV: Without a model? And yet so lifelike.

ADOLF (*apathetically*): Yes, it has a resemblance to a certain woman. It is remarkable how that woman remains in my body, just as I feel being part of her.

GUSTAV: It is not so very strange, after all. You know what transfusion is, don't you?

ADOLF: Blood transfusion? Yes.

GUSTAV: You seem to let yourself be bled more than you should. And as I now look at this figure, I begin to understand certain things that I only suspected before. You have been madly in love with her. . . .

ADOLF: Yes—so madly that I couldn't tell whether she were I or I she. . . . For when she smiles, I smile; when she weeps, I weep, and—can you imagine it?—when she bore our child, I suffered her pain.

GUSTAV: It hurts me to say this, my friend—but do you know what? You are showing the first symptoms of epilepsy.

ADOLF (*deeply shaken*): I? How can you say anything like that?

GUSTAV: Because I have seen these symptoms in a younger brother of mine who overindulged in adventures of love.

ADOLF: In which way—in which way did this—did it show?

> (*When* GUSTAV *describes the symptoms, he does so graphically.* ADOLF *listens with rapt attention and imitates* GUSTAV'S *gestures involuntarily.*)

GUSTAV: It was horrible to see. . . . But if it upsets you, I won't torment you with a description.

ADOLF (*filled with anxiety*): Go on! By all means, go on!

GUSTAV: Well—the boy had gone and married an innocent little girl with hair hanging down in curls and with the eyes of a dove, the face of a child and the pure soul of an angel. But nonetheless she succeeded in arrogating to herself the prerogatives of the male. . . .

ADOLF: What are they?

GUSTAV: Initiative, of course . . . and with the consequence that the angel came very close to carrying him off to heaven. But first he had to be crucified and feel the spikes in his flesh. It was horrible!

ADOLF (*breathlessly*): Well—what happened to him?

GUSTAV (*pacing his speech with deliberation*): We could be sitting talking—he and I—and after a while he would turn white as chalk, his arms and legs would grow rigid, and his thumbs would stiffen and turn inward, into the cramp-like palms of his hand—like this. . . . (*He demonstrates with a gesture, which* ADOLF *unconsciously repeats.*) . . . then his eyes would be bloodshot, and he would move his jaws and gnash his teeth—like this. . . . (*He imitates his brother's symptoms, and immediately* ADOLF *goes through the same motions.*) The saliva would cause a rattling in his throat, his chest would constrict as if put in a vise, the pupils of his eyes would flicker like gas flames, he would foam at the mouth, and the foam would be churned into froth by his tongue, and finally he would topple over backward—slowly—and fall into his chair, like a man who is drowning. And then . . .

ADOLF (*in a faint whisper*): Stop! Stop!

GUSTAV: And then . . . Are you ill?

ADOLF: Yes!

GUSTAV (*goes over and brings him a glass of water*): There now—drink some water—then let's talk about something else.

ADOLF (*weakly*): Thanks!—But continue. . . .

GUSTAV: Well—and when he came to, he had no recollection of what had happened to him; he had been unconscious all through it. —Have you ever had attacks like that?

ADOLF: I have had an occasional attack of vertigo, but the doctor says it is caused by anemia.

GUSTAV: Yes—that's how it begins. Take my word for it, it will turn into epilepsy if you don't take care of yourself.

ADOLF: What is there I can do about it?

GUSTAV: First of all, you must observe strict sexual abstinence.

ADOLF: For how long?

GUSTAV: For at least six months.

ADOLF: Why, I couldn't do that. It would break up our marriage.

GUSTAV: Then I may as well say goodbye to you.

ADOLF (*putting the covering back on the wax figure*): I couldn't do it!

GUSTAV: Don't you want to save your own life? —But tell me—since you have already taken me into your confidence so generously—isn't there something else that distresses you, some secret wound that weighs upon you? For you rarely find only one thing to be the cause of disharmony, life being what it is—so motley, and giving so many opportunities for misunderstandings and discord. Have you no skeleton in your closet whose presence you refuse to acknowledge to yourself? For instance, you mentioned a moment ago that you had a child and that you had placed it somewhere. . . . Why don't you have the child stay at home with you?

ADOLF: Because my wife doesn't want it here.

GUSTAV: For what reason? You can tell me frankly!

ADOLF: Because—when the child was three years old it was beginning to look like him—her former husband.

GUSTAV: Oh! Have you ever seen her former husband?

ADOLF: No, never. I have only had a fleeting glance of him in a bad portrait, but I couldn't detect any likeness between him and the child.

GUSTAV: Oh, well, portraits never look like the originals; and besides, he may have changed since it was taken. —But, in any case, you didn't let that give rise to suspicions in you, did you?

ADOLF: Not in the slightest! The child was born a year after we were married, and her husband was away, traveling, when I first met Tekla—at this very bathing resort—yes, in this very house, even. And that is the reason why we come here every summer.

GUSTAV: And so you couldn't have any suspicions. And, as a matter of fact, you need not have any, for the children of a widow, who has remarried, frequently look like her dead husband. This is unquestionably annoying, and, as you know, it was the cause of widows being burned to death in India. But tell me now, have you never been jealous of him, or of the memory she has of him? Wouldn't it make you feel disgusted if you were to meet him while out walking and—with his eyes fixed on your Tekla—hear him associate himself with her by speaking of *we two* instead of saying *I? (With sarcasm.)* We? H'm.

ADOLF: I can't deny that that thought has occurred to me more than once.

GUSTAV: There, you see! And you'll never be free of that thought! You must know that there are certain conflicts or inconsistencies you meet with in life to which there can be no solution. Let me therefore suggest that you put wax in your ears and keep on working. If you do that and let the years pass by, and you board up the door to that closet with new impressions, the skeleton will not rattle its bones.

ADOLF: Forgive me for interrupting you, but—but it is really astonishing how much you remind me of Tekla at times when you speak. You have a way of winking your right eye as if you were aiming a gun at me; and your eyes have the same mysterious power over me as Tekla's have at times.

GUSTAV: You don't say!

ADOLF: And the way you just said those words—in exactly the same kind of casual tone as she uses. "You don't say!" is one of her favorite expressions; she uses it frequently.

GUSTAV: Who knows—we may be related distantly; for that matter, we are all related to one another. In any case, it seems curious, and it will be interesting to make your wife's acquaintance and see for myself.

ADOLF: But can you imagine, she never borrows an expression from me; she seems rather to avoid my particular choice of words. And I have never seen her copy any of my gestures or special mannerisms; and generally husband and wife take on each other's peculiar characteristics and grow to be alike.

GUSTAV: Yes—but now let me tell you something: that woman has never loved you!

ADOLF: What's that you say?

GUSTAV: Now, now . . . I beg your pardon. But don't you know that a woman's love consists in taking, in accepting . . . and the man she takes *nothing* from she does not love. She has never loved you!

ADOLF: Don't you think she can love more than once?

GUSTAV: No, one lets oneself be fooled only once; after that, one keeps one's eyes open. You yourself have never been taken in—that is why you must beware of those who *have been*. They are dangerous, I assure you, they are.

ADOLF: Your words go through me like knives. I feel something being cut open inside me—and I can't do anything to prevent it. But I feel relieved by the cutting, for there are abscesses that never come to a head. . . . She has never loved me! But why did she take me then?

GUSTAV: Tell me first how she happened to take you. And was it *you* who took *her*, or *she you*?

ADOLF: God knows—I don't think I can answer that question —or how it all came about? It didn't happen so all at once!

GUSTAV: Would you like me to try guessing how it happened?

ADOLF: You couldn't.

GUSTAV: Oh, after all you have told me about yourself and your wife, I think I should be able to figure out just how it happened. Listen now and let me tell you. (*In an unimpassioned, almost jesting tone of voice.*) The husband was away on a journey for the purpose of study and of doing research, and she was left at home, alone. In the beginning, she enjoyed her temporary freedom. But then emptiness set in; for I imagine she felt rather forlorn after two weeks of living alone with herself. And then he, the other man, appeared; and little by little the vacuum is filled. By comparison, the absent husband begins to lose lustre, for the simple reason that he is far away—as in proportion to the square of the distance, you know. However, when they feel their passions stirring, they become uneasy, both for themselves and for the husband; and they also feel the pangs of their guilty consciences. In the interest of self-preservation they seek refuge by creeping behind their fig leaves, playing the game of brother and sister; and the more sensual their feelings become, the more spiritual they pretend their relationship to be.

ADOLF: Brother and sister? How can you know that?

GUSTAV: I just guessed it. Children like to play papa and mama, but when they grow older, they play brother and sister—in order to hide what should not be seen. And then they take the vow of chastity and play hide and seek— until they find themselves in a dark recess or cranny where they are sure not to be discovered. . . . *(With make-believe severity.)* But they sense that they are being seen by One who can penetrate the darkness; and now they are frightened . . . and in their terror they conjure up in their imagination an apparition of the absent husband. The ghost takes on dimensions, looms larger and larger, turns into a nightmare plaguing them in their lovers' slumber—a creditor, knocking at their door; and they see his forbidding hand between theirs when they sit down to eat—they hear his stern, unwelcome voice in the silence of the night, which ordinarily would only have been broken by the throbbing of their pulse beats. He does not interfere with their having each other, but he disturbs their serenity. And when they feel the impact of his invisible power to ruin their happiness, and finally flee—although they vainly try to rid themselves of the memory of it all, which keeps pursuing them—from the guilt they left behind, and public opinion, which frightens them; and they have not the strength to bear the burden of their own guilt—and so a scapegoat has to be found somehow, somewhere, and offered up. The two were freethinkers—but they lacked the courage to face him and speak to him frankly, saying: We love each other. In short, they were cowards, and therefore the tyrant had to be done away with. Have I guessed rightly?

ADOLF: Yes. But you forget that she educated me and gave me fresh inspiration, new thoughts. . . .

GUSTAV: No, I didn't forget. But how was it that she didn't bring up the other one also—to be a freethinker?

ADOLF: Why, he was an idiot, I know.

GUSTAV: Of course he was an idiot! But that is a rather vague description, and in her novel she describes his idiocy as primarily consisting in his inability to understand her. Forgive me for asking you—but has your wife really such a depth of mind and understanding? I can't say I have found her to be so profound in what she has written.

ADOLF: I haven't, either. And I must also confess that I find it hard to understand her myself. It is as though the cogwheels of our brains did not mesh—as though something were bursting in my head whenever I try to fathom her.

GUSTAV: Perhaps you, too, are an idiot?

ADOLF: No, I don't think I am. And it seems to me she is seldom in the right. For instance—just read this letter which I received from her today! Read it! *(He takes a letter from his wallet and hands it to* GUSTAV.*)*

GUSTAV *(reads it in a cursory manner)*: H'm. The handwriting seems very familiar. . . .

ADOLF: Almost masculine, wouldn't you say?

GUSTAV: Well, I have seen at least *one* man with a similar handwriting. —I notice she calls you "brother." So you are still playing that game! I see the fig leaves have not been removed, even though they have withered. Don't you even call her by her first name?

ADOLF: No, for then I think you lose all respect for each other.

GUSTAV: So-o? Then it is to instill respect in you that she calls herself your sister, eh?

ADOLF: I want to feel a greater respect for her than for myself—I want her to be my better self.

GUSTAV: Why don't you try to be that yourself? Although you may find it a little more awkward and uncomfortable than letting somebody else be it. You don't really want to be under your wife's thumb, do you?

ADOLF: Yes, I do. I relish the idea of being always a little inferior to her. For example, I have taught her to swim; and now when I hear her boasting that she is a better and more daring swimmer than I am, I—I like it. At the beginning I made her believe I was not nearly as good as she and somewhat of a coward, in order to give her courage. But before I knew it, one fine day I found myself really being less daring than she and actually less skillful at swimming than she. It was as if she had, in fact, robbed me of my courage.

GUSTAV: Have you taught her anything else?

ADOLF: Yes, but I tell you this in confidence: I have taught her to spell—something she didn't know how to do before. And now I'll tell you something else. When she took over our correspondence, I gave up writing; and what do you think happened? For lack of practice during these years, my grammar has begun to show traces of this neglect. But do you think she remembers that it was I who taught her? Oh, no! And so now it is I, of course, who am the idiot!

GUSTAV: Ah, so you are the idiot now, are you?

ADOLF: It's all in jest, of course.

GUSTAV: Certainly, certainly! Yet it is nothing short of cannibalism. You know what cannibalism is, don't you? The savages eat their enemies in order to take on their virtues and attributes. This woman of yours has eaten your soul, your courage—all that you know. . . .

ADOLF: And my faith in myself . . . It was I who encouraged her to write her first book. . . .

GUSTAV (*with a grimace*): You don't say?

ADOLF: It was I who kept urging her on and flattering her even when I thought what she wrote was cheap and tawdry. It was I who introduced her into literary circles, where she had an opportunity to sip honey from the lips of those luxurious plant specimens; it was through my intervention that the critics did not massacre her; it was I who blew up her courage and confidence—blew so persistently and vehemently that my breath gave out. I gave and gave and gave until nothing was left for myself! Do you know—and now I am going to tell you every blessed thing. . . . Do you know that the soul is really something quite wonderful—and it occurs to me now that when my artistic successes were on the point of putting her and her reputation in the shade, I did my best to give her fresh courage by downgrading myself and my talent and subordinating my efforts to hers. I talked about the comparatively unimportant rôle of painting so long and so incessantly, talked and talked and invented so many reasons in support of it that one fine day I found that I had persuaded myself of the worthlessness of this art form. I had erected a house of cards, and all one had to do to topple it was to blow on it. . . .

GUSTAV: Excuse me if I remind you that when we began this conversation, you mentioned that she never takes anything from you.

ADOLF: Not any more, no! Because there is nothing left for her to take!

GUSTAV: The serpent has had its fill and is now vomiting it up.

ADOLF: She may have taken even more from me than I realize.

GUSTAV: You may be sure of that. She took without your noticing it—and the name for that is *stealing*.

ADOLF: Perhaps, after all, she did not educate me.

GUSTAV: But instead you educated her! In all likelihood, that is the case. But she tricked you into thinking the opposite. May I ask how she went about it when she tried to educate you?

ADOLF: Well—first of all . . . H'm.

GUSTAV: Well . . .

ADOLF: Why, I . . .

GUSTAV: Why, no—it was she, wasn't it?

ADOLF: Come to think of it, I am not so sure now. . . .

GUSTAV: There, you see!

ADOLF: However—she had taken my faith in myself too, and that caused me to go down, until you appeared and imbued me with a new faith.

GUSTAV (*with a smile*): In sculpturing?

ADOLF (*hesitantly*): Yes . . .

GUSTAV: And you have faith in it—you believe in this abstract, out-of-date art form from the childhood days of mankind—you believe that you can make an impression with pure form in three dimensions, do you? That you can capture the minds of people in these days of realism and naturalism; that you can give illusion without the aid of color—without color, do you hear? Do you really think you can do that?

ADOLF (*crushed*): No . . .

GUSTAV: Neither do I!

ADOLF: Then why did you urge me?

GUSTAV: Because I felt sorry for you.

ADOLF: Yes—I am afraid I should be pitied! Because now I am bankrupt—finished! And the worst of it is that I no longer have *her*.

GUSTAV: What good would she be to you, if you did have her?

ADOLF: She would be what God was for me before I turned to atheism: an object I could look up to with reverence, with adulation.

GUSTAV: Forget the reverence! Let something else take its place—for example, a dose of healthy contempt.

ADOLF: I could not live without having something to worship. . . .

GUSTAV: You are a slave!

ADOLF: And I must have a woman to adore!

GUSTAV: Oh, hell! But if you absolutely have to have someone to bend your knee to, then go back to God! Imagine an atheist who still lets that superstition about women rule him! Do you realize what this unfathomable profundity, this sphinxlike attitude in your wife, really amounts to—do you? It is all stupidity—nothing but stupidity. Let me show you—she doesn't even know the difference between a consonant and a diphthong! Something is wrong with the mechanism, you see! She is like a cheap cylinder watch in a case of gold. And what makes her so irresistible? The skirts, that's all! Put her in pants—paint a mustache under her nose with burnt cork—and then listen to her with sober senses and size her up—and you'll find how differently her cackling sounds. A phonograph record —that's all—playing back your own and other people's sayings, but robbed of their essence, sapped of pith and marrow. Have you ever seen a woman in the nude? Why, of course, you have. A youth with nipples on his breast; a male not fully matured; a child that has shot up and been stunted in its growth; an anemic who suffers hemorrhages with regularity thirteen times in a year! What is to become of someone like that?

ADOLF: If what you say is true, why should I think that we are alike?

GUSTAV: It's nothing but hallucination—the mysterious, hypnotic power of a woman's skirt! Or perhaps—because you have actually grown to be like each other. The leveling has been completed, her capillary attraction has performed the equalizing miracle. . . . However, tell me one thing. . . . (*He takes out his watch and looks at the time.*) . . . we have now been talking for six hours, and your wife ought to be here any minute. Don't you think we had better end the conversation now so that you will have a chance to rest?

ADOLF: No, don't leave me! I'm afraid to be alone.

GUSTAV: Oh, your wife will be here in a short while; you won't be alone very long.

ADOLF: Yes, she'll be coming. . . . Isn't it strange, I long for her—yet I am afraid of her! She caresses me—she is tender—but there is something about her kissing that stifles me, that suffocates me, something that saps my strength —that benumbs me. . . . It is as if I were a circus child, whose cheeks are given a pinch by the clown before the child makes its entrance into the ring, to give them the appearance of flushed health to the audience.

GUSTAV: I really feel sorry for you, my friend. . . . Even though I am not a physician, I can tell that you are a dying man. A mere look at your latest paintings is evidence of that.

ADOLF: You don't mean to say . . . ? How can you tell?

GUSTAV: The color is a watery blue, flat and faded, thin and washed out. You can see the canvas right through the paint—a ghastly yellow—ashen—like a dead body. . . . It is as if I saw your hollow, putty-colored cheeks peering out at me from under the paint. . . .

ADOLF: Stop it! Stop!

GUSTAV: Yes—and that's not only my personal opinion. . . . Haven't you read the newspaper today?

ADOLF (blenching): No.

GUSTAV: There it is on the table.

ADOLF (he reaches for the newspaper without picking it up, seemingly lacking the courage): Does the newspaper say that?

GUSTAV: See for yourself. Or do you want me to read it?

ADOLF: No!

GUSTAV: I'll leave if you wish.

ADOLF: No—no—no! I can't understand—but I think I'm beginning to hate you—and yet I can't let you go! You drag me out of the icy water into which I had fallen and, the moment you have safely pulled me out, you give me a whack on the head and push me back into the water again. As long as I kept my secrets to myself, I still had my guts intact, but now I am empty, depleted, drained. There is a painting by an Italian master depicting a saint being tortured by having his intestines cranked out of him and coiled onto a windlass. The martyr lies watching himself growing more and more emaciated while the winding-drum keeps increasing in thickness. . . . In much the same way, it now seems to me as if you had increased in size after having hauled my secrets out of me; and when you leave, you'll be taking my innards with you and leaving behind an empty shell.

GUSTAV: Well, you certainly have a vivid imagination! —Any-how, your wife will come home soon and bring back your heart to you, won't she?

ADOLF: No, not after this—after you've burned her out of my heart. You have laid everything in ashes—my art, my love, my hopes, my faith!

GUSTAV: All that had already been done, without any help from me.

ADOLF: Yes, but it could have been saved. Now it is too late, you mischief-maker, you fiend!

GUSTAV: So far we have only done a little clearing of the land. Now we shall do some sowing in the ashes.

ADOLF: I hate you! I curse you!

GUSTAV: Good signs, both of them! You still have some guts left in you. And now I'll pull you up out of the hole in the ice once more. Listen to me! Will you listen to what I say—and obey?

ADOLF: Do with me whatever you will—I'll obey.

GUSTAV (*getting up*): Look at me!

ADOLF (*regards him*): Now you are looking at me again with one of those hypnotizing glances that draws me to you. . . .

GUSTAV: And listen to me!

ADOLF: Yes, but talk about yourself this time—don't talk any more about me: I am like a bleeding wound and can't bear being touched.

GUSTAV: Forget about me. I'm of no account. I'm merely a teacher of dead languages and a widower, that's all. Now, take hold of my hand.

ADOLF (*takes his hand*): What tremendous strength you must have! It's like touching a dynamo. . . .

GUSTAV: And then remember that I was once as much of a weakling as you are now. . . . Stand up!

ADOLF (*gets up and, in so doing, falls and catches hold of* GUSTAV *about the neck*): I am like a child with no legs, and my brain is laid wide open. . . .

GUSTAV: Take a few steps across the room!

ADOLF: I couldn't.

GUSTAV: You will—or I'll make you.

ADOLF (*straightening up*): What did you say?

GUSTAV: I'll make you, that's what I said.

ADOLF (*leaps backward, infuriated*): You . . .

GUSTAV: There! Now the blood went to your brain, and your self-assurance came back. Now I'll turn on the electricity. Where is your wife?

ADOLF: Where is she?

GUSTAV: Yes.

ADOLF: She is—at a—at a meeting.

GUSTAV: Are you so certain?

ADOLF: Absolutely.

GUSTAV: What kind of meeting?

ADOLF: In connection with an orphanage.

GUSTAV: Were you friends when she left?

ADOLF (*with some hesitation*): No, we—we were not.

GUSTAV: Consequently, enemies. What did you say to her that made her angry?

ADOLF: You are absolutely eerie! I am frightened of you! How could you know?

GUSTAV: That's simple. I have three given factors, and so it's easy enough to find the unknown quantity by deduction. What did you say to your wife?

ADOLF: I told her— I said only two words to her, but they were two awful words, and I reproach myself for them— I am sorry no end for saying them.

GUSTAV: You shouldn't be. Tell me what they were.

ADOLF: I called her an old flirt.

GUSTAV: What did you say after that?

ADOLF: That's all I said.

GUSTAV: Oh, no, you said something else, but perhaps you've forgotten. Perhaps you lack the courage to recall it—or have put it away and hidden it in some secret drawer? But now you must open it and let the secret out.

ADOLF: I have no recollection of anything else.

GUSTAV: But I have. This is what you said: "You ought to

be ashamed of yourself—to be flirting at your age! You know you are too old to hook another lover!"

ADOLF: Did I say that? I might have, but—but how can you possibly know?

GUSTAV: I heard her telling about it on the steamer on my way here.

ADOLF: To whom?

GUSTAV: To four young men she was in company with. Even at her age, she seems to be attracted to unspoiled, immature young men, just as . . .

ADOLF: That is an entirely innocent pastime she is indulging in.

GUSTAV: As when playing brother and sister while being husband and wife, eh?

ADOLF: So you have seen her, then?

GUSTAV: I have, yes. But you haven't, since you were not there to see her—I mean since you were not there in person. And that, you see, is why a husband can never really know his wife. Have you a photograph of her?

(ADOLF *takes a photograph of her from his wallet. He seems puzzled.*)

You were not with her when this was taken, were you?

ADOLF: No.

GUSTAV: Take a look at it. Does this look like the picture you painted of her—does it? No! The features are the same, but the expression is a different one. But that is something you can't see because you see her image through your own in the background. Look at this picture now, look at it through the eyes of a painter, and forget about the original. What does she look like? I see nothing but an affected flirt, bent on making a conquest. Do you see the cynical expression about her mouth—which she never lets *you* see? Do you see these glances in search of a man who is not you? Do you see the extreme low cut of the dress, the way she has done her hair, and how her sleeves have been loosened and pushed up? Do you see?

ADOLF: Yes—yes, I do.

GUSTAV: Watch out, my boy!

ADOLF: Watch out for what?

GUSTAV: Her vengeance! Have you forgotten that you have wounded her in the most sensitive and tender spot when you told her she could no longer attract a man? If you had said that what she wrote was nothing but trash, she would simply have laughed at your lack of taste; but believe me, if she has not taken her revenge already, you can't blame her for it.

ADOLF: That is something I must know.

GUSTAV: Try to find out!

ADOLF: Find out?

GUSTAV: Look into it! I'll help you if you want me to.

ADOLF: Well—I have to die some time, so . . . I may as well die now as later. What do you think we should do?

GUSTAV: First tell me something. Isn't there one single spot where your wife is vulnerable?

ADOLF: Not that I know of. I think she must have nine lives like a cat.

GUSTAV: There, now—there is the steamer blowing its whistle in the sound—she'll be here any minute.

ADOLF: Then I must go down and meet her.

GUSTAV: No! You will stay here—you must be rude to her. If she has a clear conscience, she will let the sparks fly thick and fast about your ears; if she is guilty, she will embrace and caress you.

ADOLF: Are you so sure of that?

GUSTAV: Not absolutely. The hare dodges and darts hither and thither, but I'll keep on her trail. My room is next to yours. . . . (*He points to the door on the left, behind the chair.*) I'll take up position inside and be the lookout, while you do your part in here. And when you have finished your act, we'll exchange rôles. Then I'll go into the cage and play out my scene with the snake, while you keep your eye glued to the keyhole. When it's over, we'll meet in the garden and compare notes. But stand your ground, and don't give in! If I see you weakening, I'll give two thumps on the floor with a chair.

ADOLF: Settled! But, whatever you do, don't go away! I must be sure you are close by—in the room next door.

GUSTAV: You don't have to worry about me—I'll be there. But don't get frightened when you observe how I dissect a human soul and place the innards on that table. They say it is a gruesome experience for a novice; but once you have been through the ordeal, you will have no regrets. But you must remember one thing—not a word to her

about having met me or anyone else while she has been
gone. Not a word, do you hear? Her vulnerable point I'll
find out myself. Sh! Here she is now—she is in her
room. . . . She is humming to herself. . . . That's a sign
she is in a frenzy. And now—stiffen up and sit down on
that chair there, then she will have to sit on the chaise
longue—and then I can have a clear view of you both.

ADOLF: We still have an hour before it is time for dinner.
I haven't heard the bell ring, so no other guests could have
arrived. Consequently we'll be alone—unfortunately.

GUSTAV: Are you wavering?

ADOLF: I am neither one thing nor another. Yes, I am afraid
of what is to come—but I can't prevent it from coming.
The stone is set in motion down the hill, but it isn't the
final drop of water that started it rolling, nor was it the
first one. It was all of them together.

GUSTAV: Then let it roll! There'll be no peace until it does.
Goodbye now for a while . . .

(*He goes out, and* ADOLF *nods a goodbye, while still
holding the photograph in his hand. Then he tears
it into pieces, throwing them under the table. He
seats himself on his chair, fidgets with his necktie
and the lapel of his coat, combs his hair, etc.* TEKLA
*enters and immediately goes to him and gives him a
kiss. She does it in a friendly, open manner, cheerfully
and charmingly.*)

TEKLA: How do you do, my little brother! How are you?

ADOLF (*on the verge of capitulating, his tone half recalcitrant,
half jocular*): What mischief have you been up to now,
since you give me a kiss?

TEKLA: Well, I'll have to tell you. . . . I have done away
with an awful lot of money.

ADOLF: But did you enjoy yourself?

TEKLA: Enormously. But not at that meeting for the orphan
children—that was boring. But what has my little brother
been amusing himself with while his little bird was away?
(*She looks around the room as if she were searching for,
or on the scent of, something.*)

ADOLF: I've been bored, that's all.

TEKLA: No one to keep you company?

ADOLF: Not a soul. All alone.

TEKLA (*with her eyes fixed on him, seats herself on the chaise longue*): Who has been sitting here?

ADOLF: On the chaise longue? Nobody.

TEKLA: That's strange. It's still warm. And here is an indentation from somebody's elbow in the upholstery. You haven't had a female visitor, have you?

ADOLF: I? You really don't believe that, do you?

TEKLA: You are blushing. Is my little brother prevaricating? Come and confess to your little sister what is troubling your conscience. (*She pulls him to her. He falls on his knees and buries his head in her lap.*)

ADOLF (*with a smile*): You are a female demon! Don't you know you are?

TEKLA: No, I am ever so ignorant about myself.

ADOLF: You never really look at yourself, do you?

TEKLA (*suspiciously observing him*): I think of nothing but myself. I am a frightful egotist. You have become very philosophical, I notice.

ADOLF: Lay your hand on my forehead!

TEKLA (*in a prattling tone of voice*): Is something disturbing you again? Would you like me to drive away your worries? Shall I? (*She kisses him on the forehead.*) There, now . . . Did your troubles fly away?

ADOLF: Yes, I feel better now.

TEKLA: Well, now tell me what you have been doing to while away the time. Did you do any painting, little brother?

ADOLF: No—I have done with painting.

TEKLA: You have—what? You have finished with painting?

ADOLF: Yes—but don't scold me for it. I can't help it if I am unable to paint any more.

TEKLA: What do you expect to do, then?

ADOLF: I am going to try sculpturing.

TEKLA: You have so many new ideas.

ADOLF: Well—but stop scolding me. . . . I'd like you to look at that figure there!

TEKLA (*removing the covering from the wax figure*): Well, what do I see? Who is it supposed to be?

ADOLF: Guess!

TEKLA (*her voice unthawing*): Is it meant to be your little squirrel? Aren't you ashamed of yourself?

ADOLF: Isn't it like you?

TEKLA: How can I tell? It hasn't any face.

ADOLF: Yes, but it has so much else—which is beautiful.

TEKLA *(with a fondling tap on his cheek)*: If you don't watch what you say, I'll give you a smack on the mouth.

ADOLF *(moving away from her)*: No, no! Somebody could come!

TEKLA: What of it? Can't I give my own husband a kiss? I am legally entitled to that prerogative, am I not?

ADOLF: Yes, but, you know—people here at the hotel don't think we are married because we kiss each other all the time. And even though we quarrel every so often—it does not change their impression, for lovers do that, too, I am told.

TEKLA: Well, then—why quarrel? Can't you always be nice—the way you are now? Don't you like to be nice? Don't you want us to be happy?

ADOLF: Yes, of course I do—but . . .

TEKLA: What is the matter with you? Why the *but?* And who is it who has put this idea of giving up painting in your head?

ADOLF: Who is it? You always suspect that somebody is behind all that I think and do. You are jealous.

TEKLA: Yes, I am jealous. I'm afraid that someone may come and take you away from me.

ADOLF: You are afraid of that—when you know that no woman could ever take your place—that I couldn't live without you?

TEKLA: Frankly, it is not my own sex I have a fear of, it is your male friends who put notions into your head.

ADOLF *(scrutinizing her)*: So you are afraid, are you? Just what is it that you are afraid of?

TEKLA *(getting up)*: Somebody has been here! Who has been here?

ADOLF: Can't you bear being looked at?

TEKLA: Not that way! You are not looking at me the way you usually do.

ADOLF: How am I looking at you, tell me.

TEKLA: You are peering at me through half-closed eyelids. . . .

ADOLF: . . . and *through yours*—to see what is hidden in the back of your mind.

TEKLA: Look as much as you like! I have nothing to hide. But —you are talking in a different tone of voice today. You are using expressions that . . . *(Eying him in a scrutinizing manner.*) You are philosophizing, aren't you? (*Coming up to him threateningly.*) Who has been here?

ADOLF: Nobody but my doctor . . .   ,

TEKLA: Your doctor? Who is your doctor?

ADOLF: The doctor from Strömstad.

TEKLA: What's his name?

ADOLF: Sjöberg.

TEKLA: What did he say?

ADOLF: He said. . . . Why, he said, among other things—that I was on the verge of coming down with epilepsy.

TEKLA: Among other things, you say. . . . What else did he say?

ADOLF: Well—something that was most disagreeable.

TEKLA: Let me hear!

ADOLF: He told me we could not live together as man and wife for a while.

TEKLA: Why! I might have imagined it. They are trying to break up our marriage. I have seen signs of it for some time.

ADOLF: You could never have noticed anything like that, since nothing like that ever happened.

TEKLA: Couldn't I? Couldn't I?

ADOLF: How could you possibly see what does not exist— unless you conjured up fears in your imagination, making you see things that never existed? Just what is it you are afraid of? Can it be that you are afraid that I might borrow somebody else's eyes to see you as you really are rather than as you appear to be? Can that be the reason?

TEKLA: Stop raving and don't let your imagination run away with you, Adolf. It is the beast in you that gives full play to such wild fancies—the beast that taints your soul!

ADOLF: Where did you learn that pretty phrase? From those pure, unsophisticated young men on the steamer, eh?

TEKLA (*without losing her composure*): Well, let me tell you —the young can teach us a lot of things. . . .

ADOLF: I could almost swear you have already reached the stage of letting yourself become infatuated with adolescents.

TEKLA: I always have been. That's why I fell in love with you. . . . Do you object?

ADOLF: No, but I would prefer to be the only object of your love.

TEKLA (*playfully; prattling*): My heart is so big, don't you know? I have enough love for more than one—for many more. . . .

ADOLF: But your little brother does not care to have any more little brothers.

TEKLA: Come here to your little squirrel now—then I'll pull your hair for being so jealous! No, I should say *envious*.

(*The sound of a chair being bumped against the floor is heard from the adjoining room.*)

ADOLF: No, I don't care to play games. I want to have an earnest talk with you.

TEKLA (*in a prattling tone*): Good heavens! He wants to be serious! All of a sudden he has become awfully serious. . . . (*She takes* ADOLF's *head in her hands and kisses him.*) Now smile—smile a little!

(ADOLF *produces a smile against his will.*)

There now!

ADOLF: You are a demon! I am beginning to believe you practice black magic!

TEKLA: Now you know it! That's why you had better not start any trouble. For, if you do, I'll cast a spell on you and spirit you away!

ADOLF (*suddenly rising*): Tekla! Sit still and pose for me for a moment. I want to get your profile so I can give your face to the figure.

TEKLA: Why not? (*She turns her head in profile.*)

ADOLF (*studying her, pretending to be modeling her*): Don't think about me now—think about someone else.

TEKLA: I'll think about my latest lover.

ADOLF: The pure, innocent young man?

TEKLA: Precisely. He had such a tiny, lovely mustache—so tiny—and his cheeks were like peaches—and they were so soft and pink, one was tempted to bite into them!

ADOLF (*with darkening expression*): Hold that expression on your mouth!

TEKLA: What expression?

ADOLF: That bold, brazen, cynical expression—which I never saw on your face before . . .

TEKLA (*making a wry face*): Like this?

ADOLF: That's just the expression, yes. (*Getting up from his chair.)* Have you heard how Bret Harte describes an adulteress? Have you?

TEKLA *(with a smile)*: No, I have never read Bret— What was his name?

ADOLF: Then let me tell you. She is a pale, bloodless female who never blushes.

TEKLA: Never, you say? But she is sure to blush when she meets her lover, even though neither Mr. Husband nor Mr. Bret is there to see it.

ADOLF: Are you so sure of that?

TEKLA *(again with a smile)*: Well, if the husband is not man enough to make the blood flow to her head, I suppose he will never witness that fascinating dramatic climax.

ADOLF *(with sudden fury)*: Tekla!

TEKLA: You little fool!

ADOLF: Tekla!

TEKLA: Call me your little squirrel, then I'll blush beautifully for you. You like to see me blush, don't you?

ADOLF *(disarmed)*: You little vixen! I am so angry at you, I could bite you.

TEKLA *(playfully)*: Come and bite me then. Come! *(She extends her arms to him.)*

ADOLF *(embracing and kissing her)*: Yes, I shall bite you to death!

TEKLA *(jokingly)*: Watch out! Someone could come!

ADOLF: I don't care! I don't care about anything else in the world so long as I have you!

TEKLA: And if you didn't have me—what then?

ADOLF: Then I would die.

TEKLA: Yes, but you have nothing to fear on that score, for I am too old for anyone to want me.

ADOLF: Tekla! Why don't you erase those words from your mind? Forget what I said that time! I take it all back!

TEKLA: Can you explain why you are jealous and at the same time so cocksure of yourself?

ADOLF: No, I can't explain anything. But it may be that the thought that someone else has possessed you still rankles in me. There are times when it seems to me as if our love were nothing but a figment of the imagination, a means of self-defense, a passion turned into a point of honor; and I can't imagine anything that would torture me more than for him to be aware of my unhappiness. Oh! . . . I have never seen him, but the mere thought of someone sitting and waiting for disaster to strike me—someone who never stops cursing me in his prayers and who would break into wild, unconstrained laughter if he could see the end of me—the mere thought of that keeps haunting me; it drives me to you, fascinates me, paralyzes me. . . .

TEKLA: Do you think I would let him have that satisfaction—do you? Do you think I would want to see his prophecy come true?

ADOLF: No, I don't wish to think that.

TEKLA: Well, why don't you quiet down, then?

ADOLF: I can't—because you never stop agitating me with your flirtatious behavior. Why do you keep up this kind of adventurous game?

TEKLA: It isn't any game at all—I simply want to be liked and appreciated.

ADOLF: Yes—but only by men.

TEKLA: Naturally. A woman can never expect to be admired by other women, you know.

ADOLF: By the way, have you heard anything from him recently?

TEKLA: Not for the past half year or so.

ADOLF: Don't you ever think about him?

TEKLA: No. We have not communicated with each other since the death of our child.

ADOLF: And you have never run into him anywhere?

TEKLA: No. But I have heard he is living somewhere on the west coast. What makes you so concerned about him?

ADOLF: I don't know. However, during these last few days while I have been alone, I've been thinking about him, about how he must have felt that time when he was alone—after you left him.

TEKLA: It sounds to me as if your conscience were troubling you.

ADOLF: It is.

TEKLA: You feel like a thief, don't you?

ADOLF: Almost.

TEKLA: That's really good! In your opinion, stealing women is as easy as stealing children and chickens, then! In other words, you look upon me as his property, his chattel! Much obliged to you!

ADOLF: No, but I think of you as his wedded wife—and that

is not a mere piece of property! It is something for which there is no substitute.

TEKLA: Oh, yes, there is. If you should suddenly find that he had remarried, all these ridiculous notions of yours would fly away. And you have taken his place with me, haven't you?

ADOLF: Have I? . . . And did you ever love him?

TEKLA: I most assuredly did.

ADOLF: But then . . . .

TEKLA: I just got tired of him.

ADOLF: Suppose you should tire of me, too.

TEKLA: I won't.

ADOLF: And if another man came along who possessed the attributes and qualities you are looking for *now*—just suppose such a man should come along—then you would leave me. Wouldn't you?

TEKLA: No.

ADOLF: Even if he captivated you so completely that you could not be without him? You would unquestionably leave me.

TEKLA: No, not necessarily.

ADOLF: You don't mean to say you could be in love with two men at one and the same time?

TEKLA: Certainly—why not?

ADOLF: I can't understand you.

TEKLA: There are many things in this world that exist, even though you wouldn't understand them. We are not all created alike.

ADOLF: Now I am beginning to understand.

TEKLA: Why, you don't say!

ADOLF: Why, you don't say! (*There is a silence.* ADOLF *seems to have difficulty in calling something to mind and gives up the effort.*) Tekla! Do you know that your frankness is becoming painful?

TEKLA: And yet you yourself taught me to speak frankly; you considered that the greatest virtue you knew.

ADOLF: Yes—but it occurs to me now that you have been concealing your true self behind this frankness of yours.

TEKLA: That is the modern strategy, don't you know?

ADOLF: I can't explain it, but I find the atmosphere is becoming distinctly unpleasant here. If you have no objection, we'll start for home this very evening.

TEKLA: What kind of freak idea is this? I have only just arrived and don't care to go traveling again.

ADOLF: But I wish to leave.

TEKLA: I don't care what you wish. But if you want to—leave!

ADOLF: I order you to come with me on the next steamer!

TEKLA: You order me? What kind of silly nonsense is that?

ADOLF: Are you aware that you are my wife?

TEKLA: Are you aware that you are my husband?

ADOLF: Yes, and there is a difference, isn't there, between the one and the other?

TEKLA: So—you are singing that tune, are you? You have never loved me!

ADOLF: Haven't I?

TEKLA: No—for if you love, you give.

ADOLF: A man *gives* his love; a woman takes, and accepts, the man's love. And I have done nothing but give, give, give. . . .

TEKLA: Pshaw! What have you given?

ADOLF: Everything!

TEKLA: Then you have certainly given a lot, haven't you? And, if so, I have received. And are you now coming with your bills for what you have given me? By accepting, I have simply shown that I loved you. A woman only takes presents from her lover.

ADOLF: From her lover, yes. There you spoke a true word! That is what I have been to you—your lover—but never your husband.

TEKLA: Yes? Well, and didn't you find it much more pleasant not to have to serve as a chaperon? But if that position is not to your liking, I'll discharge you—for I do not want a husband.

ADOLF: No, I have discovered that. Lately, when I observed that you were anxious to steal away from me like a thief and gravitate to your own kind of friends among whom you could show off with plumes borrowed from me and dazzle them with my jewels, I tried to remind you of your debt to me. Immediately I turned into a disagreeable creditor—someone a debtor likes to see transported as far away as possible—and you wanted to cancel your indebtedness. And in order not to make your debt to me still greater, you stopped dipping into my treasure box and started pilfering from others. And so I became your husband without wishing to be—and that led you to hate me. But now—whether you like it or not—since I cannot be your lover any more I am going to be your husband.

TEKLA (*playfully*): Stop talking nonsense, you little idiot!

ADOLF: I must warn you, it is dangerous to go about thinking that everybody is an idiot except yourself.

TEKLA: But there are few who do not think that.

ADOLF: And I am beginning to suspect that he—your former husband—may not have been an idiot.

TEKLA: Oh, God, I think you are beginning to feel sympathy for him. . . .

ADOLF: Not far from it!

TEKLA: Why, I—! And perhaps you should like to make his acquaintance, too, and pour out your heart to him? What a beautiful picture that would make! But even I am beginning to be drawn to him again, for I've tired of acting as wet nurse to you. He was a man, at least. The only trouble was that he was also my husband.

ADOLF: There, you see? But you must not talk so loud! People might hear us!

TEKLA: What harm in that, so long as they know that we are a married couple?

ADOLF: So you have a passion for men who are the manly type—as well as for chaste adolescents—at one and the same time?

TEKLA: My passion is boundless, as you see, and my heart is wide open to any and all, tall and short, handsome and ugly, young and old. I love the whole world!

ADOLF: Do you know what that implies?

TEKLA: No, I know nothing—I only feel.

ADOLF: It means—that your age is beginning to tell.

TEKLA: Are you harping on that again? You had better be careful!

ADOLF: Be careful yourself!

TEKLA: Be careful of what?

ADOLF (*picking up a knife from the revolving base*): Of this!

TEKLA (*prattling*): Little brother should not play with such dangerous weapons!

ADOLF: This is no game!

TEKLA: Oh, so it is serious, eh? Dead serious? Then I must show you how wrong you are. By that I mean that you shall never see and you shall never know, but the whole world will see and know—everybody but you. But you will suspect and surmise and sense; and from this day on you will never have a moment's peace! You will be conscious of your own ridiculousness, you will feel that you are being cheated and deceived—but you will never be able to prove it, for no married man can ever do that. You will get what you deserve!

ADOLF: You hate me, don't you?

TEKLA: No, I don't hate you. And I don't think I ever will. But that is probably because you are a child at heart.

ADOLF: I am a child now. But do you recall the time when the storm broke over us? Then you lay there crying like a helpless baby; then you took refuge in my lap, and I had to put you to sleep by kissing your eyelids. That time it was I who was the wet-nurse. I had to see that you did not go out with your hair in disarray, I had to send your shoes to be mended and make sure that there was food in the house. I had to sit by your side constantly, holding your hand in mine, sometimes for hours, because you were haunted by fear—fear of the whole world. And, overcome by the weight of public opinion, you realized you didn't have a friend left. I had to imbue you with new courage until my throat was parched and my head ached. I had to sit and make myself believe that I was a bulwark of strength, forcing myself to have faith in the future; and finally I succeeded in infusing you with life after you had lain there as though touched by death. Then you had admiration for me; then I was the man for you—not the athletic specimen you had just abandoned, but the high-minded, strong-souled man, the mesmerist who transfused his own nervous energy into your enervated system and charged your worn-out brain with fresh electric impulses. In that way I brought you back to life and into society, provided you with new friends, furnished you with a little court of your own followers, whom I—by taking advantage of their friendship for me—duped into heaping admiration on you, and I let you lord it over me and my home. What is more, I painted your image in my most beautiful paintings, in rosy red and azure blue against a background of gold; and there was not an exhibition where you did not occupy the choice position. I portrayed you as Saint Cecilia; as Mary

Stuart; Karin Månsdotter, who was the wife of Erik the Fourteenth; as Ebba Brahe, who was the great love of Gustav Adolf . . . and thus I created an interest in you and compelled the braying populace to see you through my own enchanted eyes. I forced your personality upon them, harassed them until you had gained their overwhelming adulation and could take the reins into your own hands. . . . When I had launched you securely upon your career, my strength was gone, and I collapsed from overexertion: I had raised you up and, in so doing, strained myself to the point of complete exhaustion. I fell ill, and my illness was an embarrassment to you because it came at the very time when—after you had waited so long—life had finally begun to smile on you. There were times when I felt that you were driven by a secret desire to rid yourself of your creditor and eyewitness. . . . Gradually your love changes to that of a supercilious sister; and, for lack of anything better, I learn to accustom myself to my new rôle of a little brother. Your tenderness does not diminish; on the contrary, you grow even more tender, but it now has a streak of pity in it that borders on contempt. And, as my talent keeps dwindling, and your sun is rising, your contempt turns into disdain. But, somehow or other, your source of inspiration seems to run dry when I no longer can supply you out of mine—or, rather, when you want to show that you refuse to draw from mine. And so we both go to ruin. And then you have to find someone to blame for it—someone else. For you are weak and haven't the strength to take the guilt upon yourself, and that is why I was chosen as the scapegoat—to be sacrificed alive. But when you deprived me of my strength, you failed to take into account that, at the same time, you were maiming and disabling yourself; for the years had joined us together so that we had grown into twins. You were an offshoot from my stem, but you tried to divorce your sprouting self from it before you were any more firmly grafted onto me. And that is why you could not grow and develop by yourself, and the tree could not live without its main branch—so we both died.

TEKLA: What you are driving at is that you have written my books. . . .

ADOLF: No, that is what *you* will say in order to make me

out a liar. I didn't express myself as crudely and unscrupulously as you did. I took the time just now to bring out all the delicate shades of meaning, all the halftones and transitions. But your hurdy-gurdy keeps grinding out the same note continually.

TEKLA: You may talk as much as you like, but the essence of it all is that you are the real author of my books.

ADOLF: No, you can't jump at such a conclusion. You can't render a chord with one single note, you can't translate a mottled, diversified life into a one-digit number. I said nothing so crude as that I had written your books.

TEKLA: But that was what you meant to imply!

ADOLF (*in a rage*): I meant nothing of the kind!

TEKLA: But the gist and substance of it, the sum total . . .

ADOLF (*in a frenzy*): There is no sum total if you don't add it up! You get merely a quotient, a long, interminable quotient of decimal fractions, when you divide and when the dividend is not evenly divisible. I have not added it up.

TEKLA: No—but I know how to add!

ADOLF: I don't doubt it—but I haven't added it up.

TEKLA: But you were eager to.

ADOLF (*closing his eyes, his strength at an end*): No, no, no—don't say another word to me or I shall have a convulsion! Be quiet! Leave me alone! You destroy my brain with your rude, heavy-handed, brutal pincers—I feel your claws clutching at my thoughts and tearing them to pieces. . . . (ADOLF *suddenly stares into space, twiddling his thumbs. He seems on the verge of unconsciousness.*)

TEKLA (*in a tender voice*): What is the matter, Adolf? Are you ill? Adolf!

(ADOLF *motions her away with a feeble gesture.*)

Adolf!

(ADOLF *shakes his head.*)

Adolf!

ADOLF: Yes . . . ?

TEKLA: Will you admit you were unjust to me just now?

ADOLF: Yes, yes, yes—I was unjust. . . .

TEKLA: And will you ask me to forgive you?

ADOLF: Yes, yes, yes—I ask you to forgive me—so long as you don't talk to me!

TEKLA: Then kiss my hand now!

ADOLF (*kissing her hand*): I'll kiss your hand—if you will only stop talking to me!

TEKLA: And now go out and get some fresh air before dinner!

ADOLF: Yes, that's just what I need. . . . And then we'll pack and leave for home.

TEKLA: No!

ADOLF (*getting up from his chair*): Why not? What is your reason?

TEKLA: The reason is that I have promised to attend the soirée this evening.

ADOLF: Oh! So that's your reason?

TEKLA: That's the reason, yes. I have already promised. . . .

ADOLF: Promised? Perhaps you merely said that you intended to go, and that doesn't prevent you from saying now that you can't go.

TEKLA: No—I don't do as you do. I keep my promises.

ADOLF: One should keep one's promises, of course, but that doesn't mean one has to stand by every chance word one lets drop. Did someone make you promise?

TEKLA: Yes.

ADOLF: In that case you can be excused from your promise, since your husband is ill.

TEKLA: No, I don't care to be. And you are not so ill that you can't come along with me.

ADOLF: Why do you always want to have me with you? Why? Does it give you any more self-assurance?

TEKLA: I don't understand what you mean.

ADOLF: That's your usual retort when I say something that you don't like.

TEKLA: Is that so? What is it I don't like now?

ADOLF (*exasperated*): Be quiet! And stop arguing! Goodbye! But mind what you do!

(ADOLF *goes out through the rear door, then turns to the right when outside.* TEKLA *is alone on the stage. Soon after,* GUSTAV *comes in. He goes directly to the table and is about to pick up a newspaper. He acts as if he did not know that* TEKLA *was in the room.* TEKLA *makes a sudden motion of astonishment, but controls her feelings.*)

TEKLA: You?

GUSTAV: Yes, it is I. I hope you'll forgive me. . . .

TEKLA: What brings you here?

GUSTAV: I came here by land, but—but I am not going to stay—now that . . .

TEKLA: By all means, stay! Well, it's been a long time since . . .

GUSTAV: A long time, yes!

TEKLA: You have changed considerably.

GUSTAV: And you are as charming as ever! You almost look younger! But you will pardon me, won't you? I don't wish to spoil your happiness by remaining. If I had known that you were staying here, I would never have . . .

TEKLA: I wish you would stay—that is, if you don't think it improper. . . .

GUSTAV: So far as I am concerned, I have no objection. But I am afraid that—no matter what I say—I may displease or irritate you. . . .

TEKLA: Sit down for a while! I am sure you won't hurt my feelings, for you were always so tactful and correct—a characteristic I am sure you have not lost.

GUSTAV: You are much too kind. But that does not mean that your husband would look upon these attributes of mine with the same indulgence as you.

TEKLA: Quite the contrary; only a while ago I heard him express a good deal of sympathy for you.

GUSTAV: Really? Oh, yes, everything has a way of disintegrating with time—like the names we carve in a tree. Not even enmity is likely to remain with us forever.

TEKLA: But as Adolf has never seen you, he couldn't possibly have a dislike for you. As for me, I have always nourished the hope that the two of you would some day come together as friends, even if only for a brief moment—or, at least, that the three of us would meet and that you two would shake hands with each other—and then part!

GUSTAV: I, too, as a matter of fact, have had a secret longing to see and convince myself that the woman I loved more than my own life was in really good hands. . . . While I have heard many good things about him and am acquainted with all that he has done as an artist, I should nevertheless like to look him straight in the eye before I grow too old—and then take his hand and earnestly beseech him to guard well the treasure that Providence has placed in his keeping. In so doing, I would at the same time put out the blind, instinctive hatred that still lingers inside me. After that, I would hope to find some peace and humility in my soul so that the rest of my dreary, painful life would be bearable. . . .

TEKLA: You have uttered my very own thoughts—and you have been so understanding! For that I thank you!

GUSTAV: Oh, I am a mere man—and much too insignificant to put you in the shade! My life, with its monotony, my restricted social circle and narrow sphere of activity, were not meant for your passionate, freedom-loving spirit—and I admit it unreservedly! But you—who have plumbed the depths of the human soul—you can understand what an effort it has been for me to acknowledge this to myself.

TEKLA: It is noble, it is magnanimous of you to recognize your own shortcomings—and not everyone is capable of that. . . . *(With a sigh.)* But you were always of a loyal, upright, dependable nature—and I respected you for it—even though . . .

GUSTAV: No, I was not—not in those days—but what we go through, the sorrows and sufferings, purify and ennoble us. . . . And I have suffered.

TEKLA: Poor Gustav! Can you forgive me—can you? Tell me you can!

GUSTAV: Forgive you—forgive you for what? It is I who am begging you for forgiveness.

TEKLA *(changing the subject)*: I believe we are both shedding tears—old as we are.

GUSTAV: Old, did you say? Yes, I am old—but you—you keep growing younger and younger!

(He seats himself on the chair to the right. TEKLA *sits down on the chaise longue.)*

TEKLA: You really think so?

GUSTAV: And you certainly know how to dress!

TEKLA: You taught me that! Don't you remember you suggested the colors that were most becoming to me? Don't you?

GUSTAV: No.

TEKLA: Why, yes. Don't you remember—h'm—I can even remember that you were annoyed whenever I didn't wear something that did not have a suggestion of flaming red in it.

GUSTAV: I wasn't annoyed! I was never annoyed or angry with you!

TEKLA: Oh, yes, you were—when you tried to teach me to think! Have you forgotten? I just couldn't learn to think.

GUSTAV: Why, certainly you could think. Who can't? And you have turned out to be really clever at it—at least in your writing.

(TEKLA *is disagreeably affected and speeds up the conversation.*)

TEKLA: Well, anyhow, Gustav dear—it is nice to see you again—and under such peaceful circumstances.

GUSTAV: Well, I was not exactly given to arguing and quarreling, I don't think, and I dare say you had it rather peaceful when you were with me.

TEKLA: Yes—almost too peaceful.

GUSTAV: So-o? But, you know, I thought that was the way you liked me to be. At any rate, that's the impression you gave me when we were engaged.

TEKLA: At such a time a woman doesn't know exactly what she wants to do. And Mama had always impressed upon me that I must use my wits and play my cards well.

GUSTAV: Well, and now you have life and bustle around you. Life among artists is full of lustre and effervescence, and your husband seems by no means to be a slow-poke.

TEKLA: Don't forget there is such a thing as getting too much of a good thing!

GUSTAV (*changing the subject*): Why, I believe you are still wearing my earrings!

TEKLA (*embarrassed*): Yes, and why shouldn't I? We have never been enemies, as you know, and so I wear them to show—and also to remind myself—that there never was any enmity between us. Besides, you may not be aware of the fact that you can't buy earrings like these any more. (*She takes off one of the earrings.*)

GUSTAV: That is all very well, but what does your husband say about it?

TEKLA: What do I care what he says?

GUSTAV: You mean you don't care? But you could do him an

injury that way, by not caring. It would hold him up to ridicule.

TEKLA (*blurting out the words as if talking to herself*): He is already ridiculous!

(*She tries to put her earring on again, and* GUSTAV *notices that she is having difficulty. He rises to help her.*)

GUSTAV: Perhaps you will let me help you . . . ?
TEKLA: Oh, thank you—yes, thank you!

(GUSTAV *tweaks her ear between his fingertips while adjusting the earring.*)

GUSTAV: That dear little ear of Tekla's! What if your husband should see us now?
TEKLA: Then, let me tell you, there would be hysterics!
GUSTAV: Is he so jealous?
TEKLA: You ask if he is jealous! Well, I should say he is!

(*A clattering sound is heard from the adjoining room.*)

GUSTAV: Who lives next door?
TEKLA: I have no idea. Well, tell me what you are doing now, and how are things with you?
GUSTAV: First tell me how things are with you.

(TEKLA *seems embarrassed by the question, and confused. Preoccupied with her thoughts, she unthinkingly removes the covering from the wax figure.*)

Why, who is that? Well, I'll be . . . Why, it's you, isn't it?
TEKLA: I think not.
GUSTAV: It looks like you.
TEKLA (*sarcastically*): So *you* think!
GUSTAV: It reminds me of the anecdote "How could Your Majesty tell?".
TEKLA (*bursts into raucous laughter*): You are absolutely mad. Do you know any new funny stories?
GUSTAV: No, but you should be able to tell some.
TEKLA: I never hear anything amusing any more.
GUSTAV: Is he bashful? Is he reserved?
TEKLA: Oh, so-so. In his speech, at least.
GUSTAV: Not in other ways?
TEKLA: He is very sick just now.

GUSTAV: The poor child! But that is what happens when our little brother sticks his nose into other people's hornets' nests.

TEKLA (*with a chuckle*): You are too, too terribly mad!

GUSTAV: We stayed here one time, in this very room, just after we were married—remember? It was furnished differently then. In front of that column over there, for instance, stood a writing desk; and the bed was over there. (*He indicates with a gesture.*)

TEKLA (*in a bantering manner*): Keep still, will you?

GUSTAV: Look at me!

TEKLA: Why not?

GUSTAV: Do you think we can ever forget something that has made a deep, indelible impression upon us? Do you?

TEKLA: No. The power that our memories wield over us is great; but stronger than any are the memories of our younger days.

GUSTAV: Do you remember when I first met you? You were an adorable little child—a miniature slate on which your parents and your governess had scribbled some crow's feet that I had to erase. Then I substituted new, different words after my own heart and liking until the time came when you felt you were crammed full with knowledge. And that, you see, is the reason why I have no desire to be in your husband's shoes. But, after all, that is his affair. Yet it is also for this reason that I find it so delightful to run across you again. We think alike in so many ways. As we now sit here talking to each other, it is as if I am uncorking a bottle of old wine which I myself had filled. I get my own wine back—but it has aged. And now that I am about to marry again, I have purposely chosen a young girl whom I can educate and bring up in accordance with my own principles and precepts, for, you see, the woman is the man's child—and, if she is not, then he will become hers. And that turns the world upside down.

TEKLA: Are you really going to get married again?

GUSTAV: Yes. I am going to tempt Fortune once more; but this time I shall break the mare in better and hitch her up so there won't be any running away.

TEKLA: Is she pretty?

GUSTAV: Yes—to me she is. But perhaps I shall turn out to be too old for her. And it is strange—now that chance

has brought me face to face with you again—now I begin
to doubt whether it is possible to start that game all over
again.

TEKLA: Why the doubt?

GUSTAV: Because my roots are still in your soil. I can feel
they are there. And the old wounds are bursting open. You
are a dangerous woman, Tekla!

TEKLA: You don't say! My young husband insists I no longer
can captivate.

GUSTAV: To put it bluntly: he no longer loves you.

TEKLA: What his idea of love can be is more than I can
fathom.

GUSTAV: You have been capering about, playing hide-and-
seek, for so long that you can't capture each other. That is
what happens sometimes. You have habituated yourself to
playing the innocent maiden, and that has made him lose
courage. So you see—changing one's habits can have its
drawbacks.

TEKLA: It sounds as though you were reproaching me.

GUSTAV: Far from it! Whatever happens is almost always
meant to happen, and if this had not come about, something
else would have. And now that this has happened, it was
meant to happen.

TEKLA: You are truly a civilized person, Gustav! In fact, I
have never known anyone with whom I would rather exchange ideas. You never preach or moralize—you ask so
little of people that one feels completely uninhibited when
with you. Let me tell you—I am jealous of this girl that
you are going to marry!

GUSTAV: And, quite frankly—I am jealous of your husband!

TEKLA (*getting up*): And yet we must part—part forever!

GUSTAV: Yes, so we must! But not without a proper goodbye!
What do you say?

TEKLA (*pacing the floor in agitation*): No!

GUSTAV (*following her about*): Yes! We must say a last goodbye to each other! Let us drown our memories in an intoxication so benumbing, leaving us so dazed, that when we
wake up we will have no recollection of the past! You
know that there are things that induce a state like that? (*He
puts his arm around her waist.*) You are letting yourself be
dragged down by a man whose soul is sick and who is con-
taminating you with his illness. I shall infuse fresh life into

you, I shall bring your talent to fruition, make it blossom anew in your autumn like the second blooming of the monthly rose. I shall . . .

(*Two* LADIES *appear on the veranda outside. They seem overtaken by surprise and laughingly point at them, then withdraw.*)

TEKLA (*tears herself away from* GUSTAV): Who was that on the veranda?

GUSTAV (*in a tone of indifference*): A couple of the guests here.

TEKLA: Stay away from me! I'm afraid of you!

GUSTAV: Why are you afraid?

TEKLA: You take my soul away from me!

GUSTAV: I gave you mine instead. For that matter, you have no soul—you merely think you have.

TEKLA: You have a faculty for saying uncivil things in such a way that one can't get angry with you.

GUSTAV: That is because you realize that I hold the first mortgage on you. And now—tell me when and where?

TEKLA: No—I can't help feeling sorry for him. After all, I think he still loves me and I don't wish to cause him any more hurt.

GUSTAV: He does not love you! And I can prove it!

TEKLA: How can you prove it?

(GUSTAV *picks up the torn pieces of the photograph from the floor and hands them to her.*)

GUSTAV: There! You can see for yourself!

TEKLA: Oh! This is outrageous!

GUSTAV: There, now you see! And so—*when* and *where*?

TEKLA: What a deceitful blackguard!

GUSTAV: When?

TEKLA: He is leaving tonight—by the eight o'clock steamer.

GUSTAV: And so . . . ?

TEKLA: Nine o'clock.

(*A rumbling is heard from the adjacent room.*)

Who can be occupying that room next door and be making such a racket?

GUSTAV (*going over to the door and peeping through the keyhole*): I'll see if I can find out. . . . I see a table lying upside down on the floor—and a water decanter, broken in pieces. . . . I can't see anything else. Perhaps they have a dog in there that they have shut in. Well, then—at nine o'clock . . .

TEKLA: Yes, nine o'clock! He has brought it upon himself! To think that he could be so false—he who always kept preaching honesty and who constantly admonished me to be completely truthful! But wait a moment—I just remember that he greeted me in a manner that was almost unfriendly—and he didn't come down to the landing place—and—then he said something about the young men on the steamer, and I acted as though I didn't understand what he was driving at. But then—how could he have known about them? Wait now—and then he took to philosophizing about women—and had visions of your ghost hovering about—and he spoke about turning to sculpture because that was *the* fine art of our time—precisely as you used to, some years ago. . . .

GUSTAV: You don't say!

TEKLA: You don't say! Ah, now I understand it all! Now I begin to realize what a scurvy blackguard you are! You have been here, you have torn the heart out of him! It was you who had been sitting there on the chaise longue; it was you who made him believe he had epilepsy—who told him to practice celibacy and that he should assert his manhood by revolting against me! Yes—you were the one! How long have you been here?

GUSTAV: I've been here a week.

TEKLA: Then it *was* you I saw on the steamer.

GUSTAV: It was I.

TEKLA: And you really imagined you would trap me, didn't you?

GUSTAV: And I have.

TEKLA: You haven't yet.

GUSTAV: Oh, yes, I have.

TEKLA: You sneaked up on my lambkin like a wolf—you came here with a diabolical scheme to destroy my happiness and had almost realized it when my eyes were opened and I put a stop to it.

GUSTAV: It didn't happen quite that way. This is what did happen. That I had a secret desire to destroy your marriage was only natural. At the same time, I was almost certain that no intervention on my part would be necessary. Furthermore, there have been so many other things that have required my attention that I have had no time for scheming. But one day, when I was on an outing, I happened to see you in company with those young men on the steamer—and it was then I thought the time was ripe to look you over! So I came here, and your little lamb threw himself without hesitation into the embrace of the wolf. Through some sort of reflex emotion—which I shan't be discourteous enough to try to explain—I gained his confidence. At first I felt compassion for him, as he was now in the very same situation that I had once found myself in. Then, however, he started to poke about in the old wound—your book, you know, and the idiot!—and that goaded me to pick him apart and scramble up the pieces so that he could never be put together again. And, thanks to the conscientious preparatory work you had done, I was successful. But I had not tackled you yet. You were the mainspring of the mechanism and you had to be unwound and taken apart also—and what a noise and buzzing that caused! When I came in here to face you, I hadn't any real idea of what to say to you. Like a chess player, I had a whole lot of thoughts in my head, but my play depended upon what your next move would be. One move led to another, chance played its part, and—before I knew it—I had you checkmated. Now you are cornered and caught!

TEKLA: Oh, no, I am not!

GUSTAV: Oh, yes, you are! What you wanted to happen least of all *has* happened. The world—in the persons of two women guests here, who quite accidentally and not of my doing, since I am not given to intrigue, happened to pass by—the world has witnessed that you have been reconciled with your former husband and crawled back into his staunch, dependable embrace, full of remorse and repentance. Is that sufficient proof?

TEKLA: It should be revenge enough for you! But will you tell me—you who are so intelligent and civilized and so logical in your thinking— how is it that you who fatalistically feel that everything that does happen has to happen, and that all our actions derive from compulsion . . .

GUSTAV (*correcting her*): To a certain degree, from compulsion.

TEKLA: It's the same thing.

GUSTAV: No!

TEKLA: . . . how is it that you, who consider me guiltless since my nature and circumstances impelled me to act as I did—how can you justify your seeking revenge?

GUSTAV: For exactly the same reason, and because my own nature, in combination with circumstances, incited me to revenge. That equalizes matters, doesn't it? But do you know why you and your husband were destined to lose in this contest . . .

(TEKLA *makes a disdainful face.*)

. . . why you allowed me to get the better of you? I'll tell you! It was because I was stronger than you—stronger and more intelligent! And you—you are the idiot—and so is he! And now you will understand that a person is not necessarily an idiot simply because he does not write novels or paint pictures! Remember that for the future!

TEKLA: You haven't the slightest bit of feeling!

GUSTAV: No, not the slightest! But, you see, that is the reason why I can think—something you show you have had scant experience in doing—and take action as well—as you have just found out!

TEKLA: And all this—simply because I hurt your vanity!

GUSTAV: And that is something that should not be trifled with! It's the one sore spot you must never touch! It's the most vulnerable spot people have!

TEKLA: You are a miserable, revengeful creature! Phew!

GUSTAV: And you are a miserable and immoral creature! Phew!

TEKLA: It's my nature, don't you know?

GUSTAV: And so it is mine, don't you know? People should learn something about human nature before letting their own nature have free play. Else it may lead to disaster, and then there'll be weeping and wailing and gnashing of teeth.

TEKLA: You will never learn to be forgiving. . . .

GUSTAV: Of course I can forgive. I have forgiven you.

TEKLA: You have?

GUSTAV: Certainly. Have I lifted a finger against either of you during all these years? No. All I did was to come here and take a look at you—and you both fell apart. Have I ever reproached you—or preached to you—or moralized?

Have I? No. I jested and played a little prank on your better half, and that proved sufficient to make him give up the ghost. And now I stand here—I, the plaintiff—defending myself! Tekla—have you nothing to reproach yourself for?

TEKLA: Nothing whatsoever! Christians maintain that Providence guides our actions, while others say that fate does. How can we therefore be held responsible for what we do?

GUSTAV: In a certain sense, yes—but you must always make allowances, as when stitching a seam in a garment; and there is where our guilt is often hidden. And sooner or later the creditors will show up. Without guilt, but not without responsibility. Guiltless before Him who no longer exists, responsible to oneself and to one's fellowmen.

TEKLA: And so you are now coming to demand your payment?

GUSTAV: I came to take back what you had *stolen*—not what I had *given* you. You stole my honor, and the only way to repair it was by taking yours from you. Don't you think I was justified in that?

TEKLA: Honor! H'm! Are you satisfied now?

GUSTAV: Now I am satisfied! (*He presses the service bell.*)

TEKLA: And now you are setting off to see your betrothed, I suppose. . . .

GUSTAV: I am not betrothed. And don't want ever to be again. And I am not going home, for I have no home—and don't wish to have any!

(*There is a knock at the door. A* WAITER *enters.*)

Will you bring me my bill? I am leaving on the eight o'clock steamer.

(*The* WAITER *bows and leaves.*)

TEKLA: Without reconciliation?

GUSTAV: Without reconciliation, you say! You use so many words that have lost their meaning. You speak of reconciliation! Would you perhaps like all three of us to live together? Would you? Rather, you should make amends by atoning for what you have done—but that is something you are incapable of! You have done nothing but take, and what you have taken, you have consumed, and so you can't give it back. . . . Will you now be satisfied if I beg you to forgive me for your having clawed my heart to pieces and for having dishonored me—to forgive me for having made me, for seven long years, the constant laughing-stock of my pupils at school—to forgive me for freeing you from the domineering influence of your parents, and for delivering you from the tyranny of ignorance and superstition—for setting you at the head of my household, giving you position and friends—for making the child you were when we met into a woman! Forgive me for all this, as I now forgive you. . . . Now—now I have canceled the bond! Now you can go and settle accounts with your other husband!

TEKLA: What have you done with Adolf? I begin to suspect—something—terrible!

GUSTAV: Done with him? Do you really love him?

TEKLA: I love him!

GUSTAV: A moment ago it was I! Did you tell the truth then?

TEKLA: I did!

GUSTAV: Then—do you know what you are?

TEKLA: You hate me, don't you?

GUSTAV: I pity you! I won't say it is a vice, but it is a failing—a peculiar failing which can have serious, harmful consequences. Poor Tekla! I don't know why it is, but—although I am no more guilty than you—I have a feeling of contrition, of self-reproach! But perhaps it will do you some good to experience what I felt that time! Do you know where your husband is?

TEKLA: Yes—I believe I know now! He is next door—in your room! And he has heard everything we have said—and seen everything! And he who has seen his guardian spirit is destined to die. . . .

(ADOLF *appears in the doorway to the veranda. His face has the pallor of death, and he is bleeding from a wound on one cheek. His eyes stare, expressionless, into space, and white froth comes from his mouth.*)

GUSTAV (*taken aback*): No—there he is now! Settle your account with him now and see if he is as generous as I have been! Goodbye! (*He goes out to the right, but suddenly stops.*)

TEKLA (*going to* ADOLF *with outstretched arms.*): Adolf!

(ADOLF *collapses against the doorstep and falls to the floor.* TEKLA *throws herself across his limp body, caressing him.*)

Adolf! My beloved child! Do you hear me? Speak, speak! Say you forgive your selfish, miserable Tekla! Please forgive me—forgive me—forgive me! Please—answer me, little brother! Do you hear me—please, please! Oh, my God— God in heaven—help us! Help us!

GUSTAV: I believe she really loves *him,* too. Poor soul!

CURTAIN

To Betty Shannon

The Stronger

(1888–1889)

A Play in One Scene

CHARACTERS

MRS. X.,
 a married actress

MISS Y.,
 an unmarried actress

A WAITRESS

A corner of a café for ladies. Two wrought iron tables; a sofa upholstered with red shag; several chairs. MISS Y. is seated at one of the tables. Before her is a half-empty bottle of ale. She is reading an illustrated periodical, which she later exchanges for others on the table. MRS. X. enters. She is dressed in winter apparel and wears a hat and cloak. She carries a Japanese shopping bag or basket, of exquisite design, on her arm.

MRS. X.: How do you do, Amelie dear! You are sitting here all by yourself on Christmas Eve—like some poor bachelor. . . .

(MISS Y. *looks up from the magazine, gives MRS. X. a nod, and resumes her reading.*)

MRS. X.: You know it hurts me to see you sitting here—alone—alone in a café, and, of all times, on Christmas Eve. It makes me feel as bad as when I once saw a wedding party in a restaurant in Paris. The bride sat reading a comic paper, while the bridegroom was playing billiards with the wedding guests. Ugh, I thought to myself, with a beginning like that, what will the marriage be like—and how will it end? *He,* playing billiards on their wedding night—And *she* reading a comic paper, you mean to say? . . . Ah, but there is a certain difference, don't you think?

(THE WAITRESS *enters with a cup of chocolate which she places before MRS. X. Then she leaves.*)

145

MRS. X.: Do you know what, Amelie! I believe you would have been better off if you had married him. . . . You remember that I urged you from the very first to forgive him. You remember that? You could have been his wife now, and had a home of your own. . . . Do you recall how happy you were last Christmas when you spent the holidays with your fiancé's parents out in the country? How you sang the praises of domestic life and literally longed to get away from the theatre?—Yes, Amelie dear, a home is the best after all—next to the theatre. And children, you know. . . . Well, but you wouldn't understand that!

(MISS Y. *expresses disdain.*)

MRS. X. (*sips a few teaspoonfuls of her chocolate. Then she opens her shopping bag and brings out some Christmas presents.*): Here—let me show you what I have bought for my little ones. (*She shows her a doll.*) Look at this one! This is for Lisa. . . . Do you see how she rolls her eyes and turns her head! Do you? Do you see?—And here is a popgun for Maja. . . . (*She loads the toy gun and pops it at* MISS Y.)

(MISS Y. *makes a gesture of fright.*)

MRS. X.: Did I frighten you? You didn't think I was going to shoot you, did you? Did you?—Upon my soul, I really think you did! If *you* had wanted to shoot *me,* I wouldn't have been surprised. After all, I have stood in your way —and I realize that you can never forget that . . . even though I was entirely blameless. You still believe that I schemed to have you dismissed from the Grand Theatre —don't you? But I didn't! You may think whatever you like, but I had nothing to do with it! I realize, however, that no matter what I say, you will still believe I was responsible for it! (*She takes out a pair of embroidered bedroom slippers from the bag.*) And these are for my better half. I embroidered them myself—with tulips. You understand, I hate tulips, but my husband has to have tulips on everything. . . .

(MISS Y. *looks up from her magazine with an expression of irony mixed with curiosity.*)

MRS. X. (*places a hand inside each slipper*): See what tiny

feet Bob has! See? And I wish you could see how ele-
gantly he walks! You never saw him in slippers, did you?

(MISS Y. *laughs aloud.*)

MRS. X.: Look, let me show you! (*She makes the slippers
walk on the table.*)

(MISS Y. *gives another loud laugh.*)

MRS. X.: And when he gets angry, he stamps his foot, like
this: "Damnation! These stupid maids who never can
learn to make coffee! And look at this! The idiots don't
even know how to trim a lamp wick!" And when there is a
draft from the floor and his feet are cold: "Heavens! It's
freezing cold, and the incorrigible fools let the fire go out
in the grate!" (*She rubs the sole of one slipper against the
top of the other.*)

(MISS Y. *gives a shriek of laughter.*)

MRS. X.: And when he comes home, he goes hunting for
his slippers which Marie has put under the chiffonier. . . .
Oh, but it's a shame to sit and make fun of my own husband like this. After all, he is so nice. He is a good little
husband. . . . You should have had a husband like him,
Amelie!—What are you laughing at, if I may ask? What
is it? What's the matter?—And the best of it is that he is
faithful to me—yes, that I know. He has told me so himself! . . . Why the sneering grin? He told me that Frédérique tried to seduce him while I was on a tour in
Norway. . . . Can you imagine such impudence! (*There
is a silence.*) I would have torn her eyes out! That's what
I'd have done, if she had come near him while I was at
home! (*Again there is silence.*) I was lucky enough to hear
about it from Bob himself before being told by some
gossip. . . . (*Silence.*) But Frédérique was not the only one,
let me tell you! I can't understand it, but women seem to
be absolutely crazy about my husband. They must think
he has something to say about the engaging of the artists,
because he is on the board of administration. . . . I would
not be surprised if you, too, had used your wiles on him!
I never did trust you too much. . . . But I know now
that he could not be interested in you—and it seemed to
me you always acted as if you bore some sort of grudge

against him. . . . *(There is a silence and they regard each other with some embarrassment.* MRS. X. *continues.)* Why don't you come home to us this evening, Amelie, just to show that you have no hard feelings—at least not against *me.* . . . I can't explain just why—but I think it is so unpleasant to be bad friends—with you especially. Perhaps it is because I stood in your way that time *(In a slower tempo.)* . . . or . . . I can't imagine . . . what the reason could have been—really . . . *(There is a silence.)*

(MISS Y. *gazes fixedly and curiously at* MRS. X.)

MRS. X. *(pensively)*: Our relationship was such a strange one. . . . The first time I saw you, I was frightened of you. I was so frightened that I didn't dare let you out of my sight. No matter when or where I went—I always found myself next to you. . . . I didn't have the courage to be your enemy, and so I became your friend. But whenever you came to our home, it always led to discord. I noticed that my husband could not bear the sight of you and it made me feel ill at ease—as when a garment does not fit. I did everything I could to persuade him to show you some friendliness, but it was no use—not until you announced your engagement! Then suddenly a violent friendship blossomed between you two! At the time it appeared as if only then you dared to show your true feelings—when it was safe for you to do so! And then—what happened afterwards? . . . I didn't feel any jealousy—and that seems strange to me now! And I can remember the scene at the christening, when you were the godmother, and I had to coax him to kiss you. When he did, you were so abashed and confused—and quite frankly, I didn't notice it at the time, didn't give it a thought. I never thought of it until —until this very moment. . . . *(She rises violently, impassioned.)* Why don't you say something? You haven't uttered one single word all this time! You have let me sit here, talking on and on! You have been sitting there, drawing out of me all these thoughts that have been lying like raw silk in the cocoon—thoughts . . . yes, even suspicions. . . . Let me see! Why did you break off your engagement? Why did you never come to our home again after that? Why won't you come to our home tonight?

(MISS Y. *seems to be about to break her silence.)*

MRS. X.: Don't speak! You needn't say a word! Now I understand everything! It was because of this—and that—and that! That's it exactly. Now the accounts are balanced! Now I know the answer!—For shame! I won't sit at the same table with you! *(She moves her things to the other table.)* That is why I had to embroider tulips on his slippers—because you liked tulips. . . . That's why we—*(She throws the slippers on the floor.)*—why we had to spend the summers at Lake Mälar—because you didn't like the open sea; that's why my son was named Eskil—because that was your father's name; that's the reason I had to wear your colors, read your authors, eat your favorite dishes, drink what you liked—your chocolate, for instance. . . . That is why . . . Oh, my God—it's frightening to think of it—horrible! Everything, everything came to me from you, even your passions! Your soul crept into mine, like a worm into an apple, worming its way, boring and boring, until nothing was left but the rind and a speck of black dust inside. I tried to get away from you, but I couldn't! You charmed me, bewitched me like a snake, with your black eyes. . . . Every time I lifted my wings to escape, I felt myself being dragged down again: I lay in the water with bound feet—and the harder I fought to keep afloat, the further down I went—down, down, until I sank to the bottom, where you lay in wait like a giant crab to seize me with your claws—and there is where I am now.

Ugh! How I detest you, hate you, hate you! But you—all you do is to sit there silent, cold and impassive! You don't care whether it's new moon or full moon, Christmas or New Year—whether people around you are happy or unhappy! You have neither the capacity to hate nor to love; you are as cold-blooded as a stork watching a rathole; you are incapable of scenting your prey and pursuing it—but you know how to hide in holes and corners and exhaust your prey. Here you sit—I suppose you know that people call this corner the rat trap, in your honor—scanning the newspapers in the hope that you may read about someone who has had bad luck or been struck by misfortune, or about someone who has been dismissed from the theatre. . . . Here you sit, lurking for victims, figuring out your chances like a pilot in a shipwreck.

Here you receive your tributes! Poor Amelie! You know, in spite of everything, I feel sorry for you, because I am aware that you are miserable—miserable like some wounded beast!—and made spiteful and vicious because of having been wounded! I find it hard to be angry with you, despite feeling that I ought to be—but, after all, you are the weaker one. . . . As for the episode with Bob—well, I shan't let that bother me. . . . It hasn't really harmed me! And if *you* got me into the habit of drinking chocolate, or if someone else did, matters little . . . (*She takes a spoonful of chocolate; then, common-sense-like.*) Besides, chocolate is a healthful beverage. And if you have taught me how to dress—*tant mieux!* My husband has become all the more fond of me as a result! That is one thing I have gained, and that you lost. As a matter of fact, judging from what I have seen, I think you have already lost him! But no doubt it was your intention that I should leave him—as you did—and which you now regret. But, you see, that's just what I don't intend to do! We must not be one-sided or selfish, you know. But why should I take only what someone else doesn't want? All said and done, perhaps I am at this moment really the stronger. . . . You never received anything from *me*—while *you gave* something to me! And now I have had the same experience as the proverbial thief had: When *you* woke up, *I* possessed what *you* had lost! And why was it that everything you touched became sterile and empty? Your tulips and your passions proved insufficient to keep a man's love—while I was able to keep it. Your authors could not teach you the art of living—as I have learned it. Nor did you bear a little Eskil—even if your father bore that name. . . . And why are you forever silent, your lips eternally sealed? I confess I used to think it a sign of strength—but perhaps it is only because you have nothing to say! Perhaps it is for lack of thoughts! (*She rises and picks up the slippers from the floor.*) Now I am going home—and I take the tulips with me. Your tulips! You found it hard to learn from others—you found it hard to bend, to humble yourself—and so you broke like a dry reed—and I survived! I thank you, Amelie, for all that you have taught me! And thank you for teaching my husband how to love! Now I am going home—to love him! (*She leaves.*)

To the memory of Clifford Backstrand

Pariah

(1889)

A Play in One Act

Mr. X.,
    an archaeologist

Mr. Y.,
    on a visit from America

Both men are of middle age.

*The action takes place on a farm
in southern Sweden.*

A plain living room in a farmhouse in a country district. In the rear, a door and windows; beyond is seen the out-of-doors. In the center of the room, a large dining table. Piled on one side of it are books, writing materials, and archaeological artifacts. On the opposite side are microscopes, boxes with insects, and alcohol jars. On the right is a bookcase. The furnishings, while simple, nevertheless bespeak the home of a farmer in comfortable circumstances.

MR. Y. enters with an insect net and a vasculum. He is in his shirt-sleeves. He goes directly to the bookcase, takes a book from one of the shelves, and starts reading it, still standing.

The bells of the country church announce the close of the service. The landscape and the interior are bathed in sunlight.

Now and then the hens are heard clucking outside.

MR. X. comes into the room; he is also in his shirt-sleeves.

(MR. Y. *gives a violent start and quickly replaces the book, upside down. He makes believe he is looking for another one.*)

153

MR. X.: This heat wears one down, doesn't it? I wouldn't be surprised if we had a thunderstorm. . . .

MR. Y.: So-oh! What makes you think that?

MR. X.: The bells have a hollow sound—the flies are biting—and the hens are clucking. I had thought of going fishing, but I couldn't find even one worm. Don't you feel nervous?

MR. Y. (*with circumspection*): I? Oh—a little, perhaps. . . .

MR. X.: But then you always act as if you were expecting a storm to break.

MR. Y. (*with a nervous twitch*): Do I?

MR. X.: Yes—and now that you are going away tomorrow it is not surprising if you should have a touch of travel fever! What's the news today, I wonder? Here is the mail. . . . (*He picks up some letters on the table.*) Oh! Whenever I open a letter, I get palpitations of the heart! Nothing but debts! Debts! Were you ever in debt?

MR. Y. (*after reflecting*): No-o!

MR. X.: Well, then you can't know how it feels to get unpaid bills in the mail. . . . (*He reads one of the letters.*) The rent is unpaid—the landlord is making threats—my wife is in despair! And here I am surrounded by gold up to my elbows! (*He opens the box with wrought iron fittings that stands on the table.*)

(*The two men seat themselves, one on either side of the box.*)

Here, you see, I have the gold that I have dug up during the past fourteen days. The metal alone is worth six thousand. And this bracelet would bring me enough to pay the three hundred and fifty I owe. With what I have here, I could make a brilliant career for myself. Of course, I would first have the drawings and the woodcuts made for my thesis—then I would have it published. And afterward I would travel. . . . Why don't I do it, do you think?

MR. Y.: I suppose you are afraid of being found out.

MR. X.: Perhaps that, too! But don't you think that an intelligent man like me should be able to arrange things so that no one could know? You see—I roam around out there alone—where no one sees what I am doing—and poke about on the slopes. Wouldn't it be easy enough for me to pocket some of the finds I come across?

MR. Y.: Yes—but it might be dangerous to dispose of them.

MR. X.: Nonsense! I would, of course, melt down every particle—and then I would make it all into coins—of standard weight, naturally. . . .

MR. Y.: Naturally!

MR. X.: That goes without saying! If I just wanted to make counterfeit, then I wouldn't have to dig for gold first, would I?

(There is a silence.)

You may say what you like, but it's strange that—if someone else were to do what I can't persuade myself to do—I would let him go free! But, as for myself, I could never exonerate myself! I would come to the defense of the thief with a glowing speech! I would prove that the gold was *res nullius*—or no man's—because it had been buried in the earth from the time before property rights existed—that it now belonged to no one but the finder, since it had not been included in the assessed value of the owner's property, and so forth. . . .

MR. Y.: And you would probably be able to accomplish this much more surely, if—h'm—the thief did not steal because of need, but instead, for example, out of a mania for collecting, out of scientific interest, out of ambition and vanity to possess a rare discovery, don't you think?

MR. X.: You mean to say that I would not be able to have him exonerated, had he stolen from need? No, you're right! That is the one thing the law does not forgive! That is plain, outright theft!

MR. Y.: And that you would not forgive?

MR. X.: H'm! Forgive! How could I very well do that when the law does not excuse it? And I may as well confess that I would find it disagreeable to accuse a collector of stealing, if he could add to his collection some artifact that he did not already possess and that he had come across on someone else's property!

MR. Y.: In other words, vanity and ambition would excuse what dire need would not.

MR. X.: And this despite the fact that need should be the stronger—as a matter of fact, the *only*—excuse. . . . However, that's the way it is. And I am no more able to change this than I am able to change my resolution never to steal, no matter what.

MR. Y.: And I suppose you consider that a special virtue—that you can't bring yourself—h'm—to steal!

MR. X.: It is as natural to me as the desire to steal is natural for others—and consequently not a virtue. *I* cannot *do it*—and *they* can't *resist!* You understand, of course, that the desire for gold is not lacking in me . . . then—why don't I take this? I can't! I just can't! It's something I would be incapable of doing. . . . And to be *lacking* in any quality is not a virtue! So . . .

(*He slams the box shut. Meanwhile, a few scattered clouds have appeared over the landscape, occasionally darkening the room. Finally, darkness sets in, as when a thunderstorm is approaching.*)

MR. Y.: It's terribly sultry, isn't it? I believe we shall have a thunderstorm. . . .

(MR. Y. *rises. He closes the door and the windows.*)

MR. X.: Are you afraid of thunderstorms?

MR. Y.: I don't see why one shouldn't take precautions. . . .

(*They sit down at the table again.*)

MR. X.: You are a curious fellow! You suddenly land here like a bombshell about two weeks ago, introduce yourself as a Swedish-American travelling about in pursuit of flies for some obscure museum. . . .

MR. Y.: We don't have to discuss me now.

MR. X.: That's what you always say, when I tire of talking about myself and want to focus the conversation on to you. Perhaps that explains why I took a liking to you—because you gave me a chance to talk about myself! Before we knew it, we were like old friends. You had no corners to rub against, no sharp points that pricked. . . . There was something so mellow and soft about you! You were considerate as only a highly cultivated person can be. You were never noisy when you came home late, made no sound when you got up in the morning. You overlooked trifles and always turned away when conflict was brewing. In a word, you were the perfect friend and companion. But at the same time you were entirely too compliant, too submissive, and altogether too silent and negative for me not to begin to reflect over it as time went on. . . . Also you are full of fears and timidity. It all points to your leading a double life. . . . Do you know that—as I sit here, facing that mirror, and see your back in it—I could almost believe I was seeing another person!

(MR. Y. *turns around and looks in the mirror.*)

MR. X.: Well, you can't see how you look from the back. Looking at you from the front, you have the appearance of a frank and fearless man who faces his fate with courage and self-reliance. But from the back . . . well, I don't wish to be discourteous . . . but from the back you look as though you were carrying a heavy burden—as if you were cringing to escape a thrashing! And as I look at your crimson suspenders crisscrossed over your white shirt—they remind me of nothing so much as a trademark on a packing case. . . .

MR. Y. (*rises*): I feel I am going to suffocate—if that thunderstorm doesn't break soon!

MR. X.: Take it easy! It will soon be here! . . . And—and then, your neck! It looks as if it were meant for another face—a face of a different type than yours! You are so frightfully narrow between the ears that I have sometimes wondered what race you really belong to!

(*There is a flash of lightning.*)

That one looked as if it struck over at the sheriff's!

MR. Y. (*disturbed*): The sheriff's?

MR. X.: I said it looked as if it did! But let's forget about the thunderstorm. . . . Sit down now, and let's have a real talk, since you are going away tomorrow. . . . You know—it is strange, but you belong in that category of people whose image I can't recall, once they are out of sight. . . . When you are out in the fields, and I happen to think of you, I invariably see before me the face of another man I was once acquainted with. . . . He didn't really look like you, yet there is a certain similarity between you. . . .

MR. Y.: Who was that?

MR. X.: I don't want to mention his name. . . . However,

for a number of years I used to have dinner at the same place where he ate. It was there I happened to meet this fair-complexioned little man with pale, harrowed-looking eyes one day at the *smörgåsbord*. He had an uncanny ability to make his way toward the head of the line, even when the place was at its most crowded. He never elbowed his way and always avoided other people's elbows. Even when he found himself far over by the door, three yards away, he could manage to get his slice of bread. . . . He always appeared happy to be among people; whenever he spotted an acquaintance, he was so delighted that he broke into boisterous laughter and would slap him on the back and embrace him, as if he hadn't come across another human being for years. If anyone stepped on his toes, he would smile as if begging the man's pardon for having been in his way.

For two whole years I saw this man, and I amused myself by making guesses about his profession and his character. But I never asked anyone who he was. I didn't want to know, for then my pleasure in studying him would have been lost. This man had the very same characteristics that you have. He was difficult to classify. One day I would think he was a teacher who hadn't attained his doctor's degree; the next, a noncommissioned officer, a pharmacist, a minor county official, or a plainclothesman. And, just like you, he seemed to be a patchwork of two different human types: the front didn't match the back.

One day I stumbled across an item in a newspaper about an enormous banknote forgery that had been committed by a well-known civil servant. Soon after, I learned that my indefinable acquaintance had been in business with the forger's brother and that his name was Stråman. I also learned that the same Stråman had formerly run a lending library, but that now he was a police reporter for a widely circulated newspaper. What connection could there possibly be between forgery, the police, and the indefinable man's strange behavior? I couldn't figure it out. . . . But when I asked a friend whether Stråman had been duly punished, he couldn't answer yes or no—he didn't know. . . .

(There is a silence.)

MR. Y.: Well, did he get—his punishment?

MR. X.: No. He went unpunished. . . .

(Again there is a pause.)

MR. Y.: What you mean to say is that this was why he was so drawn to the police and so afraid of offending people?

MR. X.: Yes.

MR. Y.: Did you get acquainted with him after that?

MR. X.: No—I didn't care to. . . .

(Silence.)

MR. Y.: Would you have cared to—if he had been punished?

MR. X.: Yes, gladly!

(MR. Y. gets up from his chair and paces back and forth a few times.)

MR. X.: Sit down! Why can't you relax?

MR. Y.: Where did you get this liberal view of human problems? Are you a Christian?

MR. X.: No, you ought to be able to tell that I am not. . . .

(A quizzical expression comes over MR. Y's face.)

MR. X.: A Christian would demand forgiveness, but I demand punishment, for the sake of restoring equilibrium—or whatever you choose to call it! And you, who have been in prison, ought to know something about that.

MR. Y. *(stops and stands motionless, regarding MR. X. first with a wild, hate-filled look, then with astonishment and admiration)*: How—could—you know—that?

MR. X.: I have eyes to see with!

MR. Y.: How—how can you—see . . . ?

MR. X.: I have made it my study. It is an art, like so many other things. But let us not talk about it any more. *(He looks at his watch, then places a document before MR. Y., dips a pen in the ink, and hands it to him.)* I must attend to my muddled affairs. Will you be good enough to witness my signature on this promissory note? I have to deliver it to the bank in Malmö tomorrow morning; so we can then take the same train.

MR. Y.: I am not going by way of Malmö.

MR. X.: No?

MR. Y.: No.

MR. X.: But, in any case, you can witness my signature, can't you?

MR. Y.: No! I have made it a rule never to put my name on any paper. . . .

MR. X.: . . . again! This is the fifth time you have refused to sign your name! The first time was on a postal receipt. . . . That's when I first began to watch you. . . . And now I see that you have a dread of using pen and ink. You haven't sent off a single letter since you came here, only a postal card—and that you wrote with a blue pencil! Do you understand now how I figured out your past misstep? To continue . . . It must be at least the seventh time that you have refused to come with me to Malmö—and you haven't been there since you arrived. And yet you came from America just to see that city! And every morning you walk three or more miles south— all the way to the slope by the windmill—merely to get a glimpse of the city's roofs! And when you stand over there by the left-hand window and peer through the third pane to the right, counting from the bottom, you can see the towers of the old castle and the chimneys of the county prison.

Now do you realize it isn't I who am so confoundedly clever, but rather you who are stupid?

MR. Y.: You have nothing but contempt for me, haven't you?

MR. X.: No!

MR. Y.: Oh, yes—you must have—you must . . .

MR. X.: No! I give you my hand on that!

(MR. Y. *kisses his outstretched hand.*)

MR. X. (*jerks his hand away*): What kind of beastly business is this?

MR. Y.: Forgive me—but you, sir, are the only person who has offered me his hand after learning about . . .

MR. X.: And now I notice that you don't even address me by my first name any longer! And it disturbs me that you—having served your sentence—no longer feel yourself rehabilitated, washed clean, as good as the next man! I am curious to know just how it came about. . . . Would you care to tell me?

MR. Y. *(turning and twisting in his chair)*: Yes—but you don't have to believe that what I tell you is the truth. . . . I'll tell you—and then you'll understand that I am not an *ordinary* criminal. . . . You'll realize that a man can make missteps that are, so to speak, inevitable, unavoidable . . . *(He turns in his chair.)* . . . that come about spontaneously, by themselves, without any desire on his own part—without the will to do wrong. . . . Do you mind if I open the door a little? I believe the storm is over. . . .

MR. X.: By all means, do.

MR. Y. *(opens the door. Then he seats himself by the table and relates the following with dry enthusiasm, theatrical gestures, and false accents.)*: Well—you see. . . . I attended the university in Lund, and while I was there I needed a loan from a bank. I had no large debts, and my father had a little money—not very much, but something. I had forwarded the promissory note for an additional signature to a man who—contrary to my expectations—returned it with his refusal to sign it. For a moment I was struck dumb by the blow. It was an unpleasant surprise—extremely unpleasant! The document lay before me on the table, and his letter next to it. . . . Disconsolate, my eyes scanned the fatal words that pronounced judgment on me. . . . While it was not a death sentence—for I could easily find someone else to become surety: as a matter of fact, as many as I cared to have—nevertheless, I found the situation very disagreeable, as I just said. And as I sat there, my eyes, after a while, remained innocently fixed on the signature at the bottom of the letter . . . the signature, which—in the right place —might have assured my future for me. It was an exceptionally neat and symmetrical handwriting. . . . Now— you know how one can sit preoccupied and clutter up a blotter with the most meaningless words . . . and . . . I had the pen in my hand . . . *(He takes the pen.)* . . . like this . . . and, before I knew it, it began to move. . . . I don't want to give you the impression that there was anything mystical, anything spiritualistic, about it . . . for I put no faith in any such things. . . . It was a purely unreflecting, absentminded, mechanical act—as I sat there copying the well-formed signature over and over again—

naturally, without the slightest intention of making it work to my advantage. Finally, when I had scribbled all over the letter, I had attained complete dexterity in signing the man's name . . . (*He casts away the pen violently.*) . . . and then I forgot about the whole matter. When I went to sleep that night I slept heavily and soundly; when I awoke I was aware that I had been dreaming—but I couldn't recall what I had dreamt. . . . At moments, however, it was as if a door had been opened: I saw the writing table with the promissory note on it—much like a memory, a remembrance. . . . And when I got up out of bed, I was driven by a compulsion to go to the desk— exactly as if, after due deliberation, I had made the irrevocable decision to sign the name to the fatal document. I gave no thought to the consequences and felt no fear of the risk I was taking. I had no hesitation whatsoever. It was as if I were fulfilling a sacred duty—and I penned the signature! (*He jumps up.*) What would you call this? Could it have been an impulse—of the kind you call hypnotic suggestion? Could it? But suggested by whom? No one but I was sleeping in the room! Could it have been my own uncivilized nature—the primitive savage who recognizes no laws—who, while my conscience was asleep, emerged with his criminal instincts, incapable of calculating the consequences of his actions? Tell me— what do you think?

MR. X. (*makes an effort to speak bluntly*): To tell the truth, your story does not satisfy me completely. It has gaps in it . . . yet that may be because you don't remember all the details any longer. I have done some reading about criminal tendencies and impulses, I recollect—h'm. . . . But, never mind, you have learned the hard way . . . and you have been courageous enough to acknowledge your mistake. So let us speak no more about it.

MR. Y.: Yes, yes, yes—we must discuss it, we must discuss it! We'll discuss it from beginning to end, until I feel entirely convinced that I am an innocent victim. . . .

MR. X.: You are not convinced of it yet?

MR. Y.: No! I am not.

MR. X.: Well . . . and that, you see, is the very thing that troubles me; *that* is what worries me. . . . Has it never occurred to you that we—all of us—have a skeleton in the closet? Didn't we all pilfer and lie when we were children? You may be sure we did. Yes—and there are some who remain children all through life and never learn to conquer their lawless instincts. All they need is the opportunity—and the criminal is in the making! But what I can't understand is that you don't feel that you are innocent! If a child is considered morally unaccountable for its actions, why shouldn't a criminal also be held unaccountable? It's strange, but—well, what does it matter? I may regret it later on. . . .

(There is a pause.)

I once killed a man—yes, and I have never felt any remorse!

MR. Y. *(with irrepressible interest)*: You—you—have killed?

MR. X.: I did—yes! Perhaps you will shrink from taking my hand now?

MR. Y. *(blithely)*: Ah, how you talk!

MR. X.: Yes—but I was not punished for it!

MR. Y. *(confidentially, with a superior air)*: So much the better for you! How did you get out of it?

MR. X.: There was no one to prosecute me—no suspicions —no witnesses. This is how the incident happened. A friend of mine had invited me, one Christmas, to go hunting with him outside of Uppsala. He sent a sottish old farmhand to fetch me; the man kept falling asleep on the box, turned over in a ditch, and time after time he let the vehicle graze against posts and gateways. I can't say that my life was in danger, but in a fit of impatience I gave him a jab on the chin—merely to make him alert, to wake him up. . . . But the consequence of it was that he never woke up again. He died on the spot!

MR. Y. *(craftily)*: Well . . . and didn't you report how it happened?

MR. X.: No—for the following reasons: the man had neither relatives nor others who needed him. He had lived out his life—his place could immediately be taken by somebody who needed it more. While I, on the other hand, was indispensable to my parents' happiness—and, perhaps, even to science. . . . And, besides, the incident had already taught me my lesson: I would never again succumb to the temptation of striking anyone. And I didn't want to ruin both my parents' and my own life in order to satisfy an abstract justice. . . .

MR. Y.: So—that's the way you judge human worth?

MR. X.: In this particular case, yes. . . .

MR. Y.: But have you no feeling of guilt whatsoever? . . . And how do you manage to maintain your equanimity?

MR. X.: I have no feeling of guilt—for I haven't committed any crime. . . . As a boy I both took and gave back many a blow. It was simply my ignorance of its effect on an elderly person that caused his death.

MR. Y.: Well—but even for causing death by accident you get a two-year sentence—the same time you are given for —for forging a signature. . . .

MR. X.: Don't think I haven't thought about that, too! I have! And many a night I have dreamt that I was in prison. . . . Whew! Tell me—is it really as horrible as they say—to be locked up behind bars?

MR. Y.: You may be sure it is! First they disfigure you by shaving off your hair. If you don't look like a criminal before, you will then. You take a look at yourself in the mirror and you are convinced you *are* one.

MR. X.: Perhaps it's simply that the mask is torn off! It isn't such a bad idea!

MR. Y.: You may jest all you like! And then they reduce the size of your portions at mealtime until you finally feel you are hovering between life and death. . . . All the vital functions deteriorate, you feel yourself shrinking, and your soul—which was to be cleansed and made well by the expiation of your crime—is placed on a starvation diet and is pushed back through the ages, to its primitive state. . . . All you are given to read is books fit for savages from the time of the exodus. . . . All you hear is what will never come to pass in heaven. But what happens on earth remains a dark secret. . . . You are torn loose from your surroundings. You are demoted to a class below you and are under the thumb of people far beneath you; you have visions of living in the Bronze Age and feel as if you were going about in an animal skin, living in a cage, and eating out of a trough! Oh!

MR. X.: Well—but I must say there is some common sense in that! Anyone who behaves as if he were living in the Bronze Age must expect to appear in his historical garb.

MR. Y. *(in a rage)*: You are being sarcastic! You, who have behaved like a creature of the Stone Age—and yet are permitted to live in the golden age!

MR. X. *(scrutinizing him; sharply)*: What do you mean by those words—the golden age?

MR. Y. *(slyly)*: Nothing at all!

MR. X.: You lie! You haven't the courage to speak your mind!

MR. Y.: I am a coward, am I? That's what you think, eh? I wasn't a coward when I dared to come here, where I have suffered so much. . . . But do you know what one suffers the most from when he is put behind bars? Well, I'll tell you! It's—that the others are not also behind bars!

MR. X.: Which others?

MR. Y.: The ones who go unpunished!

MR. X.: Are you alluding to me?

MR. Y.: Yes!

MR. X.: I have committed no crime.

MR. Y.: Oh, so! Haven't you?

MR. X.: No. An accident is not a crime.

MR. Y.: Is that so? Is committing a murder an accident?

MR. X.: I have committed no murder.

MR. Y.: So-o? Beating a person to death—is that not murder?

MR. X.: No—not necessarily! There is murder, accidental murder, manslaughter, assault and battery resulting in death—with various degrees of intent and lack of intent. However, now I am getting to be really afraid of you! For you belong in the most dangerous category of human beings: the stupid ones!

MR. Y.: So-o, you think I am stupid, do you? Now, you listen to me! Would you like me to prove to you that I am a very shrewd, canny person? Would you?

MR. X.: Go on! Let's hear!

MR. Y.: You will acknowledge that I am both intelligent and logical when you hear my reasoning. . . . You were the cause of an accident, for which you might get two years of hard labor. You have escaped this infamy completely —up until now. . . . And here you see a man, who—who has been the *victim* of an accident—of a subconscious impulse—and he has had to suffer two years of hard labor. . . . Only through some great scientific accomplishment can this man clear himself of the stigma with which

he—through no fault of his own—has been branded. . . .
But in order to carry out this work, he needs money—a
great deal of money—and needs it immediately! Now
—don't you think that the other man—the one who went
unpunished—might restore the equilibrium of their human
relationship if a demand were made upon him for a
reasonable amount as penance? Don't you think so?

Mr. X. *(calmly)*: Why, yes!

Mr. Y.: Well—then we understand each other! H'm!

(There is a silence.)

What do you think would be a reasonable amount?

Mr. X.: Reasonable? The law has determined compensation
of not less than fifty crowns. But as the deceased has no
heirs or relatives, all talk about compensation is useless.

Mr. Y.: Oh, so you refuse to understand! Well, then, let me
speak a little plainer: it is to me you are to pay the
restitution. . . .

Mr. X.: I have never heard that someone who has committed
manslaughter should compensate a forger. And, furthermore—we have no prosecutor here!

Mr. Y.: Oh, is that so? Well—here he is! I am the prosecutor!

Mr. X.: Now I am beginning to see what you are up to! How
much are you asking for becoming an accessory to the
murder?

Mr. Y.: Six thousand crowns!

Mr. X.: That's too high! Where am I to get the money from?

(Mr. Y. points to the box.)

No—I won't do it! I will not be a thief!

Mr. Y.: Stop your acting! You mean to say that you haven't
pilfered from it before?

Mr. X. *(as if he were talking to himself)*: To think that I
could have been so completely mistaken! But that's the way
these smooth, slippery creatures work! A soft nature appeals
to us, and therefore we are easily fooled into thinking that
we are liked in return. . . . That is exactly why I have
always been on my guard against people to whom I have
taken a liking! So, now . . . it's your definite conviction
that I have helped myself to the contents of that box
before?

MR. Y.: Precisely!

MR. X.: And if you don't get the six thousand, you will report me?

MR. Y.: You may be certain of that! This is one time you won't get out of it! So you had better not try!

MR. X.: And you think that I would allow my father to have a son who is a thief, my wife to have a thief for a husband, my children a thief for a father, and my co-workers a thief for associate? No—that is something that will never happen! Now I am going to the sheriff to give myself up. . . .

MR. Y. (*jumps up and starts collecting his luggage, etc.*): Wait a second!

MR. X.: For what?

MR. Y. (*with a stutter*): I only thought that . . . since I have nothing more to do here, there is no need for me to remain . . . and so I may as well be on my way. . . .

MR. X.: No—you are not going to leave! Now—sit down where you sat before—at the table—then the two of us will have a little talk.

MR. Y. (*seats himself after first putting on a dark coat*): What —what do you plan to do now?

MR. X. (*keeps looking in the mirror behind* MR. Y.): Now I see it all! Ah!

MR. Y. (*worried*): What is it you see—that is so remarkable? . . .

MR. X.: Looking in the mirror I can see that you are a thief —a plain, ordinary thief! A moment ago, when you sat there with your white shirt on, I noticed that something was amiss on the bookshelf. But I couldn't tell just what was wrong, for I wanted to listen to you and observe you as well. But as you grew more and more unbearable, my senses sharpened. And when you put on your black coat just now, it brought into contrast and helped to offset the red back of that book there. . . . I failed to notice it before because of your red suspenders. And now I know where you got your forgery story from! And your concoction about subconscious impulses! You read it in Bernheim's treatise on subconscious desires and impulses! But when you replaced it on the shelf, you placed it upside down! So you stole even that story idea! Therefore I can only

conclude that you committed your crime either out of
need or from a desire to satisfy your appetite for pleasure!

MR. Y.: From need! If you only knew . . .

MR. X.: If you knew what poverty I have endured—and still
do! But that's neither here nor there. . . . Let us proceed!
That you have been in prison, there is no doubt. But it
was in America, for you described American prison conditions. . . . And, another thing—I could almost swear that
you never served time for the offense you committed
here. . . .

MR. Y.: What makes you say such a thing? . . .

MR. X.: Wait until the sheriff arrives. He will be able to tell
you.

(MR. Y. *rises abruptly from his seat.*)

MR. X.: You see! The first time I mentioned the sheriff in
connection with the thunderstorm, you were just as eager
to get away! And when a man has been in prison, he
doesn't go to a mill on a hillside to take a peek at one—or
keep gazing through a window pane at one. . . . In brief,
you are both a punished and an unpunished culprit! And
that's why it was so frightfully difficult to make you out!

MR. Y. (*completely crushed*): May I leave now?

MR. X.: Now you may go—yes!

MR. Y. (*collecting his things*): Are you angry with me?

MR. X.: Yes—but perhaps you would prefer that I feel pity
for you. . . .

MR. Y. (*ill-temperedly*): Pity? Do you think you are any
better than I am?

MR. X.: Of course I do—because I *am* better than you! I
am more intelligent than you are, and more trustworthy
when it comes to other people's property.

MR. Y.: You are rather clever, I admit, but not as crafty as
I am! You may have put me in check, but by the next
move you may be checkmated—despite your cleverness!

MR. X. (*staring fixedly at* MR. Y.): Do you want another
joust? What demoniacal scheme are you up to now?

MR. Y.: That remains my secret!

MR. X.: Let me look at you! You intend to write an anonymous letter to my wife and tell her my secret. . . .

MR. Y.: Yes—and you can't stop me! You wouldn't dare to

put me in prison—and so you have to let me go. . . . And, once away from here, I can do what I please!

MR. X.: Oh, you swine! You stepped on my Achilles heel that time. . . . Are you trying to force me to be a murderer?

MR. Y.: A wretch like you could never commit murder!

MR. X.: Do you see now that all men are not alike? You sense that I could never commit such acts as you could. . . . That is why you have the upper hand over me. But—suppose you forced me to do the same to you as I did to the old driver! *(He lifts his hand as if about to strike him.)*

MR. Y. *(gives* MR. X. *a hard look)*: You couldn't! Any man who hasn't the nerve to save his own skin by helping himself from that box there wouldn't have the courage!

MR. X.: Then you don't think I have helped myself, do you?

MR. Y.: You are too much of a coward! Just as you were a coward when you didn't tell your wife that she was married to a murderer. . . .

MR. X.: You are an entirely different person from what I am. . . . I don't know whether you are stronger or weaker. And whether you are more or less of a criminal is none of my business. . . . But one thing is certain: you are more stupid! You were stupid when you signed another's name, instead of going begging—as I was forced to do! You were stupid when you stole ideas from that book. *(Points to the bookshelf.)* You might have known that I had read it. . . . You were stupid when you imagined yourself to be shrewder than I and that you could entice me to steal. . . . You were stupid when you had the notion that there could be equilibrium in the world by having two thieves instead of one. . . . But the most ridiculous was your idea that I could have built my life's happiness on an unsafe foundation! And now—get to work on your anonymous letter to my wife and tell her that her husband is a murderer! . . . I told her at the time we were engaged! Are you satisfied now?

MR. Y.: Do you mind if I go?

MR. X.: You are going at once—this very minute! Your belongings will be sent after you! Get out!

CURTAIN

To Charles A. Perera

Simoon

(1889)

A Play in One Act

CHARACTERS

BISKRA,
  an Arabian girl

YOUSSEF,
  her lover

GUIMARD,
  lieutenant in the Zouaves

*The action takes place in Algeria
in the 1880s.*

An Arabian Marabout, a sepulchral chamber with a sarcophagus in the center. Prayer rugs are scattered about. In the corner, left, a pile of bones. Double doors in the rear; the doors have air holes and are covered with hangings. Apertures in the rear wall. Here and there, sand heaps; also a mound of uprooted aloes, palm leaves, and alfalfa plants.

SKRA (*enters. She wears a burnous pulled down over her face. On her back she carries a guitar. She throws herself on a rug and starts to pray, her arms crossed. The wind can be heard whining outside*): La ilâha ill allâh!

OUSSEF (*enters swiftly*): The Simoon is coming! Where is the Frank?

SKRA: He should be here any moment. . . .

OUSSEF: Why didn't you stab him to death? Why didn't you?

SKRA: Because—he shall take his own life! If I had killed him, the foreigners would exterminate all of us—our whole tribe! For they know that I was Ali the guide—but they do not know that I am also the girl Biskra. . . .

OUSSEF: You say—he shall take his own life? How?

SKRA: You know that the Simoon dries up the foreigners' brains like dates—they see nightmares so horrible that life becomes intolerable, and they flee into the great unknown. . . .

OUSSEF: I have heard that. . . . And at our last encounter with them, six Franks took their own lives before they reached their destination. But you must not depend on the Simoon today. Snow has fallen in the mountains—and in

173

another half-hour the storm may have passed. . . . Biskra! Is your hate still aflame?

BISKRA: You ask if my hate is aflame! My hatred is as boundless as the desert. It is burning like the sun—stronger even than my love! Every moment of passionate joy stolen from me by the murder of Ali has turned into a poison, like that secreted in the viper's fangs . . . and what the Simoon may not have the strength to do, I have!

YOUSSEF: Well spoken, Biskra—and you shall bring it about. . . . As for myself, since I set eyes on you, my hatred has withered like the alfalfa grass in autumn. Draw strength from me—be the arrow to my bow!

BISKRA: Hold me close, Youssef! Fold me in your embrace!

YOUSSEF: Not here—not in the presence of the Holy One! Later, later—when you have earned your reward. . . .

BISKRA: You proud man! You proud sheik!

YOUSSEF: Yes . . . the woman who is to bear my son under her heart must prove herself worthy.

BISKRA: No other woman shall bear your son, Youssef! No one but I, Biskra—the despised one, the ugly one—but also the strong one!

YOUSSEF: So be it! Now I shall go below for a little sleep by the spring. Need I instruct *you* in the secrets of magic— you who were taught by the great Marabout Siddi Sheik? You have practiced them in the market places since you were a child.

BISKRA: No, I have no need of instruction. . . . I know all the secret magic that is needed to bring terror to a cowardly Frank and make him die—these cowards who steal upon the enemy, after firing their leaden bullets! I know all there is to know—even the art of ventriloquy. And what my wiles fail to accomplish, the sun will take care of—for the sun is the ally of Biskra and Youssef. . . .

YOUSSEF: The sun is the friend of the Moslems. But it is not to be relied on. It may burn you, Biskra. . . . Take a drink of water. . . . I see your hands are shriveled, and . . . *(While speaking, he has removed a rug and opened a trapdoor leading to the cellar. He descends and returns with a dipper of water, which he offers to* BISKRA.)

BISKRA *(takes it and drinks)*: My eyes are seeing red—my lungs are drying up—I hear. . . . I hear. . . . Do you see the sand beginning to sift through the roof? The strings of the guitar are trembling—the Simoon is here! But the Frank—he is not yet here!

YOUSSEF: Come below with me, Biskra, and let the Frank die out there by himself!

BISKRA: First hell, and then death! Did you think I would weaken? *(Empties the dipper of water on the sand heaped inside.)* Water on the sand will make my revenge grow. . . . I shall dry up my heart. . . . Grow, hatred! Burn fiercely, sun! Choke and suffocate, O wind!

YOUSSEF: Hail to you, mother of Ibn Youssef—for *you* shall bear Youssef's son . . . and he shall be the avenger! You, Biskra!

(The wind increases steadily. The hangings before the door stir. A red glow lights up the stage. In the next moment, the glow has changed to yellow.)

BISKRA: The Frank is coming—and the Simoon is here! Leave me now!

YOUSSEF: In half an hour I shall see you again. There is the hourglass. . . . *(He points to a pile of sand.)* Heaven itself measures out the time for the hell of the infidels!

(BISKRA is alone. GUIMARD enters. His face is pale, his feet unsteady. His mind is deranged, and he speaks in a faint voice.)

GUIMARD: The Simoon is here. . . . Where do you think my men have gone?

BISKRA: I led your men from west to east. . . .

GUIMARD: West to—east . . . Let me think—that is straight east—and west! . . . Help me to a chair, and give me some water. . . .

BISKRA *(leads GUIMARD to the mound of sand and places him on the floor, letting his head rest on the heaped-up sand)*: Do you feel comfortable now where you are sitting?

GUIMARD *(gazing at her)*: I am not sitting quite straight. Put something under my head.

BISKRA *(piles the sand higher under his head)*: There! I have put a pillow under your head. . . .

GUIMARD: My head? You mean my feet, don't you? . . . Isn't it under my feet?

BISKRA: Why, of course!

GUIMARD: That's what I thought. . . . Now let me have a footstool under—under my head. . . .

BISKRA (*drags the aloe over to him and places it under his knees*): Here is a footstool for you.

GUIMARD: And then—some water . . . Water!

BISKRA (*takes the empty bowl and fills it with sand. Then she gives it to* GUIMARD): Drink while it is cold!

GUIMARD (*takes a sip from the bowl*): It's cold—but it doesn't quench my thirst. . . . I can't drink it—I abhor water. . . . Take it away!

BISKRA: There is the dog that bit you. . . .

GUIMARD: Which dog? . . . I have never been bitten by any dog!

BISKRA: The Simoon has crippled your memory. . . . Watch out for the delusions that the Simoon conjures up! Don't you remember the mad greyhound that bit you at one of the hunts at Bab-el-Ouëd? Don't you remember?

GUIMARD: The hunt at Bab-el-Ouëd . . . You are right—yes! It had the color of a beaver, didn't it?

BISKRA: Yes—a beaver-colored bitch. I knew you would remember! She bit you in the leg—in the calf of the leg! Can't you feel the sting of the wound? Don't you feel it?

GUIMARD (*he touches his leg with his hand and pricks himself on the aloe*): Yes, I feel it! Water! Water!

BISKRA (*hands him the bowl of sand*): Drink! Drink!

GUIMARD: No, I can't! Holy Mary, Mother of God. . . . I have the rabies! (*He barks ferociously like a mad dog.*) I'll bite you! I'll bite you!

BISKRA: Have no fear—I shall heal you and drive out the demon with the all-powerful aid of music. . . . Listen!

GUIMARD (*screams out*): Ali! Ali! No music! I can't bear to hear music! And how can it help me?

BISKRA: If music can tame the evil spirit of the snake, why shouldn't you believe it can conquer a mad dog? Listen! (*She sings, accompanying herself on the guitar.*) Biskra—Biskra—Biskra—Biskra—Biskra—Biskra . . . Simoon! Simoon!

YOUSSEF (*from below*): Simoon! Simoon!

GUIMARD: What is it you are singing, Ali?

BISKRA: Did I sing? . . . Now, look! Look, now I take this palm leaf and put it in my mouth. . . . (*She places a palm leaf between her teeth. She sings:)* Biskra—Biskra—Biskra—Biskra—Biskra—Biskra . . .

YOUSSEF *(from below)*: Simoon! Simoon!

GUIMARD: What kind of satanic illusion is this!

BISKRA: Now I shall sing.

BISKRA AND YOUSSEF *(in unison)*: Biskra—Biskra—Biskra—Biskra—Biskra—Biskra . . . Simoon!

GUIMARD *(rises)*: Who are you, Satan—singing with two voices? Are you man or woman—or both?

BISKRA: I am Ali, the guide. . . . You don't recognize me because your senses are deranged. But if you wish to save yourself from the delusions of your mind and your eyes, you must believe me, believe what I say and do what I tell you to do.

GUIMARD: There is no need for you to tell me—I know that everything you say is true. . . .

BISKRA: There, you see—idolater!

GUIMARD: Idolater?

BISKRA: Yes! Show me the idol you wear next to your heart!

(GUIMARD shows her a medal he wears around his neck.)

BISKRA: Trample it under your foot and pray to God, the one and only One, the Merciful One, the Compassionate One. . . .

GUIMARD *(hesitates)*: Saint Édouard, my patron saint . . .

BISKRA: Can he save you? Can he?

GUIMARD: No, he can't. . . . *(His mind becomes suddenly lucid.)* Yes, he can!

BISKRA: Let's see if he can! *(She opens the doors. The hangings move, the grass stirs.)*

GUIMARD *(covers his mouth)*: Close the door!

BISKRA: Down with the idol!

GUIMARD: No, I can't!

BISKRA: You see! The Simoon doesn't harm a hair on my head, but you—you, the infidel, suffer death from it! Throw away the idol!

GUIMARD *(tears the medal from his breast and throws it on the floor)*: Water! I die!

BISKRA: Pray to the Only One, the God of Mercy, the God of Compassion!

GUIMARD: What shall I pray?

BISKRA: Repeat after me!

GUIMARD: Speak the words. . . .

BISKRA: God is One, only One. There is no other God than He, the God of Mercy, the God of Compassion. . . .

GUIMARD: God is One, only One. There is no other God than He, the God of Mercy, the God of Compassion. . . .

BISKRA: Lie down on the floor!

(GUIMARD *obeys her unwillingly.*)

BISKRA: What do you hear?

GUIMARD: I hear the purling water of a spring. . . .

BISKRA: You see! God is one, and there is no other God than He, the Merciful One, the Compassionate One. . . . What do you see?

GUIMARD: I see the purling water of a spring. I hear a lamp that is lit—in a window—in a window with green shutters—in a street, shining white. . . .

BISKRA: Whom do you see in the window?

GUIMARD: My wife—Élise . . .

BISKRA: Who stands behind the curtains—with his arm around her waist?

GUIMARD: It's my son—Georges!

BISKRA: How old is your son?

GUIMARD: He'll be four on St. Nicholas' Day.

BISKRA: And he is old enough to stand behind the curtains and hold another man's wife in his embrace?

GUIMARD: Why, of course not. But it is he. . . .

BISKRA: Four years old—and already he has a blond moustache!

GUIMARD: A blond moustache, you say? Oh, that is—that is Jules—my best friend. . . .

BISKRA: . . . who stands behind the curtains and has his arms around your wife's neck!

GUIMARD: You Satan!

BISKRA: Do you still see your son?

GUIMARD: No—I don't see him any longer. . . .

BISKRA (*imitates the ringing of church bells on the guitar*): What do you see now?

GUIMARD: I see bells ringing—and I sense the taste of dead bodies—my mouth smells of rancid butter—faugh!

BISKRA: You hear the priest chanting the litany for the dead body of a child, don't you?

GUIMARD: Wait, wait! I can't hear him. . . . (*Despondent-*

ly.) . . . But since you say so—then . . . yes, now I can hear him. . . .

BISKRA: Do you see the wreath on the coffin they are carrying?

GUIMARD: Yes . . .

BISKRA: With purple ribbons—and stamped with silver letters: "Farewell, my beloved Georges. From Your Father."

GUIMARD: Yes, that's what it says! . . . (*He sobs.*) My Georges! Georges! My beloved child! Élise, my wife, comfort me! . . . Help me. . . . (*He gropes about in the air.*) Where are you? Élise! Have you abandoned me? Speak the name of your beloved!

A VOICE (*from the roof*): Jules! Jules!

GUIMARD: Jules! . . . That's not my name. . . . What is my name? . . . My name is Charles . . . and she called me Jules! . . . Élise, my dearest one, answer me—for your spirit is here—I can feel you near me—and you promised me solemnly never to love anyone else. . . .

(THE VOICE *breaks out into laughter.*)

GUIMARD: Who laughs?

BISKRA: Élise—your wife!

GUIMARD: Kill me! Let me die! I don't care to live any longer. . . . Life sickens me—it sickens me to live—sickens me like sour wine, like food fit for pigs. . . . (*Spits out of loathing, as if nauseated.*) I have no saliva left! Water! Water! . . . or I'll bite you.

(The storm rages full force outside.)

BISKRA (*covers his mouth; she coughs*): You are dying, Frank! Write your last will, while there is still time! Where is your notebook?

GUIMARD (*manages to take out his notebook and pencil*): What shall I write?

BISKRA: When a man is dying, he thinks his wife—and his children, doesn't he?

GUIMARD (*struggling to write*): "Élise . . . I curse you! Simoon—I am dying. . . ."

BISKRA: And now—sign your last will and testament, or it will have no force. . . .

GUIMARD: How shall I sign it?

BISKRA: Write: La ilâha ill allâh!

GUIMARD (*writes*): It is written! Please let me die now!

BISKRA: Yes—now you shall die—die like a cowardly soldier who has left his men to their fate! And the jackals will give you a fine funeral, I think. They will howl the litany over your dead body! (*She strums an attack signal on the guitar.*) Do you hear the drums? They are giving the signal for attack! The infidels, who have the sun and the Simoon as their allies, advance from their ambush . . . (*She strums on the guitar.*) . . . their fire comes from everywhere—the Franks are prevented from reloading their rifles—the Arabs deploy in orderly manner and charge—the Franks are on the run. . . .

GUIMARD (*gets to his feet*): The French never flee!

BISKRA (*plays "Retreat" on a flute that she produces*): The Franks are fleeing—or they would not blow to retreat. . . .

GUIMARD: They are retreating—it's the retreat—and I am here. . . . (*He tears off his epaulettes.*) I am dead! (*He falls to the floor.*)

BISKRA: Yes, you are dead! You were dead long ago and you didn't know! (*She goes to the bone pile and brings back a skull.*)

GUIMARD: I am dead—am I dead? (*He touches his face.*)

BISKRA: Yes . . . and have been dead a long time. Look at yourself—look at yourself in the mirror! (*She holds the skull before him.*)

GUIMARD: Oh! Is this . . . Is this I?

BISKRA: Don't you recognize your high cheekbones—can't you see where the vultures have plucked out your eyes—don't you see the hole where your right molar was extracted—and the dimple in the chin which was covered by the handsome little goatee you affected—and which your Élise loved to stroke? Don't you see where your ear used to be—that your little Georges used to kiss each morning at breakfast? And can't you see where the broadax left its mark at the nape of the neck—when the executioner put an end to the deserter's life? . . .

(GUIMARD, *who has listened to her words with terror, staring at his image with glazed eyes, falls dead.*)

BISKRA (*who has been kneeling beside* GUIMARD, *rises. She feels his pulse, then she says*): Simoon! Simoon! (*She opens the doors. The hangings flutter in the wind. She covers her mouth and falls on her back.)* Youssef!

YOUSSEF *(enters from the cellar. He sees* GUIMARD's *body and examines it. Then he looks about for* BISKRA *and discovers her lying on the floor. He lifts her in his arms.)*: Are you alive?

BISKRA: Is the Frank dead?

YOUSSEF: If he is not, he will be! Simoon! Simoon!

BISKRA: Then I want to live! But bring me some water!

YOUSSEF *(carries her toward the trapdoor)*: There! And now Youssef is yours!

BISKRA: And Biskra will be the mother of your son! Youssef, my great Youssef!

YOUSSEF: My strong Biskra! Stronger than the Simoon!

CURTAIN

The First Warning

(1892)

A Comedy in One Act

CHARACTERS

AXEL BRUNNER,
   aged 37

OLGA BRUNNER,
   his wife, 36 years of age

ROSA,
   15 years old

THE BARONESS,
   her mother, 47 years old

A MAID

*The action takes place in Germany,
shortly before the turn of the nineteenth century.*

*A German dining room. A long table
in the center of the room, a large cabinet to the left. A parlor stove and other pieces. The center door is wide open,
showing vineyards on a hillside, the
spire of a church, etc. A wallpapered
door to the right. A traveling bag on a
chair beside the cabinet.*

MRS. BRUNNER *is seated at the table,
writing. A bouquet of flowers and a pair
of gloves lie on the table.*

MR. BRUNNER *(enters)*: Good morning!—Although it is
noontime. How did you sleep?

MRS. BRUNNER: Splendidly—under the circumstances.

MR. BRUNNER: Well, we might have left the party a little earlier last evening. . . .

MRS. BRUNNER: I seem to recall that you said the same thing
repeatedly last night. . . .

MR. BRUNNER *(fingering the bouquet)*: I am surprised that
you can remember that!

MRS. BRUNNER: I also remember that you objected to my
singing so many songs. —Will you stop picking my flowers
to pieces?

MR. BRUNNER: Are they the Captain's flowers?

MRS. BRUNNER: Yes, and no doubt they were the gardener's
before they became the florist's. But they are mine now.

MR. BRUNNER *(flings away the bouquet)*: It's a fine custom
the men in this place have, sending flowers to married
women!

MRS. BRUNNER: Perhaps you should have gone home and
gone to bed a little earlier, my dear.

MR. BRUNNER: No doubt the Captain would have liked that. But since I had only one choice—to stay and be ridiculous, or to go home by myself and be ridiculous— I chose to stay.

MRS. BRUNNER: And became comic!

MR. BRUNNER: Can you explain why you want to be the wife of a man who appears a fool? I would hate to be the husband of a woman who appears ridiculous.

MRS. BRUNNER: I pity you!

MR. BRUNNER: You do, do you? I pity myself—and not infrequently. But I challenge you to guess the tragedy of my position. . . .

MRS. BRUNNER: I'll let you answer that question yourself. You'll do it much more cleverly than I could.

MR. BRUNNER: It's because—because I am still in love with you—after fifteen years of married life.

MRS. BRUNNER: Fifteen years! Do you carry a pedometer with you?

MR. BRUNNER (*seats himself beside her*): On my thorny path? No, indeed! But you who are dancing along on roses— perhaps you ought to begin to count *your* steps. . . . To me you are—unfortunately—just as young as ever, while I am turning gray. But as we are both of the same age, you can take a look at me and see that you, too, are approaching the dangerous age. . . .

MRS. BRUNNER: That's what you are waiting for, hoping for. . . .

MR. BRUNNER: Precisely! Oh, how often haven't I longed to see you old and ugly—wished that you had been marked by chicken pox or had lost your teeth—only so that I would be able to keep you for myself and put an end to this anxiety which never leaves me!

MRS. BRUNNER: How beautiful! And as soon as you saw me ugly and old, you would feel at peace—until some other worry caught hold of you—and then you would let me sit there, hemmed in by all that serenity and tranquility!

MR. BRUNNER: No, I wouldn't.

MRS. BRUNNER: Oh, yes, you would! For I have noticed that your love cools the moment you think you have no reason to be jealous. I only wish to remind you of last summer, when we lived on that God-forsaken island. You were away all day, fishing and hunting, you acquired an appetite,

and grew fat, and took on an assurance in your behavior
that bordered on arrogance.

MR. BRUNNER: And yet, I remember, I was jealous of the
handyman.

MRS. BRUNNER: Oh, my God!

MR. BRUNNER: Yes, I discovered that you carried on a conversation with him when you should have been giving him
an order, that you inquired about his health, his plans for
the future, and his love life before sending him off to chop
some wood. . . . I think you are turning red in the face. . . .

MRS. BRUNNER: Out of shame for my husband! . . .

MR. BRUNNER: . . . your husband, who . . .

MRS. BRUNNER: . . . who is completely lacking in shame!

MR. BRUNNER: Yes, you can accuse me of that, as of so
much else. . . . But I wish you would tell me why you hate
me.

MRS. BRUNNER: I have never hated you. I have only had
contempt for you. Why? For the same reason, no doubt,
that I am contemptuous of all men as soon as they—what
is it they call it?—fall in love with me. That's how it is—but
why it is so, I haven't the faintest idea.

MR. BRUNNER: I have noticed that—and that is why I have
wished desperately that I might grow to hate you . . . and
that *then* you might fall in love with me. I pity the man
who is in love with his wife!

MRS. BRUNNER: You are really to be pitied—and so am I! I
pity myself! But what can we do to remedy the situation?

MR. BRUNNER: Nothing. We have been roving about for the
last seven years—I in the hope that circumstances, chance,
would send something our way that would bring about a
change. I have tried hard to fall in love with someone else,
but without success. Meantime, your constant scorn and
contempt, and my everlasting ludicrousness, have robbed
me of my courage, my faith in myself, and my ability to
act. Six times I have fled you—and now I am about to try
the seventh. (*He rises and takes the traveling bag from the
chair.*)

MRS. BRUNNER: So? Your little private excursions were
escape attempts, were they?

MR. BRUNNER: Unsuccessful attempts! The last time I got as
far as Genoa. I visited the museums, but saw no paintings
—I saw only you. . . . I went to the Opera—but heard

neither music nor singing—only your voice in all imaginable nuances. . . . I happened into a Pompeian café—and the only woman who charmed me there resembled you—or grew to resemble you!

MRS. BRUNNER (*agitated*): You went to places like that?

MR. BRUNNER: Yes—that is how far my love for you carried me astray. But my virtue—which was a source of embarrassment to me—made me appear ridiculous.

MRS. BRUNNER: This, you know, spells the end—it's all over between us!

MR. BRUNNER: I am afraid so, since you are incapable of being jealous of me.

MRS. BRUNNER: Yes, that's one sickness I have never had. . . . I couldn't even be jealous of Rosa, whose infatuation for you borders on madness.

MR. BRUNNER: How ungrateful I am—not to have noticed it! On the other hand, I have had certain suspicions of the old Baroness. She is forever making it her business to be poking about in the big cabinet there. But since she is our landlady, and the furniture is hers, I could very well be mistaken as to her motives for roaming around in our rooms. . . . Now I am going to get dressed. In half an hour I'll be gone—and without any leave-taking, I beg of you. . . .

MRS. BRUNNER: Do goodbyes generally upset you?

MR. BRUNNER: Yes, and from you especially! (*He goes out.*)

(MRS. BRUNNER *is alone for a moment. Then* ROSA *enters. She is carelessly dressed, her hair is hanging down, and she wears a kerchief around her head, tied under the chin, as though she were suffering from toothache. The somewhat abbreviated dress has a hole in the left sleeve. She carries a big basket, filled with flowers.*)

MRS. BRUNNER: Oh, it's you, Rosa! How are you, my child?

ROSA: Good morning, Mrs. Brunner. Oh, I have such a toothache. I wish I were dead!

MRS. BRUNNER: You poor child!

ROSA: And tomorrow I have to take part in the Corpus Christi procession and I have to make the wreaths of roses today. Mr. Brunner promised to help me with them. . . . Oh, my teeth! . . .

MRS. BRUNNER: Let me look at your teeth—let me see if you have a cavity. . . . Open your mouth wide! Why, my dear, your teeth are like pearls! *(She kisses* ROSA *on the lips.)*

ROSA *(annoyed)*: You mustn't kiss me, Mrs. Brunner—I don't like being kissed. Please don't! *(She climbs up on the table and stretches her legs onto a chair.)* Besides, I don't know what I want. But I did want to go to the party yesterday—and then I had to stay at home alone and study my lessons, as if I were a little child. How I hate to have to sit on the same bench with those awful brats in school! And I am not going to let that captain tickle me under the chin again! I am no longer a child! And if Mother ever pulls my hair again—I don't know what I'll do to her!

MRS. BRUNNER: Rosa, my dearest, what's the matter with you? What has happened?

ROSA: I don't know what's come over me. . . . But my whole head is throbbing—and so are my teeth. . . . It feels as if I had a red-hot iron down my back, and life nauseates me. . . . I feel like jumping into the river. I would like to run away—go roaming around and sing at fairs and in marketplaces—I'd like to be accosted and seduced by bold, impertinent men. . . .

MRS. BRUNNER: Rosa! Listen—listen to me!

ROSA: I would like to have a baby! Oh, I wish it wasn't considered shameful to have a baby! —Oh, Mrs. Brunner! *(She notices the bag.)* Who is going away?

MRS. BRUNNER: It's—my husband. . . .

ROSA: Then you have been mean to him again, Mrs. Brunner! Where is he going? Is he going far away? When is he coming back?

MRS. BRUNNER: I have no idea—not the slightest.

ROSA: You don't mean it! And you haven't asked him? *(She rummages in the bag.)* I can see he is planning to go far away. Here is his passport. . . . Far away! Very far? Oh, Mrs. Brunner, why can't you show some kindness to him—he who is so good to you? *(She throws herself into* MRS. BRUNNER's *arms, weeping.)*

MRS. BRUNNER: Oh, my dearest child! You are crying, poor little girl! Poor thing!

ROSA: I am so very fond of your husband!

MRS. BRUNNER: And you feel no shame, Rosa, telling this to me, his wife? And you want me to console you—my

little rival! Weep, dear child! It does you good to have
a cry. . . .

ROSA (*tears herself away*): No—I am not going to cry unless
I feel like it, do you understand? And if I feel like picking
up what you throw away, I'll do it! I am not going to
ask anyone for permission to like whomever I want to
like and have whatever I feel like having.

MRS. BRUNNER: Well, well! What's this I hear? But are you
so sure that *he* likes *you?*

ROSA (*seeks* MRS. BRUNNER'S *embrace again, weeping*): No—
that's just it—I am not!

MRS. BRUNNER (*tenderly, babying her*): Perhaps you would
like me to speak nicely to my husband and ask him to be
nice to you? Shall I do that?

ROSA (*in tears*): Yes! —But he must not go away! He must
not! Be nice to him, Mrs. Brunner, then he won't go away!

MRS. BRUNNER: How shall I behave then, you poor little mad-
cap?

ROSA: I don't know—but you should let him kiss you as
much as he wants to. . . . You think I didn't see you in the
garden the other day, when *he* wanted to, and *you* didn't?
And then I couldn't help thinking . . .

(THE BARONESS *enters.*)

THE BARONESS: Forgive me for disturbing you, Mrs. Brunner, but if you don't mind, I should like to get into the
cabinet. . . .

MRS. BRUNNER (*rises*): Whenever you like, my dear Baroness.

THE BARONESS: Oh, there is Rosa. . . . So you are up—and
I thought you were sick in bed. . . . Go at once and study
your lessons!

ROSA: Tomorow is a holy day, and we have no school: you
know that, Mama!

THE BARONESS: Just the same, go! And don't be coming in
here again and disturbing Mr. and Mrs. Brunner!

MRS. BRUNNER (*going toward the door, center rear*): Oh,
Rosa doesn't disturb us at all. We are as good friends as we
can possibly be. . . . We were just going down into the
garden to pick some flowers—and then I was going to
ask Rosa to try on the white dress that she is going to
wear tomorrow.

ROSA: Thank you, Mrs. Brunner. . . . *(She goes out through the center door, nodding to* MRS. BRUNNER *in secret understanding.)*

THE BARONESS: I am afraid you are completely spoiling my Rosa.

MRS. BRUNNER: A little kindness spoils no one, my dear Baroness, least of all Rosa. She is a child who has not only an exceptional heart but a rare understanding.

*(*THE BARONESS *rummages in the cabinet.* MRS. BRUNNER *stands in the doorway, center.* MR. BRUNNER *enters from the door, right. He exchanges a glance with* MRS. BRUNNER, *and the two smile as they watch* THE BARONESS. MR. BRUNNER *carries several parcels, which he places in the traveling bag.* MRS. BRUNNER *leaves.)*

THE BARONESS: Forgive me for disturbing you—but I'll be through in a moment. . . .

MR. BRUNNER: You don't have to apologize, Baroness.

THE BARONESS *(advances to the center of the room)*: Are you thinking of going away again on another trip, Mr. Brunner?

MR. BRUNNER: Yes.

THE BARONESS: Are you going far?

MR. BRUNNER: Perhaps. Perhaps not.

THE BARONESS: You don't know?

MR. BRUNNER: To tell the truth, ever since I placed my fate in someone else's hands, I have had no idea what the future might hold in store for me.

THE BARONESS: Do you mind if I ask an inquisitive question, Mr. Brunner?

MR. BRUNNER: That depends. . . . Are you friendly with my wife?

THE BARONESS: Well—as friendly as two women can be. At my age, with my experience of life, and my temperament . . . *(She stops abruptly.)* However—I can see you are not happy—and I, too, have suffered as you are suffering. . . . I know that only time can heal what ails you. . . .

MR. BRUNNER: Do you really think it is I who am sick? Isn't my behavior completely normal? Am I not, in reality, suffering because I see the abnormality, the sickness in other people's behavior?

THE BARONESS: . . . I was married to a man, whom I
loved. . . . You smile—you don't think a woman is capable
of love, because—because . . . However, I loved him, and
he loved me. . . . But he loved other women, too. . . .
And so I fell prey to jealousy—frightfully so! I became
intolerable to him. . . . He went away to war—he was an
army officer, you see—and he never returned. It was said
that he had fallen in battle, but his remains were never
found. . . . And now I can't erase from my mind the
thought that he still lives, and that he is wedded to another woman. Can you imagine—I am still jealous of my
dead husband! I dream of him at night—dream that he
is with that other one—with someone else. . . . Oh, Mr.
Brunner, have you ever felt that kind of excruciating torment—have you?

MR. BRUNNER: I ask you to believe me—I have! —But how
did it ever occur to you that he might be alive? (*He busies
himself with the traveling bag.*)

THE BARONESS: I had had certain little suspicions, based on
a variety of circumstances. But the years passed without
my finding anything to justify my imaginings. . . . Then
you came here—four months ago. By some weird fate,
there is a striking resemblance between you and my husband. I observed it immediately. This acted as a reminder
—and when my fancies, as it were, took concrete form,
my former doubts grew into certainties—and now I have
a positive feeling that he is still alive. I am tormented by this
jealousy that constantly plagues me—and that is why I
understand you. . . .

(MR. BRUNNER, *who has been listening somewhat dis-
interestedly at first, shows attentiveness as she comes
to the conclusion of her story.*)

MR. BRUNNER: You say your husband looked like me. . . .
Won't you sit down, Baroness?

(THE BARONESS *seats herself by the table, her back toward the garden.* MR. BRUNNER *sits down beside her.*)

THE BARONESS: In appearance he resembled you, and in
character, too—save for his weaknesses. . . .

MR. BRUNNER: And he would be about ten years older than I . . . and he had a scar on his right cheek, as if from a pin or a needle, didn't he?

THE BARONESS: Why, yes—he did!

MR. BRUNNER: Then I have met your husband—one night in London!

THE BARONESS: Then he is alive?

MR. BRUNNER: I can tell you in a little while—not at this precise moment—I have to figure it out. . . . Let me see. . . . It is five years now—in London, as I said. . . . I had been out at a gathering with some ladies and gentlemen. The atmosphere there had been depressing all evening, and on my way home I started to converse with the first man I laid eyes on, to get a chance to talk myself out of my low spirits. As luck would have it, we hit it off from the very first, and our conversation turned into a sidewalk chat that lasted for hours—and during which the man confided to me his life story, after he had learned that I came from the same part of the world as he.

THE BARONESS: Then he is alive?

MR. BRUNNER: He didn't die in the war, at least, for he was taken prisoner—fell in love with the mayor's daughter in the town—she deserted him—he escaped to England—he took to gambling, but had bad luck. . . . When we parted in the wee hours, he gave the impression of being a lost soul, of being done for. . . . And he made me promise that if fate should cause me to cross your path one year from that day and if, meantime, he had given no sign of life through an advertisement in the *Allgemeine Zeitung*—which I take regularly—I could take it for granted that he was dead. And, if I should ever meet you, he asked me to kiss your hand for him, and your child's brow, and beg you to forgive him. (*He kisses* THE BARONESS'*s hand.*)

(ROSA *is seen on the veranda, regarding the scene with a wild look in her eyes.*)

THE BARONESS (*moved*): Then he is dead!

MR. BRUNNER: Yes. And I should, of course, have delivered his message long before this, had the man and his name not escaped my memory.

(THE BARONESS *crumples her handkerchief. She seems to hesitate.*)

Is your mind at rest now?

THE BARONESS: In a way, yes. But now all hope is gone, too. . . .

MR. BRUNNER: The hope that you might suffer once more the sweet pangs of pain?

THE BARONESS: Perhaps. . . . Aside from my child, the only other thing that gave me any interest in life was my anxiety for him. . . . Isn't it strange that we even miss the agony of grief?

MR. BRUNNER: If you'll forgive me for saying so, I think you miss your jealousy even more than you miss your lost husband.

THE BARONESS: Perhaps. . . . Apart from my child, the only chained to the illusion all this time. . . . But now—with nothing left for me . . . (*She takes hold of* MR. BRUNNER'*s hand.*) You who brought me this last greeting, you are for me a living memory. . . . We have both suffered!

MR. BRUNNER (*anxiously rising, he looks at his watch*): Forgive me, but I must—I must leave by the next train!

THE BARONESS: That is just what I wanted to ask you not to do! Why must you go? Aren't you happy here?

(ROSA *disappears.*)

MR. BRUNNER: During these stormy days, I have had my happiest moments here in your home, and it is with great sorrow that I leave it. But I must. . . .

THE BARONESS: Because of what happened last evening?

MR. BRUNNER: Not entirely—it just happened to be the last straw. —Excuse me. I have to pack. . . . (*He busies himself with the bag.*)

THE BARONESS: If you have definitely made up your mind—let me help you. No one else seems to be giving you a hand.

MR. BRUNNER: Thank you ever so much, my dear Baroness, but I have almost finished. And I beg you to make the leave-taking brief—it will be less painful that way. . . . Your tenderness toward me has been a great comfort in my distress, and it is as much of an ordeal to say goodbye to you as . . .

(THE BARONESS *is moved.*)

. . . as to a good mother! I could read in your eyes what you felt for me when, out of delicacy, you expressed your sympathy by silence. At times it seemed as though your company had a good effect upon my relations with my wife —for your age gave you a certain right to say things that a young woman is reluctant to hear and would resent from one of her own age.

THE BARONESS (*with some hesitation*): May I tell you, then, that your wife is no longer a young woman?

MR. BRUNNER: Yes, she is—to me she is!

THE BARONESS: But not to others.

MR. BRUNNER: How much better it would be if she would face it. . . . Her coyness and coquettishness are getting to be more and more repugnant to me. Her winning ways don't make up for her exaggerated demands and pretensions. People will soon begin to laugh at her. . . .

THE BARONESS: They are doing it already.

MR. BRUNNER: You mean that? Poor Olga! (*He becomes pensive, but is roused out of his reflections by the sound of chimes.*) The chimes in the bell tower. I am leaving in half an hour.

THE BARONESS: You can't leave without breakfast!

MR. BRUNNER: I am not hungry—and besides, I feel train-sick already. My nerves are shaking like telephone wires in frosty weather.

THE BARONESS: Then I'll go and fix you a cup of coffee. You'll let me do that, won't you? And then I'll send the maid up to help you finish your packing, shall I?

MR. BRUNNER: You are so very kind, Baroness. I almost feel tempted into weaknesses I might regret!

THE BARONESS: You will not regret it, if you follow my advice. I do wish you would! (*She goes out.*)

(ROSA *enters through the door, center rear.*)

MR. BRUNNER: Good morning, Rosa. How do you feel?

ROSA: Why do you ask?

MR. BRUNNER: Why? Why, your head is swathed in bandages!

ROSA (*tears off the kerchief and puts it in her pocket*): There

is nothing wrong with me! I am entirely well! You intend
to leave us, don't you?

MR. BRUNNER: Yes, I am leaving.

(THE MAID *enters.*)

ROSA (*to* THE MAID): What do you want?

THE MAID: The Baroness asked me to help Mr. Brunner to
pack.

ROSA: There is no need for that! —Go!

(THE MAID *hesitates; she starts to leave.*)

Go, do you hear!

(THE MAID *leaves.*)

MR. BRUNNER: Are you being discourteous to me, Rosa?

ROSA: No, I am not. I want to help you myself. But you are
the impolite one. You are going back on your promise to
help me with the flowers for tomorrow's feast day. . . .
But I don't care about that. I am not going to the feast.
I am not. . . . I don't know where I'll be tomorrow. . . .

MR. BRUNNER: What's the meaning of this? . . . .

ROSA: Isn't there anything I can help you with, Mr. Brunner?
Couldn't I brush your hat?

(*She takes his hat and starts to brush it.* MR. BRUNNER
tries to take it away from her.)

No, let me be! —Now see what you have done! You have
torn my dress! (*She puts her fingers into the hole in her
sleeve and tears it wide open.*)

MR. BRUNNER: Rosa, you are acting very strangely today. I'm
afraid you will cause your mother distress—the restless
way you behave.

ROSA: What do I care whether Mother is distressed or not?
On the contrary, it would make me feel good, even though
it would hurt you a little, perhaps. . . . But I don't care
about you any more than I care about the cat in the kitch-
en or the rats in the cellar. . . . And if I were your
wife, I would hate you and go so far, far away that you
would never be able to find me any more! —Phew! Kissing
another woman! Phew!

MR. BRUNNER: Oh, so, my child, you saw me kiss your
mother's hand. . . . Let me tell you, then—that kiss was a

last greeting from your father. I met him abroad—that was after the war—and I have a greeting from him for you, too. . . .

> *(He advances toward her, takes her face in his hands, and is about to press a kiss on her forehead when* ROSA *throws back her head and presses her lips against his. At the same moment* MRS. BRUNNER *appears on the veranda. Looking shocked, she leaves.)*

Rosa, my child, I merely wanted to give you an innocent little kiss on the forehead. . . .

ROSA: An innocent kiss! Ha ha! Yes, very innocent! And you believe in Mother's fairy tales about my father? He died several years ago. He was a man who knew what love was! He was not afraid to love! He didn't tremble when he was kissed or wait to be invited! If you don't believe me, come up to the attic with me, and I'll let you read his letters to his mistresses! Come along! *(She opens the wallpapered door, behind which the stairs are visible.)* Ha ha ha! You are scared—afraid I'll seduce you, aren't you? You look shocked! You are amazed that I, a girl who has been a woman for three years, should already know that love is not an innocent game! You don't believe that babies are born through the ear, do you? . . . Now I can see that you despise me, but that's just what you shouldn't do—for I am neither better nor worse than any of the rest. . . . That's how I am!

MR. BRUNNER: Rosa! Go and change your dress before your mother comes!

ROSA: Do you think my arms are so ugly? Or don't you dare to look at them? Now I begin to understand why—why your wife—why you are jealous of your wife!

MR. BRUNNER: Now—this is going a little too far!

ROSA: You are turning red in the face! Is it on my account or your own? Do you know how many times I have been in love?

MR. BRUNNER: Never.

ROSA: Never with a timid man, no! Now you despise me again, don't you?

MR. BRUNNER: Yes, a little . . . Take good care of your heart, Rosa. Don't hang it on your sleeve, to be pecked to pieces by the birds, and to be soiled! You say you are a woman, but you are a very young woman—or what is commonly called a girl.

ROSA: And so—and so . . . But I can grow into a woman. . . .

MR. BRUNNER: But since you are not one yet—let us postpone this sort of conversation. . . . Give me your hand on that, Rosa. . . .

ROSA (*bursting into tears of anger*): You! Never! Never!

MR. BRUNNER: Are we not going to part as friends? We— who have had so many happy days together during this dismal winter and this long-drawn-out spring?

(MRS. BRUNNER *enters with a coffee tray. She is somewhat preoccupied and gives the impression that she does not see* ROSA.)

MRS. BRUNNER: I thought you might find time to drink a cup of hot coffee before you take off.

(ROSA *tries to take the tray from* MRS. BRUNNER.)

Thank you, my dear little friend. I can manage. . . .

MR. BRUNNER (*regarding* MRS. BRUNNER *with questioning, somewhat ironic glances*): You had a good idea there, Olga. . . .

MRS. BRUNNER (*without meeting his eye*): I am glad—that. . . .

ROSA: Perhaps you will let me say goodbye now—to Mr. Brunner. . . .

MR. BRUNNER: Are you going to leave us now, Rosa?

ROSA: I suppose I have to—since Mrs. Brunner is angry with me. . . .

MRS. BRUNNER: I? Why, my dear young lady. . . .

ROSA: You promised you would help me to try on my dress, didn't you?

MRS. BRUNNER: Yes, but not just this minute, my child. Or perhaps you wish to keep my husband company, and I'll go and try it on. . . .

MR. BRUNNER: Olga!

MRS. BRUNNER: What is it?

(ROSA, *with her finger in her mouth, is embarrassed and angry.*)

If the young lady is going to see Mr. Brunner off at the train, I would suggest that she go and put on a suitable dress!

(ROSA, *as before, still upset.*)

And take the flowers along, in case you would like to shower him with them. . . .

MR. BRUNNER: Now you are cruel, Olga!

ROSA (*with a curtsy*): Goodbye, Mr. Brunner.

MR. BRUNNER (*grasping* ROSA *by the hand*): Rosa! Take good care of yourself and you will soon grow up and turn into a nice, big girl. . . .

ROSA (*takes her flowers*): Goodbye. (*She runs out.*)

(MR. *and* MRS. BRUNNER *both seem embarrassed.* MRS. BRUNNER *averts her face from her husband.*)

MRS. BRUNNER: Is there anything I can help you with?

MR. BRUNNER: No, thank you. I am almost ready.

MRS. BRUNNER: You have so many people to help you, anyhow.

MR. BRUNNER: Let me look at you! (*He tries to take her face in his hands.*)

MRS. BRUNNER (*tears herself away from him*): No, let me be!

MR. BRUNNER: What's the matter?

MRS. BRUNNER: Perhaps you think I am—I am jealous. . . .

MR. BRUNNER: I had no such thought—but, now that you mention it, I believe you really are!

MRS. BRUNNER: Jealous of a little schoolgirl like her! Oh!

MR. BRUNNER: The object matters little when it comes to love. Wasn't I jealous of a handyman? Wasn't I? You must have seen, then, that . . .

MRS. BRUNNER: . . . that you kissed her!

MR. BRUNNER: No—it was she who kissed me!

MRS. BRUNNER: Shameless! But those little hoydens are like monkeys!

MR. BRUNNER: They imitate their elders!

MRS. BRUNNER: You seem to enjoy their attentions just the same!

MR. BRUNNER: Being unused to such attentions!

MRS. BRUNNER: Possibly from such young ladies. You seem to be less afraid of the more mature. . . .

MR. BRUNNER: Oh, so? You saw that, too?

MRS. BRUNNER: No—Rosa told me. Just the same, you are a regular ladies' man—that's exactly what you are!

MR. BRUNNER: I suppose I must be! I only wish I could profit by it!

MRS. BRUNNER: Well, you'll soon be free to choose a younger and more attractive wife!

MR. BRUNNER: Nonsense, I couldn't possibly . . .

MRS. BRUNNER: . . . Now that I am old and ugly.

MR. BRUNNER: I can't understand what's come over you! Let me look at you once more! (*He goes toward her.*)

MRS. BRUNNER (*hides her head in his arms*): No, you mustn't look at me!

MR. BRUNNER: What in the world is this? Don't tell me you are jealous of a schoolgirl—or a widowed old lady?

MRS. BRUNNER: I have bitten off—a piece of one of my front teeth! I don't want you to look at me!

MR. BRUNNER: Oh, you baby! The first tooth comes in with pain—and with grief the first one goes!

MRS. BRUNNER: And now you will want me no longer?

MR. BRUNNER: That's where you are wrong! (*He closes the traveling bag.*) Tomorrow we'll go together to Augsburg to get you a new tooth—a gold tooth!

MRS. BRUNNER: And then we'll never come back here again—will we?

MR. BRUNNER: Never—if that's the way you want it!

MRS. BRUNNER: And you are no longer restless, are you?

MR. BRUNNER: No—not for the next week or so, anyway.

(THE BARONESS *comes in with a coffee tray.*)

THE BARONESS: Excuse me, I thought . . .

MR. BRUNNER: Thank you, Baroness, but I have already had my coffee. However, since you have gone to the trouble, I'll take another cup. . . . And if you . . .

(ROSA *appears in the doorway in her white dress.*)

And if you and Rosa would like to join us, we have no objection. We would even enjoy it. My wife and I are leaving. We take the first train from here tomorrow morning. . . .

CURTAIN

To Amandus Johnson

Debit and Credit

(1892)

A Play in One Act

CHARACTERS

TURE,
  a gardener

ANNA,
  TURE's wife

A WAITER

AXEL,
  TURE's brother; a Doctor of Philosophy and leader of an
  African expedition

THE GROOM IN WAITING

LINDGREN

THE FIANCÉ

CECILIA

MARI

*The action takes place in AXEL's suite
in a hotel in Stockholm.
The time is the 1890s.*

An attractive room in a hotel. A door on each side of the room.

TURE *and his* WIFE *have just entered the room and are looking about with curiosity. Both are plainly dressed and visibly unsophisticated.*

TURE: This is certainly a fine room! But then it is a fine man who lives in it, too!

THE WIFE: Yes, I should say it is! I have never met your brother, of course, but I have heard him talked about often enough.

TURE: Don't talk like that! *My* brother, the doctor, has traveled all through Africa—and that is something not everybody has done! —And even if he did drink a lot of toddies when he was young, why . . .

THE WIFE: Your brother the doctor, yes! But what is he if not a schoolmaster?

TURE: Oh, no, he is a Doctor of Philosophy. . . .

THE WIFE: Well, that's a schoolmaster, isn't it? The same as my brother, who teaches school at Åby.

TURE: Your brother is a very fine man, but he is nothing but a public schoolteacher, and that isn't the same as being a Doctor of Philosophy. And I am saying that without boasting.

THE WIFE: He may be whatever he likes, and you may call him whatever *you* like, but he has cost us plenty!

TURE: That's true—but he has also done much for which we should be glad.

THE WIFE: Glad, ha! Having had to lose house and home on his account!

TURE: Yes, you are right, of course! But we still don't know if it is neglectfulness or if there were other reasons over which he had no control that account for his failure to attend to the loan. I imagine it can't be so very easy to send remittances from darkest Africa.

THE WIFE: Whether he has any trumped-up excuses or not, it doesn't do us any good. However, if he should want to do something for us, it would be nothing but his duty.

TURE: Let us wait and see! Let us wait and see! —Nevertheless . . . Have you heard he has been given four different decorations?

THE WIFE: Well, what good does that do *us?* That will only make him still more vain and conceited, I'm afraid. Oh, no—I am not going to forget so soon that the sheriff came to us with the papers and brought in all those people to be witnesses . . . and then—and then the auction— when all the neighbors came in and started to tear through our belongings! And do you know, Ture, what grieved me most?

TURE: The black . . .

THE WIFE: Yes—the thought that my own sister-in-law should have my black silk dress knocked down to fifteen crowns! Fifteen crowns!

TURE: Don't worry! Don't worry! We'll get you a new silk dress. . . .

THE WIFE: Yes, but it won't be the same dress—the one my sister-in-law took from me at the auction.

TURE: Never mind, we'll get you another dress! (*He notices a three-cornered hat lying on a table.*) Look at that grand hat lying there! It must be some royal chamberlain who is in there with Axel!

THE WIFE: What do I care!

TURE: Oh, don't you think it's nice that someone bearing the same name as you and I is honored like this, being visited by one of the King's intimates, eh? I seem to remember that you yourself jumped with joy for fourteen days after your brother the teacher had been invited to have dinner with the bishop.

THE WIFE: I don't remember that!

TURE: No, of course not!

THE WIFE: But I *can* remember the fourteenth of March, when we had to give up the farm because of him, after having been married two years—and having a child to worry about. . . . Oh! And then—when the steamer came with all those passengers, just as we were moving out. . . . I'll never forget it for all the three-cornered hats in the world! *(With a sarcastic glance at the hat.)* Anyhow, what do you think a king's chamberlain cares about a gardener and his wife who have been evicted?

TURE *(suddenly seeing an open jewelry case containing four decorations on the writing table)*: Look at this! What kind of medal is this? Look at them—his decorations! —Look at this one! *(He takes one of the decorations from the case and fondles it in his hand.)*

THE WIFE: Rubbish!

TURE: Don't be contemptible about decorations, Anna! We never know where we may end up. . . . The gardener at Stäringe was promoted a director, and made a knight of the Order of Vasa the other day. . . .

THE WIFE: What good does that do us?

TURE: I admit it doesn't do us any good—but these . . . *(Indicating the decorations in the jewelry case.)* . . . these may, in one way or another, help us to advance. . . . *(With a glance at the door leading to an inner room.)* But it looks as if we were in for a long wait, so we may as well sit down and make ourselves at home. Come here and let me help you off with your coat, Anna. Come!

THE WIFE *(after a moment of mild resistance)*: Do you really think we will be welcome—do you? I have a feeling we won't be staying long in this place.

TURE: Oho! And if I know Axel at all, you'll see we'll be getting a good dinner here. If he only knew we were here, he would . . . Oh, here—you'll see! *(He presses a bell. A moment later* A WAITER *comes in.* TURE, *to his* WIFE:*)* What would you like? A sandwich, perhaps? *(To* THE WAITER.) Bring us some sandwiches and some beer —Wait a second! A schnapps for me—corn brandy! *(To* THE WIFE.) We'll take care of ourselves, don't worry!

*(*AXEL *and the King's* GROOM IN WAITING *come from the room on the right.)*

AXEL *(to* THE GROOM IN WAITING): At five o'clock, then, and white tie . . .

THE GROOM IN WAITING: And decorations!

AXEL: Is that absolutely necessary?

THE GROOM IN WAITING: Absolutely, if you don't wish to seem discourteous. And, being a democrat, you wouldn't want to be discourteous to anyone, would you? Goodbye, Doctor!

AXEL: Goodbye!

(THE GROOM IN WAITING *bows curtly to* TURE *and his* WIFE *as he departs. They do not acknowledge his greeting.*)

Why, look who is here! The old boy himself! After all these years! And there I see your wife, too! Welcome, welcome!

TURE: Thank you, Brother Axel! And welcome back yourself from your long journey!

AXEL: Yes, it was indeed a long journey. . . . I assume you have read about it in the newspapers?

TURE: I surely have!

(*There is a silence.*)

Father wants to be remembered to you. . . .

AXEL: Yes, but—isn't he still angry with me?

TURE: Ah, but you know the old man and his ways. . . . If only *you* had not been on that expedition, he would have considered it one of the seven wonders of the world. But because *you* were a member of it, it was all sheer humbug.

AXEL: So he hasn't changed, then. Because I am his son, nothing that I do, no matter what, is any good. He is not vain, at least! —Well, that's that! But how are things with you these days?

TURE: Not so good. That old bank loan . . .

AXEL: Oh, yes, of course! I forgot! Well, how did it turn out?

TURE: Why, it turned out so that I had to pay it.

AXEL: That was terrible. But we'll no doubt be able to take care of things at the first opportunity.

(THE WAITER *comes in with a breakfast tray.*)

What is this?

TURE: Oh, I—I took the liberty of ordering a sandwich. . . .

AXEL: That was sensible of you. But I suppose we ought to have a glass of wine and drink a toast to my sister-in-law, since I couldn't be present at the wedding.

TURE: No, thank you, nothing for us! Not so early in the day! But thank you just the same!

AXEL (*gestures to* THE WAITER *to leave*): I should, of course, have asked you to stay for dinner, but I am invited out myself. Can you guess where?

TURE: You are not invited to the royal palace, are you?

AXEL: Yes, I have been invited by the Prince himself!

TURE: Well, I'll be . . . What do you think of that, Anna?

(THE WIFE *turns and twists in her chair. Painfully touched by the conversation, she cannot answer.*)

AXEL: I suppose the old man will turn republican after this —when he hears that His Royal Majesty deigns to associate with me. . . .

TURE: Listen, Axel, you must excuse me for bringing up a subject which is quite unpleasant but which we must discuss.

AXEL: I assume it is that confounded loan.

TURE: Yes, but it is not only the loan. In a few words—because of you, we have had to sell everything at public auction and we are now left penniless. . . .

AXEL: What a nuisance! But why didn't you renew the loan?

TURE: Well, tell me that! Where was I to find another mortgagor when you were away?

AXEL: Couldn't you have gone to one of my friends?

TURE: I did go. And—it turned out the way it did! Now—can you help us?

AXEL: How can I possibly help you? And just at this time—when all my creditors are after me? How can I start taking out new loans now, at the very moment when an attempt is being made to find me a position? There is no worse recommendation than being in debt. If you will just wait a little, everything will be taken care of.

TURE: Do you think we can wait without going under completely? This is just the time of year when a garden has to be cared for; this is the time for digging and planting so that things will take root and come up at the right time. Can't you find us a place?

AXEL: Where would I get a garden from?

TURE: Through your friends.

AXEL: My friends have no gardens! —Do not stand in my way now when I am trying to save myself! As soon as *I* am saved, I shall save you.

TURE (*to his* WIFE): He doesn't want to help us, Anna. . . .

AXEL: I *cannot!* Not now! Not at present! Does it seem reasonable to you that I—who am seeking a position myself— should go looking for one for somebody else? What would people say? This is what they would say: Imagine, now we will have not only him but his relatives on our back as well! And so they will drop me. . . .

TURE (*looking at his watch; then, to his* WIFE): Let us go!

AXEL: Where are you going so soon?

TURE: We have to go to the doctor with the child.

AXEL: Good Lord, have you children, too?

THE WIFE: Yes, we do. . . . And we have a sick child—sick because we had to move out into the kitchen when the auction was being held.

AXEL: And for this I am responsible! I am going mad from all this! All this because of me! So that I could win fame! What can I do for you? But would I have been better off if I had remained at home? No—worse, for then I would still be a poor schoolteacher—and then would probably have been even less able to do anything for you than I am today! Listen to me! Go to the doctor, and come back after a little while—then I shall have thought of what can be done. . . .

TURE (*to* THE WIFE): You see—he wants to help us. . . .

THE WIFE: And he should be able to!

TURE: He can do whatever he sets his mind to!

AXEL: However, don't depend on it, for then the last disappointment may turn out to be worse than the first! Oh, God in heaven, to think that you have a sick child also! And all because of me!

TURE: Oh, I don't suppose it's as serious as it sounds!

THE WIFE: You say that—you, who know nothing about it. . . .

TURE: Goodbye, then, for a while, Axel!

(LINDGREN *appears in the doorway.*)

THE WIFE *(to* TURE*):* Did you notice—he didn't introduce us to the King's groom in waiting!
TURE: What of it? Why should he?

(They leave. LINDGREN, *who has not been noticed by* AXEL, *enters the room. He is dressed somewhat plainly. He looks as if he is still not awake, is unshaven, and gives the impression of having had too much to drink.* AXEL *gives a start when he sees him.)*

LINDGREN: Don't you recognize me?
AXEL: Yes, now I do. . . . But you have changed considerably!
LINDGREN: You think so?
AXEL: Yes—I do, and it surprises me that three years could make such a difference. . . .
LINDGREN: Three years can be a long time! —Aren't you going to ask me to sit down?
AXEL: Oh, yes—but I am in somewhat of a hurry. . . .
LINDGREN: You were always in a hurry.

(He takes a seat. There is a silence.)

AXEL: Say something unpleasant now!
LINDGREN: It's coming—it's coming!

(He wipes his eyeglasses. Again a silence.)

AXEL: How much do you need?
LINDGREN: Three hundred and fifty.
AXEL: I haven't that much, and I can't get it.
LINDGREN: Oh, yes, you can. —Pardon me if I help myself to a schnapps. . . . *(He pours a drink.)*
AXEL: Won't you do me a favor and take a glass of wine instead?
LINDGREN: No—why?
AXEL: Well, it looks bad—to be guzzling liquor like this without eating anything.
LINDGREN: How delicate you have become!

AXEL: No—but it hurts my standing, my reputation—my credit. . . .

LINDGREN: If your credit is good, then you can help me to come up again, since you dragged me down.

AXEL: In other words, you are making a demand.

LINDGREN: I am merely calling to your attention the fact that I am one of your victims.

AXEL: Then let me—with the gratitude I owe you—remind you that, at the time you helped me and paid for the publication of my doctor's thesis so that I could get my university degree, you had an income. . . .

LINDGREN: . . . and that I taught you the method of study which became decisive for your scientific career; that I—who at that time was leading an orderly life—had a beneficial influence upon your careless habits and behavior; that I, in brief, *made* you; and finally—after I had applied for the grant for the expedition—that you blocked my way and appropriated the grant yourself!

AXEL: I was awarded it! Awarded it—because they thought I was the man for the post, and not you!

LINDGREN: And that finished me! When one is raised up, another one is shunted aside. Did you think that was a decent thing to do to me?

AXEL: It was ungrateful, as they call it, but the exploit was achieved, science was advanced, the honor of our country was vindicated, and new regions were opened up for the benefit of coming generations!

LINDGREN: *Skål!* You have trained yourself in oratory! Have you any idea how disagreeable it is to be made a tool of by someone and then to be cast away, discarded?

AXEL: I imagine it feels much the same as the ungrateful one feels, and I congratulate you on not being in my false position. —But let us get back to reality! What can I do for you?

LINDGREN: What do you suppose?

AXEL: For the moment, nothing!

LINDGREN: And the next moment you are gone! And after that I'll never see you again! (*He pours himself another drink.*)

AXEL: Do me a favor and don't finish the bottle, so that the waiters will suspect me.

LINDGREN: Don't be impudent!

AXEL: You don't think it is a pleasure for me to have to correct you in this manner, do you?

LINDGREN: Listen, can you get me a ticket for the festivities tonight?

AXEL: I am sorry to say I don't think they would let you in.

LINDGREN: Because of . . .

AXEL: Because you are drunk!

LINDGREN: Thank you, old friend! Listen, will you let me look at your botanical collections, then?

AXEL: No. I have to put them in shape myself for the Academy.

LINDGREN: Your ethnographic collections, then?

AXEL: No, they are not mine alone.

LINDGREN: Will you—will you let me have twenty-five crowns, then?

AXEL: I can't let you have more than ten. All I have is twenty.

LINDGREN: Damn it to hell!

AXEL: Such is the position of the envied one! Do you think there is anyone with whom I can enjoy myself? I have no one! For those at the bottom hate the one who has come to the top, and those at the top fear the one who has risen from the bottom.

LINDGREN: Yes, you are indeed unfortunate!

AXEL: Yes—and you know that—after what I have gone through this past half-hour—I would be inclined to change my position for yours. How undisturbed and inaccessible one can be when one has nothing to lose; how interesting and sympathetic to be one of the little people, one of the misunderstood, one of those who have been passed by. You have only to stretch out your hand and, presto, you have a coin in it; you offer your arm—and you have friends who put their arms around you! And so you have hosts of kindred spirits who are a mighty stronghold of support! You are to be envied, and you don't know how fortunate you are!

LINDGREN: So you look on me as having fallen so low, and upon yourself as having risen so high. . . . Then tell me—have you by chance read what this newspaper says? (*He takes out a newspaper.*)

AXEL: No, and I am not interested either.

LINDGREN: But you ought to be—for your own sake.

AXEL: I am not going to read it, not even to please you. You say to me, "Come here and let me spit on you," and then you are naïve enough to demand that I come to you! Let me tell you something. During these few minutes I have arrived at the firm conclusion that if I should happen upon you in a dense bamboo jungle, I would without compunction mow you down with my breechloader.

LINDGREN: I quite believe you to be a rapacious beast!

AXEL: One should never balance the books with one's friends, or with persons whom one has lived with intimately, for one never knows who has most of the figures on the debit side. But when you present your bill, I shall look it over carefully! —Don't you think I realized soon enough that behind your beneficence lurked an unconscious desire to get the chance to transform me into the strong arm that you lacked—so that you could perform what you were unable to do yourself? *I* was possessed of a gift of invention and initiative; all *you* had was money and personal connections. Therefore, I am to be congratulated that you did not devour me, and I may be excused for devouring *you*—for I had no other choice than to eat or be eaten!

LINDGREN: You are a predatory animal!

AXEL: And you—a rodent! Who could not elevate yourself into a predatory animal—as you so intensely desired! Just as, at this moment, you have no wish to elevate yourself to my level, but rather to see me lower myself to yours! If you have anything to add that is of importance, do it quickly—I am expecting a caller.

LINDGREN: Your fiancée, eh?

AXEL: So you have sniffed that out, too?

LINDGREN: Why, of course! And I know what Mari—whom you jilted—thinks and says. . . . And I know what has happened to your brother and your sister-in-law. . . .

AXEL: You know my Cecilia? She is not my fiancée yet, you know.

LINDGREN: No, but I know her intended!

AXEL: Just what do you mean by that?

LINDGREN: She has been seeing another man right along. . . . Oh—so you didn't know that?

AXEL (*listening in the direction of the entrance door*): Why, yes, I knew that, but I thought she had broken with him. . . . Listen, come back in fifteen minutes—then I shall have tried to arrange *something* for you. . . .

LINDGREN: Is this some sort of polite brush-off, eh?

AXEL: Why, no—I am merely trying to discharge an obligation. I mean it—seriously!

LINDGREN: In that case, I shall leave. And I'll be back. . . . Until we see each other again. . . .

(*There is a knock at the door.* AXEL *goes to open it.* THE WAITER *enters.* THE FIANCÉ *appears in the doorway, dressed in black.*)

THE WAITER: There is a gentleman here to see you, sir.

AXEL: Ask him to come in.

(THE WAITER *goes out, leaving the door open.* THE FIANCÉ *enters.* LINDGREN *looks him over intently.*)

LINDGREN (*to* AXEL): Well, goodbye, Axel. And good luck to you! (*He leaves.*)

AXEL: Goodbye.

(THE FIANCÉ *is self-conscious.*)

With whom have I the honor . . . ?

THE FIANCÉ: My name is not important. Unlike you, I have no reputation that I can boast of. And the reason for my coming is an affair of the heart.

AXEL: You are not . . . Do you know Cecilia . . . ?

THE FIANCÉ: Yes—I am the one!

AXEL (*at first hesitant, then with determination*): Please sit down. (*He goes to the entrance door, opens it, and summons* THE WAITER. *To* THE WAITER:) See that I get my bill—pack my baggage in the other room—and have a cab ready for me in half an hour.

(THE WAITER *bows and leaves.* AXEL *returns to* THE FIANCÉ *and seats himself.*)

Go ahead, please!

THE FIANCÉ (*after a pause, unctuously*): Two men lived in the same city. One was rich, the other one was poor. The rich man had sheep and cattle in abundance; the only thing the poor man possessed was a little lamb. . . .

AXEL: What has this to do with me?

THE FIANCÉ (*continuing as before*): . . . a little lamb, which he had bought and which he raised. . . .

AXEL: This is taking too much time! What is it you want? Are you still engaged to Cecilia?

THE FIANCÉ (*with a sudden change in tone*): Have I said anything about any Cecilia? Have I?

AXEL: Listen, my dear man, come to the point, or you will be shown the door! But hurry up, and don't go round-about—no twisting and turning. . . .

THE FIANCÉ (*offering* AXEL *his snuffbox*): Care for some snuff?

AXEL: No, thank you!

THE FIANCÉ: A great man has no such petty foibles.

AXEL: Well—since you will not speak out, then I shall. It is, of course, none of your concern, but it will do you good to know about it anyhow, since you don't seem to be aware of it. I am engaged to Cecilia, whom I have been told was once engaged to you.

THE FIANCÉ (*overcome*): Have been told—once . . . ?

AXEL: Yes—she broke off her engagement to you.

THE FIANCÉ: That's news to me!

AXEL (*takes out a ring from his vest pocket*): That you should not be aware of it is inexplicable. But you know it now. Here you see my engagement ring.

THE FIANCÉ: She has broken off her engagement to me?

AXEL: Yes—she could not very well be engaged to both of us at the same time. And since she was no longer in love with you, she had to break the engagement. I would have told you this in a more delicate manner if you had not acted so scornfully when you came here.

THE FIANCÉ: I have not treated you with scorn!

AXEL: Cowardly and lying, servile, creeping, and flamboyant!

THE FIANCÉ (*meekly*): You are a hard man, Doctor!

AXEL: No—but I shall be! You did not spare my feelings a moment ago—you sneered and scoffed at me—which is something I did not do. . . . This is the end of this conversation.

THE FIANCÉ (*with true emotion*): She was my only lamb, and I was afraid you would take her away from me. . . . But you won't do it—you, who have so many. . . .

AXEL: Assume that I really would not—are you, then, so sure that she would remain with you . . . ?

THE FIANCÉ: Think of my plight, Doctor. . . .

AXEL: Yes, if you will think of mine!

THE FIANCÉ: I'm a poor man. . . .

AXEL: So am I. But—judging by what I see and hear—you have eternal bliss waiting for you beyond this life. I have not. Besides, I have taken nothing from you. I have merely accepted what was offered me. Precisely as you have.

THE FIANCÉ: And I who had dreamed of a future for this girl—a future so bright . . .

AXEL: Forgive me for telling you a piece of discourtesy, since you have been discourteous to me. . . . Are you so sure that this girl's future would not be even brighter at my side?

THE FIANCÉ: Are you reminding me of my humble circumstances as a workingman . . . ?

AXEL: No, I am alluding to this girl's future, which lies so close to your heart. And when I hear that she no longer feels any affection for you, but loves me instead, I feel free to think that her future would be brighter with a man she loves than with someone she does not love.

THE FIANCÉ: You have all the advantages on your side, and we poor people exist merely to be sacrificed.

AXEL: Come now, I have been told that you pushed aside a rival of yours for Cecilia's favors, and that by not too honorable means. What do you think that victim thought of you, eh?

THE FIANCÉ: He was a wicked, sinful fellow!

AXEL: From whom you saved the girl! Now I save her from you! Goodbye!

(CECILIA *suddenly enters.*)

THE FIANCÉ: Cecilia!

(CECILIA *is taken aback.*)

You seem to have found your way here already!

AXEL (*to* THE FIANCÉ): Take yourself off!

CECILIA (*feeling faint*): Give me a glass of water!

THE FIANCÉ (*picking up the brandy bottle*): There is nothing left in the bottle! —Watch out for that man, Cecilia!

AXEL (*pushing* THE FIANCÉ *out of the door*): There is no need for you to remain here! Get out!

THE FIANCÉ: Watch out for that man, Cecilia! (*He departs.*)

AXEL: This was a most disagreeable, scandalous scene, which you could have saved me from if you had openly broken with him and if you had refrained from seeking me out here in my rooms!

CECILIA (*starts to weep*): Are you going to reproach me, too?

AXEL: I had to find out who brought all this about. And now that it has been cleared up, let us talk about something else! To begin with, how are you?

CECILIA: Oh, so-so.

AXEL: That means, not too well?

CECILIA: How do you feel yourself?

AXEL: Excellent—only a little tired.

CECILIA: Are you coming with me to my aunt's this afternoon?

AXEL: No, I can't—I am invited out—to a dinner party.

CECILIA: And that's more interesting, I suppose! You are invited out so often, and I never go anywhere.

AXEL: H'm.

CECILIA: Why do you say "h'm"?

AXEL: Because your remark made an unpleasant impression on me.

CECILIA: One gets so many unpleasant impressions these days. . . .

AXEL: For example?

CECILIA: When one reads the newspapers!

AXEL: So you have read those scandalous articles about me? Do you really believe what they say? Do you?

CECILIA: I don't know what to believe.

AXEL: Then you actually do harbor a suspicion that I could be so lacking in honor as I am accused of in these articles? But since you nonetheless want to marry me, I must assume that you are prompted by purely practical reasons, and not by personal inclination or affection.

CECILIA: You speak so unfeelingly—as if you didn't love me at all.

AXEL: Cecilia! Will you come with me? Will you leave with me in a quarter of an hour?

CECILIA: A quarter of an hour? Where?

AXEL: To London.

CECILIA: I wouldn't come with you until we are married!

AXEL: Why?

CECILIA: Why must we leave in such a hurry?

AXEL: Because—it's so suffocating, so stuffy here! If we stay here I'll be so hampered and dragged down that I'll never be able to extricate myself!

CECILIA: That's strange! Are things that bad?

AXEL: Are you coming with me, or are you not?

CECILIA: Not before we have been married, for then you wouldn't marry me at all!

AXEL: That's what you think, is it? Well, sit down for a moment while I go inside and write a couple of letters.

CECILIA: You want me to sit alone in here—with the door open?

AXEL: Don't close the door, or we'll be lost for good. (*He goes out to the right.*)

CECILIA: But don't stay away too long!

(*She goes over to the entrance door, closes it, and turns the key. MARI enters through the same door a moment later.*)

Wasn't the door locked?

MARI: No, I didn't find it locked. Why, was it supposed to be locked?

CECILIA (*superciliously*): With whom have I the honor . . . ?

MARI: I ask you the same.

CECILIA: What concern is that of yours?

MARI: How polite! Ah, now I understand. . . . So, you are the one! Then I am your victim—for the present!

CECILIA: I don't know you.

MARI: I know *you* so much the better!

CECILIA (*gets up and goes over to the door on the right*): Well . . . (*In the doorway, to AXEL.*) Come here for a moment!

(*AXEL comes out and sees MARI. He is taken aback.*)

AXEL: What are you doing here?

MARI: One never knows. . . .

AXEL: Please leave!

MARI: Why?

AXEL: Because our relations ended three years ago!

MARI: And now you have found another to throw on the scrapheap!

AXEL: Did I ever make any promises to you which I did not keep? Do I owe you anything? Did I ever promise to marry you? Have we any children between us? Have I alone shared your favors?

MARI: But you seem to want to be alone—with that one! *(With a gesture toward* CECILIA.*)*

CECILIA *(coming up to* MARI*)*: Shut up! I don't know you!

MARI: But you knew me when we walked the streets once upon a time—then you knew me! And when we solicited in the square, I remember everybody knew us by our first names! *(To* AXEL.*)* And now you intend to marry that one! You know—you are much too good for her!

AXEL *(to* CECILIA*)*: Have you known this girl before?

CECILIA: No!

MARI *(to* CECILIA*)*: Have you no shame? I didn't recognize you at first—you have become so elegant. . . .

*(*AXEL *regards* CECILIA *fixedly.)*

CECILIA: Come, Axel! I'll go with you!

AXEL *(reflectively)*: At once! Just wait a moment! I am going in to write one more letter. —But we must close the door first.

MARI: No, thank you, I don't want to be shut in the way she was just now.

AXEL *(pricking up his ears)*: Was the door locked?

CECILIA *(to* MARI*)*: Have you the temerity to say that the door was locked?

MARI: Since you showed surprise that it was not locked, I suppose you had locked it so badly that it didn't catch.

AXEL *(giving* CECILIA *a searching look; then, to* MARI*)*: Mari, you were always a good girl, as I recall. Will you give me back the letters I wrote to you?

MARI: No!

AXEL: What do you want with them now?

MARI: I have heard I can sell them, now that you have become so famous.

AXEL: And in that way you can get revenge, eh?

MARI: Exactly!

AXEL: Is it Lindgren who. . . .

MARI (*pointing toward the entrance door*): Yes—and here he is in person!

(LINDGREN, *in fine humor, enters.*)

LINDGREN: Look at this! So many girls! And Mari is here, too—like the rudd when it's spawning! Listen, Axel. . . .

AXEL: I can hear you, even when I don't see you. You are in unusually good humor! What evil could have befallen me now?

LINDGREN: I felt a little low this morning before I had a chance to pull myself together, but then I went out and had a beefsteak. . . . Well—you see, Axel, you owe me nothing, really. . . .

(AXEL *shows a perplexed countenance.*)

. . . for what I did for you, I did out of the kindness of my heart, and that redounds to my honor, as well as giving me pleasure. And what I have given you, was given to you, and you have not borrowed it.

AXEL: Now you are being entirely too modest and generous!

LINDGREN: Don't say that! However, one service deserves another. Will you put your name to this note for me?

(AXEL *hesitates.*)

You don't have to be afraid. I am not going to put you in the same predicament as your brother did. . . .

AXEL: What do you mean? Don't you know that it was I who put him in his present precarious situation. . . .

LINDGREN: For two hundred crowns, yes. But you stood surety for the five-year lease on the farm. . . .

AXEL: In heaven's name!

LINDGREN: What was that? H'm—h'm!

AXEL (*looking at his watch*): Wait a few minutes—I have to go in and write a couple of letters.

(CECILIA *tries to follow him, but he holds her back.*)

Just a few minutes, darling. . . . (*He kisses her on the*

forehead.) Just a few minutes. (*He goes toward the door on the right.*)

LINDGREN (*to* AXEL): Here is the note. Do it at once!

AXEL: Give it to me!

> (LINDGREN *hands the note to* AXEL, *who determinedly goes out, right.*)

LINDGREN (*to the two women*): Well, are you two little girls friends again now?

MARI: Yes, indeed! And before we leave here together, we'll be even closer friends.

> (CECILIA *makes a face.*)

I feel like having some kind of fun today.

LINDGREN: Come out with me—I'll have some money now.

MARI: No!

> (CECILIA *places herself uneasily on a chair near the door through which* AXEL *went out, as though she were seeking support from within.*)

LINDGREN: We'll go and look at the fireworks tonight, so that we can see what a great man looks like by the light of Roman candles! What do you say, Cecilia?—Cecilia!

CECILIA: Oh, I am going to be sick if I stay here much longer!

MARI: It wouldn't be the first time!

LINDGREN: Go ahead and squabble, girls! I want to hear you! Batter each other! Let the blows come thick and fast! Go ahead! Ugh!

> (TURE *and his* WIFE *enter.*)

Ah! Old acquaintances! How are you?

TURE: We are well, thank you!

LINDGREN: And the child?

TURE: The child?

LINDGREN: So-o, have you forgotten you have a child? Have you the same difficulty remembering names?

TURE: Names?

LINDGREN: Yes—signatures! He is taking a horribly long time writing in there!

TURE: Is my brother the doctor in there?

LINDGREN: I don't know whether the doctor is in there—but

your brother went in there just now. We may as well go in and find out. . . . *(He knocks at the door.)* Silent as the grave! *(He repeats the knock.)* Well—I am going in!

(He goes into the other room. There is general uneasiness and excitement.)

CECILIA: I wonder what he is doing in there?

MARI: We'll soon find out.

TURE: What has been going on here?

THE WIFE *(to* TURE*)*: *Something* is going on here. . . . You'll see, he won't help us!

*(*LINDGREN *comes out of the inner room, carrying a vial and some letters.)*

LINDGREN: What does it say here? *(Trying to read the label on the vial.)* Potassium cyanide! How could that sentimental fool be so stupid as to take his life for such a bagatelle. . . .

(All give a scream.)

So-o, you were not a predatory animal after all, my dear Axel! But. . . . *(He peers into the room again.)* But he is not there. . . . And his baggage is gone! Consequently, he has left! And the vial hasn't been opened. . . . That means —that he had intended to take his life, but changed his mind. . . . Here are the letters he wrote. . . . "To Miss Cecilia." . . . There seems to be something round inside— probably the engagement ring. . . . *(He hands the letter to* CECILIA.*)* This is for you. *(He looks at another letter and holds it against the light.)* "To my Brother Ture." It has a blue piece of paper in it—it is a promissory note for what he owes you. . . . That should be welcome!

*(*THE FIANCÉ *appears in the doorway, left.)*

TURE *(who has opened his letter)*: You see, he did help us, after all!

THE WIFE: Yes, in that way, yes!

LINDGREN: And here—here is my note! But without any security! What a hard man! What a devil of a fellow!

MARI: And so there will be no fireworks, then!

THE FIANCÉ: Didn't he leave anything for me?

LINDGREN: Oh, yes, I think he leaves a fiancée—over there! *(He makes a gesture toward the back of the room, where*

CECILIA *is sitting.*) But just think what a man he was, after all, to be able to clear up tangled affairs like that! Of course, it annoys me that I allowed myself to be duped —but I just wonder whether I wouldn't have done exactly the same. . . . And, who knows, perhaps *you* would, too? Eh?

CURTAIN

In the Face
of Death

(1892)

A Tragedy in One Act

CHARACTERS

MONSIEUR DURAND,
   keeper of a *pension;* formerly an employee of the State
   Railways

ADÈLE   27 years old
ANNETTE   24 years old   his daughters
THÉRÈSE   18 years old

ANTONIO,
   a lieutenant in the Italian cavalry

PIERRE

*The action takes place in French Switzerland
in the 1880s.*

A dining room with a long rectangular table. In the rear, a door, which stands open. Through the doorway can be seen the tops of the churchyard cypresses and, beyond, Lake Leman with the Savoyard Alps and the French bathing resort Évian.

On the right, a door leading to the kitchen. On the left, a door to the Durand family's living quarters.

DURAND stands looking out across the lake through a pair of binoculars. ADÈLE enters from the kitchen. She is wearing an apron, and her sleeves are rolled up. She is carrying a coffee tray.

ADÈLE: Haven't you gone for the bread for the coffee yet, Father?

DURAND: No, I sent Pierre for it. I have been so short of breath for the last few days. . . . I can't climb that steep hill. . . .

ADÈLE: You sent Pierre again. . . . That means paying him three sous! Where are we going to get the money from? For the last two months we have only had one guest in the *pension*.

DURAND: I know that, of course. Why couldn't Annette go for the bread?

ADÈLE: That would be the quickest way of ruining our credit altogether! And that's what you have been doing all these years.

DURAND: Must I hear that from you, too, Adèle?

ADÈLE: I have been holding my tongue longer than the rest! But I am getting tired of it, too!

DURAND: Yes, that you have—and I have to admit you have shown yourself to be a little more human than Thérèse and Annette! They have been torturing me! . . . You and I have managed to keep the house going since your mother died. You had to stay in the kitchen like poor Cinderella—and I had to look after the guests and sweep and scrub and start the fire—and run errands. . . . But if you are tired, what about me, then?

ADÈLE: You've no right to be tired! You have three children you have to support and provide for—now that you've squandered our inheritance!

DURAND (*listens to a sound from outside*): Do you hear the tolling of bells and the rolling of drums over at Cully? If they have a fire over there, they will be lost! I can tell by the waves on the lake that the foehn is starting to blow.

ADÈLE: You paid the fire insurance on the house, didn't you?

DURAND: Yes, I did. If I hadn't paid it, I wouldn't have been able to get the last mortgage.

ADÈLE: How much of the property is still unencumbered?

DURAND: Only a fifth of the insurance value. And you know how property values decreased here after the railroad passed us by and was detoured to the east.

ADÈLE: Oh, how I would welcome a change! Anything!

DURAND (*in a severe tone*): Adèle!

(*There is a pause.*)

Will you put out the fire in the kitchen?

ADÈLE: I can't do it until the coffee bread comes. . . .

DURAND: Well—it's here now.

(PIERRE *enters with a basket.*)

ADÈLE (*looks inside the basket*): No bread! Nothing but a bill! Two . . . three! (*She holds up the bills.*)

PIERRE: Yes—the baker said he couldn't give any more credit until he was paid. And when I passed the butcher's and the grocer's, they gave me these bills. . . . (*He goes out.*)

ADÈLE: Oh, God in heaven—then we are at the end of our rope! —But what is this? (*She takes out a package and unwraps it.*)

DURAND: It's some candles I bought to light for my beloved René. . . . It's the anniversary of his death today.

ADÈLE: You spend money on things like that!

DURAND: Yes—I bought them with the tips I made. . . . Don't you think I feel the humiliation—having to keep my hand out every time a guest is leaving? . . . Can't you let me have the one joy I still cherish—contemplating my grief one day in each year? —To live over in my memory the most beautiful thing that this life has given me? . . .

ADÈLE: Had he been alive today, you probably would not find him so beautiful!

DURAND: There may be some truth in your sarcasm . . . but, as I remember him, he was nothing like you girls are today!

ADÈLE: I am going to leave it to you to entertain Monsieur Antonio when he comes down for his coffee and finds there is no bread. Oh, if only Mother were alive today! She could always cope with such embarrassing predicaments, no matter what! She knew how to manage and make ends meet—while you would stand around not knowing what to do!

DURAND: Your mother had many good sides!

ADÈLE: And you—you only found fault with her!

DURAND: Here comes Monsieur Antonio. . . . Step outside now, while I have a talk with him.

ADÈLE: It would be better if you went out and borrowed some money so that we would be spared humiliation. . . .

DURAND: I couldn't borrow another sou! I have been borrowing for the last ten years! I'd rather see everything collapse this very minute—everything—just so that there would be an end to all this!

ADÈLE: An end for you, yes! But what about us? You never think of us!

DURAND (*with resignation, wounded*): No, I have never thought of you—never!

ADÈLE: Are you exacting payment again for bringing us up?

DURAND: I only object to your unfair reproach. If you will leave me now, I shall meet the storm, as I always do! . . .

ADÈLE (*mocking him*): As I always do! H'm! (*She leaves.*)

ANTONIO (*enters through the door, rear*): Good morning, Monsieur Durand.

DURAND: You have already been out for a walk—eh, Lieutenant?

ANTONIO: Yes, I took a walk down toward Cully and watched the men put out a chimney fire. And now a cup of coffee would certainly taste good!

DURAND: I am sorry to have to tell you . . . indeed, it gives me a great deal of pain . . . to have to confess that I can't continue my business any longer. . . . I haven't the means to keep going. . . .

ANTONIO: What has happened?

DURAND: Speaking plainly, we are bankrupt.

ANTONIO: But, my dear Monsieur Durand, there must be some way of getting you out of your situation—isn't there? It is only a temporary difficulty, I hope.

DURAND: No, this time there is no way out! For the past several years the situation has been getting increasingly worse—and I'd rather see the whole business go to the wall now than to have to be in constant anxiety, day and night, over what will eventually have to come to pass.

ANTONIO: Yet I can't help thinking you are much too pessimistic. . . .

DURAND: I can see no reason why you should doubt my word, Lieutenant. . . .

ANTONIO: . . . For the simple reason that I should like to be of some help to you. . . .

DURAND: I don't care to be helped! Poverty and necessity will force my children to live a different life from now on. They have done nothing but toy with life. With the exception of Adèle, who runs the kitchen and who *does* work, what do the two others do? They sing and play, they go for walks and engage in flirtation . . . and as long as there is a piece of bread in the house, they will never learn to do anything useful.

ANTONIO: That may be—but while your economy is being untangled, you must have food in the house. If you don't mind, I'll stay on another month and pay my bill in advance.

DURAND: No! I thank you just the same—but this time we must drive on to the end of the road—even if it should land us in the lake! I don't want to continue with this kind of business, which does not even give us our bread—only humiliation! Let me tell you what happened last spring. . . . The house had been empty of guests for three months. . . . At last an American family came to our rescue. The very first morning after their arrival, I found the son embracing my daughter Thérèse, trying to kiss her! What would you have done in my place?

ANTONIO (*puzzled, confused*): I don't know. . . .

DURAND: I know what I, as her father, ought to have done! But—as her father—I didn't do it! The next time I will know what to do!

ANTONIO: That's the very reason, it seems to me, that you ought to take precautions and carefully consider what you are doing, so that your daughters are not left to the hazards of the future. . . .

DURAND: Monsieur Antonio, you are a young man—and for some inexplicable reason I feel sympathetic toward you. Whether you appreciate this confidence of mine or not— I beg of you one thing: form no opinion whatsoever either of me personally or of my behavior. . . .

ANTONIO: Monsieur Durand, I give you my word, if you will only answer this one question: Are you a native-born Swiss, or are you not?

DURAND: I am a Swiss citizen.

ANTONIO: I know you are—but I asked you whether you were born in Switzerland.

DURAND (*in an uncertain voice*): Yes—I was. . . .

ANTONIO: I merely asked because . . . because I was interested. However, since I must believe you when you tell me that the *pension* is to be closed, I want to pay my bill. It is only a pittance—ten francs—but I don't want to leave without settling it.

DURAND: I have no way of knowing whether the amount is correct or not. I don't keep the books. But if you are trying to cheat me, you will be held accountable. I'll go and get the bread now. Then we'll see. . . . (*He goes out.*)

(THÉRÈSE *enters a moment later, a mousetrap dangling from one hand. She is dressed in a negligee, and her hair is hanging loose.*)

THÉRÈSE: Ah, it is you, Antonio! I thought I heard the old man's voice. . . .

ANTONIO: Yes, he said he was going to get the bread for the coffee.

THÉRÈSE: Hasn't he gone after it yet? No—we can't have that old fool hanging around here much longer!

ANTONIO: You look so beautiful today, Thérèse—but that mousetrap isn't becoming to you!

THÉRÈSE: And it isn't any good, either. I have been putting bait in it for a whole month and haven't caught a single mouse. Yet every morning the bait is gone. —Have you seen Mimi this morning?

ANTONIO: You mean the cat? She always seems to be here— whether you want her around or not. But today I have been spared from seeing her!

THÉRÈSE: You should speak nicely about those not present! Remember that he who loves me, loves my cat! (*She places the mousetrap on the table and takes an empty saucer from the floor.*) Adèle! Adèle!

ADÈLE (*in the doorway to the kitchen*): What is it Her Grace commands so loudly?

THÉRÈSE: I command some milk for my cat and a cheese rind for your mice!

ADÈLE: Go and get them yourself!

THÉRÈSE: Is that the way to answer Her Grace?

ADÈLE: It's the answer you deserve! And I ought to give you a special scolding for appearing before strangers with your hair uncombed!

THÉRÈSE: We are all old friends here, and . . . Antonio, go over to Aunt Adèle and speak nicely to her—and perhaps she will let you have some milk for Mimi.

(ANTONIO *hesitates.*)

THÉRÈSE: Well—aren't you going to do what I tell you?

ANTONIO (*gives her a short answer*): No!

THÉRÈSE: What kind of answer is that? Would you like to have a taste of my riding crop?

ANTONIO: Don't be impudent!

THÉRÈSE (*taken aback*): What did you say? What—did—you say? Are you trying to remind me of what I am—to put the blame on me for my weakness?

ANTONIO: No—I simply want to remind you of what I am— my guilt—and my weakness!

ADÈLE (*takes the empty saucer*): Now, listen, my two friends! What kind of linguistic exercises are you practic- ing, anyhow? Why don't you make up—and then in a minute I'll give you a good cup of coffee! *(She goes into the kitchen.)*

THÉRÈSE *(in tears, to* ANTONIO*)*: You have tired of me, Antonio! You are thinking of leaving me! . . .

ANTONIO: Stop weeping! It makes your eyes so ugly!

THÉRÈSE: They may not look as beautiful to you as Annette's. . . .

ANTONIO: Oh, it's Annette now? Well, now—all jesting aside —I think we have waited long enough for the coffee, don't you?

THÉRÈSE: You would be the right one to have for a husband! You can't even wait a second for your coffee! . . .

ANTONIO: And what a charming wife you would make! You would nag your husband at the slightest provocation—the moment you did something stupid!

ANNETTE *(enters. She is dressed, and her hair is arranged.)*: You are not quarreling so early in the morning, are you?

ANTONIO: Why, there is Annette—and already dressed!

THÉRÈSE: Yes, Annette is splendid in every way—and, besides, she has the advantage of being older than I. . . .

ANNETTE: If you don't keep your mouth shut, I'll . . .

ANTONIO: Now, now! Don't be ugly now, Thérèse! *(He grabs her by the waist and kisses her.)*

DURAND *(appears in the doorway. He stops short, taken aback.)*: What's this?

THÉRÈSE *(tears herself away from* ANTONIO*)*: What?

DURAND: Did my eyes deceive me?

THÉRÈSE: What did you see?

DURAND: I saw you allowing this man, this stranger, to kiss you!

THÉRÈSE: That's a lie!

DURAND: Have I lost my eyesight—or have you the audacity to lie in my face?

THÉRÈSE: You talk about lying—you, who keep lying to us and to everybody, saying that you were born a Swiss, although you were born a Frenchman!

DURAND: Who has told you that?

THÉRÈSE: Mother told me!

DURAND *(to* ANTONIO*)*: Lieutenant! . . . We have settled our accounts—and I ask you to leave this house immediately! Immediately—or . . .

ANTONIO: Or? . . .

DURAND: You may choose your weapons!

ANTONIO: I wonder just what weapons you would resort to? You would fight shy and take to your heels!

DURAND: If I didn't choose to cane you, I would use my rifle from the last war! . . .

THÉRÈSE: A fine soldier you are! A deserter!

DURAND: Your mother told you that, too, didn't she? I don't know how to fight the dead—but I can beat the life out of the living! *(He lifts his thick stick and advances toward* ANTONIO.)

(THÉRÈSE *and* ANNETTE *throw themselves between the two men.)*

ANNETTE: Think of what you are doing!

THÉRÈSE: You will end on the guillotine!

ANTONIO *(draws back and starts to leave)*: Goodbye, Monsieur Durand! You have my contempt—and my ten francs! Keep them!

DURAND *(takes a gold coin from his vest pocket and throws it after* ANTONIO): I curse you and your money, you swine!

THÉRÈSE AND ANNETTE *(call after* ANTONIO): Don't go! Don't go! Father will kill us!

DURAND *(breaks the cudgel in two)*: If I can't kill, I can at least die!

ANTONIO: Goodbye—and now you can grieve without me—the last rat from the sinking ship! *(He leaves.)*

THÉRÈSE *(to* DURAND): You certainly have a fine way of treating your guests! No wonder our business is crumbling!

DURAND: A fine way, you say! Guests like him! Tell me, Thérèse . . . my child. . . . *(He takes her face between his hands.)* Tell me, my dearest child . . . tell me, if I saw wrong just now—or if you told an untruth. . . .

THÉRÈSE *(sullenly)*: What do you mean?

DURAND: You know very well what I mean! It isn't so much the thing in itself—it might have been just an innocent flirtation. . . . What I want to know is whether I can trust my senses—that's what interests me most. . . .

THÉRÈSE: Why don't you talk about something else—talk about what we are going to eat and drink today instead! Besides, it's a lie that he kissed me!

DURAND: It's not a lie! In heaven's name—I saw the whole thing!

THÉRÈSE: Prove it!

DURAND: Prove it? With two witnesses—or one policeman! *(To* ANNETTE.*)* Annette, my child . . . will you please tell me the truth?

ANNETTE: I didn't see anything!

DURAND: That's the right answer! One must never let one's sisters down! Oh, how like your mother you are today, Annette!

ANNETTE: Don't say anything bad about Mother! Oh, if she had been alive today!

ADÈLE *(to* DURAND*):* Here is your milk. But what became of the bread?

DURAND: I didn't get any bread, my child . . . but there will be bread, as there always has been. . . .

THÉRÈSE *(snatches the glass from his hand):* You are not going to get a thing—not a thing! You—throwing away money—and letting your children starve!

ADÈLE: He threw away the money, did he? The wretch! He should have been put away in a madhouse that time, when Mother said he was ripe for it! Look—here is another bill that somebody just delivered in the kitchen! *(She throws it at* DURAND.*)*

> *(*DURAND *glances at the bill and gives a start. Then he pours a glass of water, which he drinks. He seats himself and lights his pipe.)*

ANNETTE: He can afford to spend money on tobacco! That he can afford!

DURAND *(tired and resigned):* My dear children—this tobacco didn't cost any more than a glass of water. . . . It was given to me six months ago—so don't work yourselves up about that! It isn't necessary!

THÉRÈSE *(removes the matches from the table):* But at least you are not going to waste any matches!

DURAND: If you knew, Thérèse, how many matches I wasted on you when I got up in the night to make sure you hadn't kicked off your bedclothes. . . . If you knew, Annette, how many times I have stolen to your bed and brought you water when you cried for thirst! Your mother thought it was bad for children to drink water. . . .

THÉRÈSE: That's so long ago, it doesn't interest me in the

slightest! Besides, it was nothing but your duty, wasn't it? You said so yourself. . . .

DURAND: So it was, yes—but I did it! And what's more, I did a little more than I might have done. . . .

ADÈLE: Well—keep on doing it! Or else nobody knows what will become of us! Three young girls left without protection or anything else—without a sou to live on! You know what necessity and poverty can drive a young girl to, don't you?

DURAND: I've tried to instill that in you for the last ten years . . . but you paid no attention to me! And twenty years ago I prophesied that this was what would happen! And I haven't been able to stave it off. I have been sitting here like a lonely brakeman on an express train—have seen it coming closer and closer to the brink of the abyss —and I haven't been able to get near the engine's brake-wheel to prevent it.

THÉRÈSE: And now you want us to thank you for wrecking the train and leaving us in the ditch?

DURAND: No, my child! All I ask is that you treat me a little more kindly. . . . You give the cream to the cat, but you begrudge your father even a sip of milk—your father, who hasn't had a decent meal for such a long time. . . .

THÉRÈSE: So it's you who drink up the cat's milk!

DURAND: Yes—it's I, yes!

ANNETTE: Perhaps he's also the one who has been eating up the bait in the trap?

DURAND: Yes—it's he!

ADÈLE: What a pig!

THÉRÈSE (*with a laugh*): Just imagine—if there had been poison on it!

DURAND: You mean: If there had *only* been poison on it!

THÉRÈSE (*to* DURAND): Well—you wouldn't have minded that, would you? You have been talking about putting a bullet through your head long enough—but you haven't done it yet!

DURAND: Why haven't I shot myself? That's nothing short of reproach! Well—do you know why I haven't done it? Because, my beloved daughters, I didn't want you to have to jump in the lake! . . . Now try to find some other mean things to say! Your words are like music to my ears— music from the good old days. . . .

ADÈLE: Oh, why don't you stop your chattering! It won't get you anywhere—it won't do you any good! Do something instead—do something!

THÉRÈSE: Do you realize what will happen if you leave us in this predicament?

DURAND: I suppose you will become prostitutes. . . . That's the threat your mother always made when she had spent the money for the household on lottery tickets.

ADÈLE: Shut up! And don't say another word about our dear, beloved mother!

DURAND (*babbling to himself*): There burns a light—in this house tonight—and when the light has burned . . . our fortune has turned. . . . I suppose I should have said: When the light has burned out . . . then the foehn comes along—sweeping and strong. . . . Yes! No!

(*It has started to blow outside, and it grows dark.* DURAND *listens to the wind and suddenly jumps up, turning toward* ADÈLE.)

Put out the fire in the stove—the foehn is coming!

ADÈLE (*looks him straight in the eye*): The foehn is not coming!

DURAND (*gradually his voice becomes more and more frantic*): Put out the fire in the stove! If we have a fire there, we won't get a sou of the insurance money! Put out the fire in the stove, I tell you! Don't you hear what I say? Put it out!

ADÈLE: I can't understand you!

DURAND (*gazes into her eyes while he takes hold of her hands*): Will you do as I tell you—(*Pleading fervently.*) please! Do as I tell you!

(ADÈLE *goes out into the kitchen, leaving the door ajar.*)

DURAND (*to* THÉRÈSE *and* ANNETTE): Go upstairs and close your windows, children . . . and look after the dampers! But first, come here and give me a kiss—for I am going on a journey—a journey that may bring its rewards . . . and help to give you security. . . .

(ANNETTE *goes out.*)

THÉRÈSE: You can get us some money, can you?

DURAND: I have a life insurance policy—I am hoping to cash it in. . . .

THÉRÈSE: How much will you get on it?

DURAND: Six hundred francs if I sell it—five thousand if I die. . . .

(THÉRÈSE *seems puzzled.*)

DURAND: Say what's on your mind, my child! No, let's not be unnecessarily cruel. . . . Tell me, Thérèse, are you in love with Antonio? I mean—so much in love that you would be unhappy if you didn't get him? Are you?

THÉRÈSE: Yes—I am. . . .

DURAND: Well—then you ought to marry him, if—if he—is in love with you! But you must never be unkind to him. . . . If you are, you will never be happy! Farewell, my dearest, dearest child! (*He embraces her and kisses her on both cheeks.*)

THÉRÈSE: You are not going to die, Father! . . . Oh, no, you must not die!

DURAND: You don't begrudge me some peace at last?

THÉRÈSE: No—not if you wish it . . . if you really wish it. . . . Forgive me, Father, for all the many times I have been unkind to you!

DURAND: Nonsense, my child!

THÉRÈSE: I have been meaner to you than anyone!

DURAND: If you have, I noticed it less—for I loved you the most! Why, I don't know. . . . And now—go and close the windows!

THÉRÈSE: Here are your matches, Father. . . . And—here—here is your milk. . . .

DURAND (*with a wan smile*): Oh—my child!

THÉRÈSE: Well—what else is there that I can do? I haven't anything else that I can give you. . . .

DURAND: You gave me so much happiness and joy when you were a child that you owe me nothing. Go now! And try to give me the same friendly smile you used to give me then. . . .

(THÉRÈSE *smiles at him and starts to go. Then she sud denly turns and throws herself into his arms.*)

There, there, my child. . . . Now I am happy again. . . .

(THÉRÈSE *runs out.* ANNETTE *enters.*)

Farewell, Annette.

ANNETTE: Are you going away? I don't understand all this. . . .

DURAND: I am going away, yes. . . .

ANNETTE: But you are coming back, aren't you, Father?

DURAND: None of us know whether we shall survive each day that we live. . . . But, no matter what, we can say goodbye to each other anyhow, can't we?

ANNETTE: Well—goodbye, then, Father! And I hope you have luck on your journey! And don't forget to bring something home for us, as you used to do. . . . (*She goes out.*)

DURAND: You still remember that, Annette, even though it is a long time since I bought anything for you children. . . . Goodbye, Annette! (*He babbles to himself.*) For good and ill—in big and small—what you have sowed—will others till. . . .

(ADÈLE *enters.*)

DURAND: Adèle! Now I want you to listen to what I have to say . . . so that you will understand everything! If I speak in veiled terms, it is only because I wish to spare your conscience from knowing more than you should. First of all, I want you to be completely at ease! I have told the children to go to their rooms. . . . And now I want you to ask me this question, to begin with: "Is your life insured?" Well? . . . Well? . . .

ADÈLE (*with an inquiring look, hesitantly*): Is your life insured?

DURAND: No. I did have a policy, but I sold it long ago. I had a feeling that somebody was eager to have it fall due. . . . I have, however, insurance against fire! Here is the policy—hide it in a safe place! And now let me ask you a question: Do you know how many candles there are to a pound of vigil lights—the kind you pay seventy-five centimes for?

ADÈLE: Six.

DURAND (*with a gesture toward the package of candles*): How many are there in the package there?

ADÈLE: There are only five.

DURAND: That's because the sixth is standing high up in the attic, very close to . . .

ADÈLE *(screams)*: Lord Jesus!

DURAND *(takes out his watch)*: In five minutes, or not much more—it will have burned down—burned to the end!

ADÈLE: No—no!

DURAND: Yes, yes! Do you see any other way out? Any other light in this darkness? No! And therefore . . . well, so far I have only been talking about things of a material nature. . . . Let us now talk about something else! If Monsieur Durand, your father, should leave this world as an . . . *(He whispers the word.)* . . . as an arsonist . . . that is something that really matters little. . . . But that— all through his life—he has lived as a man of honor. . . that is something that his children should be aware of and know. . . . Very well! I was born in France—and there was no necessity for me to admit it to any rascal who might come along. . . . Shortly before I had reached the conscription age, I fell in love with her whom I later married. . . . In order to be able to marry, we came here to Switzerland and we took out naturalization papers. . . . When the last war broke out, and it looked as if I might be forced to bear arms against the land of my birth, I joined the franc-tireurs, fighting the Germans! I was never a deserter, as you now hear—but your mother fabricated that story out of whole cloth!

ADÈLE: Mother never told lies!

DURAND: There! Now the corpse is come to life again, and it comes between us as it always has done! I can't be the plaintiff against the dead, but I swear that what I am telling you is the truth! Do you hear me—*the truth!* And as far as your dowry is concerned—I mean, the inheritance from your mother—the facts are these: first of all, your mother—through extravagance and childish speculations— wasted every sou of my paternal inheritance, so that I was forced to resign from my position and start this *pension*. In order to provide you with an education, some of the money she inherited from her mother was used up. . . . Would you call that reckless spending by me? Would you? So, you see—this, too, was an untruth. . . .

ADÈLE: Well—that's not what Mother said when she was dying. . . .

DURAND: Then I can only say that your mother lied on her deathbed, as she did all through life! And it is this curse that has followed me like a ghost ever since! Do you realize how you have tortured me innocently with these two lies all these years? I didn't want to inflict anxiety and uneasiness on you young ones and cause you to doubt your mother's good character. . . . That is why I kept quiet! I had carried the cross for her throughout our whole married life. . . . I bore all her shortcomings and defects on my back, took upon me all the consequences of her mistakes—until, at last, I began to feel and believe that I was the guilty one. And it didn't take her long to come to the conclusion, first, that she was without blame, and, finally, that she was the victim! I used to say to her, whenever she had enmeshed herself in some serious muddle, "Blame it on me!" And she did! And I carried the brunt of the load and suffered for it! But, the more deeply she became indebted to me, the more she hated me with all the boundless hate of a debtor! And at last she began to nourish a contempt for me in order to strengthen the delusion within her that she had outwitted me! And, to top it all, she taught you to have contempt for me, too—for she needed support in her weakness! I had thought and hoped that this evil, but weak, soul of hers would die with her. . . . But the evil lingers on: it grows like a disease or an affliction—while what is sound and wholesome lasts only so long; then it stops, and it goes downward. And when I tried to bring about a change in what was a wrong and abnormal way of running the house, I was met with a cry from you: "Mother said so and so!" and "Mother did so and so!" And that is why it was true and why it was right! And so I became nothing but a poor fool in your eyes whenever I did anything good, a miserable creature when I showed any sensibility, a base villain after you had managed to get the upper hand and finally ruined us all!

ADÈLE: It's noble of you to make accusations against her who is dead and therefore can't defend herself!

DURAND (*speaking with great rapidity and growing exaltation*): I am not dead yet—but it won't be long now. . . . Will you defend me when I am gone? No—and you needn't! But help to defend your sisters—and give them, my little chil-

dren, your every attention and thought, Adèle! Keep a
mother's eye on Thérèse—she is the youngest one. . . and
she is full of life—she is quick to do both good and evil—
thoughtless and indiscreet—and she has her weaknesses. . . .
See to it that she gets married soon—try to arrange it so
that she does marry! Now I—I can smell burning straw. . . .

ADÈLE: God Almighty—save us!

DURAND *(he empties the drinking glass)*: He will—He will!
And you must try to find a position for Annette as a
teacher! She must come out into the world and meet nice
people. . . . When the insurance is paid, I want you to
look after the money wisely. I don't want you to be mi-
serly; I want you to outfit the girls so that they are presentable and can be out among people. . . . And don't try
to save anything from the fire—except my personal
papers which lie in my chiffonier—in the middle drawer—
here is the key. . . . The insurance policy you have. . . .
(Smoke is seeping down through the ceiling.) It won't be
long now before everything will be over! We'll soon hear
the bells tolling from St. François. . . . Promise me just
one thing: never speak one word to your sisters about this!
They would not have a moment's peace if they knew!
(He seats himself by the table.) One thing more: never a
word to them about their mother! Her portrait also lies
in the chiffonier. . . . I never told you—because I thought
it was enough to have her invisible spirit hovering about the
house. Give my last farewell to Thérèse, and ask her to
forgive me! And don't forget to buy her the very best you
can find when you go shopping for clothes. . . . You know
her weakness for fine clothes—and where this weakness
might lead her! . . . And tell Annette . . .

> *(A dull tolling of bells is heard from outside. Smoke is
> seen pouring into the room. MONSIEUR DURAND puts
> his head in his hands and lets it sink down on the
> table.)*

ADÈLE: It's burning! It's burning! . . . Father! What's wrong
with you? You'll burn to death!

> *(DURAND lifts his head weakly, pushing aside the drink-
> ing glass with a telling gesture.)*

ADÈLE: You . . . you haven't taken poison? . . . Have you?

DURAND *(confirms her suspicions with a feeble nod of the head)*: You—have—the—policy, haven't you? Tell Thérèse —and Annette . . . *(His head drops on the table.)*

(The bells toll again, followed by the sound of anxious murmurs, excited throngs, and the shuffling of boots against rotted branches and debris, outside.)

CURTAIN

o the memory of Frank L. Davis

Motherlove

(1892)

A Play in One Act

CHARACTERS

THE MOTHER,
  once a prostitute; 42 years old

HÉLÈNE,
  her daughter, an actress; 20 years of age

LISEN,
  aged 18

AUNT AUGUSTA,
  a dresser in a theatre

*The action takes place in a fisherman's cottage
at a seaside resort.*

*A glassed-in veranda in the rear. Be-
yond, a view of a cove in the skerries.*

THE MOTHER *and* AUNT AUGUSTA *each
sit smoking a cigar, while sipping stout
and playing cards.* HÉLÈNE *is seated by
the window. Her eyes are fixed on the
scene outside.*

THE MOTHER: Come here and join us now, Hélène! We
need a third.

HÉLÈNE: Do I have to play cards on a beautiful day like
this?

AUNT AUGUSTA *(sarcastically)*: Always trying to please her
mother!

THE MOTHER: You shouldn't sit there on the veranda! You'll
get burned in the sun!

HÉLÈNE: I'm not getting burned. . . .

THE MOTHER: Well—but it's drafty there! *(To* AUNT AU-
GUSTA.*)* It's your turn to shuffle—here you are! *(She hands
her the deck of cards.)*

HÉLÈNE: May I go for a swim with the girls today?

THE MOTHER: Not without your mother! You know that!

HÉLÈNE: Yes—but the girls know how to swim, and you
don't, Mother. . . .

THE MOTHER: It is not a question of who can swim or who
can't! You know perfectly well I don't allow you to go
out without your mother, Hélène!

HÉLÈNE: I know it only too well! Haven't I heard it from
the time I first was able to understand what you were
saying? . . .

AUNT AUGUSTA: That shows you have a loving mother,

Hélène, always looking out for what is best for her child, doesn't it? It certainly does!

THE MOTHER (*offers her hand to* AUNT AUGUSTA): Thanks! Thank you for those words, Augusta! Whatever I may have been in other ways, well . . . I have certainly been a good, tender mother. . . . I can truthfully say that!

HÉLÈNE: Well—then I suppose it's no use asking you to let me go and play a game of tennis?

AUNT AUGUSTA: You have no right to be impertinent to your mother, young lady! If you don't want to give even that much joy to your dear ones by joining them in their innocent little pleasures, it's nothing short of audacity to ask to be allowed to amuse yourself in other people's company! That's what I think!

HÉLÈNE: Yes—yes—yes! I know every word of that by heart! I've heard it before!

THE MOTHER: Are you being impudent and nasty again? Why don't you do something useful? Don't sit there doing nothing! You are a big girl!

HÉLÈNE: If I am a big girl, then why do you treat me like a child?

THE MOTHER: Because you *act* like a child!

HÉLÈNE: Why reproach me for that? Isn't that just what you want me to be? Isn't it?

THE MOTHER: Tell me, Hélène—I seem to notice that you have become quite worldly-wise of late. . . . Whom have you been keeping company with recently?

HÉLÈNE: With you two, among others!

THE MOTHER: Are you keeping something from your mother?

HÉLÈNE: It's about time I did, I think—isn't it?

AUNT AUGUSTA: Have you no shame, you little brat, talking back to your own mother?

THE MOTHER: Why don't we do something worth while instead of arguing? Why don't you study your part, for instance, and then let me hear you read it?

HÉLÈNE: Our director has told us we mustn't read for anyone—he's afraid we'll learn our rôles the wrong way.

THE MOTHER: That's the thanks I get for trying to help you! No matter what I do, it's wrong, of course, and stupid!

HÉLÈNE: Then why do you want to help? And why should I be blamed for your stupid errors?

AUNT AUGUSTA: You mean to say, you are rebuking your mother for having no education? I have never heard anything so outrageous! Never!

HÉLÈNE (*to* AUNT AUGUSTA): You tell me I mean to do that! I don't mean that at all, and am not doing it! But when Mother wants to teach me to read my part the wrong way, then I must speak out, or I would find myself without an engagement—and then we would be left penniless!

THE MOTHER: Now we find out that you are *supporting* us! But do you know what we have to thank your Aunt Augusta for? Do you know that it was she who took care of us and looked after us when your disreputable father abandoned us both? It was she who supported us! That's why you owe her a debt that you can never repay! Do you know that? Do you?

(HÉLÈNE *is silent*)

THE MOTHER: Do you know that? Answer me!

HÉLÈNE: I am not going to answer you!

THE MOTHER (*in a loud, angry voice*): Can't you answer?

AUNT AUGUSTA: Calm yourself, Amélie! The neighbors can hear us, and they'll start gossiping! Now calm yourself!

THE MOTHER (*to* HÉLÈNE): Now put your clothes on and we'll all go for a walk. . . .

HÉLÈNE: I don't want to go for a walk just now!

THE MOTHER: This is the third day in a row you refuse to take a walk with your mother! (*She seems to be weighing something in her mind.*) Can it be possible? . . . Go outside on the veranda, Hélène, while I have a talk with Aunt Augusta. . . .

(HÉLÈNE *withdraws to the veranda.*)

THE MOTHER: Do you think it could be possible? . . .

AUNT AUGUSTA: What could be possible?

THE MOTHER: That she has heard something?

AUNT AUGUSTA: It doesn't seem possible!

THE MOTHER: Anything is possible! Not that I believe that anyone could be so cruel as to tell the child to her face! I once had a nephew who never found out that his father had committed suicide until he was thirty-six years old. . . . Yes—there is something behind Hélène's changed behavior. . . . Eight days ago I had already noticed that she was ill at ease when we were together—when we went out walking! She only wanted to go where we wouldn't meet anyone; and, when we did meet anybody, she looked away—she was nervous—I couldn't get a word out of her—and she wanted to go straight home! Yes, there—there *is*—something, I am sure!

AUNT AUGUSTA: You mean to say—or could I have misunderstood you?—you mean to say she is ashamed to be seen with you—to be seen with her own mother?

THE MOTHER: That's exactly what I mean!

AUNT AUGUSTA: No—that's going just a little too far! Really!

THE MOTHER: Oh, but the very worst is . . . Can you imagine? When we went on that boat trip, and some of her acquaintances came over to us, she didn't even introduce me to them!

AUNT AUGUSTA: Do you know what I think? She has met someone who has come here during the last eight days! That's what I think. . . . Let's go down to the post office and find out who the latest summer arrivals are!

THE MOTHER: You are right! That's what we'll do! (*She calls out toward the veranda.*) Hélène! We are going down to the post office for a few minutes—look after the house while we are gone! . . .

HÉLÈNE: Yes, Mother! . . .

THE MOTHER (*to* AUNT AUGUSTA): It's exactly as if I had dreamt all this before. . . .

AUNT AUGUSTA: Well—dreams have a way of coming true sometimes. . . . I know! . . . But never the pretty dreams!

(*They go out, left.* HÉLÈNE, *alone, waves to someone outside.* LISEN *comes in. She is dressed for tennis, all in white, and wears a white hat.*)

LISEN: Have they gone out?

HÉLÈNE: Yes, just for a few minutes.

LISEN: Well, what did your mother say?

HÉLÈNE: I didn't dare ask her! She has such a quick temper! . . .

LISEN: Poor Hélène! Aren't you coming along to the picnic? I had so much looked forward to having you! . . . If you only knew how very much I like you! (*She embraces and kisses her.*)

HÉLÈNE: And if you only knew how glad I am to have met you—and to be asked to your home! It has meant so much to me! I have never been out among cultured people before. . . . Can you imagine how I must feel—having been brought up in a hovel, with stale, musty air, and with shady people of uncertain livelihood moving about me, whispering, nagging, arguing, quarreling—where I never received a kind word, much less a caress—and where I was watched as if I had been a criminal, a convict? Oh! I am talking about my own mother—and it hurts me so frightfully, so frightfully! . . . You will have nothing but contempt for me now! . . .

HEN: Nobody can help what their parents are, and . . .

HÉLÈNE: No—but one has to suffer for what they are! There is a saying that we could live with our parents to the end of our days and never really know what kind of human beings they are. I don't doubt there is some truth in that. . . . Yet—even if we found out the worst, we would not believe it.

HEN (*warily*): You have not been hearing any gossip, have you?

HÉLÈNE: Yes—I have. When I was down at the bathhouse the other day I heard, through the partition, a couple making remarks about Mother. Do you know what they said?

HEN: I wouldn't pay any attention to it. . . .

HÉLÈNE: I heard them say that she had been a loose woman! I didn't want to believe it—I still don't believe it—yet I can't help feeling that it is true. Everything points to it—and I feel ashamed, mortified! Ashamed to show myself in her company. Everybody seems to be staring at us—I seem to feel the men ogling us! It's frightful! But can it really be true? Do you think it can be true? Tell me!

HEN: People tell so many lies—but I haven't heard anything. . . .

HÉLÈNE: Yes—you *have* heard something—you *do* know! You just don't want to say anything. And I feel grateful to you for that. Just the same, I couldn't be more unhappy—whether you tell me or not!

HEN: Hélène dear, you must forget what you heard! And come over to our place today. . . . There you will meet

people you will like. My father came home this morning
and he is anxious to meet you. I must tell you that I hav
written to him about you in my letters—and I thin
Cousin Gerhard has done so, too. . . .

HÉLÈNE: You have a father, yes. . . . I had a father, too
when I was young, very young. . . .

LISEN: What became of him?

HÉLÈNE: He left us, Mother says, because he was a good
for-nothing!

LISEN: You can't be so sure of that. . . . However, there
another thing I wanted to tell you. If you'll come wit
us today, you'll meet the director of the Grand The
atre. . . . You can never tell what it may lead to—perhap
he will engage you. . . .

HÉLÈNE: Really?

LISEN: Yes, that's right! He is already interested in yo
You see, Gerhard and I have been talking to him abou
you—and you know how sometimes just a little thing lik
that can decide someone's fate. A personal approach, th
right word at the right time. . . So you simply can't sa
no, unless you want to stand in your own way!

HÉLÈNE: Lisen, my dearest! You ask if I would like to! Yo
know only too well I would like to come. But I never g
anywhere without Mother.

LISEN: Why? Can you give me *one* good reason?

HÉLÈNE: I don't know. . . . She drummed it into me when
was a child, and it still sticks. . . .

LISEN: Has she made you promise her that?

HÉLÈNE: No—she didn't need to. . . . She simply said, *"Th
is what you must say!"* And I have followed her advi
ever since. . . .

LISEN: Do you feel you would be doing her an injustice
you were away from her for a few hours?

HÉLÈNE: I don't think she would miss me especially. . .
When I am at home, she always has something to rema
about. . . . Just the same, it would hurt me to go an
where, if she were not invited. . . .

LISEN: Have you ever thought of bringing her to see us?

HÉLÈNE: No—that hadn't occurred to me. No.

LISEN: Have you ever thought about the day when you mig
get married?

HÉLÈNE: I am never going to marry!

LISEN: Has your mother taught you to say that, too?

HÉLÈNE: She may have. Yes, she has always warned me against men.

LISEN: Married men also?

HÉLÈNE: I suppose so.

LISEN: Listen to me, Hélène! It's about time you become emancipated!

HÉLÈNE: Indeed not! That's one thing I don't want to be— emancipated!

LISEN: Oh, no, I don't mean it the way you mean it! I mean—you need to set yourself free—to stop being dependent on others. You are grown up! And you don't want to ruin your life, do you?

HÉLÈNE: I don't think I can ever learn to be independent. Do you realize that I have been riveted to my mother from the time I was born? Never have I dared to think a thought that was not hers—never could I express a desire that she didn't have! I am aware that it stands in my way, that it is an obstacle . . . but there is nothing I can do about it!

LISEN: But some day—when you no longer have your mother with you—you will be standing quite alone—and you will be helpless for the rest of your life!

HÉLÈNE: I'll have to take that chance. . . .

LISEN: You have no acquaintances of your own—no friends! And none of us can live a solitary life. . . . You must try to find some way out of it! Have you never been in love?

HÉLÈNE: I don't know. I have never dared to think of such things—and Mother doesn't allow young men even to look at me! How about you? Do you ever think about love?

LISEN: Well—if someone should take a liking to me . . . and if I should like him . . .

HÉLÈNE: Then I suppose you will marry your cousin Gerhard.

LISEN: No, I could never marry him! He is not in love with me. . . .

HÉLÈNE (*surprised, quizzically*): No?

LISEN: No! He is in love with you!

HÉLÈNE (*unbelieving*): With me?

LISEN: Yes! And one reason for my coming here is this: he wants to ask if he may call on you. . . .

HÉLÈNE: Here? Oh, no—that would never do! You don't think I would want to step between you two, do you? And you don't imagine I could possibly take your place in his affections—you, who are so beautiful and charming? . . . *(She takes* LISEN's *hands in hers.)* What a beautiful hand you have! And such a dainty wrist! I looked at your feet, Lisen dear, the last time we went swimming. . . .

*(*LISEN *sits down.* HÉLÈNE *kneels at her feet.)*

What a sweet little foot—not a bruised nail! And such well-shaped toes—as lovely and pink as a baby's . . . *(*HÉLÈNE *kisses* LISEN's *foot.)* You are truly a thoroughbred—and so much finer and nobler than I!

LISEN: You must stop this now, and don't talk such nonsense! *(She rises.)* If you only knew. . . . But I . . .

HÉLÈNE: And I am sure you are just as good as you are beautiful. . . . We—who only see your kind from a distance—with your fair, delicate faces, free from the ravages of poverty and need, and untouched by the ugly scars that envy marks us with. . . .

LISEN: Stop it, Hélène! One would almost think that you had taken a romantic fancy to me!

HÉLÈNE: That's just it! I have! I've been told that I look a little like you—as a blue anemone resembles a white one—and that's why I see in you my better self: what I would like to be, yet never *can* be. . . . You crossed my path like a shining light—white as an angel—during these last days of summer. . . . Now autumn is here, and the day after tomorrow we go back to the city. . . . And then we'll never see each other again. . . . You will never be able to lift me up out of my drab surroundings—while I might drag you down; and that is something I would not want to do! I want to put you on a pinnacle—away up high, and so far away that I can't see your shortcomings! And so, Lisen, my first and only friend—goodbye. . . .

LISEN: Oh, no—I have heard enough! —Hélène! Do you know who I am?

*(*HÉLÈNE *is puzzled.)*

Very well—I am your sister!

HÉLÈNE: You—my sister? . . . What are you saying?

LISEN: You and I have the same father!

HÉLÈNE: You are my sister! My little sister! . . . But then who is my father? I assume he is a naval commander, since that's what your father is. . . . How stupid I am! But he is married now—he must be, of course, since . . . Is he good to you? He was not so good to Mother, you know. . . .

LISEN: How do you know? —But aren't you glad that you have found a little sister now? One who doesn't cry all the time? . . .

HÉLÈNE: Of course I am—I am so happy I don't know what to say! . . .

(They embrace.)

But I can't be as glad as I would like to be, for I don't know what will happen now! What will Mother say? And what will happen when we meet my father?

LISEN: Let me take care of your mother! She can't have gone very far, I imagine. . . . But be sure to keep in the background until you are needed. . . . Now, my little one, come and give me a kiss first!

(They kiss each other.)

HÉLÈNE: My sister! How strange that word sounds—as strange as the word "father"—since I have not used it before. . . .

LISEN: Let's not chatter aimlessly now. Let's stick to the matter at hand. Do you believe that your mother would refuse to let you go, if you were invited to see us? Your sister and your father?

HÉLÈNE: Without Mother, you mean? Oh, she hates your— she hates my father—hates him indescribably!

LISEN: But suppose she had no cause to hate him? If you only knew how full of lies and delusions the world is! And of errors, mistakes, and misapprehensions! My father once told me about a fellow cadet of his when he first went into the navy. . . . A gold watch disappeared from the cabin of one of the officers, and the young cadet was suspected of being the thief, God only knows why. . . . His comrades soon shunned him, and this embittered him so, changed him to such a degree, that it became impossible to have anything to do with him. He was constantly getting into fistfights, and he was finally forced to leave the service. Two years later the thief was apprehended—he was a boatswain. But what restitution could possibly be made to the innocent young man, since he had never been anything but a suspect? Yet the suspicion hung over him for the rest of his life, even though his innocence had been established. A malicious nickname given the youngster, he never lost, either! The whole evil thing had grown up like a house, his bad reputation was built up and expanded—and when they tried to tear down the false foundation, the building remained, dangling in the air like the castle in *A Thousand and One Nights*. . . . So you see what can happen in this world! But even stranger things can happen! Take the case of the instrument-maker in the city of Arboga, for instance! He was branded an arsonist because someone had set fire to his place of business! . . . Or the case of a certain Andersson. This man was disgraced by being given the nickname of Andersson the Thief, because he had been the *victim* of a notorious theft!

HÉLÈNE: What you mean to say is that my father is not the kind of man I *think* he is?

LISEN: That's exactly what I mean.

HÉLÈNE: That's how I have seen him sometimes in my dreams—after having lost the remembrance of him. . . . Isn't he quite tall—and hasn't he a dark beard—and large blue eyes—a sailor's eyes?

LISEN: Yes—he is not unlike that.

HÉLÈNE: And . . . wait. . . . Now I remember. . . . You see this watch? You see this tiny compass attached to the chain? Where North is, the dial has an eye engraved on it. . . . Who gave it to me? Do you know?

LISEN: My father gave it to you. I was with him when he bought it.

HÉLÈNE: Then it is he I have seen so many times in the theatre, when I've been playing. . . . He would always sit in a box to the right of the stage and keep his opera glasses fixed on me. . . . I didn't dare mention it to Mother—she was always trying to keep me sheltered. . . . One time he threw a bouquet of flowers across the footlights—but Mother promptly burned them. . . . Could that have been he, do you think?

LISEN: Yes, that was he . . . And, believe me, he has kept
an eye on you all these years—as closely as he watches
his compass needle. . . .

HÉLÈNE: And now you tell me I am going to meet him—
that he would like to see me? This is almost like a fairy
tale. . . .

LISEN: But now it's no longer a fairy tale! I hear your
mother coming—she is here. . . . You stay out of sight—
let me come under fire first! . . .

HÉLÈNE: I feel as if something terrible were going to happen! I can feel it! Why can't there be peace and goodwill
among human beings? Oh, if this were only over with!
If only Mother would try to be good! . . . I'll say a prayer
to God, asking Him to make her good. . . . But I wonder
whether He can—or perhaps He does not wish to. I
don't know. . . .

LISEN: He both can and will—if you will only have faith . . .
a little faith in luck, at least—and in yourself, in your
own ability. . . .

HÉLÈNE: Ability? To do what? To be inconsiderate and in-
sincere? I can't do that, I can't! And we won't enjoy our
happiness if it is bought with the tears of others—not for
very long. . . .

LISEN: Quick—hurry up—go outside!

HÉLÈNE: I don't understand how you can think this will
end happily.

LISEN: Ssh!

(HÉLÈNE *withdraws to the veranda.* THE MOTHER *enters.*)

LISEN: My dear Mrs. . . .

THE MOTHER: Miss, if you please . . .

LISEN: Your daughter . . .

THE MOTHER: Yes, I have a daughter—even though I am not
married. . . . I am not the only one—and I am not
ashamed of it. . . . What is it you want?

LISEN: I really came to ask permission for Hélène to come
to a picnic that some of the summer guests have arranged.

THE MOTHER: Hasn't Hélène told you her answer?

LISEN: Yes, she answered quite correctly that I should see
you. . . .

THE MOTHER: That's not a frank answer. (*Goes to the ve-*

randa door and calls to HÉLÈNE.) Hélène! My child! Would
you like to accept an invitation without your mother being
asked?

HÉLÈNE *(enters)*: Yes, if you have no objection. . . .

THE MOTHER: If I have no objection! Why should I make
a decision for you—a big girl like you? You must tell this
young lady yourself what you want to do. If you would
like to see your mother sit shamefully alone at home,
while you are out having a good time . . . if you would
like to have the guests at the picnic ask you where your
mother is—so that you won't have to say, "Mother was
not invited because of this and that and so forth and so
on." . . . Make your own decision now!

LISEN: Madam, let us not quibble over words. I know what
Hélène would like to do in this case. And I also know
your habit of making her say what you want her to say.
If you really care as much for your daughter as you say
you do, you would do everything that was for her own
good—even if you thought it humiliating for you.

THE MOTHER: Listen to me, my child! I know who you are
and what your name is—even if I haven't had the honor
of being introduced to you! I just wonder if you—at your
age—can teach me anything, at my age. . . .

LISEN: Who knows? For the past six years—since my mother died—I have spent my time trying to bring up my
younger brothers and sisters. . . . And I have found that
there are some people who can never learn anything from
life, no matter how old they may be.

THE MOTHER: Just what are you trying to tell me, young
lady?

LISEN: What I want to tell you is this! Your daughter has
an opportunity to come out among people—and, perhaps,
either to advance her career and gain recognition, or to
become engaged to and marry a young man of a good,
respectable family. . . .

THE MOTHER: All that sounds fine, but where do I come in?

LISEN: We are not discussing you now—we are discussing
your daughter! Can't you, for one moment, think of her
without thinking about yourself?

THE MOTHER: Let me tell you something, miss! When I
think about myself, I am also thinking about my daughter,
for she has learned to love her mother. . . .

LISEN: I don't believe a word you say! She has clung to you merely because you kept her apart from everybody—and because she has to have somebody to cling to after you tore her away from her father. . . .

THE MOTHER: What's that you say?

LISEN: I am saying that you took her away from her father, after he refused to marry you! Refused to marry you because you had been unfaithful to him! You refused to let him see his own child—and you took revenge for your crime on both her and her father!

THE MOTHER: Hélène! Don't believe a word she says! Oh, to think that I would have to live to see this happen—to have a stranger come into my home and disgrace me before my own child!

HÉLÈNE (steps forward; to LISEN): You mustn't say anything bad about my mother! . . .

LISEN: I can't help it—I simply can't! I have to defend my father! . . . But I can tell that this conversation is nearing its end. . . . I merely wish to give you a piece of advice before leaving. Get rid of that bawdy woman, that procuress, who lives in this house under the name of Aunt Augusta! That is, if you don't want to destroy your daughter's reputation completely! That is point number one! Then get together all your receipts for money given you by my father for Hélène's upbringing and education—for you will soon be asked to account for every penny! That's point number two! And now I shall give you an extra piece of advice. Stop disgracing your daughter with your company on the streets—and above all, at the theatre . . . or she will soon have every door to advancement shut to her! And then you would be just as quick to sell her charms as you in the past have been eager to buy back your lost reputation at the expense of her future!

(THE MOTHER *collapses*.)

HÉLÈNE (to LISEN): Leave this house! You—for whom nothing is sacred—not even motherhood!

LISEN: Sacred—yes . . . As sacred as the boys are when they spit out their prayers! That's holiness, too!

HÉLÈNE: It looks to me now as though your only reason for coming here was to tear down, not to mend. . . .

LISEN: Yes—I came here to see my father given restitution

—my father who was as innocent as the man accused of arson, you remember. . . . I also came here to raise you up—after you had been made the victim of a woman who can only be rehabilitated if she withdraws to some place where no one will molest her, and where she won't bother others. That is why I came here. And now it is done—so, goodbye!

THE MOTHER: Don't go yet, miss! I have something I want to say to you first! You didn't come here just to speak about . . . what you just said. . . . You came to ask Hélène to your home, didn't you?

LISEN: I did, yes. We wanted her to meet the director of the Grand Theatre . . . he is interested in Hélène.

THE MOTHER: You really mean it? The director himself! And you didn't say one word about that! Why, certainly . . . certainly Hélène will come! Yes, alone—without me!

(HÉLÈNE *makes a confused gesture of disapproval.*)

LISEN: Well, now—now I see—that you are human, after all. Hélène, your mother is giving you permission to come! Do you hear?

HÉLÈNE: But I don't care to go now. . . .

THE MOTHER: What nonsense is this?

HÉLÈNE: No! I won't fit in there! I won't feel at home among people who have contempt for my mother!

THE MOTHER: Stop acting silly! Do you want to stand in your own way and ruin your career? Put your clothes on and get dressed right away, so that you are presentable. . . .

HÉLÈNE: No—I am not going! I can't leave you alone, Mother—now that I know everything. I can never be happy again. . . . I can never have any faith in anything. . . .

LISEN (*to* THE MOTHER): Now you are reaping the fruits of what you have sown. . . . If ever a man should come along and marry your daughter, you will be sitting alone in your old age and have time to regret your indiscretions! Goodbye! (*She goes over to* HÉLÈNE *and kisses her on the forehead.*) Goodbye, my sister!

HÉLÈNE: Goodbye!

LISEN: Look me in the eye and let me see a gleam of hope!

HÉLÈNE: I can't. And I can't thank you for your good intentions, either. You have done me more harm than you think. . . . I was slumbering in the sunshine on a wooded hillside, and you woke me with a snakebite.

LISEN: Go back to sleep, and I'll come and wake you with a song and with flowers. . . . Goodnight now! And sleep well! *(She leaves.)*

THE MOTHER: An angel of light dressed in white, ha! Why, she is a regular demon! A regular demon! That's what she is! And you! What a fool you are! What kind of silly nonsense is this? You don't have to be so sensitive when people behave so brutally!

HÉLÈNE: But when I think of all that you have told me! So much that is untrue! And making me tell lies about my father all these years. . . .

THE MOTHER: Ah! What's the good of worrying about the snows of yesteryear?

HÉLÈNE: And then . . . there is Aunt Augusta. . . .

THE MOTHER: Keep quiet! Aunt Augusta is a thoroughly fine woman, and you owe her a great deal. . . .

HÉLÈNE: That isn't true, either! . . . You know that it was my father who paid for my education!

THE MOTHER: Yes—but I had to live, too, didn't I? You are so petty, so small-minded. And vindictive, too. Can't you overlook an innocent little lie? Ah, there is Aunt Augusta! Come now, let's enjoy ourselves as best we can—in our own small way. . . .

AUNT AUGUSTA *(enters gustily)*: Why, yes—it was really he! You see, I wasn't so very wrong, after all, was I?

THE MOTHER: Yes—but let's not bother about that worthless creature anymore. . . .

HÉLÈNE: Don't call him that, Mother! You know it isn't true!

AUNT AUGUSTA: What isn't true?

HÉLÈNE: Come on and let us play a game of cards! I can't pull down the walls it has taken you two so many years to build up! Let's play! *(She seats herself at the card table and starts shuffling the cards.)*

THE MOTHER: Well . . . I am glad to see you are being a sensible girl at last!

CURTAIN

To Sven Åhman

Playing with
Fire

(1892)

A Comedy in One Act

CHARACTERS

THE FATHER,
  60 years old; a rentier

THE MOTHER,
  58 years old

THE SON,
  27 years old; a painter

HIS WIFE,
  24 years old

THE FRIEND,
  26 years old

THE COUSIN,
  a girl of 20

*The action takes place at a seaside resort,
in the summer, during the 1890s.*

A glass veranda, furnished like a drawing room, with a door leading to a garden. There is also a door on either side.

THE SON *is seated, painting. His* WIFE *enters, dressed in a morning frock.*

THE SON: Is he up yet?

THE WIFE: Axel! How should I know?

THE SON: I thought you might have looked.

THE WIFE: Have you no shame? If I were not convinced that you could never be jealous, I might suspect that you were!

THE SON: And if I didn't know that you could never be unfaithful, I might begin to have doubts.

THE WIFE: Why? Why just now?

THE SON: You heard what I said. I said *if.* . . . And, as far as our friend Axel is concerned, you know, of course, that I value his company more than anyone else's; and since you, fortunately, share my sympathy for the poor distressed soul, then everything is well, of course.

THE WIFE: He is an unfortunate human being, but I must say he behaves rather strangely at times. Why, for example, did he depart so suddenly last summer—without even saying goodbye—and leaving his belongings behind? . . .

THE SON: Yes, that is a curious story! I thought he was in love with cousin Adèle.

THE WIFE: You did?

THE SON: Yes, but I don't any more. Mama was under the impression that he had gone back to his wife and children.

THE WIFE: What's that you say? Aren't they divorced?

THE SON: Not yet—not completely . . . but he expects the final decree to come through any day.

THE WIFE: You think he was actually in love with Adèle? And you didn't say a word about it to me? —Yes, if they *could* get together, I think it would be a good thing.

THE SON: Who knows? Adèle is a bore. . . .

THE WIFE: Adèle? Then you don't know her.

THE SON: She has a fine figure, but whether she is passionate—that is something I can't say.

THE WIFE: *If* she is passionate!

THE SON: Is she?

THE WIFE: Well—once she breaks out . . .

THE SON: No—really?

THE WIFE: That seems to interest you. . . .

THE SON: In a way, yes.

THE WIFE: In which way?

THE SON: You know that she modeled for me when I did the painting of "The Girl Swimmer.". . .

THE WIFE: Yes, of course I know that. Who hasn't modeled for you? But I don't see why you should show your sketches to every person who comes along. . . . Ah, here is the old lady!

(THE MOTHER *enters. She is carelessly dressed, wears a large Japanese hat, and carries a shopping bag.*)

THE SON: You look like the devil himself today, Mama!

THE MOTHER: How polite you are!

THE WIFE: Knut is terrible, I must say. But what have you been shopping for?

THE MOTHER: Oh, I bought some fine flounders. . . .

THE SON (*rummaging in the shopping bag*): Oh, hell! —But what is this? Wild ducklings?

THE WIFE: They could have a little more meat on them. . . . Feel here—under the breast. . . .

THE SON: I am an admirer of beautiful breasts.

THE WIFE: Shame on you!

THE MOTHER: Well, so your mutual friend came to visit you again last evening?

THE SON: Our friend? He is Kerstin's friend! She is completely mad about him! I thought they were going to kiss each other last evening when he arrived!

THE MOTHER: You must not tease like that, Knut, for—he who plays with fire . . .

THE SON: I know—but I am too old, you see! And, besides, do I look as though I had reason to be jealous?

THE MOTHER: Love has nothing to do with looks. . . . or does it, Kerstin?

THE WIFE: I haven't the faintest idea what you are driving at . . .

THE MOTHER (*pats her gently on the cheek*): Kerstin! Be careful, Kerstin!

THE SON: Kerstin is so terribly innocent, and you must not come here and spoil her, you old frump.

THE WIFE: You have such an abominable way of jesting, one never knows when to take you seriously.

THE SON: I always speak seriously.

THE WIFE: I can almost believe you, for you never even smile when you say these horrid things.

THE MOTHER: I believe you are both in a quarrelsome mood this morning. Didn't you sleep well?

THE SON: We didn't sleep at all.

THE MOTHER: Shame on you! Shame on you! —No, now I must go, otherwise Papa will give me a scolding.

THE SON: Papa! Yes—where is he?

THE MOTHER: I suppose he's gone out for his usual morning walk with Adèle.

THE SON: And you are not jealous, Mother?

THE MOTHER: Huh!

THE SON: Well, but I am!

THE MOTHER: Jealous of whom, if I may ask?

THE SON: Of the old man, of course.

THE MOTHER: Now you see, Kerstin, what a nice family you have come into!

THE WIFE: Yes, if I didn't know Knut as well as I do, and if I didn't already know that artists are a breed apart, I might have difficulty telling exactly where I belong at times.

THE SON: Yes, I am an artist, but Papa and Mama are prosaic and unimaginative.

THE MOTHER (*without any sign of malice*): It's you who are prosaic and unimaginative; for, as old as you are, you never earned your own bread. And certainly your father was neither prosaic nor unimaginative when he built this house for a good-for-nothing like you!

THE SON: Well, I am not the only son for nothing! You had better be on your way now, or you will get your scolding right here—and I don't care to listen to it! Hurry up now! The old man is coming!

THE MOTHER: Then I'll go out this way. *(She leaves.)*

THE SON: There is a damnable draft here in this house—from two directions!

THE WIFE: Yes—I wish your father and mother would leave us a little more to ourselves. And this idea of having our meals with them and not letting us run the house.

THE SON: Precisely as crumbs are put out for the sparrows on the window ledge—so that one can have the pleasure of watching them eat!

THE WIFE *(in a listening attitude)*: You must be quiet now! Try to put the old man in a good humor so that we don't have to listen to the usual morning tirade.

THE SON: I only wish I could! But he doesn't always respond to my subtle jokes!

(THE FATHER *enters, dressed in a white waistcoat and a black velvet jacket, wearing a rose in his lapel buttonhole. Adèle,* THE COUSIN, *enters. She strolls about the room, then starts to dust.)*

THE FATHER *(without removing his hat)*: It is cold these mornings. . . .

THE SON: So I notice.

THE FATHER: You notice . . . ?

THE SON: I see that your head is cold, anyway!

(THE FATHER *gives him a look of contempt.)*

THE WIFE: How rude you are, Knut!

THE FATHER: A fool creates grief for himself, and the father of a fool can have no happiness.

THE SON: Where do you get all your sayings?

THE WIFE *(to* THE COUSIN): This room has already been dusted today, my dear.

THE FATHER: Wise women build the home, but a fool can tear it down by his stupidity.

THE SON: Do you hear that, Adèle?

THE COUSIN: You mean me?

THE SON: Yes! Tell me, where do you find this proverb: "A beautiful woman without chastity is like a sow with a gold bucket on her snout"?

THE WIFE: Knut! Behave!

THE FATHER: You had a visitor come to see you last evening. He came late, didn't he?

THE SON: Did you think it was too late?

THE FATHER: I didn't think anything! But it seems to me a young man could choose a more fitting time for paying a visit.

THE SON: So-o? Then you do think it was too late!

THE FATHER: Had you invited him beforehand?

THE SON: What kind of inquisition is this? Have you brought the thumbscrews with you?

THE FATHER: No, you have taken charge of them! For I have merely to ask a question, and you threaten to leave —despite the fact that I built this house for you so that we may at least see you during the summer. And when one is as old as I am, one feels a need of living for others.

THE SON: Why, you are not an old man yet! With that rose in your buttonhole, one would suspect that you had been out courting.

THE FATHER: There is a limit—even to jesting! What do you think, Kerstin?

THE WIFE: Oh, Knut is terrible! And if I didn't know that he doesn't mean anything by it . . .

THE FATHER: If he doesn't mean anything by what he says— then he is an idiot! *(He regards a newly started portrait of* THE FRIEND.*)* Who is this supposed to be?

THE SON: Don't you see it is my friend—our friend?

THE FATHER: He has an unpleasant expression. He looks like a questionable character to me—judging by this portrait.

THE WIFE: Oh, but he isn't!

THE FATHER: A person who has no religion is a bad human being, and a person who breaks up his marriage is also bad.

THE WIFE: But he didn't—he had it dissolved by the court.

THE FATHER: There was a time when Knut didn't speak too highly of your friend. How does it happen that he now is so fond of him?

THE SON: Because I didn't really know him then. But I do now. —Are you through with your morning broadside?

THE FATHER: Have you ever heard this proverb . . .

THE SON: I have heard all your proverbs and all your anecdotes!

THE FATHER: There is a time for loving—and there is a time for hating! Good morning! *(He goes out.)*

THE WIFE *(to* THE COUSIN, *who is about to water the plants)*: The flowers have been watered, my dear!

THE COUSIN: Why do you call me "dear" when you know you don't like me? You hate me!

THE WIFE: I don't hate you, even though you are the cause of all the dissension in our family.

THE COUSIN: Ah, so now *you* are starting, too?

THE WIFE: I wish I could see some sort of kindliness back of your solicitude about my home, but there is always a touch of reproach in your attitude. . . . And, whenever you do anything for me, you seem to be finding fault.

THE COUSIN: You feel that way because you neglect your home and your child. But I have only one thought in mind—and that is to be of some use here, so that I shan't feel as if I were living on charity. But you—you—you . . .

THE SON *(goes over to* THE COUSIN *and regards her)*: You have a temper? Then you must also have passion!

THE WIFE: What have you to do with her passion?

THE COUSIN: Yes—if one is poor one must have no likes or dislikes, no opinions, no will, no passions! But anyone who makes a rich marriage and has a fine wedding can do whatever he or she wants, can live any way they want, crawl into a comfortable bed and do whatever they like—day and night!

THE WIFE: Shame on you!

THE COUSIN: But look out for me, you . . . ! I have ears—and eyes to see with. . . . *(She leaves.)*

THE SON: I believe the devil is loose today!

THE WIFE: Not yet, but he might get loose. Better watch out for that girl! Has it ever occurred to you that your mother might die?

THE SON: Well, what of it?

THE WIFE: Then your father might marry again.

THE SON: Marry Adèle?

THE WIFE: Yes.

THE SON: Bah! We would be able to put a stop to that, I should think. . . . In other words, she would then be my stepmother, and her children would come in for a share of the inheritance.

THE WIFE: I have heard that your father has already made his will in Adèle's favor.

THE SON: What do you think about their relationship?

THE WIFE: Everything—and nothing! But one thing is certain: he is in love with the girl.

THE SON: In love with her! Perhaps—but that is all.

THE WIFE: So much so that he was already jealous of Axel a year ago.

THE SON: Well—can't we get the two of them to marry, then?

THE WIFE: Axel is not so easy to tie down.

THE SON: He—who catches fire so easily—like all those who have been married before?

THE WIFE: Oh, but it would be a pity. . . . He is much too good for a demon like her.

THE SON: I don't know what is happening this year, but it seems to me as if the air had thickened. I feel as though a storm were brewing, and I am beginning to have a terrible longing to go abroad.

THE WIFE: Yes, but you don't seem to be able to sell any of your paintings—and, if we leave here, your father will withdraw his support from us. We must talk this over with Axel. He always knows how to find a way out for others, even though he can't take care of himself.

THE SON: I don't know whether it is wise to let outsiders know too much about one's family troubles. . . .

THE WIFE: You call our one and only friend an outsider?

THE SON: Well, be that as it may—one is always closer to one's own. . . . And besides—I don't know. . . . The old man has a habit of saying, "Always treat your friends as though they were to become your enemies."

THE WIFE: So-o, now you are quoting your father's sayings! But he also has another horrible saying: "Fear him whom you love!"

THE SON: Yes, he is incorrigible once he gets started!

THE WIFE (*calling outside*): Well, at last! (*She goes toward* AXEL.) Good morning, deep sleeper!

(THE FRIEND *enters. He is wearing a light summer suit with a blue tie and tennis shoes.*)

THE SON: Good morning to you!

THE FRIEND: Good morning, my good friends! You haven't been waiting for me, have you?

THE WIFE: We certainly have!

THE SON: My wife has been in absolute agony because you didn't get any sleep last night!

THE FRIEND (*puzzled*): How so? How so?

THE SON (*to his* WIFE): You see how shy he is!

(THE WIFE *looks fixedly and curiously at* THE FRIEND.)

THE FRIEND: It's a beautiful morning—and, after having slept under the roof of two such happy human beings as you, life can still smile on one!

THE SON: Do you really think we are very happy?

THE FRIEND: Yes—and one who is doubly happy is your father, for he has his children and grandchildren with whom he can relive a happy life. Few people are blessed with that in their old age.

THE SON: You must not be envious!

THE FRIEND: I am not. On the contrary, I take delight in seeing how pleasantly life can turn out for some. . . . It gives me hope that it may treat me more kindly in the future. Particularly when one considers what a painful life your father has had to endure: financial ruin, being exiled from his country and ostracized by his family . . .

THE SON: . . . and now rich in property and other worldly goods, his son happily married. . . . Don't you think so?

THE FRIEND: Yes, there is no doubt about that!

THE SON: Tell me—I could swear you were in love with my wife last year. Weren't you?

THE FRIEND: No, I can't say that I was. But I dare say I was more than a little fond of her. But I am all over that now.

THE WIFE: I imagine you are very fickle, aren't you?

THE FRIEND: Yes, as far as my romances are concerned—luckily—for me!

THE SON: But why did you leave us so precipitately last summer? Could it have been because of that other lady—or perhaps because of Adèle?

THE FRIEND (*confused*): Your question is a little blunt, a little indiscreet.

THE SON (*gloating*): It was because of Adèle! You see, Kerstin? You see?

THE WIFE: Why should he be scared of her?

THE FRIEND: The ladies don't scare me. . . . I am only afraid of my own feelings for them!

THE SON: You have an exceptional ability to wriggle out of things. One never knows just where you are.

THE FRIEND: Why should you keep a closer eye on me than on someone else?

THE SON: Do you know what my father remarked about your portrait just a moment ago?

THE WIFE: Knut!

THE SON: He said you looked like a questionable character.

THE FRIEND: It could be, of course, that the portrait does resemble the original. I really am very wicked just now.

THE WIFE: You are always bragging about how wicked you are. . . .

THE FRIEND: Perhaps I do that to cover up.

THE WIFE: Oh, no—you are a good fellow, much better than you would like people to think you are. But you must not frighten your friends away from you.

THE FRIEND: Are you afraid of me?

THE WIFE: Yes, occasionally—when I can't understand you.

THE SON: You must get married again—that's all there is to it.

THE FRIEND: All there is to it? And to whom?

THE SON: To Adèle, for instance.

THE FRIEND: I beg you not to talk about this any more.

THE SON: Aha! We did touch the tender spot! So-o, it was Adèle, after all!

THE FRIEND: And now, my friends—now perhaps I ought to go and change, put on a dark coat. . . .

THE WIFE: No—you are not going to do anything of the kind. That suit is perfectly lovely, and Adèle will fall in love with you in it.

THE SON: You hear? My wife thinks you are charming.

THE WIFE: Is there anything so terrible about saying that a man's suit is becoming to him?

THE SON: It is at least a little unusual for a woman to pay compliments to a man. But then, of course, we are not ordinary people.

THE FRIEND: Will you come with me later when I go out to look for a room?

THE WIFE: What's that? Aren't you going to stay here with us?

THE FRIEND: Why, no! That was not my intention at all.

THE SON: Well, well, well!

THE WIFE: Why don't you want to stay here with us? Why?

THE FRIEND: I don't know—I think you should be left to yourselves. And we might get tired of one another.

THE WIFE: Are you tired of us already? . . . Now you listen to me—it simply won't do for you to stay in the village. Then people would certainly have something to talk about. . . .

THE FRIEND: To talk about? Talk about what?

THE WIFE: Heavens, you know how people make up stories. . . .

THE SON: You just stay here, that's all there is to it! Let them talk! If you stay here, you are, of course, my wife's lover; if you take a room in the village, then naturally you must have committed an indiscretion, and been chased out of the house. And, when all is said and done, I think it's more to your credit to be taken for my wife's lover. What do you think?

THE FRIEND: You express yourself plainly enough, but in this case I would prefer to consider what is correct, as far as your interests are concerned.

THE WIFE: I think you must have some secret reason that you don't care to tell us about.

THE FRIEND: Quite frankly—I don't dare! Yes, yes—yes, it is so easy to become part and parcel of the existence of others, to share their happiness with them, until finally one's feelings are interwoven with theirs—and then it becomes a hardship to separate.

THE SON: Then why separate? All nonsense aside, you are staying with us! Now offer your arm to my wife, and we'll go for a walk.

(THE FRIEND *offers* THE WIFE *his arm with a sign of embarrassment.*)

THE WIFE: I believe you are shaking! He is shaking, Knut!

THE SON: Why, you make a very nice, attractive couple! But you are right, he is really shaking. If you have a chill, then stay at home!

THE FRIEND: If you don't mind, I should like to stay here and read the newspapers.

THE WIFE: You most certainly may. And I'll send Adèle in to keep you company. Knut and I are only going out to do some shopping. (*She waves to someone outside.*) Come here, Adèle! I have something for you!

(ADÈLE *enters.*)

THE FRIEND: Would you care to keep me company while our friends go shopping?

THE COUSIN: Keep you company? Are you afraid of the dark?

THE FRIEND: Terribly!

(THE SON *and* THE WIFE *leave.* THE FRIEND *makes certain that they are alone.*)

As a relative, you are one of the family. Now that we are alone, I would like to take this opportunity to talk with you in confidence. May I?

THE COUSIN: Do!

THE FRIEND: You know how fond I am of my two young friends. . . . You smile . . . and I know what is in your mind. I admit that Kerstin, being a young woman, has a certain attraction for me; but I assure you that I know how to discipline my feelings—and only for a passing instant did I have to worry about holding on to myself.

THE COUSIN: It doesn't surprise me in the least that you should be smitten by Kerstin. Knowing her as I do, I realize she has the ability to captivate. But how you can find Knut's company so attractive is something I cannot understand. Why, he is just an insignificant nobody, much inferior to you in talent and experience.

THE FRIEND: You mean to say he is a child—nothing but a child. But that is exactly what I find so restful, after having spent the whole winter associating with people who do nothing but argue and talk.

THE COUSIN: Playing with children is a restful pursuit that may prove tiring, but you never get tired of Knut. Why is it that you don't?

THE FRIEND: I haven't given it a thought, but you seem to have. What do you think?

THE COUSIN: That you—without being conscious of it—are in love with Kerstin.

THE FRIEND: I don't think I am, for I love them as though the two of them were one person; I don't enjoy their individual company as much as being with both of them. If I were constantly alone with only one of them, it would drive me from both! But suppose it were true, as you say, that I am in love with Kerstin—what would it matter, so long as I hid my feelings?

THE COUSIN: Feelings have a habit of communicating themselves, and fire spreads quickly.

THE FRIEND: That may be, but I see no danger of that here. You can rest assured that I, who have only recently been through all the tortures of a divorce, would neither care to experience another nor to be the cause of one. Besides— Kerstin loves her Knut.

THE COUSIN: Loves? She has never been in love. Their love is merely a passive conjugal liking. But Knut has a passionate nature, and someday he may grow tired of strawberries and milk. . . .

THE FRIEND: You must have been engaged once—weren't you?

THE COUSIN: What makes you think that?

THE FRIEND: You seem to be so very familiar with things of this sort! And so I am going to probe a little deeper. It seems to me there has been quite a change here since last year.

THE COUSIN: In which way?

THE FRIEND: There is a different atmosphere here, I find— a different way of talking and thinking. . . . There is something here that disturbs me, makes me feel uneasy. . . .

THE COUSIN: You have noticed that, too, have you? Yes, it's a strange family! The father is inactive—lives on the interest of his money—does nothing but clip coupons; the son is an idler, who has been given a yearly income to live on. They eat, sleep, and spend their time as pleasantly as they can, biding their time until their departure from this earth. No aim in life—no ambition or aspirations— no passion; but you hear much of the wisdom of Solomon the Preacher! Have you noticed that there is one expression you hear every other hour in this house? "He is an evil creature!" It is served up like bread—with everything.

THE FRIEND: It is remarkable how well you speak. And how keen your observation . . .

THE COUSIN: Yes—like my hatred!

THE FRIEND: Anyone who hates as you do should also be able to love.

THE COUSIN: H'm.

THE FRIEND: Adèle, now that we have been speaking ill of our friends, you and I must be friends. Whether we wish to or not . . .

THE COUSIN: Whether we wish to or not!

THE FRIEND: Let us shake hands on that! But you must promise not to hate—me!

THE COUSIN (*takes his hands, which he holds out to her*): How cold your hands are!

(THE WIFE *appears momentarily in the doorway.*)

THE FRIEND: Yours are so much warmer!

THE COUSIN: Sh! Kerstin is here!

THE FRIEND: Then we'll have to continue our conversation some other time. . . .

(*There is a silence.* THE WIFE *enters the veranda.*)

THE WIFE: How quiet you are, suddenly! Did I disturb you?

THE COUSIN: Not at all. But perhaps I am disturbing you?

THE WIFE (*handing* THE FRIEND *a letter*): Here is a letter for you. I can see it's from a woman.

(THE FRIEND *looks at the envelope and turns pale.*)

How pale you suddenly are! If you still feel cold, I'll lend you my shawl. (*She takes off her shawl and puts it over his shoulders.*)

THE FRIEND: Thank you! It keeps me warm, at least!

THE COUSIN: Perhaps you would like to have a pillow under your feet, too?

THE WIFE: It would be better if you asked the maid to make a fire in his room upstairs. Whenever it rains for a couple of days, the dampness from the sea immediately penetrates into the house.

THE COUSIN: Yes, you are right.

THE FRIEND: Oh, but—must you go to so much trouble just for my sake?

THE COUSIN: Why, it's no trouble at all! (*She leaves.*)

THE FRIEND: How quiet it suddenly became!

THE WIFE: Just like a moment ago. What secrets were you two telling each other?

THE FRIEND: I had an opportunity to unburden myself a little, so I took advantage of it.

THE WIFE: Unburden yourself to me a little, then! You are unhappy. . . .

THE FRIEND: Above all, because I can't work. . . .

THE WIFE: And you can't work because . . .

THE FRIEND: Because . . . ?

THE WIFE: Are you still in love with your wife?

THE FRIEND: No, not with her—but with the memory of her.

THE WIFE: Then revive your memories of her!

THE FRIEND: Never!

THE WIFE: Was it to her that you fled last fall?

THE FRIEND: No, it was not to her—it was to someone else—since you ask.

THE WIFE: Shame on you! Shame!

THE FRIEND: Well, when you have been stung by a gadfly, you seek relief by rolling in the dirt. It hardens your skin—makes it tough.

THE WIFE: Shame on you!

THE FRIEND: Oh, but there is legitimate dirt—and illegitimate.

THE WIFE: Just exactly what do you mean?

THE FRIEND: You are a married woman, and we are not a couple of innocents—consequently, I mean that in marriage one reposes, as it were, on consecrated ground; and when one is not married, on unconsecrated ground. But say what you will, they are both of the earth earthy.

THE WIFE: You don't mean to compare . . .

THE FRIEND: Yes, that's exactly what I am doing.

THE WIFE: Just what sort of woman were you married to?

THE FRIEND: A respectable girl from a most respectable family.

THE WIFE: And you loved her?

THE FRIEND: Much too much.

THE WIFE: And then? . . .

THE FRIEND: Then we came to hate each other.

THE WIFE: But why? Why?

THE FRIEND: That is one of the many questions that life leaves unanswered!

THE WIFE: Nevertheless—there must have been some reason for it. . . .

THE FRIEND: That is what I used to think, too—but then we suddenly realized that it was hate that was at the root of our hostility. The dissensions were not what brought about the breach; dissension set in when love ceased to exist.

That is why the so-called loveless marriages are the most successful, you see.

THE WIFE (*naïvely*): Yes, I must say Knut and I have never had any serious disagreements.

THE FRIEND: There you spoke a little too frankly, Kerstin!

THE WIFE: What did I say?

THE FRIEND: You confessed you never loved your husband.

THE WIFE: Loved? Well—what is love?

THE FRIEND (*gets up*): What is love? What a question—from a married woman! Well, it is one of those things that are done—and that should not be expressed in words.

THE WIFE: Was your wife an attractive woman?

THE FRIEND: Yes—to me she was. She resembles you, as a matter of fact.

THE WIFE: Am I attractive, do you think?

THE FRIEND: Yes.

THE WIFE: My husband didn't think so—until you told him. Strange to say, the moment you come out here, he is suddenly overcome with affection for me. It is as though your presence fired him with love.

THE FRIEND: You don't say! Then that is why he likes to have me come here. And what about you?

THE WIFE: I?

THE FRIEND: Don't you think we ought to stop now—before we go too far?

THE WIFE (*shows anger*): What do you mean? What kind of opinion have you of me?

THE FRIEND: I meant nothing by it, Kerstin! Nothing whatever! Forgive me if I offended you!

THE WIFE: You have hurt me frightfully. But I know what a low opinion you have of us women.

THE FRIEND: Not of all women! To me you are . . .

THE WIFE: Yes?

THE FRIEND: . . . the wife of my friend, and therefore . . .

THE WIFE: And if I were not . . . ?

THE FRIEND: Shall we stop right here? Kerstin, you give me the impression that you are not accustomed to being made a fuss over by men. . . .

THE WIFE: No, you are quite right, and that is why I am grateful when anyone shows that he likes me—even if ever so little.

THE FRIEND: Even if ever so little! You really have just the right temperament to be a happy woman—asking so little of life.

THE WIFE: What do you really know of my demands on life?

THE FRIEND: Are you ambitious? Have you any aspirations? Could you possibly have an urge to do something, to rise in the world and become something?

THE WIFE: No—nothing like that. But this monotonous life, with nothing to occupy oneself, with no excitement, and without anything ever happening! Do you know that sometimes I am caught by a cruel feeling of wanting some horrible disaster to strike: an epidemic, or a great fire, or . . . *(In a whisper.)* . . . that my child should die . . . that I should die myself!

THE FRIEND: Do you know what that comes from? From doing nothing—from an overabundance of earthly blessings —and perhaps from something else. . . .

THE WIFE: What?

THE FRIEND: Passion!

THE WIFE: What did you say?

THE FRIEND: I hate to repeat the word, especially because I believe you did hear it; but since I don't use it in a derogatory sense, I don't think that I could have offended you!

THE WIFE: I must say you are not like other human beings! You strike your friends in the face—and it doesn't even seem to hurt.

THE FRIEND: And there are women who love to be struck, they say.

THE WIFE: I am beginning to be afraid of you!

THE FRIEND: By all means, be afraid!

THE WIFE: Who are you? What is it you want? What are you after?

THE FRIEND: Don't be curious, Kerstin!

THE WIFE: Still another impertinence!

THE FRIEND: Simply a bit of friendly advice. —Have you noticed that we always quarrel when your husband is not present? That does not bode well.

THE WIFE: For what?

THE FRIEND: A long-lasting friendship. It indicates the need for a change.

THE WIFE: Sometimes I feel as though I could hate you.

THE FRIEND: That's a good sign! But have you never felt as though you could love me?

THE WIFE: Yes—at times . . .

THE FRIEND: When? Tell me!

THE WIFE: I have a good mind to answer you just as frankly. . . . Yes, when you are talking with Adèle.

THE FRIEND: This passion of yours strikes me as being like your husband's, which flares up for you whenever I am present. Adèle and I seem to have been given the task of kindling the fire.

THE WIFE (*bursts into laughter*): The way you say it, it sounds so ridiculous that I can't even get angry.

THE FRIEND: You should never get angry, for it is more unbecoming to you than to others. But let us talk about something else. Where is your husband? (*He gets up and looks through the window.* THE WIFE *does the same.*) I didn't mean to attract your attention to what is going on down there in the garden. . . .

THE WIFE: As if I hadn't seen Knut kissing Adèle before . . .

THE FRIEND: That Adèle does not make you jealous of your husband—that worries me. There is so much in this house that worries me this year. Do you know what? I could swear that there is something rotting here.

THE WIFE: How so? I haven't noticed anything. —Oh, but Adèle and Knut—they only do it in fun.

THE FRIEND: Yes—playing with fire—with knives—and finally with dynamite! To me this is a gruesome game!

(THE FATHER *enters. He does not remove his hat.*)

THE FATHER: Is Knut here?

THE WIFE: No, he went out to do some shopping. Did you want anything special?

THE FATHER: Of course, since I am asking for him. Have you seen Adèle, then?

THE WIFE: No, not for quite a while.

THE FATHER (*notices* THE FRIEND): Excuse me, I didn't see you! How are you?

THE FRIEND: Fine, thank you. I hope you are also feeling well.

THE WIFE (*to* THE FATHER): Is there anything I can do for you?

The Father: Yes, if you would be so kind . . . But perhaps I am disturbing you. I'll come back later.

The Wife: You, disturbing us? . . .

The Father: You see, the trouble is this—I have mosquitoes in my bedroom—and so I thought I would ask you if you would let me sleep in the attic room.

The Wife: How annoying! We just gave that room to Axel.

The Father: Oh—then he is going to stay! If I had known that, I certainly wouldn't have brought up the matter.

The Friend: I would never have accepted your invitation to stay here had I known that you . . .

The Father: Oh, don't let me stand in the way. . . . I have no desire to be caught between the bark and the tree!

(There is a silence.)

Has Knut started his painting yet?

The Wife: No. He is in no mood for it just now.

The Father: He is never in the mood for any work—and now less than ever.

The Wife: Is there anything else you wish to say?

The Father: Oh, no—it doesn't matter. . . . Yes, I'd rather you didn't mention anything to Knut about the bedroom.

The Wife: I'll be only too glad not to.

The Father: You understand, it's not at all pleasant to start wrangling—over nothing. If the bedroom had been unoccupied, and I could have slept there, it would have been a different matter. But now that it is already taken, why . . . Well—goodbye for a while . . . *(He goes out.)*

The Friend: Will you excuse me, Kerstin, if I leave you for a few moments?

The Wife: Where are you going all of a sudden?

The Friend: I—I can't tell you.

The Wife: You are going out to get a room! I won't let you!

The Friend *(having picked up his hat)*: Do you think I could stay in your house after having been shown the door in this manner?

The Wife *(tries to take his hat from him)*: No—you are not going! Knut and I were not the ones who showed you the door; and, besides . . .

The Son *(enters)*: What's going on here? Are you fighting? Or is this a declaration of love?

THE WIFE: We are merely having a lovers' quarrel. . . . But can you imagine, Knut—this restless man insists upon going out and finding himself a room because your father came in and asked if he might sleep in the attic room.

THE SON: Wanted to sleep in the attic room! He was just curious to see what you were doing, of course! And that is the reason you want to leave? Get down on your knees and ask her to forgive you!

(THE FRIEND *kneels before* THE WIFE.)

Kiss her foot! She has a lovely foot, I can tell you!

THE FRIEND (*goes through the motions of kissing* THE WIFE's *foot, then gets up*): Well, now I have asked to be forgiven for going out to rent a room! See you later! (*He leaves in haste.*)

THE WIFE (*irritated*): Axel! (*After a pause.*) I really think it's indecent of the old man to come in here and interfere like this and disturb the peace in our home! From now on, we shan't have any peace at all—neither day nor night!

THE SON: Well, we'll just have to get used to it. But I do think you might have tried not to show your feelings so openly!

THE WIFE: My feelings! What feelings? What do you mean? Perhaps you—perhaps you are jealous?

THE SON: What? Now I suppose I don't know what I am talking about! I am talking about the way you spoke to my father!

THE WIFE (*trying to change the subject*): Let us stop talking about feelings—and put on this necktie so that you will at least look human. (*She takes a small parcel from her pocket while she is speaking.*)

THE SON: Am I to have a new tie again? And, of all things, another blue one!

THE WIFE (*tying the tie*): Well, you don't want to go about with a soiled tie, do you? And then I want you to get rid of your moustache. . . .

THE SON: Oh, no! Now you are going a little too far!

THE WIFE: How?

THE SON: Next, I suppose, you would like me to put on a light suit and tennis shoes?

THE WIFE: Yes, that would suit you perfectly, for you are

beginning to put on weight—you are getting to be quite
plump. . . .

THE SON: And so you would like me to shave off a little flesh
and look like a skeleton. The only other thing I have to
do is—to get a divorce.

THE WIFE: Why, Knut, I believe you are jealous!

THE SON: Perhaps I have already passed that state! But this
is really fantastic! I am jealous, yet I feel neither envy
nor bitterness. I am so fond of this man that I couldn't
deny him anything. Nothing!

THE WIFE: Nothing! You are making a very broad statement.

THE SON: Yes—but that is how it is. It is shameful, repre-
hensible, insane—but if he asked me to let him sleep with
you, I couldn't say no—I would let him.

THE WIFE: Now you really shock me! I have heard you say
a lot of things and I have tolerated much from you. . . .

THE SON: I just can't help it, but it is a fact! Do you
know . . . there are times when I see before me—both when
I am awake and in my sleep—I see you two together . . .
and it doesn't cause me pain; on the contrary, I feel happy
about it, I revel in it as at the sight of something very
beautiful!

THE WIFE: Why, this is absolutely frightful!

THE SON: I may be a rare case—but you must admit it is
damnably interesting!

THE WIFE: You know, I sometimes think you want to get
rid of me.

THE SON: But you don't believe that, do you?

THE WIFE: Yes, I do—at times. It seems to me as if you
were trying to push Axel into my arms—to urge him on,
so that you would have grounds for divorce and could get
rid of me.

THE SON: This is unheard of! Tell me, Kerstin, have you two
never kissed each other?

THE WIFE: Upon my soul, never!

THE SON: Will you promise me—if that should happen—that
you will tell me straight to my face, quite openly, "This
is how it is!"

THE WIFE: Listen, Knut! You had better be careful that you
don't lose your mind!

THE SON: You are right! You see—I hate to be deceived!
That is something I don't want to be the victim of! And

to lose you—that I don't want either . . . but rather that than to be deceived!

THE WIFE: Suppose you put a stop to your preaching now and let me start with mine. What is your relationship with Adèle?

THE SON: You know what my relationship with her is, and you approve of it.

THE WIFE: I have never approved of any breach of the marriage vow!

THE SON: Aha! Now you are singing another tune. What was an innocent pastime yesterday is a crime today.

THE WIFE: Exactly like my innocent relations with Axel a moment ago.

THE SON: Today they may be innocent, but who knows what they will lead to tomorrow!

THE WIFE: Then why don't you wait until tomorrow?

THE SON: No, I don't care to wait until it is too late.

THE WIFE: Then—what is it you want?

THE SON: I don't know. Yes—an end to this . . . if there is an end. We have tied the net ourselves, and now we are caught in it! Oh, how I hate him when he is not here! But the moment I set eyes on him again, and he glances at me with his big eyes, then I love him—like a brother—or a sister. . . . Now I am beginning to understand how you could have come under his influence. But I fail to understand how *I* could have been so swayed. I wonder whether it isn't because I have been all alone here among females until I have become womanish in my feelings and allowed your love for him to infect me. . . . You must love him boundlessly, without being conscious of it.

THE WIFE: That is true! And now you wish to free yourself of all blame!

THE SON: As you are doing!

THE WIFE: You mean you!

THE SON: I mean you! Oh, I am going insane!

THE WIFE: I can quite believe it!

THE SON: And you don't feel the slightest compassion!

THE WIFE: You want me to feel compassion for you when you torment me like this?

THE SON: You have never loved me!

THE WIFE: You have never loved me!

THE SON: Ah! Now we have come to the quarreling stage, which will go on until doomsday!

THE WIFE: Then let us call a halt before it is too late. Go and take a swim so that you can cool off!

THE SON: You want to be alone . . .

(THE FRIEND *enters.*)

THE FRIEND (*gaily and openheartedly*): Well, I certainly am in luck! Just as I was about to leave, I ran into Adèle—and she had a room. . . .

THE WIFE: Adèle—has a room to let?

THE FRIEND: She knew where I could get one.

THE WIFE: That girl—is there anything she doesn't know?

THE FRIEND (*to* THE SON, *offering him a cigarette*): Cigarette?

THE SON (*abruptly, brusquely*): No, thanks!

THE FRIEND: What a good-looking tie you are wearing!

THE SON: You think so?

THE FRIEND: You have been talking about me behind my back while I was gone! I can tell by your faces.

THE SON (*in agitation*): Excuse me! I must go and have my swim! (*He leaves abruptly.*)

THE FRIEND: What's troubling him?

THE WIFE: He is jealous.

THE FRIEND: Really? But he has no cause to be.

THE WIFE: Knut says he has. Where is that room Adèle spoke to you about?

THE FRIEND (*absently*): Adèle? Oh, right across the way from you—at the pilot's.

THE WIFE: She certainly knows how to arrange things. From your room over there you can look directly into hers. What an intriguing female!

THE FRIEND: I don't believe that dear Adèle even gave that a thought.

THE WIFE: Dear Adèle? So you have become that intimate with her?

THE FRIEND: Kerstin, don't arouse ghosts that will stir up feelings which ordinarily would not be seen in the light of day! Don't do it, or . . .

THE WIFE: Are you planning to leave us again, suddenly? But I won't let you—you have no right to go away. . . .

THE FRIEND (*lighting a cigarette*): Perhaps it is my duty!

THE WIFE: If you are my friend, you won't leave me unpro-

tected in this house! My honor is in danger here. My repre-
hensible husband—aided and abetted by his parents—
is likely to allow himself all kinds of degrading, disreputable liberties. Can you imagine, he has gone so far in
boorishness as to say that he would relinquish me, if
need be, give me up—to you!

THE FRIEND: Why, what a charming form of jealousy! And
what did you reply to that?

THE WIFE: What could I say?

THE FRIEND: You ask me that?

THE WIFE (*hysterically*): You are like a cat playing with its
prey! Can't you see how I am caught in your net—how I
suffer, how I struggle to get out of it? Yet I can't! Have
pity on me—give me at least one friendly glance—and don't
sit there like an unfeeling image, waiting to be worshiped
and to receive a sacrifice! (*She falls to her knees.*) You
are so strong, so virile—you know how to control your
passions, you are so proud, so honorable, and it is because
you have never been in love—never loved as I now love
you!

THE FRIEND: Haven't I? Get up, Kerstin! Get up and sit
down over there in that armchair! There! Now it is my turn
to say something. . . . (*He remains seated, cigarette in
hand.*) I have loved you—as the saying goes—from the moment I first set eyes on you. Do you remember the sunset
when we first met last year? Your husband was down in
the valley below, painting, when I passed by. I was introduced to you, and we stood there talking until we were
tired; and you sat down on the grass and invited me to
sit beside you. But the grass was damp with dew, and I
did not care to get wet. And so you unfastened your cloak
and spread out one of the flaps for me to sit on. To me
that was as if you had taken me in your embrace and let
me rest in your lap. I was very miserable, felt very tired
and lonely, and it looked so soft and warm and comfortable
inside your cloak. I was actually tempted to crawl inside
and hide myself at your young virgin bosom, but I was
ashamed when I noticed a faint smile in your innocent
eyes, as though you wondered how a man like me could
be so shy. . . . After that we met again—time after time.
Your husband seemed to revel in my admiration for you;
it almost seemed as if I had discovered his wife for him.

I became your captive, and you played with me; your
husband showed no reluctance about teasing me in front
of others—even when many persons were present. His
egotism and cocksureness offended me sometimes—and
there were moments when I was tempted to push him
aside and try to take his place. Do you remember the afternoon when I had invited you both to my birthday party?
You were to come late; after we had waited for you for
an hour, you entered the drawing room, dressed in a
skirt the color of a pansy, and with a shirtwaist of a light-
colored, flowery pattern. And you wore a large, broad-
brimmed summer hat with cheek-bands; it was covered
with yellow lawn, which threw a sunshine of gold over
your entire being. And then, when you handed me your
bouquet of roses with the timid daring of a girl of fourteen,
you seemed to me so overwhelmingly beautiful that I
couldn't utter a word: I could neither bid you welcome
nor thank you for the flowers—I hastily left the room and
I wept.

THE WIFE: You do know how to hide your feelings. That
you do!

THE FRIEND: Do you remember what happened later that
night, after we had had supper and then exchanged memories for hours and our souls met in an embrace? Knut
practically invited me—and I believe you had induced him
to do so—to come and live with you in the city during the
winter. And do you recall what I answered?

THE WIFE: You answered, "I don't dare!"

THE FRIEND: The next morning I was gone.

THE WIFE: And I wept the whole day—and so did Knut!

THE FRIEND: Just think how many tears will be shed this
time!

THE WIFE: This time?

THE FRIEND: Sit still! Now that everything has been said,
nothing remains for us but to part.

THE WIFE: No—no! We can't part! Why can't things remain
the way they are? You are so composed, and I am not at
all disturbed or agitated. What has Knut to do with our
feelings for each other as long as we know how to control
them? We can sit h⌐re, as you see, in all tranquillity, and
discuss what once has been—like an old married couple
who talk about the love of their youth.

THE FRIEND: Oh, what a child you are! I don't understand what kind of marriage yours has been if you think that friendship can be nothing but that after a declaration of love. I am as composed as a keg of gunpowder beneath a percussion cap; I am as cold as a fired-up steam boiler. . . . Oh, I have fought—I have tormented myself—but I can't be responsible for what I may do.

THE WIFE: But I can!

THE FRIEND: Yes, I quite believe you can. You extinguish the fire whenever it flames up, but I—I have to live with myself. Oh, what a horrible thought! And do you think that, after what has happened, I could stay here in this house and accept the crumbs from the rich man's table, breathe the air here, and drink in the fragrance from his garden—and still have a clean conscience?

THE WIFE: Why shouldn't you have a clean conscience, when *he* has no qualms about having a mistress whom he openly fondles and kisses?

THE FRIEND: No, no—don't try to shift the blame—for then we will have come to the edge of the precipice, and there will be nothing left for us but to jump into the sea! No, let us do something original for once—let us set an example to the world and show how honest, decent people behave. The moment Knut comes back, we say to him, "This is the way things are. We love each other. Help us to decide what to do!"

THE WIFE: That is a great idea! It is a noble one! Yes—that is what we'll do, come what may! And we can do it with a clear conscience—for we have not committed any crime!

THE FRIEND: And after that? He will, of course, ask me to leave.

THE WIFE: Either that—or to stay.

THE FRIEND: On what condition? That everything be as it was in the past? No, I can't accept that! Do you think that after this I could stand to see you caressing each other—to listen to the door of your bedroom shutting after you? . . . No! I see no end to this! But he must be told, else I shall never be able to look him in the face again, never be able to press his hand again! We must tell him everything—then let us see what happens!

THE WIFE: Oh, if only the next hour were over! Tell me

that you love me, or I shall never have the courage to put the knife into him! Tell me you love me!

THE FRIEND (*remains seated, as does* THE WIFE): I love you—body and soul! I love your dainty little foot, which I see sticking out from under the hem of your dress . . . I love your little white teeth—your mouth, flirting for a kiss—your ears and your sensually inviting eyes . . . I love every inch of your light, ethereal body, which I should like to throw over my shoulder and run away with to the woods! When I was young, I once snapped up a girl from the street, lifted her up in my arms, and ran up four flights of stairs with her. . . . I was young in those days—but now, think of it—now I am grown up!

THE WIFE: But you must love my soul, too!

THE FRIEND: I love your soul because it is weaker than mine, ardent and fiery like mine, faithless like mine. . . .

THE WIFE: May I not get up now and come to you?

THE FRIEND: No, you mustn't!

THE WIFE: I hear Knut coming—I know his step—and I won't have the courage to speak until I have kissed your brow.

THE FRIEND: Is that he coming?

THE WIFE: Sh!

> (THE FATHER *comes in. With his hat on his head, he goes straight to* THE FRIEND, *who gives a start and gets up.* THE FATHER *takes a newspaper from a table behind* THE FRIEND.)

THE FATHER: Excuse me for disturbing you. I only wanted this newspaper. (*To* THE WIFE.) Have you seen Adèle?

THE WIFE: This is the fifth time today you have asked for Adèle!

THE FATHER: Oh! You are keeping count! —Aren't you going for a swim before breakfast?

THE WIFE: No—not today.

THE FATHER: You make a mistake if you neglect taking a swim when your health is so poor.

> (*There is a silence.* THE FATHER *leaves.*)

THE FRIEND: No—I can't stay here another day! I wouldn't be able to stand it!

THE WIFE *(going up to him, looking at him passionately)*: Shall we go away from here?

THE FRIEND: No! But I am going!

THE WIFE: Then I shall go, too! Let us die together!

THE FRIEND *(taking her in his arms and kissing her)*: Now we are lost! Whatever made me do this? This is the end of faith and honor—of friendship—of peace of mind! A fire from hell that burns and sears all that was green and blooming!

(They separate and go back to their former seats.)

THE SON *(enters rapidly)*: Why are you sitting so far apart from each other?

THE WIFE: Because . . .

THE SON: And why do you look so agitated?

THE WIFE: Because we . . . *(There is a long pause.)* . . . because we love each other!

THE SON *(regarding each one for a moment, then turning to THE FRIEND)*: Is that true? *(He sits down on a chair and appears to be overwhelmed.)* Why did you have to tell me?

THE WIFE: That's the thanks I get for being honest!

THE SON: That is very original—but it is indecent!

THE WIFE: You told me yourself that if this should ever happen . . .

THE SON: Yes, so I did. And now it has happened. Come to think of it, I knew it before—and yet it seems like such a new thing that I can't grasp it. Who is to blame? No one—and all three of us. What are we to do—and what is going to happen now?

THE FRIEND: Is there anything you can reproach me for?

THE SON: Nothing whatsoever! You fled when you saw danger was near—you refused our invitation to come and live with us—you concealed your feelings so completely that Kerstin thought you hated her. But why did you come back again?

THE FRIEND: Because I believed that my feelings for her were dead.

THE SON: That sounds plausible, and I believe you. However, we are sitting here faced with a fact that we neither brought about nor were able to stave off. We tried to prevent the danger by our forced openness, we jested about it—but it has come ever closer and has finally overtaken us. What are we going to do? Let us discuss things calmly and try to remain friends to the last. What are we to do?

(Silence.)

Neither of you has an answer? We can't sit here looking on while the house is on fire and not do anything about it. *(He gets up.)* Let us think about the consequences. . . .

THE FRIEND: I think the decent thing would be for me to withdraw.

THE SON: I think so, too.

THE WIFE: No—I won't let you go! If you do, I'll go with you!

THE SON: Is this what you call speaking calmly?

THE WIFE: Nothing about love is ever calm! *(She approaches THE FRIEND.)*

THE SON: You might at least spare me the sight of your carnal lust. Have a little consideration for my feelings, since I am comparatively innocent, and am always the one who has to suffer.

THE WIFE *(putting her arms around THE FRIEND's neck)*: You must not leave, do you hear?

THE SON *(takes hold of THE WIFE by the arm and pulls her away from THE FRIEND)*: You might behave like decent people and wait until I am out of the room. . . . *(To THE FRIEND.)* Listen, my friend! We must come to a quick decision, because the breakfast gong is going to sound in a few minutes. I can see that there is nothing that will subdue your love, while I think I could conquer mine if I made a slight exertion. If I were to continue to live with a woman who is in love with another man, it would not be a complete marriage: I would always feel I was living in polyandry. That is why I shall withdraw—but not until after I am assured that you will marry her.

THE FRIEND: I don't know why, but your noble, generous offer humiliates me more than the consciousness of having committed a crime would have done—if I had stolen her.

THE SON: I don't doubt that, but it humiliates me less to give than to be robbed. I will give you five minutes to make your arrangements. So—farewell, for a moment or two. *(He goes out.)*

THE WIFE: Well?

THE FRIEND: Don't you see how ridiculous I appear now?

THE WIFE: No, there is nothing ridiculous about being honest.

THE FRIEND: Not always—but in this case the husband seems to be the less ridiculous one. And someday you will come to despise me.

THE WIFE: Is that all you have to say to me at a moment like this? Now that nothing stands between us, and you should be able to open your arms to me with a clear conscience—now you hesitate. . . .

THE FRIEND: Yes, I hesitate—because this openness is beginning to take on the appearance of boldness—this honesty smacks of heartlessness. . . .

THE WIFE: So-o! So-o!

THE FRIEND: And now I am becoming aware of the fact that all that smell of something rotting, which I have noticed in this house, comes from you. . . .

THE WIFE: Or from you! It was you who seduced me with your timid glances, with your brutalities that excited my passions like a whip! And now the seducer is playing the part of Virtue! Ha!

THE FRIEND: Or perhaps it was this way: It was you who . . .

THE WIFE: No! It was you, you, you! (*She throws herself on the sofa and shrieks:*) Help me! I am dying! I am dying!

(THE FRIEND *stands immobile.*)

Why don't you help me? Have you no compassion? You are a beast! Don't you see I am sick? Help me! Help me!

(THE FRIEND *does not move.*)

Call a doctor! At least do me that favor—any human being would do that even for a stranger! Call Adèle!

(THE FRIEND *goes out.*)

THE SON (*enters*): Well? What is this? (*To* THE WIFE.) Couldn't you get along together?

THE WIFE: Stop it! Don't say another word!

THE SON: But why did he disappear through the garden in such a hurry? I thought he would take both trees and bushes with him, and he raced along as though the seat of his pants had been on fire.

(THE MOTHER *and* THE COUSIN *enter.*)

THE MOTHER: Well, would you like to come and have your breakfast now?

THE SON: Thank you—yes.

THE MOTHER: But where is Axel? Should we wait for him, perhaps?

THE SON: We are going to do nothing of the kind, for he has already departed.

THE MOTHER: Well, I must say, he is a curious one! And I went to the trouble of frying some flounder for him. . . .

(THE FATHER *enters.*)

THE SON (*to* THE FATHER): Now you can have the attic room if you want it.

THE FATHER: Thanks—but now I don't need it.

THE SON: It's remarkable how changeable you are!

THE FATHER: I am not the only one—there are others. But he who governs his own mind is better off than he who conquers cities. . . .

THE SON: And here is another saying: Don't tell your friend to go away, and, later, to come back and stay!

THE FATHER: Why, that's an excellent one! Where did you get that from?

THE SON: I learned that one from Kerstin!

THE FATHER: Kerstin. Well . . . (*To* THE WIFE.) Have you been for a swim yet?

THE SON: No, she only had a cold rubdown!

(*The sound of a gong is heard.*)

THE MOTHER: There, now! Come and sit down to breakfast!

THE SON (*to* THE FATHER): Give my wife your arm, and I'll offer mine to Adèle!

THE FATHER: No, thank you! You keep Kerstin to yourself!

CURTAIN

To Joseph Mitchell

The Bond

(1892)

A Tragedy in One Act

CHARACTERS

THE JUDGE,
  25 years old

THE PASTOR,
  60 years old

THE BARON,
  42 years old

THE BARONESS,
  40 years old

ALEXANDER EKLUND

EMANUEL VICKBERG

KARL JOHAN SJÖBERG

ERIK OTTO BOMAN

ERENFRID SÖDERBERG

OLOF ANDERSSON OF VIK

KARL PETER ANDERSSON OF
  BERGA

AXEL VALLIN

ANDERS ERIK RUTH

SVEN OSKAR ERLIN

AUGUST ALEXANDER VASS

LUDVIG ÖSTMAN

THE CLERK OF THE COURT

THE SHERIFF

THE CONSTABLE

THE ATTORNEY

ALEXANDERSSON,
  a farmer

ALMA JONSSON,
  a housemaid

THE DAIRY MAID

THE FARMHAND

Male and female SPECTATORS,
  young and old

*The play takes place in the 1890s
in a small community in Sweden.*

*A village hall, in which circuit court is
held. In the rear is a door with windows on each side. Through the windows can be seen the churchyard and
a detached bell tower. To the left, a
door. To the right, the judge's seat:
a high desk on a platform. The desk
is embellished with gilt ornamentations
of the sword of justice and a pair of
scales. On each side of the desk, tables
and chairs for the twelve jurymen. In
the center of the hall are benches for
the spectators. The walls are lined
with built-in closets, to the doors of
which are tacked reports listing current
official market prices for the county,
announcements and communications,
bulletins, etc.*

THE SHERIFF: Did you ever see such a lot of people at a summer session?

THE CONSTABLE: No—not for the last fifteen years—not
since the time of the famous Alder Lake murder.

THE SHERIFF: Well—this case, I dare say, is as good as any
double murder—even of your own parents. That the
Baron and the Baroness are divorcing each other, that
alone is a scandal; but when their two families start wrangling about property and land holdings, too—then you can
well imagine what a blaze it will be. All that's missing
now is a fight over their only child—and then King
Solomon himself wouldn't be able to sit in judgment.

THE CONSTABLE: Well, what's behind it all, anyhow? Some

people say one thing, others say something else—but somebody is to blame, wouldn't you think?

THE SHERIFF: It's never the fault of one when two people quarrel, as the saying goes. And then again, it may be the fault of only *one* of them that they do. Take my old porcupine at home, for example. They tell me she storms hither and thither, quarreling with herself, when I am away. But in this case it's not a question of a mere quarrel; this is a full-blown criminal case as large as life. And in most such cases one of the parties is the plaintiff—meaning that he has been wronged; and the other party, the defendant, meaning that he is the one who has done wrong. Who the guilty one is in this case—that is not easy to say, for both parties are plaintiffs and at the same time defendants.

THE CONSTABLE: Well, well . . . Yes, we live in strange times, we do. One would think women had gone crazy. Every now and then my old woman comes out with the idea that if there was any justice in the world I ought to bear children, too! As if the Lord didn't know just what He was doing when He created us human beings! And then she dribbles out long harangues about her being human, too—as if I didn't know that before—as if I had ever said she wasn't—and that she is fed up with being a servant to me . . . when the truth is that I am the one who really slaves for *her*.

THE SHERIFF: Is that a fact? So you, too, are suffering from the same plague in your house? My old woman has the habit of reading a newspaper she brings home from the manor house; and one time she will tell me that a young Dalecarlian woman has taken up bricklaying—as if that was something so remarkable—and another time she will tell me that some old crone has attacked her sick husband and given him a beating! What in the world is the meaning of all this is more than I can fathom; but it looks to me as if she, my wife, was peeved at me because I am a man!

THE CONSTABLE: Yes, I must say it is all very strange. (*He offers* THE SHERIFF *some snuff.*) We are certainly having beautiful weather! The rye looks like a rug of fur, and we soon saw the end of the frosty nights.

THE SHERIFF: I have nothing in the field to harvest, and good years are bad years for me; no distress to levy on anyone, and no auctions. Do you know the new circuit judge who is to sit in court today?

THE CONSTABLE: No, but I have heard people say he is a young man who only recently took his bar examination and today is sitting on the bench for the first time.

THE SHERIFF: I have also heard that he is a bit of a pietist. . . . H'm.

THE CONSTABLE: H'm. H'm. —The church service for the opening of the court session is taking a long time today. . . .

THE SHERIFF *(places a large Bible on* THE JUDGE'*s desk and twelve smaller ones on the jurymen's desks)*: They can't be much longer now. They have been in there almost a whole hour.

THE CONSTABLE: He is a wonder at preaching, the pastor is, once he gets started. *(There is a pause.)* Will the Baron and the Baroness be here themselves—I mean in person?

THE SHERIFF: Both he and she! So there is sure to be an uproar. . . . *(The bell in the bell tower starts ringing.)* There, now—it's over! Go over the tables with a dust rag—then we'll be all ready to start.

THE CONSTABLE: And the inkwells are filled, aren't they?

THE BARON *(enters. In a subdued tone to* THE BARONESS): And so, before we separate for a year, we are agreed, entirely agreed, on all points, aren't we? But first of all: no recriminations before the court!

THE BARONESS: Do you think I would lay bare all the intimate details of our married life before a lot of curious peasants?

THE BARON: Exactly! Furthermore, you will have the child with you during the period of the interlocutory decree, provided that he may visit me whenever I so desire, and that he is educated in accordance with the principles I stipulated, and which you approved.

THE BARONESS: That's right!

THE BARON: Further, that—during the year of separation—I provide for you and the child with three thousand crowns from the net income of the estate.

THE BARONESS: I agree.

THE BARON: Then I have nothing to add, and so I only wish to bid you goodbye. Why we are divorcing, only you and I know; and for the sake of our son, no one else must know. And for his sake also, I beg of you not to enter into any contest so that we will be provoked into soiling the names of his parents. Who knows—once he has come out into life, he may yet have to suffer because his parents are divorced.

THE BARONESS: I shall start no contest as long as I may keep my child.

THE BARON: That settled, let us concentrate our attention solely upon our child's welfare and forget what has come between us two. And remember one thing more: if we start fighting about the child and challenge each other's fitness as guardians, the judge might take him away from both of us and place him with some pietists, and they would bring him up to hate and despise his parents.

THE BARONESS: He couldn't do that!

THE BARON: Yes, my dear—for that is the law!

THE BARONESS: It's a stupid law!

THE BARON: Perhaps it is—but it *is* the law; and the law is the same for you and me as for everybody else!

THE BARONESS: Why, that's monstrous, unheard of! And I would never submit to it!

THE BARON: But you don't need to, as we have decided not to challenge each other. We have never been able to agree in the past, but on this point we are of one mind, are we not—that we are to part without any ill feeling on either side? *(To* THE SHERIFF.*)* Is it permissible for the Baroness to wait inside?

THE SHERIFF: You are very welcome! Step in here! *(*THE BARON *escorts* THE BARONESS *to the door, left; then he goes out through the door in the rear.* THE ATTORNEY, THE HOUSEMAID, THE DAIRY MAID, *and* THE FARMHAND *enter.)*

THE ATTORNEY *(to* THE HOUSEMAID*)*: You see, my friend—that you have stolen, I don't doubt for a moment. . . . But as long as your employer, farmer Alexandersson, has no witness to prove it, you are innocent. But because your employer has called you a thief in the presence of two witnesses, *he* is guilty of slander. Therefore you are now the plaintiff, and he is the defendant. And just remember this one rule: the first duty of an accused offender—is to deny!

THE HOUSEMAID: Yes, but you just said that I am not an offender, but that farmer Alexandersson is.

THE ATTORNEY: You are an offender because you have stolen; but because you have demanded a lawyer, it is my positive

duty to wash you clean and try to have your employer
convicted. And so I say again, for the last time: Deny!
(To the witnesses.) And as for the witnesses, what are they
going to witness to? Listen carefully, now! A good witness
sticks to the matter at hand. And therefore you must
constantly bear in mind that it is not a question of whether
Alma Jonsson has stolen or has not stolen; the only question before the court is whether Alexandersson has said
that she has stolen—for, and note this well, Alexandersson
has no legal right to prove what he said—but we have.
Just why it is so, only the devil knows! And, anyhow—
that's none of your concern. Consequently: Keep your
tongues straight in your mouth and your hands on the Bible!

THE DAIRY MAID: Lord in heaven! I am scared. . . . I have
no idea what to say!

THE FARMHAND: You just say after me, and you won't be
telling any lies.

(THE JUDGE and THE PASTOR enter.)

THE JUDGE: I want to thank you for your sermon, Pastor.

THE PASTOR: Oh, don't mention it, Judge.

THE JUDGE: Well—as you know, this is the first time I am
presiding in a court. I confess I was timid about entering
a legal career in the beginning. I really took it up against
my will—it was foisted upon me. Because, for one thing,
our laws are so imperfect, our judicial institutions so
unsatisfactory, and human nature so made up of falsehood
and hypocrisy that I have often wondered how any judge
could even dare to express an honest, resolute opinion. And
today, in your sermon, you brought to life my old mis-
givings.

THE PASTOR: To be conscientious is our rightful, natural
duty; but to be sentimental—that will never do. And since
everything else on earth is so lacking in perfection these
days, we can't expect judges and their decisions to be
perfect.

THE JUDGE: That may be, but that does not prevent me from
feeling a tremendous responsibility when I hold the fate of
a human being in my hand. Particularly since a pro-
nouncement of mine can affect generations to come. I am
especially thinking of this divorce suit between the Baron
and his wife; and I feel I should ask you—since you were

the one who, as the head of the Vestry Board, communicated the two required warnings to them—what you feel their mutual relationship and respective guilt may be.

THE PASTOR: In short, you would put me in the position of sitting in judgment . . . or you would let your decision be influenced by what I say. But all I can do is to refer you to the minutes of the Vestry Board.

THE JUDGE: Well, the minutes . . . I have read them. What I want to know is what is *not* in the minutes.

THE PASTOR: The accusations the Baron and the Baroness made against each other at a private hearing remain my secret. Besides, how can I know which one told the truth and which one did not? I have to tell you the very same thing that I told them: "I have no reason to believe one of you more than the other."

THE JUDGE: But I should imagine you would have formed some sort of opinion as to their respective guilt during these hearings?

THE PASTOR: When I had heard one of them, I formed one opinion; but when I heard the other one, I had a different opinion. Therefore, you see, I can have no definite or final opinion in this matter.

THE JUDGE: But I—who have no knowledge of what has happened—I am expected to give a final opinion.

THE PASTOR: That is the grave task a judge has. I would never undertake to bear that responsibility!

THE JUDGE: But I should think . . . could not witnesses be produced who could give evidence?

THE PASTOR: No, the Baron and the Baroness have never accused each other publicly. Furthermore, two false witnesses are enough to furnish valid proof of guilt—and a perjurer can do as much. Do you think that I would ever base a decision on the gossip of servants, the loose talk of envious neighbors, or on the biased and spiteful intrigues of vindictive relatives? Do you?

THE JUDGE: You are an incorrigible skeptic, Pastor!

THE PASTOR: After having lived sixty years and having cared for people's souls for forty, one can't help being a skeptic. The habit of prevaricating is as ingrown in us as original sin, and all of us are liars, I believe. As children, we lie out of fear; as grown-ups, out of self-interest, necessity, out of a feeling of self-preservation—and I have known people who have lied out of pure human kindness. In this particular case, involving the Baron and the Baroness, I think you will have an exceedingly hard task to find out who is speaking the truth; and I feel I must warn you not to let yourself be prejudiced by any preconceived opinion. You yourself are newly married and are likely to be under the spell of a young woman's witchery. As a consequence, you may easily be influenced in favor of a young and charming lady who is not only an unfortunate wife but a mother as well. On the other hand, you have recently become a father, and as such you cannot escape being moved by the impending separation of the father from his one and only child. Be on your guard against compassion for either side—since compassion for one may spell cruelty to the other.

THE JUDGE: There is one thing, at least, that will make my task somewhat easier; and that is the fact that both parties are in mutual agreement on the main issues.

THE PASTOR: Don't rely too much on that—for that is what they all say! But once they have come before the court, then the fireworks begin. All that is needed in this case is a spark—and then the conflagration is set. Here come the jurymen now. . . . Goodbye for the time being! I am staying—but I'll keep out of sight!

(The twelve JURYMEN *enter and take their places.* THE SHERIFF, *in the open doorway, summons the participants with a bell.* THE JUDGE *takes his seat, while spectators and witnesses crowd into the courtroom.)*

THE JUDGE: Referring to the regulations of the Penal Code, in Chapter 11, paragraphs 5, 6, and 8, I herewith declare the proceedings of this court opened. *(He whispers to* THE CLERK OF THE COURT *and then says:)* Will it please the members of the jury, who have been selected to take the oath . . .

THE JURYMEN *(rise. They place their right hands on their respective Bibles, then speak in unison, except when their individual names are called):*
I, Alexander Eklund,
I, Emanuel Vickberg,
I, Karl Johan Sjöberg,
I, Erik Otto Boman,

I, Erenfrid Söderberg,
I, Olof Andersson of Vik,
I, Karl Peter Andersson of Berga,
I, Axel Vallin,
I, Anders Erik Ruth,
I, Sven Oskar Erlin,
I, August Alexander Vass,
I, Ludvig Östman,
(All together, in a low-pitched, measured tone of voice)
promise and swear before God and on his holy Gospel
that I will and shall, according to the best of my judgment
and conscience, decide fairly in all cases, no less for the
poor than for the rich, and give judgment according to
the laws of God and the statute laws of the Kingdom of
Sweden—*(In a higher pitch and somewhat louder.)*—never
to twist or distort the law, or support what is not right,
neither for the sake of close or distant kinship, friendship,
envy or enmity, nor out of fear, nor for bribes nor gifts,
nor for any cause whatsoever, no matter what form it may
take, nor cause him to be judged guilty who is without
guilt, nor him judged innocent who is guilty.
(In a louder tone of voice.) Furthermore, I shall, neither
before judgment is passed nor afterward, neither to those
who are parties to any action nor to any others, disclose
any deliberations that may be held by this Court behind
closed doors. All this I will and shall, as an honest and
upright member of the Jury, faithfully keep without perfidy,
subterfuge or deception. . . . *(There is a pause.)* . . . Upon
my life and soul, so help me God! *(The* JURORS *seat themselves.)*

THE JUDGE *(to* THE SHERIFF*)*: Call the case of Alma Jonsson
versus the farmer Alexandersson.

   *(*THE SHERIFF *calls the case, and* ALEXANDERSSON, THE
   HOUSEMAID, THE ATTORNEY, THE FARMHAND, *and*
   THE DAIRY MAID *enter.)*

THE SHERIFF *(calls out)*: The housemaid Alma Jonsson versus
the farmer Alexandersson.
THE ATTORNEY: I desire to present my power of attorney. I
appear on behalf of the plaintiff, Alma Jonsson.
THE JUDGE *(examines the document, then says)*: The housemaid Alma Jonsson has in a summons served on her former

employer, Alexandersson, brought charges under the sixteenth chapter, paragraph 8, of the Penal Code, providing for six months of imprisonment or a fine, accusing said Alexandersson of having called her a thief, without proof or support for this accusation and without bringing legal action against her for this alleged theft. What have you to say in your defense, Alexandersson?

ALEXANDERSSON: I called her a thief because I caught her stealing.

THE JUDGE: Have you any witnesses who saw her steal?

ALEXANDERSSON: No, it so happened that I had no witnesses with me, for I usually walk about by myself.

THE JUDGE: Why didn't you institute proceedings against the girl?

ALEXANDERSSON: Because I don't believe in lawsuits. And, besides, employers like me are not in the habit of doing anything about household thefts; partly because they are such common occurrences, and partly because we don't want to do anything to hurt their future.

THE JUDGE: Alma Jonsson—what have you to say to this?

ALMA JONSSON: Why, I . . . I . . .

THE ATTORNEY *(to her)*: You say nothing! *(To the Court.)* Alma Jonsson, who in this case is not the defendant but the plaintiff, requests that the Court hear the witnesses in order that they may prove the fact that Alexandersson has slandered her.

THE JUDGE: Since Alexandersson has already admitted that he did slander her, there is no necessity for witnesses. But on the other hand, it is of importance for me to know whether Alma Jonsson is guilty of stealing. For, if Alexandersson had good grounds for calling her a thief, this will serve as a mitigating circumstance when the judgment is handed down.

THE ATTORNEY: I ask for permission to take exception to the statement just made by the Court. According to Chapter 16, paragraph 13, of the Penal Code, anyone charged with having slandered another shall be denied the right to present evidence as to the truth of his offensive remarks.

THE JUDGE: I ask the parties in the case, the witnesses, and the spectators to empty the courtroom that the court may deliberate. *(All leave except* THE JUDGE *and the members of the Court.)*

THE JUDGE: Is Alexandersson a man whose word can be believed?

THE JURY (*as one*): Alexandersson is a reliable man.

THE JUDGE: Has Alma Jonsson the reputation of being an honest person?

BOMAN: I had to discharge Alma Jonsson last year for petty thievery.

THE JUDGE: In any case, I have to sentence Alexandersson to pay a fine. There is no other way out. Is he a poor man?

ÖSTMAN: He still owes the government for taxes, and last year he had a bad harvest. I'm afraid a fine will be more than he can stand.

THE JUDGE: Despite this, I see no grounds for postponing the suit. The case is clear, as long as Alexandersson is not permitted to give his side of the story. —Is there anything more to add, or has anyone any objection?

EKLUND: I simply would like to make a general observation. . . . A case like this—where the one party is not only innocent but has also been injured and yet has to take the punishment, while the thief has his so-called honor and good character restored—a case like this can have dire consequences. People will be likely to be less forbearing toward their fellowmen and neighbors, and lawsuits may become more frequent.

THE JUDGE: That may be so, but general reflections have no place in the official records, and sentence has to be meted out. For that reason I shall only ask you, the jury, this one question: Is Alexandersson guilty according to Chapter 16, paragraph 13, of the Penal Code, or is he not?

THE JURYMEN (*in unison*): Guilty.

THE JUDGE (*to* THE SHERIFF): Summon the parties in the case and the witnesses!

(THE SHERIFF *summons the parties in the case. They, the* SPECTATORS, *and others, not members of the Court, enter. The* SPECTATORS *seat themselves.*)

THE JUDGE: In the case of Alma Jonsson versus farmer Alexandersson, the latter is sentenced to pay a fine of one hundred crowns for slandering the plaintiff, Alma Jonsson.

ALEXANDERSSON: But I saw her do it—I caught her stealing! That's what one gets for being charitable!

THE ATTORNEY (*to* ALMA JONSSON): Now, do you see? If

one only keeps denying and contesting, the case is won! Alexandersson was a fool not to contest. If I had been his attorney and had contested your case against him, I would immediately have challenged and taken exception to your witnesses—and then you would have been left high and dry! Now let us go outside and settle our account. *(He,* ALMA JONSSON, *and her witnesses leave.)*

ALEXANDERSSON *(to* THE SHERIFF): And now I suppose I have to give Alma Jonsson a letter of reference and swear that she has been honest and dependable!

THE SHERIFF: That's something that doesn't concern me!

ALEXANDERSSON *(to* THE CONSTABLE): And for this I have to lose my farm and everything I own! Who would have thought that justice works like this—that the thief reaps the reward and the victim gets flogged! Hell and damnation! —Come and let's have a cup of coffee with something strong in it! Come as soon as you get through, Öman. . . .

THE CONSTABLE: I'll be with you in a little while—but don't make any noise!

ALEXANDERSSON: Yes, by all the devils, I'll make a noise—even if it should cost me three months!

THE CONSTABLE: Don't make any noise! Don't make any noise—and I'll be there!

THE JUDGE *(to* THE SHERIFF): Call the divorce suit between Baron Sprengel and his wife, née Malmberg. . . .

THE SHERIFF *(calls out)*: The divorce suit between Baron Sprengel and his wife, née Malmberg!

(THE BARON *and* THE BARONESS *come in.)*

THE JUDGE: In the proceedings brought by Baron Sprengel against his wedded wife, Baron Sprengel declares that it is his intention to continue the marriage no longer, and he requests that—as the warnings of the Vestry Board have proved to be of no avail—the couple be given a year's separation from bed and board. Has the Baroness anything to say with regard to this request?

THE BARONESS: I have no objection to the separation itself, but I have one condition to make: I insist that the child remain with me.

THE JUDGE: The law recognizes no stipulations made in advance in such cases. It is for the court to decide about the child.

THE BARONESS: This seems to me exceedingly strange.

THE JUDGE: And for that reason it is of the utmost importance to the court to learn which one of the two parties is the cause of the dissension that has resulted in the suit before it. According to the appended minutes of the Vestry Board, it appears that the wife admits to having shown at times a quarrelsome, difficult disposition; the husband, on the contrary, has admitted to no misbehavior or misconduct. Thus the Baroness seems to have acknowledged . . .

THE BARONESS: That is a lie!

THE JUDGE: I find it difficult to believe that the minutes of the Vestry Board—which have been witnessed by the rector and eight other trusted men—can be inaccurate.

THE BARONESS: The minutes are false!

THE JUDGE: Outbursts like these cannot be made with impunity before this court.

THE BARON: I should like to draw the court's attention to the fact that I voluntarily offered to surrender the child to the Baroness on certain conditions.

THE JUDGE: I repeat once again what I said a few moments ago—that it is the Court and not the plaintiff and the defendant that will pass judgment in this case. Consequently, Baroness, you deny you are the cause of the differences between you and the Baron.

THE BARONESS: Yes, I do. And it is never the fault of one that two quarrel.

THE JUDGE: This is no quarrel—it is a legal action, a breach of the law! And if I may say so, it seems to me that the Baroness is plainly showing a quarrelsome temperament and a reckless behavior.

THE BARONESS: Then you don't know my husband!

THE JUDGE: Will you be good enough to explain yourself? I can't base a decision on innuendo.

THE BARON: In that case, I must ask to have my suit withdrawn and I'll seek a divorce in other ways.

THE JUDGE: The case has already been taken cognizance of and must proceed to its determination. . . . You assert, then, Baroness, that your husband is to blame for your estrangement. Can you prove this?

THE BARONESS: Yes, it can be proved.

THE JUDGE: Will you please do so? But give due consideration to the fact that the question of the Baron's being the father is at stake, and with it the rights to the estate and property.

THE BARONESS: *That* he has forfeited many times over, not least when he denied me both sleep and food.

THE BARON: I feel compelled to mention that I have never denied the Baroness her sleep. I have merely asked her not to sleep all through the morning, because by so doing she neglected the household, and the child failed to get proper attention. And as to the food, I have always left those matters to the concern of the Baroness. I have only disapproved of certain unnecessarily extravagant social affairs, since, with the household being neglected, such expense was not justified.

THE BARONESS: He has let me lie in bed, ill, and has refused to summon a physician.

THE BARON: The Baroness had a habit of always becoming sick whenever she couldn't have her own way; but invariably such sickness would disappear before very long. After I had called in a professor from the city one time and he had diagnosed her ailment as mere sham, I refrained from summoning a doctor the next time the Baroness was taken sick. That was the time she found that the new pier-glass cost fifty crowns less than intended.

THE JUDGE: All these things are not of the nature that can be taken into consideration in judging a case of this seriousness. There must be deeper motives than that.

THE BARONESS: It seems to me that when a father refuses to let the mother of their child look after its education and upbringing, this can be counted as a motive.

THE BARON: First of all, the Baroness has had a maid to look after the child; and whenever she herself tried to care for the boy, she did everything the wrong way. Secondly, she has tried to bring up the boy as one of her own sex. She had him wear dresses until he was four years old, for instance; and to this very day, at the age of eight, his hair is the length of a girl's. And she makes him sew and crochet and has him play with dolls. All this I consider detrimental to the child's normal development toward manhood. On the other hand, she amuses herself with dressing up the daughters of the farmhands and servants as boys, has their hair cut short, and puts them to do such work as boys usually perform. In a word: When I noticed symptoms

of psychotic aberration and deviation of the kind that lead
to conflict with Chapter 18 of the Penal Code, I took the
boy's upbringing in hand myself.

THE JUDGE: And despite this you are still willing to entrust
the child to his mother's care?

THE BARON: Yes, because I never could think of being so
cruel as to take away a child from its mother, and because
the mother has promised to mend her ways. Besides, my
promise to her was a conditional one. It was only given
with the provision that it did not conflict with the law and
that no appeal to the courts was to be made. But now that
we have come to the point that accusations and recriminations have been made, I have changed my mind—especially
since I, instead of being the plaintiff, have now been made
the defendant.

THE BARONESS: That is the way this man always keeps his
promises!

THE BARON: My promises, like those of others, have always
been conditional; and as long as the conditions have been
fulfilled, I have kept my part of the bargain.

THE BARONESS: Furthermore, when we were married, he
assured me that I would have my personal freedom in
everything. . . .

THE BARON: So I did, providing that the laws of common
decency were not violated. But when her transgressions
went too far and license took the place of freedom, I felt
she had overreached herself and was imposing upon my
good will.

THE BARONESS: And after that he tormented me with the
most outrageous jealousy! That alone is enough to make it
unbearable to live together! And, to make matters worse,
he made himself ludicrous by being jealous even of my
doctor.

THE BARON: This so-called jealousy consisted in nothing more
or less than my advice to her not to accept the services of
a notorious and gossipy masseur for an ailment which is
customarily treated by a woman. However, the Baroness
may have in mind the time I showed the superintendent of
our estate the door for smoking in the drawing room and
offering my wife a cigar.

THE BARONESS: As we have started backbiting and revealing
our intimate secrets, we may as well let out the whole

truth. The Baron is guilty of adultery. Is that not enough to make him unfit to bring up my son?

THE JUDGE: Can you prove this, Baroness? *(She hands* THE JUDGE *a packet of letters.* THE JUDGE *glances through some of them.)* When did this occur?

THE BARONESS: A year ago.

THE JUDGE: According to the statute of limitation, the time for legal prosecution has expired; but the circumstances in themselves weigh heavily against the husband and may result in his losing the child and the right to a share of the common property. Does the Baron acknowledge this breach of the marriage pledge?

THE BARON: Yes—and with both shame and remorse. But there were circumstances which should be regarded as extenuating. I had been forced into a humiliating celibacy, a cold and calculated scheme of the Baroness'. And this despite the fact that I simply asked, in a decent way, to be given—as a favor—what the law prescribes as my conjugal right. I grew tired of having to pay for her love. For she had introduced prostitution into our married life. First she sold her favors for power; and later, in return for gifts and money! At last I found myself driven to seek an irregular intimacy outside the marriage—a relationship the Baroness explicitly consented to.

THE JUDGE: Did you consent to this, Baroness?

THE BARONESS: That is not true! I demand the Baron prove this!

THE BARON: It is true that I cannot give proof, as long as my only witness, my wife, denies it.

THE JUDGE: A fact need not be untrue merely because it cannot be proved. However, a bargain of this sort is contrary to existing laws. It constitutes moral turpitude, and it has no standing before the law. Thus far, Baron, the evidence I have heard is not in your favor.

THE BARONESS: And as the Baron has acknowledged his guilt with shame and remorse, I—being now the plaintiff and no longer the defendant—request that the Court proceed to render a decision since there is no need for further evidence.

THE JUDGE: As the presiding officer of this court, I would like to hear what the Baron may have to say in his defense, or at least in justification of his act.

THE BARON: I have already admitted my guilt as an adulterer and have mentioned as extenuating circumstances that it was partly due to desperate need—when, after having been married ten years, I suddenly found myself deprived of my conjugal rights—and partly because it was done with the wholehearted consent of the Baroness herself. As I now, however, have every reason to believe that all this was done for the purpose of entrapping me and making me seem guilty, it is my duty, for the sake of my son, to go a little further and . . .

THE BARONESS *(with an involuntary exclamation)*: Axel!

THE BARON: The real cause of my breaking my marriage vows—was the Baroness' unfaithfulness!

THE JUDGE: Have you any proof, Baron Sprengel, that the Baroness was unfaithful to you?

THE BARON: No! What proof I had at one time I destroyed in order to protect the family honor. But I dare say that the Baroness will still admit to the confession she once made to me.

THE JUDGE: Does the Baroness admit to this breach of your marriage vow? And if so, did it occur prior to the Baron's aberrant conduct, so that it might be assumed to have been the cause of it?

THE BARONESS: No!

THE JUDGE: Are you prepared to take an oath on your innocence with regard to this charge?

THE BARONESS: Yes.

THE BARON: God in heaven! No! She must not do it! She must not perjure herself for my sake!

THE JUDGE: I ask you once more: Are you willing to swear to it, Baroness?

THE BARONESS: Yes!

THE BARON: Allow me to point out that the Baroness is now the plaintiff in the case and as such is not required to take the oath.

THE JUDGE: As long as you have accused her of an offense, she is a defendant. What is the opinion of the jury?

VICKBERG: As long as the Baroness is a party to the proceedings, it seems to me she can hardly be a witness in her own behalf.

ERLIN: It is my opinion that if the Baroness is allowed to witness under oath, the Baron should have the same right;

but as it is against the law to put oath against oath, the whole matter remains in the dark.

VASS: But in this case it can't be a question of taking an oath as a witness; here it is a question of an oath in defense of a party's innocence.

RUTH: Then that is the first question we have to settle, I suppose.

VALLIN: We can't do that in the presence of the two parties in the case; and we can't deliberate in public.

SJÖBERG: The jury has the right of free speech, and it is not limited by any condition of secrecy.

THE JUDGE: With so many opinions to choose from, I have very little to guide me. But as the guilt of the Baron can be proved, I must ask that the Baroness take the oath and swear that she is innocent.

THE BARONESS: I am ready!

THE JUDGE: No—wait just a moment! Baron, could you—if you were given time to do so—could you produce witnesses, or proof of your assertions?

THE BARON: I neither can nor wish to do that. I am not anxious to have my disgrace spread abroad.

THE JUDGE: The deliberations of the Court are adjourned while I hold a discussion with the chairman of the Vestry Board.

(THE JUDGE *leaves the bench and goes out, left.* THE JURYMEN *are deliberating between themselves in subdued voices.* THE BARON *and* THE BARONESS *remain in the background. The* SPECTATORS *are gathered in groups, discussing the testimony, etc.*)

THE BARON (*to* THE BARONESS): You do not hesitate to commit perjury?

THE BARONESS: I shrink from nothing when my child is at stake!

THE BARON: But suppose I had proof?

THE BARONESS: But you haven't!

THE BARON: The letters are burned—but the certified copies are still in existence.

THE BARONESS: You are just lying to frighten me!

THE BARON: To show you how deeply I love my child and in order to save his mother—since I seem to be doomed anyhow—here you will find the proof. . . . And don't show yourself ungrateful now. *(He hands her a packet of letters.)*

THE BARONESS: That you were a liar—that I knew before; but that you were so low as to stoop to have the letters copied, that I could not have believed!

THE BARON: That's the thanks I get! But now we shall both be done for!

THE BARONESS: Yes—let us both go down—then at least there will be an end to this struggle!

THE BARON: Do you think it is better for the child to lose both his parents and to be left alone in the world?

THE BARONESS: That would never happen!

THE BARON: Your preposterous conceit, which makes you think yourself above both the law and your fellowmen, has incited you to take up this battle in which there can be only one loser—our son! What could you have been thinking of when you commenced this attack, which could not help but draw a defense? You could not have thought of the child! No—it must have been revenge you had in mind! But revenge for what? For my discovering your guilt!

THE BARONESS: The child? Did you think of the child when you stood here befouling my name just now before this rabble?

THE BARON: Hélène! We have clawed each other bloody like two wild beasts, we have shamelessly stripped ourselves naked before all these people who are now reveling in our downfall—for we haven't a friend among those who are here. From now on our child will never be able to speak of his parents as respectable people. A good word from his father and mother will be of no help to him when he starts out in life. He will see how they and their house are shunned—how they have to sit at home in their old age, lonely and despised! And one day—he will turn his back on us. . . .

THE BARONESS: What do you propose, then?

THE BARON: Let us leave here—let us sell the estate, and then live abroad. . . .

THE BARONESS: And start wrangling all over again! I know what it will be like! You will be meek as a lamb for a week or so and then you'll start abusing me again.

THE BARON: Think of it—now our fate is being decided by them in there. . . . You can't have much hope that the pastor will speak a good word for you after you have just called him a liar. And since I am known to be no Christian I can't expect that they will show *me* any mercy either. —Oh, I should like to hide myself in the woods under the roots of a huge tree and put my head under a rock! That is how much I feel my shame. . . .

THE BARONESS: You are quite right. The pastor likes neither one of us. It may happen as you say. . . . You ought to have a talk with him!

THE BARON: About what? About a reconciliation?

THE BARONESS: About anything you please—if you don't think it is too late! Just think—if it were too late already! . . . What is that man Alexandersson doing here? He is sneaking around us continually. I have a fear of that man!

THE BARON: Alexandersson is a decent fellow.

THE BARONESS: To you he is—but not to me! I have seen those eyes of his before. —Go and see the pastor now . . . but first take hold of my hand. . . . I have a fear of something. . . .

THE BARON: Of what, my dear? Of what are you afraid?

THE BARONESS: I don't know—of all of them—of everything—

THE BARON: You are not afraid of me, are you?

THE BARONESS: No—no longer! It is as if we had been dragged into a mill with our clothes caught between the wheels. . . . And all these malicious persons standing about, looking at us and laughing! What have we done? What is it we have done in our anger and bitterness? Just think how they will revel in seeing the Baron and the Baroness standing here in their nakedness, flogging each other! . . . Oh, I feel as if I were standing here absolutely naked— *(She buttons her coat.)*

THE BARON: Calm yourself, my dear! This is not the place to tell you what I have already told you before: that you have only one friend and one home—and we *could* start all over again! God alone knows. . . . No, we can't—we can't! . . . It has gone too far—it is the end! And this last accusation—yes, I hope it will be the last! But after all the other things, *that* had to come, too! . . . No—we are enemies for life! And if I let you keep the child, then you might marry again—I see that now! And then my child would have a stepfather—and I would have to see my wife and my son in the company of another man. . . . And I myself might be seen walking arm in arm with somebody else's strumpet. No—either you or I! One of us must be punished! You or I!

THE BARONESS: You! For if I let you have the child, you might marry someone else—and I might have to see another woman as the mother of my child! Oh—the very thought of it could make me commit murder! A stepmother for *my* child!

THE BARON: You should have thought of that before! But when you saw me chafing restlessly at the bond of love that held us together, it never occurred to you that I could love anyone but yourself.

THE BARONESS: Do you think I ever loved you?

THE BARON: Yes—one time, at any rate—when I had been unfaithful to you! That time you were sublime in your love. . . . And your pretense at scorn made you irresistible. But you also came to respect me after my transgression. Whether it was the male or the culprit in me that you admired most, I do not know—but I have a feeling it was both. It must have been both, because you are the most female of women I have ever known! What a pity that you became my wife! As my mistress you would have reaped an unchallenged victory, and your infidelities would only have provided the bouquet for my new wine.

THE BARONESS: Yes, your love was always of the sensual kind.

THE BARON: Sensual as everything spiritual; spiritual as everything sensual! My weakness for you, which was the very source from which my feelings took their strength, gave you the idea that you were the stronger one, while in reality you were merely more malicious, more brutal, and more ruthless than I.

THE BARONESS: You—the stronger one? You—who keep changing your mind every two minutes—you who never know what you want?

THE BARON: Oh, yes—I know very well what I want, but in me there is room for both love and hate—and one minute I can love you, while I can't the next! And now I can only hate you!

THE BARONESS: But have you also thought about the child?

THE BARON: Yes—now and forever! And do you realize why? Because he is the embodiment of our love. He is the memory of our beautiful moments—the bond that links our souls together, the focal point where we will always meet without intending to. . . . And that is why we shall never be able to be parted, even if our divorce should separate us. Oh, if I could only hate you as I would like to hate you!

(THE JUDGE *and* THE PASTOR *enter, engaged in conversation. They walk downstage, where they stop.*)

THE JUDGE: I realize, therefore, how absolutely hopeless it is to try to get at the truth and to attain justice. And to me it seems as if the laws were several centuries behind our conception of justice. Was I not compelled to sentence Alexandersson, who was innocent, and fine him, and let her—who was guilty of theft—get away with a clean character? And as for this divorce suit, I am at a loss to know what the facts are, and I haven't the conscience to pass judgment.

THE PASTOR: But a decision has to be made.

THE JUDGE: Not by me! —I shall resign my office and choose another profession!

THE PASTOR: Oh! That would cause a scandal and would only make you a laughingstock—and it would bar you from most any other career. Just keep going, and after presiding as judge for a few years, you will soon see how much easier it will be to crush a few human fates like egg shells. Moreover, if you want to stand apart from this particular case, let the jurors outvote you—and then the responsibility will be theirs.

THE JUDGE: That is one way—and I am quite sure they will be almost totally against me. For I have formed an opinion about this case, although it is based merely on intuition, so that I can't be absolutely certain. . . . Thank you for the advice.

THE SHERIFF (*who has been speaking with* ALEXANDERSSON, *walks over to* THE JUDGE): In my capacity as public prosecutor, I wish to report that the farmer Alexandersson will be a witness against Baroness Sprengel.

THE JUDGE: With relation to the adultery charge?

THE SHERIFF: Yes.

THE JUDGE *(to* THE PASTOR*)*: This is something that may bring us a little closer to a solution.

THE PASTOR: Oh, there may be many such loose ends floating about, if you only knew how to catch hold of them.

THE JUDGE: Just the same, it is sad to see two human beings, who once loved each other, now tearing each other apart in this manner. It's like seeing two animals being led to slaughter.

THE PASTOR: Well, such is love, my dear Judge!

THE JUDGE: What, then, is hate?

THE PASTOR: Hate is the lining inside the garment.

(THE JUDGE *walks over to the* JURYMEN *and talks to them.)*

THE BARONESS *(comes up to* THE PASTOR*)*: Help us, Pastor! Help us!

THE PASTOR: As a clergyman, I cannot and must not! And you will remember, I warned you not to play with things that are so grave. It was such a simple matter to get a divorce, you said. Well, get rid of each other, then! The law does not prevent you, so don't blame the law!

THE JUDGE *(who has seated himself)*: The Court will now resume its deliberations. According to the report of Sheriff Viberg, the public prosecutor, a witness against Baroness Sprengel has come forward, and this witness is affirming that the adultery charge made against her is valid. *(In slightly raised voice.)* Farmer Alexandersson.

ALEXANDERSSON *(steps forward)*: Here I am.

THE JUDGE: How can you prove your allegation?

ALEXANDERSSON: I saw it happen.

THE BARONESS: He is lying! Let him prove it!

ALEXANDERSSON: Prove it! I'm a witness this time!

THE BARONESS: Your statement is no proof, even if you are called a witness for the moment.

ALEXANDERSSON: Perhaps a witness has to have a couple of other witnesses, and the other witnesses still a couple of *other* witnesses!

THE BARONESS: Yes, it might well be called for when one has no assurance that they are not lying—all of them!

THE BARON *(steps forward)*: Farmer Alexandersson's testimony will not be needed. Permit me to deposit with the court all of the correspondence, which will completely prove the Baroness' marital infidelity. —Here are the original letters. The copies are in the possession of the defendant.

(THE BARONESS *gives a shriek, but soon recovers.*)

THE JUDGE (*to* THE BARONESS): The Baroness was willing to take an oath on her innocence a moment ago.

THE BARONESS: But I didn't! And now I think it's about time that the Baron and I call it quits.

THE JUDGE: The law does not cancel crime with crime! Each one's account has to be settled separately.

THE BARONESS: Then, while we are here, I want to file a claim against the Baron for my dowry, which he has squandered.

THE JUDGE: If the Baron has spent the Baroness' dowry recklessly, there is every reason for settling it now.

THE BARON: When the Baroness and I were married, she brought with her six thousand crowns in stocks. This stock could find no buyers and later became valueless. As the Baroness, when she married, was employed as a telegrapher and refused—as she said—to be supported by her husband, we entered into a marriage settlement in which it was stipulated that each one of us was to be self-supporting. But after being married, she lost her position, and since then I have been supporting her. This I have done without protest, but now that she comes with a bill and asks for payment, I shall request permission to offer a bill of my own in return. It adds up to thirty-five thousand crowns and amounts to one third of the household expenses during the years we have been married. This means that I myself accept two thirds of the total expenses.

THE JUDGE: Was this agreement made in writing, and, if so, is it in your possession?

THE BARON: No, it was a verbal agreement.

THE JUDGE: Have you, Baroness, anything to prove that you entrusted your dowry to the Baron?

THE BARONESS: When I did, it never occurred to me that it was necessary to get a receipt! I took it for granted that I was dealing with a man of honor!

THE JUDGE: Then it will be impossible for me to take the matter under consideration. Will the members of the jury please retire to the small courtroom and consider the evidence and then come to a decision. . . .

(THE JURY *and* THE JUDGE *go out to the left.*)

ALEXANDERSSON (*to* THE SHERIFF): This here justice is more than I can make any sense out of!

THE SHERIFF: I think it would be wise of you to go straight home now—or you might have the same experience as that farmer in Mariestad. . . . Did you hear what happened to him?

ALEXANDERSSON: No, I didn't.

THE SHERIFF: Well, he went to court as a spectator—was dragged into a case as a witness—and ended up by getting twenty lashes!

ALEXANDERSSON: Hell and damnation! But it doesn't surprise me! I wouldn't put it past them! (*He leaves.*)

(THE BARON *goes downstage to* THE BARONESS.)

THE BARONESS: You seem to find it difficult to keep away from me—

THE BARON: Hélène! I have stabbed you, thrust a knife into you—and I am bleeding—for your blood is mine. . . .

THE BARONESS: And you certainly know how to conjure up charges!

THE BARON: No—only countercharges! Your courage is the courage of despair, of one who is condemned to die! And once you have come away from this, you will fall into a collapse. . . . For then you will no longer have me to load your guilt and grief upon—and you will be tormented by your conscience. . . . Do you know why I have not killed myself?

THE BARONESS: Because you lacked the courage!

THE BARON: No—it was not out of fear for the fires of hell—I put no credence in that—but because I kept thinking that, even if you should be awarded the child, you will be gone in five years!

(THE BARONESS *gives him a startled glance.*)

For that is what the doctor told me! And then the boy would be without both father and mother! Think of that—alone by himself in the world!

THE BARONESS (*frantically*): Five years! —That is a lie!

THE BARON: Five years! And then—whether you want it or not—the child will be with me!

THE BARONESS: Oh, no—never! My family would bring suit and take the child away from you! Even if I die, my will shall survive!

THE BARON: Yes, evil has a way of surviving! It's true—it never dies! But I would like you to tell me why you are so set against my having the boy—and why you begrudge him his father, when you know that he needs me. Is it out of sheer malice and revengefulness that you so punish the child?

(THE BARONESS *does not answer.*)

Do you know what I told the pastor? I told him I thought you might have some doubts about the child's parentage, and that this might be the reason for your refusing to let me have the child—thinking you did not wish me to build my happiness on a false foundation. . . . He answered me, "No, I cannot think she could have any such noble motive!" —And I do not believe you yourself know why you are so fanatical on this point. But I suppose it is our struggle for survival and continued existence that impels us to keep our hold. Our son has your body but my soul—and the soul is something you cannot destroy. In him you will have me back again when you least expect it; in him you will read my thoughts, you'll find my tastes and nature and passions . . . and that is why one day you will come to hate him as you now hate me! That is what I dread!

THE BARONESS: You still seem to fear that he shall be mine!

THE BARON: Because you are a woman and a mother, you hold an advantage over me with those who sit in judgment on us. Even though justice may cast its dice blindfolded, the dice are almost always loaded.

THE BARONESS: Even though we are about to part, you know how to pay compliments. Perhaps, after all, you don't hate me as much as you pretend.

THE BARON: To be quite frank, I think it is not so much you that I despise as it is my own dishonor and disgrace. But I could hardly say that I don't hate you. And why—why this abominable hate? Perhaps I lost sight of the fact that you are nearing your forties and that something masculine is beginning to take root in you. Perhaps it is this touch of the male, which I have felt in your kisses, in your embraces, that I find so repulsive. . . .

THE BARONESS: Perhaps it is. For I have never told you before that my greatest sorrow in life has been that I was not born a man!

THE BARON: And so, perhaps, your sorrow has in turn brought about the greatest sorrow of *my* life! And now you are avenging yourself for one of nature's tricks by bringing up your son as a woman. —Will you promise me one thing?

THE BARONESS: Will *you* promise *me* one thing?

THE BARON: What good does it do to promise? You know we never keep our promises!

THE BARONESS: No, you are right. Let us make no more promises.

THE BARON: But will you answer a question truthfully?

THE BARONESS: Even if I told you the truth, you would believe it was a lie!

THE BARON: Yes—I would.

THE BARONESS: Can you see now that all is over between us—forever?

THE BARON: Forever! And we once vowed to love each other for eternity!

THE BARONESS: What a shame to be forced to make such a vow!

THE BARON: Why do you say that? Marriage is a bond, isn't it—even such as it is?

THE BARONESS: I could never endure any bond!

THE BARON: Would it have been better, do you think, if we had not bound ourselves?

THE BARONESS: For me it would have been better, yes.

THE BARON: I wonder! And, in that case, you would have had no hold on me.

THE BARONESS: Nor you on me.

THE BARON: And so it would have been much the same thing as—as when you reduce a fraction. Consequently, it is not the fault of the law, nor our own fault, nor can anyone else be given the blame. And still we have to assume the responsibility.

(THE SHERIFF *approaches* THE BARON *and* THE BARONESS.)

And now—now the judgment is being handed down. . . Goodbye—Hélène!

THE BARONESS: Goodbye, Axel!

THE BARON: Parting is hard. Living together—is impossible. But, at any rate, the fight is over!

THE BARONESS: If only it were! —But I fear it is just about to begin.

THE SHERIFF: The parties in the case will retire while the Court is deliberating!

THE BARONESS: Axel! A word with you before it is too late! We have to be prepared for the possibility that the child will be taken from us both. Won't you drive home and take the boy to your mother—then let us flee from here, far away from here!

THE BARON: I can't help feeling you are trying to trick me again.

THE BARONESS: No, I am not! I am no longer thinking of you—and I am not thinking of myself—I have forgotten about revenge! Only save the child, do you hear? Do it, please. . . .

THE BARON: I'll do what you say. But if you are deceiving me . . . Never mind, I'll do it!

(*He hastens out.* THE BARONESS *goes out, rear.* THE JURY *and* THE JUDGE *enter and resume their places.*)

THE JUDGE: We have weighed all the evidence in this case, and I shall now ask the members of the jury to express their respective opinions before sentence is passed. For my own part, I find it only reasonable that the child should be awarded to its mother. While both husband and wife are equally responsible for their estrangement, the mother is by nature better fitted to care for the child than is the father.

(*There is a silence.*)

EKLUND: According to the law presently in force, the wife's position and status is determined by her husband's, and not vice versa.

VICKBERG: And the husband is the rightful guardian of the wife!

SJÖBERG: In the marriage service—which, as we know, gives validity to the marriage—the wife is enjoined to be subservient to the husband; therefore it seems to me that the man is superior to the woman.

BOMAN: And the children must be brought up in the faith of their father.

SÖDERBERG: From this it is consequently clear that the children go with the father and not the mother.

ANDERSSON OF VIK: But since husband and wife, in the case before us, are equally guilty and—judging by what the Court has heard—equally unfit to rear a child, it is my opinion that the child be taken away from both.

ANDERSSON OF BERGA: Being in agreement with Olof Andersson, I should like to call to your attention that the judge in such cases appoints two reputable men to look after the children and the property involved. The income from the property shall be used for the subsistence of the husband and his wife and the child or children.

VALLIN: In that case, I should like to propose as guardians Alexander Eklund and Erenfrid Söderberg, both of whom are known for their righteousness and dependability and for their Christian character and disposition.

RUTH: I concur with Olof Andersson of Vik concerning the separation of the child from both father and mother, and with Axel Vallin concerning the two guardians, whose Christian character makes them unusually well fitted to look after the child and its upbringing.

ERLIN: I concur with what juryman Ruth has just said.

VASS: I concur.

ÖSTMAN: I concur.

THE JUDGE: As the majority of the jurymen have expressed an opinion contrary to my own, I shall ask the jury to proceed to vote on the question. Perhaps I ought first of all to put this question to you: Is Olof Andersson's proposal that the child be taken from both father and mother acceptable to you? And are you all unanimously in favor of it?

THE JURYMEN (*in unison*): Yes.

THE JUDGE: If there is any one of you who is not in accord with this, he will please raise his hand!

(Silence; no movement.)

The verdict of the jury has consequently nullified my own judicial opinion; however, I shall enter my exception in the record against this decision, which to me seems unnecessarily cruel. —Husband and wife are to be sentenced to a year's separation from bed and board under the penalty of imprisonment if, during this period, they should seek each other out. *(To* THE SHERIFF.*)* Call in the parties!

(THE BARONESS *enters. People stream in.)*

THE JUDGE: Is Baron Sprengel not present?

THE BARONESS: The Baron will be here immediately.

THE JUDGE *(curtly)*: Whoever fails to be present has only himself to blame. The decision of the Circuit Court is as follows: In the case of Sprengel versus Sprengel, the husband and the wife are sentenced to one year's separation from bed and board; and their child shall be removed from the parents and given into the custody of two guardians for upbringing and education. The court has selected and approved as guardians two members of the jury, Alexander Eklund and Erenfrid Söderberg.

(THE BARONESS *lets out a scream and falls to the floor.* THE SHERIFF *and* THE CONSTABLE *lift her up and place her in a chair. Meantime, some of the* SPECTATORS *saunter out.* THE BARON *enters. He is out of breath.)*

THE BARON: Your Honor! I just heard the Court's verdict outside, and I ask permission to take exception to it. I challenge its validity—and also the entire jury, all of whom are my personal enemies—and the selection of the two guardians, Alexander Eklund and Erenfrid Söderberg, neither of whom possesses the financial security that is demanded of guardians. Furthermore, I shall prefer charges against Your Honor for a lack of judgment and understanding in the exercise of your office, because you failed to recognize that the one who first offends against the marriage laws is the one who is guilty of causing the mate to commit a similar offense; thus the degree of their guilt is not the same.

THE JUDGE: If anyone is not in agreement with the decision rendered, he has recourse to a higher court where he may appeal the judgment within the time limit stipulated by law! —Will the jury please come with me now and inspect the parsonage in connection with the lawsuit pending against the assessors of the communal council. . . .

(THE JUDGE *and* THE JURYMEN *go out, rear. The remaining* SPECTATORS *also leave.* THE BARON *and* THE BARONESS *are alone on the stage.* THE BARONESS *sits up.*)

THE BARONESS: Where is Emile?

THE BARON: He was not there.

THE BARONESS: You lie!

THE BARON (*after a silence*): Yes! —I did not take him to my mother, for I can't depend on her. I took him to the parsonage.

THE BARONESS: To the pastor!

THE BARON: Your one and only dependable enemy, yes! What other person could I have dared to trust? And I did it because I read something in your eyes a while ago that told me you might have in mind to do away with the child and yourself. . . .

THE BARONESS: And you saw that! —Oh, how could I have let you deceive me into believing you?

THE BARON: And what have you to say now—about all this?

THE BARONESS: I don't know. . . . I am so exhausted, I wouldn't even feel another blow. . . . It almost soothes me, comforts me, to have been given the final stab.

THE BARON: You give no thought to what will come *after* this: how your son will be reared by two peasants whose ignorance and lack of breeding, and crude habits, will torment the child and, little by little, bring about his death; how he will be oppressed by his environment and brought down into their narrow outlook; how his mind will be strangled by religious superstition; how he will be taught to have contempt for his father and mother. . . .

THE BARONESS: Stop! Don't tell me any more or I shall lose my mind! My Emile, living with peasant wives who don't know enough to wash themselves, whose beds are infested with vermin, and who never look to see whether a comb is clean or not! My Emile—no—it must never happen. . . .

THE BARON: But it is all true—all of it—and you have no one but yourself to blame!

THE BARONESS: Myself? Yes—but did I create myself? Did I implant evil in myself, sow hatred and wild passions in my heart? No! Who could have robbed me of the will and the power to fight against these evils? I look at myself now, and I feel I ought to be pitied! Don't you think I should be?

THE BARON: Yes, I do. We are both to be pitied! We tried to avoid the rocks that marriage so often breaks upon, and so we decided to live together as husband and wife without being married. But even then we quarreled, for we had sacrificed one of the greatest rewards that life has to offer— the respect of our fellow-beings. And so we were married. But we still wanted to outwit society and its laws: we would not have a regular marriage ceremony; instead, we slithered into a civil marriage. We were to be completely independent of each other, we were to keep separate accounts, we were not to be possessive of each other—but again we fell back into the old rut! Without any marriage ceremony—and with a marriage contract! And the marriage went to pieces! I forgave you your infidelity, and we lived together—free to do what we pleased—in voluntary separation—and all for the sake of the child! But I grew tired of presenting my friend's mistress as my wife, and so it came to the point when we had to part! Do you know—do you know what we have been fighting against? You call it God—I call it Nature! And Nature drove us to hate each other, just as it impels us to love each other. And now we are condemned to inflict pain on each other as long as we have a spark of life in us. . . . There will be new proceedings in the higher courts, the case will be reopened, the Vestry Board will be asked its opinion, the cathedral chapter will be requested to comment—and then the Supreme Court will give its decision! And finally will come my complaint to the Department of Justice, my plea for guardianship, your exceptions and challenges, your countersuits—in short, from guillotine to guillotine, without any hope of finding a merciful executioner! The property neglected—financial ruin—the child's education ignored! Then, why don't we put an end to our miserable lives? Because the child holds us back! I see you are weeping— but I can't weep! Not even when I think of the night in store for us in our desolate home! And you, poor Hélène, you shall now have to go back to your mother again—your mother, whom you once left with happiness in your heart, glad to have a home of your own! To be a daughter to her again . . . Yes, you may find it worse than being a wife! One year—two years—many years . . . How much longer do you think we can endure this suffering?

THE BARONESS: I shall never go back to my mother—never! I shall haunt the highways and the forests and find a place to hide, where I can scream—scream myself into exhaustion against God, who has allowed this fiendish love to come into the world as a torment to us human beings . . . and when darkness falls, I shall lay myself down in the pastor's barn so that I may be near my child when I fall asleep.

THE BARON: You think you can sleep tonight? Do you?

CURTAIN

The Pelican

(1907)

A Tragedy in One Act

CHARACTERS

THE MOTHER,
  Élise, a widow

FREDRIK,
  her son, a law student

GERDA,
  her daughter

AXEL,
  her son-in-law, married to Gerda

MARGRET,
  cook and general servant

*A drawing room. A door, rear, leads
to the dining room. At left, French
windows, opening onto a corner balcony.*

*A bureau-desk, a writing table, a chaise
longue covered with a slipcover of
worsted shag, also a rocking chair and
several other chairs, a pedestal with a
palm, etc.*

THE MOTHER *enters. She is dressed in
mourning. She seats herself apathetically
in an easy chair. From outside can be
heard the strains of Chopin's* Fantaisie
impromptu, oeuvre posthume, opus 66.
MARGRET *enters from the rear door.*

THE MOTHER: Shut the door, will you, please?

MARGRET: Are you alone, Mrs. Hult?

THE MOTHER: Will you shut the door, please. . . . Who is
that playing?

MARGRET: What terrible weather this evening, windy and
rainy . . .

THE MOTHER: Will you please shut the door—I can't bear
the odor of carbolic acid and spruce. . . .

MARGRET: I know you can't—and that's why I kept saying
that Mr. Hult should have been taken to the crypt as soon
as he passed away. . . .

THE MOTHER: It was the children who wanted the funeral
to be held here. . . .

MARGRET: Why do you want to live here now? . . . Why don't
you move?

THE MOTHER: The landlord won't let us break the lease—so we have to remain where we are. . . .

(There is a pause.)

Why did you remove the slipcover from the red chaise longue?

MARGRET: I am sending it out to be cleaned. *(Pause.)* It was on the chaise longue that your husband drew his last breath—you know that, don't you? Then why don't you get rid of it? . . .

THE MOTHER: I have no right to touch a thing until the inventory has been made. That's why I am sitting here like a shut-in—and I don't like to go into the other rooms. . . .

MARGRET: Why?

THE MOTHER: The memories—all the unpleasant memories—and the awful odor . . . Is that my son playing?

MARGRET: Yes . . . He doesn't feel at home in here. He feels uncomfortable—and he is always hungry. . . . He says he has never had enough to eat. . . .

THE MOTHER: His health has always been poor—ever since he was born. . . .

MARGRET: A bottle baby must have nutritious food after it has been weaned. . . .

THE MOTHER *(bitingly)*: Is that so? Well—has there ever been a lack of anything here?

MARGRET: I wouldn't say that exactly—but, just the same, you shouldn't have bought the cheapest and poorest food. . . . And to send children to school on nothing but a cup of chicory and a piece of bread—it just isn't right. . . .

THE MOTHER: My children have never complained about what they get to eat. . . .

MARGRET: That may be! Perhaps not to you! No—they wouldn't have dared. . . . But when they were growing up, they used to come to me in the kitchen. . . .

THE MOTHER: We have always been in modest circumstances. . . .

MARGRET: How can you say that? I read in the newspaper once that Mr. Hult was paying taxes on twenty thousand a year. . . .

THE MOTHER: It doesn't take long before money is gone.

MARGRET: Yes, yes—but the children are not very strong. . . .

Take Miss Gerda—she is not yet fully developed although she has passed her twentieth birthday. . . .

THE MOTHER: What are you talking about?

MARGRET: Yes, yes! *(Pause.)* Don't you want me to make a fire for you? It's cold in here.

THE MOTHER: No, thank you. We can't afford to be burning up our money. . . .

MARGRET: But young Mister Fredrik is frozen all day long, and he tries to keep himself warm by going out for a walk or by playing the piano. . . .

THE MOTHER: He has always been frozen. . . .

MARGRET: I wonder why?

THE MOTHER: Watch out, Margret! . . .

(There is a silence.)

Is somebody walking about inside?

MARGRET: No, nobody is walking inside. . . .

THE MOTHER: You don't think I am afraid of ghosts, do you?

MARGRET: How would I know? . . . But one thing I do know —I am not going to stay here much longer. . . . From the day I came into this house, it was as if it had been my fate to watch over the children. . . . I wanted to leave when I saw how you mistreated your servants—but I couldn't—I didn't feel free to. . . . But now that Miss Gerda is married, I feel my mission here is at an end; and soon the hour of relief will be at hand—not quite yet, though. . . .

THE MOTHER: I don't understand a word you are saying. . . . Everybody in the world knows how I have sacrificed myself for my children—how I have done all I could to take care of my home and responsibilities. . . . You are the only one to cast aspersions on me—but I am not going to let it disturb me. You may leave any time you like. Now that the young people are moving in with me, I don't intend to keep any servants. . . .

MARGRET: I wish you luck! Children are generally not too grateful by nature, and mothers-in-law are not too highly regarded—unless they can supply the wherewithal.

THE MOTHER: You needn't worry—I'll pay my own way. . . . And, what is more, I'll help with the household chores. Besides, my son-in-law is not like any other son-in-law. . . .

MARGRET: Isn't he?

THE MOTHER: No, he isn't! He doesn't treat me at all like a mother-in-law, but rather as a sister, even a friend. . . .

(MARGRET *makes a wry face.*)

THE MOTHER: I noticed the face you just made! I like my son-in-law—and that's my privilege—and he deserves to be liked. . . . My husband didn't care for him; he was envious, not to say jealous. Yes—he paid me a compliment by being jealous, even if I am not so very young any longer. . . . What did you say?

MARGRET: I didn't say anything! But I thought I heard someone come in. . . . It's Mister Fredrik—I can hear him coughing. —Don't you want me to make a fire?

THE MOTHER: It isn't necessary.

MARGRET: Mrs. Hult, I have frozen in this house, and I have starved, and I am not going to speak about that—but let me have a bed, a decent bed to sleep in, now that I am old and worn out. . . .

THE MOTHER: A fine time to ask for that—now that you are leaving. . . .

MARGRET: You are right. I forgot. But if you have any respect for your house and home, take my bedclothes, which people have slept in and died in, and burn them, so that you won't have to be ashamed in front of whoever takes my place—if you should ever get anybody!

THE MOTHER: Nobody will take your place!

MARGRET: But if anybody should, they wouldn't stay. . . . I have seen fifty maids come and go. . . .

THE MOTHER: Because they were no good—none of you are. . . .

MARGRET: Thank you! . . . And now—now your day will come, madam! We all have our day—it comes and goes by turns!

THE MOTHER: Have you finished now?

MARGRET: Yes, soon! Very soon! Sooner than you think! (*She goes out.*)

(FREDRIK *enters. He carries a book and is coughing. He stutters slightly.*)

THE MOTHER: Shut the door, will you, please. . . .
FREDRIK: Why?

THE MOTHER: Is that a way to answer me? What do you want?

FREDRIK: Do you mind if I sit in here? I can't read in my room—it is too cold in there.

THE MOTHER: Oh, you are always frozen.

FREDRIK: With no heat, you feel the cold much more when you are sitting still.

(*Silence.* FREDRIK *pretends to read.*)

Has the inventory been completed yet?

THE MOTHER: Why do you ask? Can't you wait until we are out of mourning? Don't you miss your father?

FREDRIK: Yes, I do—yes—but he is well off where he is, I am sure—and I am glad he has found peace at last. But that does not prevent me from wanting to know just where I stand—whether I shall be able to graduate without having to borrow money. . . .

THE MOTHER: You know that your father left nothing—except, perhaps, debts. . . .

FREDRIK: But his business must be worth something, don't you think?

THE MOTHER: You can't call it a business when it carries no stock of any kind—no commodities or wares, you understand.

FREDRIK (*after a moment's thought*): But the firm—its name and good will—its customers . . .

THE MOTHER: How can you sell a firm's customers?

(*There is a silence.*)

FREDRIK: Why, yes, they say that . . .

THE MOTHER: Have you been to see an attorney?

(*Silence.*)

So that's the way you mourn your father?

FREDRIK: No! But let us take one thing at a time! Where are my sister Gerda and her husband?

THE MOTHER: They came home this morning from their wedding trip and went to a *pension* for the night.

FREDRIK: Then they will at least get enough to eat!

THE MOTHER: You don't do anything but talk about food! Have you ever had reason to complain about the meals you get at home?

FREDRIK *(with suppressed sarcasm)*: Oh, no—never!

THE MOTHER: Tell me something! During the last few months
—when your father and I were living apart, you remember—did he ever mention anything about his firm's financial
condition?

FREDRIK *(engrossed in his book)*: No-o—nothing in particular . . .

THE MOTHER: Can you explain why he should not have
left something, when he had an income of twenty thousand
the last few years of his life?

FREDRIK: I know nothing about Father's business—but I did
hear him say that the household took a good deal of money
to run—and then he spent quite a lot of money recently
when he bought the new furniture.

THE MOTHER: He said that, did he? I wonder whether he had
any debts?

FREDRIK: I don't know. He did have some, but he paid them.

THE MOTHER: Where did the money go? Did he make a
will? . . . He hated me—and several times he threatened
to leave me without a penny. Could he possibly have
hidden away some money somewhere?

(There is a silence.)

Is somebody walking about inside?

FREDRIK: No, I don't hear anybody.

THE MOTHER: I am a little nervous, because of everything
that has happened—the funeral . . . and the business.
—However, you know that your sister and your brother-
in-law are taking over the apartment here—so you shall
have to look for a room for yourself somewhere else.

FREDRIK: Yes, I know.

THE MOTHER: You don't like Gerda's husband, do you?

FREDRIK: No, there is no love lost between us.

THE MOTHER: Nevertheless, he is a fine young man, a splendid
young man . . . and you ought to like him. He deserves it.

FREDRIK: He doesn't like me—and, besides, he behaved badly
to Father.

THE MOTHER: Whose fault was that?

FREDRIK: Father was never mean.

THE MOTHER: No?

FREDRIK: Now I think I do hear somebody inside. . . .

THE MOTHER: Put on some lights. . . . But only a couple!

(FREDRIK *switches on a couple of lights. There is a pause.*)

THE MOTHER: Wouldn't you like to have Father's portrait in your room? The one hanging on the wall?

FREDRIK: Why?

THE MOTHER: I don't like it—his eyes have such a mean look. . . .

FREDRIK: They don't to me! (*Takes down the portrait from the wall.*) Yes, I'll take it. . . .

(*There is a pause.*)

THE MOTHER: I am waiting for Axel and Gerda. . . . Wouldn't you like to see them?

FREDRIK: No! I have no wish to—and I think I'll go to my room. I only wish I could have a fire in my stove.

THE MOTHER: We can't afford to burn up our money. . . .

FREDRIK: I have heard that for twenty years—and yet we have had money to go traveling abroad, merely in order to boast about it, and we spend enough on a hotel dinner to buy four fathoms of birch wood—four fathoms on one dinner!

THE MOTHER: You talk nothing but nonsense!

FREDRIK: There certainly was something wrong here, but now I think it will come to an end—as soon as the settlement is made. . . .

THE MOTHER: What do you mean?

FREDRIK: I mean the inventory, and all the rest. . . .

THE MOTHER: What? . . . The rest?

FREDRIK: Possible debts and unfinished business. . . .

THE MOTHER: Oh! So-o?

FREDRIK: In the meantime, may I have some money for some woolen underwear?

THE MOTHER: You ask for money for things like that at a time like this? Isn't it time that you began to think about earning some money yourself?

FREDRIK: Yes—as soon as I have graduated. . . .

THE MOTHER: You have to borrow, then, I suppose, like everybody else. . . .

FREDRIK: Who would lend money to me?

THE MOTHER: Your father's friends!

FREDRIK: Father had no friends! An independent man has

no friends. Friendship is nothing but an attachment formed
for the purpose of mutual admiration. . . .

THE MOTHER: How wise you are! That's something you
learned from your father, isn't it?

FREDRIK: Yes, he was a wise man—but now and then he
committed stupidities.

THE MOTHER: Listen to him! —Have you thought about getting married?

FREDRIK: No, thanks! To keep a companion to entertain
young men about town—to act as legal protection for a
flirtatious woman—to supply ammunition to one's best
friend, which is the same thing as one's worst enemy, in a
tug of war against oneself . . . Oh, no, I take care not to do
that!

THE MOTHER: Well, I never heard . . . Go to your room—I
have had enough for today! You must have been drinking!

FREDRIK: That's something I always have to do—it alleviates
the cough and makes me forget my hunger.

THE MOTHER: Are you complaining about the food again?

FREDRIK: There is nothing wrong with the food, except that
it is so meager that it tastes more like air. . . .

THE MOTHER *(taken aback)*: Now you have to go!

FREDRIK: . . . Or it is so full of salt and pepper that you feel
hungry after eating it! You might call it spiced air!

THE MOTHER: I believe you are drunk! Get out of here!

FREDRIK: Yes—I'll get out! I'd like to add something—but
this will have to do for today! Yes! *(He goes out.)*

(THE MOTHER *walks back and forth, ill at ease, ner-
vously pulling out one table drawer after another.*
AXEL *enters breezily.)*

THE MOTHER *(greets him affectionately)*: At last you are
back, Axel! I have been longing for you. . . . But where
is Gerda?

AXEL: She'll be here a little later. Well, how are you? And
how is everything?

THE MOTHER: Sit down, and let me ask you a question first—
we haven't seen each other since the wedding. Why did
you come back so soon? I thought you had planned to be
away for eight days—and you have only been away three.

AXEL: Well, it got to be a little tedious, you know. There
was nothing more to talk about—and then the loneliness

started to get oppressive. . . . And we had become so used to your company that we began to miss you.

THE MOTHER: You mean that? Yes, we three have stuck together through all sorts of stormy weather—and I dare say I have been of some help to you.

AXEL: Gerda is still a child, and she doesn't understand the art of living. . . . She has her prejudices and is a little stubborn . . . in some respects she is even fanatical. . . .

THE MOTHER: And—what did you think of your wedding?

AXEL: Very successful, very! And the verses—how did you like the verses?

THE MOTHER: The verses to me, you mean? Why, I don't believe any mother-in-law ever had such verses dedicated to her on her daughter's wedding day. . . . Do you remember the verse about the pelican who gives her blood to her young? You know, it made me cry—yes, it really did. . . .

AXEL: But not for long. Because afterward you danced every dance, every single one. Gerda almost became jealous of you. . . .

THE MOTHER: Well, it wouldn't have been the first time! She wanted me to come to the wedding in black—because of our mourning, she said. But I paid no attention to her. You don't expect me to take orders from my children, do you?

AXEL: Why, of course not; why should you? Gerda is a little absurd at times. If I so much as look at a woman, she . . .

THE MOTHER: What? You are not happy together?

AXEL: You say "happy." . . . What does it mean to be happy, anyhow?

THE MOTHER: So? You have already quarreled?

AXEL: Already? We never did anything but quarrel when we were engaged. . . . And, to add insult to injury, I had to resign my lieutenant's commission in the regular army and go into the reserves. . . . It's really amusing, but it appears as though she likes me less without the uniform!

THE MOTHER: Well, why don't you wear your uniform, then? I must admit I hardly recognize you in civilian clothes. You are really quite another person. . . .

AXEL: I can only wear my uniform on active duty and on parade.

THE MOTHER: You mean you are not permitted to?

AXEL: No—those are the regulations. . . .

THE MOTHER: Whatever the reason, I can't help feeling sorry for Gerda. She was engaged to a lieutenant—and finds herself married to a bookkeeper!

AXEL: Well, but there is nothing that can be done about it, is there? One has to live. . . . A propos—is there any news of the family affairs?

THE MOTHER: Quite frankly, I don't know. . . . But I am beginning to be suspicious of Fredrik. . . .

AXEL: How so?

THE MOTHER: He was talking so mysteriously this evening. . . .

AXEL: He's such a boor!

THE MOTHER: People like him can be sly; I am not so sure that there isn't a will hidden somewhere—or that he didn't have some savings. . . .

AXEL: Have you looked around?

THE MOTHER: I have looked in every drawer. . . .

AXEL: In Fredrik's room, you mean?

THE MOTHER: Yes, of course. And I always go through his wastebasket, since he writes letters and tears them up. . . .

AXEL: That doesn't mean anything—but have you been through the old man's bureau-desk?

THE MOTHER: Certainly . . .

AXEL: I mean thoroughly . . . Every one of the drawers?

THE MOTHER: Every single one!

AXEL: Bureau-desks can have secret drawers, you know.

THE MOTHER: I never thought of that!

AXEL: Then we have to investigate. . . . (*He goes over to the bureau-desk.*)

THE MOTHER: No—don't touch anything—it's been sealed by the public administrator!

AXEL: Can't we look for it without touching the seal?

THE MOTHER: No! No!

AXEL: Yes—if we loosen the boards in the back . . . All secret drawers are in the back. . . .

THE MOTHER: You need tools for that. . . .

AXEL: Oh, no—we can manage without tools. . . .

THE MOTHER: But Gerda must never know!

AXEL: Why, certainly not! She would immediately tell her brother. . . .

THE MOTHER (*closes and locks the doors*): Just to be on the safe side, I am locking the doors.

AXEL *(examines the back of the bureau-desk)*: Why, someone has already been here! There is a board loose—I can reach inside with my hand. . . .

THE MOTHER: Fredrik has been here! . . . You see? I was right in my suspicions. . . . Hurry up—someone is coming!

AXEL: Here—I can feel some papers!

THE MOTHER: Hurry! Hurry—someone is coming!

AXEL: It's an envelope—a large envelope. . . .

THE MOTHER: I can hear Gerda coming! Give me the papers! Quick!

AXEL *(gives her a large envelope)*: Here—hide it!

(She hides it in her bosom. There is a sound of the door being pulled, followed by a knock.)

AXEL *(to THE MOTHER, in anger)*: Why did you lock the doors? What excuse can we offer now?

THE MOTHER: Keep quiet!

AXEL: You are a fool! . . . Open the door! —Or I'll open it myself! Out of my way! *(He opens the door.)*

GERDA *(enters, looking disturbed and dejected)*: Why did you lock the door?

THE MOTHER: Because it has a way of opening of itself, and I am tired of closing it every time anybody goes in or out. —Now . . . shouldn't we discuss how you are going to furnish your apartment, now that you are going to settle down here? That is what you plan to do, isn't it?

GERDA: I presume we have to. . . . It's immaterial to me. What do you say, Axel?

AXEL: Why, yes—no question about our being comfortable here—and it will be pleasant for your mother, too, since we all get along so well together. . . .

GERDA: But where is Mama going to sleep?

THE MOTHER: In here, my child, in here. I'll just put in a bed.

AXEL: Are you going to put a bed in here, in the drawing room, Élise?

GERDA *(pricks up her ears on hearing AXEL address her mother by her first name)*: Do you call Mother . . .

AXEL: I mean Mother. —But we'll find a way out, don't worry. . . . We have to help one another, and what Mother will pay us, we can live on. . . .

GERDA *(brightening)*: And then I'll have someone to help me with the household chores. . . .

THE MOTHER: Certainly, my child—but I refuse to do the dishes!

GERDA: Why, that is out of the question! —Yes, I think it will all work out very well—as long as I can have my husband to myself! I won't let anyone even look at him! That was the trouble at that *pension,* and that is why our trip was cut short. . . . And if anyone should ever try to take him from me, she'll die! There—I have said it!

THE MOTHER: Now let us go in and start to arrange the furniture. . . .

AXEL (*looking meaningfully and fixedly at* THE MOTHER): Yes, and Gerda can start in here. . . .

GERDA: Why should I . . . ? I don't like to be left alone in here. . . . I won't feel really at home until we have moved in. . . .

AXEL: Since you are afraid of the dark, let us all three go in together. . . .

(*All three go inside.*)

(*The curtain falls for a brief instant.*)

•   •   •

SCENE
TWO

The stage is empty. Outside, a wind is blowing, and it can be heard whining past the windows and through the parlor stove. The door in the rear starts to slam, sheets of paper from the writing table whirl around the room, the palm on the pedestal is shaken violently, a portrait falls from the wall. Then FREDRIK'S *voice is heard calling, "Mama!" and, immediately afterward, "Close the window!" Then there is a pause. The rocking chair starts to rock.*

THE MOTHER *(enters furiously, reading a sheet of paper that she holds in her hand)*: What is this? *(Her eyes are suddenly riveted on the rocking chair; she looks frightened.)* The chair is rocking! . . .

AXEL *(follows her in)*: What is the matter? Is it the will? What does it say? Let me read!

THE MOTHER: Close the door! We'll be swept off our feet! But I must open a window to get rid of this odor! No— it was not his will—it was a letter to Fredrik, in which he maligns me—and you!

AXEL: Let me read it!

THE MOTHER: No—you will only be poisoned by it—I'm tearing it up! What luck that it didn't fall into Fredrik's hands. . . . *(She tears up the letter and throws the pieces into the parlor stove.)* Think of it: he has risen from the dead and is speaking from the grave—he is not dead! I can't stay here. . . . He writes that I murdered him. . . . I didn't, I didn't! He died of apoplexy—the doctor said so in his certificate. . . . And he says a lot of other

things, too—and they are all lies! He says that I ruined
him! . . . Listen, Axel, you must see to it that we get
out of this apartment—the sooner the better! I can't
endure it here! Promise me that you will! —Look, look
at the rocking chair!

AXEL: It's the draft that is doing it!

THE MOTHER: Let us get away from here! Promise me!

AXEL: I can't promise you! I expected that there would be
an inheritance—that's what you dangled before me—or
else I would not have married. . . . Now we have to make
the best of things as they are, and you have to treat
me like a son-in-law who has been tricked, cheated, and—
ruined! We have to stick together in order to live; we
have to save, and you have to help us!

THE MOTHER: You don't mean that I am to be used as a
servant in my own home, do you? That's something I will
never be!

AXEL: Necessity has no laws. . . .

THE MOTHER: You are a scoundrel, that's what you are!

AXEL: Take care, you old witch!

THE MOTHER (*contemptuously*): Your servant! The idea!

AXEL: At least you won't feel the pinch that your maids
had to endure—having to starve and freeze! . . .

THE MOTHER: I still have my annuity. . . .

AXEL: That won't pay even for a room in an attic, but
here it will help to pay the rent, if we remain. . . . And if
you don't stay, I'll pack up and get out!

THE MOTHER: You mean you would leave Gerda? Then
you have never loved her!

AXEL: You ought to know that better than I. . . . You
rooted her out of my mind, pushed her out—except from
the bed chamber, where you allowed her to stay—and,
if we should have a child, you would take that away
from her, too. . . . She is still in ignorance of it all, but
she is beginning to wake up from her sleep. And when
her eyes are opened, take care!

THE MOTHER: Axel! We have to stick together! We must
not be separated! I could never live by myself! I'll submit to anything—but I will not sleep on that chaise
longue! . . .

AXEL: No! I will not have the drawing room used as a
bed chamber. Now you know!

THE MOTHER: Then let me get another chaise longue. . . .

AXEL: No, we can't afford it; and this one is attractive enough. . . .

THE MOTHER: Ugh! It looks like a bloody slaughter bench!

AXEL: Such nonsense! But if you don't like it, then nothing remains for you but to live alone in some room in an attic—or in a poorhouse—and—go to prayer meetings!

THE MOTHER: I promise!

AXEL: You are wise!

(Silence.)

THE MOTHER: Just imagine, he writes to Fredrik that he was murdered!

AXEL: There is more than one way to murder . . . and *your* way of doing it had the advantage of falling outside the penal law!

THE MOTHER: Why don't you say *our* way? For you were an accomplice when you forced him into a violent rage and brought him to despair. . . .

AXEL: He stood in my way and refused to step aside—so I had to give him a push. . . .

THE MOTHER: The only thing I hold against you is that you tempted me and persuaded me to leave my home. . . . And I shall never forget that evening—the first one I spent in your house—when we sat at the festive table and suddenly heard those frightful cries from below. . . . We thought they came from the prison yard or the insane asylum. . . . Do you remember? . . . But it was he who was moving about down there in the tobacco patch, in the dark, and the rain, crying hysterically because he had lost his wife and children. . . .

AXEL: Why do you bring this up just now? And how do you know it was he?

THE MOTHER: He speaks of it in his letter!

AXEL: Well, why should we let ourselves be concerned about that? *He* was no angel. . . .

THE MOTHER: No, he was not, but sometimes he showed that he had human feelings. . . . Yes—more than you have!

AXEL: Your sympathies are beginning to make a complete about-face. . . .

THE MOTHER: Now, don't get angry! We have to keep calm, you know. . . .

AXEL: So we do . . . or we are doomed. . . .

(From inside is heard a hoarse shouting.)

THE MOTHER: What is that? Do you hear? It is he. . . .

AXEL *(brutally)*: Which he?

(THE MOTHER *stands listening.)*

AXEL: Who is it? The boy? I suppose he has been drinking again. . . .

THE MOTHER: Is it Fredrik? It sounded so like *him*, I thought . . . I'll never be able to bear this! What is the matter with him now, I wonder?

AXEL: Go in and find out! I suppose the scamp is drunk!

THE MOTHER: Is that a way to talk? After all, he is my son.

AXEL: Yes, he is that—after all. *(He looks at his watch.)*

THE MOTHER: Why are you looking at your watch? Aren't you going to stay for supper?

AXEL: No, thanks. I don't feel like drinking insipid tea or eating rancid anchovies—or porridge. And, besides, I have to go to a meeting this evening.

THE MOTHER: What sort of meeting?

AXEL: Business matters that are none of your business! Are you trying to act the rôle of stepmother now?

THE MOTHER: Are you going to leave your wife alone the first night you are in your home?

AXEL: That is none of your business, either!

THE MOTHER: Now I know what is in store for me—and my children! Now comes the unmasking. . . .

AXEL: So it does!

(The curtain falls for a fleeting moment.)

• • •

SCENE
THREE

The setting is the same. From outside can be heard the Berceuse from Godard's Jocelyn. GERDA *is seated at the writing table. There is a long pause.*

FREDRIK *(enters)*: Are you alone?

GERDA: Yes. Mama is in the kitchen.

FREDRIK: Then—where is Axel?

GERDA: He went to a meeting. . . . Sit down and keep me company, Frederik. Let us talk!

FREDRIK *(seats himself)*: Yes . . . I don't think we ever have had a talk—we avoided each other—there seemed to be no sympathy between us. . . .

GERDA: You always sided with Father, and I with Mother.

FREDRIK: Perhaps you will change now. . . . Did you really know your father?

GERDA: What a strange question! But, to tell the truth, I saw him only through Mother's eyes. . . .

FREDRIK: But couldn't you see that he was fond of you?

GERDA: Why did he try to prevent my engagement, then? Why did he want me to break it off?

FREDRIK: Because he didn't think Axel was the right man for you.

GERDA: And for that he was punished when Mother left him!

FREDRIK: Could it have been your husband who induced her to leave?

GERDA: It was both he and I! We wanted him to experience how it felt to be separated—as he wanted to separate Axel and me.

FREDRIK: And that is what shortened his life. . . . And,

believe me, there was nothing he wanted more than to
see you happy!

GERDA: You stayed with him that time. . . . What did he
say? How did he take it?

FREDRIK: I couldn't begin to tell you how deeply he suffered. . . .

GERDA: What did he say about Mama?

FREDRIK: Nothing . . . But—having seen what I have seen—
I shall never get married!

(There is a silence.)

Are you happy, Gerda?

GERDA: Yes, I am. Having found the man I had been waiting for, I am happy.

FREDRIK: Why does your husband leave you alone on your
first night home?

GERDA: He is out on business—he has gone to a meeting. . . .

FREDRIK: At a restaurant?

GERDA: What did you say? Are you sure?

FREDRIK: I thought you knew. . . .

GERDA *(puts her head in her hands and weeps)*: Oh, God!
Oh, my God!

FREDRIK: Forgive me for hurting you!

GERDA: Yes, you hurt me, you hurt me! Oh, I want to die!

FREDRIK: Why didn't you stay away longer?

GERDA: He was disturbed about some business matters—
and he was anxious to see Mama. He doesn't like to be
away from her, you know. . . .

(They exchange glances.)

FREDRIK: Oh, I see.

(There is a silence.)

Did you enjoy your trip otherwise?

GERDA: Oh, yes!

FREDRIK: Poor sister!

GERDA: Why do you say that?

FREDRIK: Well, you know how inquisitive Mother is, and
when it comes to using the telephone, she can use it as
no one else can!

GERDA: What are you saying? Has she been spying?

FREDRIK: When doesn't she? I should not be surprised if she were standing behind one of the doors now, listening to what we are saying. . . .

GERDA: You always think bad thoughts about Mother. . . .

FREDRIK: And you, nothing but good! How can you? You know how she is. . . .

GERDA: No, I don't! I don't care to know. . . .

FREDRIK: That's another thing—you don't want to know! It is in your interest not to. . . .

GERDA: Be quiet! I know I am walking in my sleep, and I don't wish to be awakened! If I were, I wouldn't be able to live!

FREDRIK: Don't you think that we all walk in our sleep? I am studying law, as you know—judicial proceedings. I read about hardened criminals who are unable to explain just why they committed their crimes . . . and who thought they did nothing wrong—until they were discovered . . . and woke up! If they are not dreaming, it must be that they walk in their sleep!

GERDA: Let me be asleep! I know I shall wake up some day—but I hope it will be a long time before I do. Ugh! All this—all these things that I know nothing about, and yet can suspect! Do you remember when we were children—and people called us petty and mean when we told the truth. . . . "You are so mean," they would tell me, whenever I declared that something which was bad was bad. . . . And so I taught myself to say nothing. Then people praised me for my good behavior! In time I got into the habit of saying what I didn't mean—and soon I was prepared to go out into life.

FREDRIK: It is true that we ought to overlook our neighbors' little faults and weaknesses—but it can easily lead to our becoming two-faced and prone to flatter people. . . . It is difficult to know just how to act! There are times when it is our duty to speak out! . . .

GERDA: You must not say any more!

FREDRIK: I won't.

(There is a pause.)

GERDA: No—I like you to talk—but not about *that!* I can hear you thinking through the silence. . . . When human beings get together, they talk, talk endlessly, merely to conceal their thoughts—to forget, to deaden their feelings. . . . They are not averse to hearing some tale about others—but when it comes to their own secrets or troubles, they like to keep them to themselves.

FREDRIK: Poor Gerda!

GERDA: Do you know what the greatest of all sorrows is? *(Pause.)* The greatest sorrow is to discover how empty happiness can be!

FREDRIK: There you spoke the truth!

GERDA: I am freezing! Let us have a little heat!

FREDRIK: Are you frozen, too?

GERDA: I have always been freezing, always hungry!

FREDRIK: You, too? This is a strange house! If I should go out and bring in some wood now, we'd never hear the end of it—not for a week or more!

GERDA: There may be some logs in the fireplace already. . . . Mama will sometimes put some in—just to fool us.

FREDRIK *(goes over to the parlor stove and opens the shutters)*: Yes—there really are a few puny logs here! . . . *(Pause.)* But what is this? A letter—a torn-up letter! We can use it to light the fire with. . . .

GERDA: Fredrik, don't make a fire! We'll get nothing but nagging—and we'll never hear the end of it! Come and sit down again, and let us talk.

(FREDRIK resumes his seat; he places the letter on the table beside him. There is another silence.)

GERDA: Have you any idea why Father hated Axel the way he did?

FREDRIK: Yes. Axel came and took both his daughter and his wife away, and left him in loneliness. And he also noticed that someone else was given better cuts and portions at table than he was. You three locked yourselves in the drawing room, where you played the piano and read aloud—but always the sort of literature our father didn't like. He was ejected from his own house, eaten out of it! And that is why he took to drinking!

GERDA: We didn't realize what we were doing! Poor Father! But there is one thing we can be glad of: that our parents had an unimpeachably good name and reputation! For that we can be thankful. . . . Do you remember our parents' silver wedding anniversary—the speeches that were made —the verses they received?

FREDRIK: I remember. . . . But to toast and do honor to a marriage as having been one of great happiness when it has been nothing but a sham, a cat and dog fight— that is to make nothing but a mockery out of marriage!

GERDA: Fredrik!

FREDRIK: I can't help it . . . but you know yourself what kind of life they led together. . . . Don't you remember the time that Mama tried to jump out of the window and we had to hold her back?

GERDA: Don't remind me of it!

FREDRIK: Why she did it, we never knew. . . . And while the divorce proceedings were going on—when I was look- ing after Father—he seemed to be about to confide in me several times . . . but he couldn't get the words out. . . . I sometimes dream about him. . . .

GERDA: I do, too! And when I see him then, he looks only thirty. . . . He looks at me in a friendly and meaningful way, but I can't make out what he wants. . . . Occasional- ly Mama is there. . . . He shows no ill feeling toward her—for he loved her, despite everything, to the very last. . . . You remember how beautifully he spoke of her at their silver wedding—*despite everything.* . . .

FREDRIK: Despite everything! It was a little too much— and still much too little.

GERDA: But it was beautiful to hear! No matter what— there is one thing that she deserves credit for. She looked after her home!

FREDRIK: Well—that may be argued! Did she?

GERDA: What's that you say?

FREDRIK: You see, now you are on *her* side again! The moment we discuss the household, you are as one. . . . It's like freemasonry—or the camorra! Even when I have asked old Margret about the frugality of the house- hold—and Margret is my friend—when I have asked her why I never felt satisfied after a meal, she, too, al- though she is generally talkative, keeps her mouth shut and gets angry! Can you explain that?

GERDA (*curtly*): No!

FREDRIK: I can hear that you are a freemason, too!

GERDA: I haven't the faintest idea what you mean!

FREDRIK: Sometimes I wonder whether Father didn't fall victim of this camorra, which he must have discovered!

GERDA: There are times when you talk foolishly. . . .

FREDRIK: I remember that Father sometimes used the word "camorra" in jest. But toward the end he never did. . . .

GERDA: It's frightful how cold it is in here—cold as the grave. . . .

FREDRIK: I'm going to light a fire, come what may! *(He picks up the torn letter, at first unreflecting; then suddenly he finds himself reading it, and his eyes open wide.)* What is this? *(Pause. He reads:)* "To my son"! . . . It is a letter from Father! *(Pause.)* It's written to me! *(He continues reading, then he collapses into a chair and reads in silence.)*

GERDA: What is it you are reading? What does it say?

FREDRIK: This is frightful! *(Pause.)* It is absolutely horrible!

GERDA: Tell me—what does it say?

　　(There is a pause.)

FREDRIK: This is too horrible! . . . *(To* GERDA.*)* This letter is from my dead father—to me! *(He resumes reading.)* Now I have been awakened from my sleep! *(He throws himself on the chaise longue and lets out hysterical screams of anguish, while he stuffs the letter in his pocket.)*

GERDA *(kneels at his side)*: What is it, Fredrik? Tell me what it is! Brother dear, are you ill? Tell me, tell me!

FREDRIK *(sits up)*: I don't want to live any longer!

GERDA: Please tell me, tell me . . .

FREDRIK: It is too unbelievable! *(He collects himself and gets up from the chaise longue.)*

GERDA: It may not have been true!

FREDRIK *(angered)*: Oh, no, he would not lie from his grave!

GERDA: He may have been deceived by sickly delusions. . . .

FREDRIK: Camorra! There it is again! And, just because of that, I shall tell you everything! . . . Now listen!

GERDA: I seem to know it all beforehand—but I won't believe it—no!

FREDRIK: You won't believe it! But whether you do or not,

you are going to hear it now! She, who gave us life, is a thief of the very worst kind!

GERDA: Oh, no!

FREDRIK: She kept a part of the household money; she made out fraudulent bills; she bought the poorest quality and charged the top-quality price; she ate her own meals in the kitchen before we had ours and gave us diluted soup and warmed-up food; she skimmed the cream off the milk—and that is why we two children are misfits today, always hungry and sick; she stole some of the money for the firewood and let us freeze. . . . When Father discovered this, he warned her. She promised to mend her ways, but she kept on with her cheating and hit upon substitutes, such as soy and cayenne pepper!

GERDA: I don't believe a word you say!

FREDRIK: Camorra! But now I'm coming to the most horrible of her crimes! That filthy swine who is now your husband, Gerda, has never been in love with you! He is your mother's lover!

GERDA: Oh! Oh!

FREDRIK: When Father found this out, and found out that your husband was borrowing money from your mother—from *our* mother—the blackguard covered up his infamy by proposing to you! There you have the story in broad strokes! What the details are like, you can well imagine!

GERDA (*crying into her handkerchief*): I knew this before—and still I didn't . . . It didn't really penetrate my mind—for it was more than I could endure!

FREDRIK: But what can we do now to save you from this debasement?

GERDA: I must go away!

FREDRIK: But where?

GERDA: I don't know!

FREDRIK: Therefore, we must wait and see what happens next.

GERDA: One is defenseless against one's own mother. . . . We have to show her reverence. . . .

FREDRIK: Like the devil!

GERDA: Don't say such things!

FREDRIK: She is as cunning as a beast, but her egotism often blinds her. . . .

GERDA: Let us get away from here!

FREDRIK: Where? No, let us stay—until the blackguard drives her out of the house! —Keep quiet! I hear the wretch coming. . . . Be quiet! Now, Gerda, we two must make a pact—let's be freemasons! I'll give you the watchword: "He struck you on your wedding night!"

GERDA: Remind me of it often—or I'll forget it! I would like so terribly to forget it!

FREDRIK: Our life has been ruined. . . . Nothing to revere, nothing to look up to . . . To forget is impossible. . . . Let us devote ourselves to clearing our father's memory, and to repairing our lives. . . .

GERDA: And seeking justice!

FREDRIK: Say revenge!

(AXEL *enters.*)

GERDA *(acting gay)*: Well, here you are! Did you enjoy the meeting? Did you get anything good to eat?

AXEL: The meeting was canceled.

GERDA: Did you say it was closed?

AXEL: I said it was canceled!

GERDA: Well, are you going to look after the household from now on?

AXEL: You are acting so curiously tonight—but then Fredrik must be an amusing companion. . . .

GERDA: We have been playing freemasons. . . .

AXEL: Watch out for that! . . .

FREDRIK *(goes over and sits down in the rocking chair)*: Then let's play camorra instead—or vendetta!

AXEL *(uncomfortable)*: You talk so mysteriously, you two! What's going on here? Secrets?

GERDA: You don't let us share *your* secrets, do you? Or perhaps you haven't any?

AXEL: What's been going on here? Has anyone been here?

FREDRIK: Gerda and I have been communicating with the beyond. . . . We have had a visit from a departed spirit. . . .

AXEL: Don't you think we might put an end to the jesting? —Or it might lead to unpleasantness. . . . Although I must say it is becoming to you, Gerda, to be in a happy mood. Usually you are gloomy and glum. . . .

(He tries to give her a pat on the cheek, but she draws away from him.)

You are not afraid of me, are you?

GERDA *(evades him)*: Not in the least! There are feelings that resemble fear but are something else; there are gestures that are more telling than facial expressions, and words that hide what neither gestures nor facial expressions can reveal. . . .

(AXEL, taken aback, fingers the books in the bookcase.)

FREDRIK *(gets up from the rocking chair, which keeps rocking until THE MOTHER enters)*: Here comes Mother with the porridge!

AXEL: Are we to . . .

THE MOTHER *(enters. Seeing the rocking chair in motion, she seems horrified, but calms herself)*: Won't you all come and have some porridge?

AXEL: No, thanks! If it is oatmeal porridge, you can give it to the hunting dogs, if you have any. If it is rye meal porridge, use it as a poultice. . . .

THE MOTHER: We are poor and have to save. . . .

AXEL: With twenty thousand, you can't call yourself poor!

FREDRIK: Yes, if you lend it to someone who doesn't pay it back!

AXEL: What did he say? Is the boy mad?

FREDRIK: No—but perhaps he has been!

THE MOTHER *(beckoning)*: Are you coming?

GERDA: Come, let us go in. . . . Courage, gentlemen! I'll give you both a beefsteak and a sandwich. . . .

THE MOTHER: You will . . . ?

GERDA: Yes, I—and in my house. . . .

THE MOTHER *(in a tone of sarcasm mixed with trepidation)*: That sounds intriguing!

GERDA *(with a gesture in the direction of the door)*: If you please, gentlemen!

AXEL *(to THE MOTHER)*: What is all this?

THE MOTHER: There are snakes in the grass!

AXEL: It sounds that way!

GERDA *(beckoning)*: If you please, gentlemen. . . .

(They all move toward the door.)

THE MOTHER *(to* AXEL*)*: Did you notice that the rocking chair was moving? *His* rocking chair!

AXEL: No, I didn't. But I noticed something else!

(THE MOTHER *leaves, frightened.)*

(The curtain falls for a few fleeting moments.)

. . .

SCENE
FOUR

The setting is the same. The strains of
the waltz "Il me disait" by Ferraris are
heard. GERDA *sits reading a book.*

THE MOTHER *(enters)*: Do you recall this tune?

GERDA: The waltz? Yes!

THE MOTHER: Your wedding waltz, which I danced until early in the morning!

GERDA: I . . . Where is Axel?

THE MOTHER: I don't care where he is.

GERDA: Oh, so! So you have quarreled already?

(There is a silence, with an exchange of glances.)

THE MOTHER: What are you reading, my child?

GERDA: The cookbook. —But why doesn't it say how long a thing must cook?

THE MOTHER *(embarrassed)*: Well, you see, it varies. People have such different tastes. One person cooks a thing one way, another person does it in a different way.

GERDA: I can't see why. . . . A meal has to be served fresh from the stove, otherwise it's warmed up—and that means it is not fresh. Yesterday, for instance, it took you three hours to cook a grouse; and for the first hour the whole apartment was permeated with a delightful odor of wild game. But then it suddenly grew silent in the kitchen— and, when the grouse was served, it lacked fragrance, and it tasted of nothing so much as mere air! Can you explain that?

THE MOTHER *(embarrassed)*: I can't understand that at all!

GERDA: Can you explain why there was no gravy served with it? Where did the gravy disappear to? Who got the gravy?

355

THE MOTHER (*brazenly, obstinately*): I haven't the faintest idea!

GERDA: But I have been making a few inquiries here and there, and I have found out something. . . .

THE MOTHER (*interrupts her*): I know all that, and you don't have to teach me anything! But now I'll teach you how to keep house. . . .

GERDA: You mean how to use soy and cayenne pepper. . . . I know how to use them both, and how to choose dishes that nobody will eat when you give a party, so that there will be enough left over for the next day; and I know how to give a party when the cupboard is full of leftovers —all that I already know . . . and that is why *I* am taking charge of the household from now on!

THE MOTHER (*in a rage*): You expect *me* to be *your servant!*

GERDA: I'll be yours, and you be mine—we must help each other! —Here comes Axel. . . .

AXEL (*enters, carrying a heavy walking-stick*): Well, how do you like the chaise longue?

THE MOTHER: Oh, it will do. . . .

AXEL (*threateningly*): Isn't is comfortable? Is there anything wrong with it?

THE MOTHER: Now I begin to understand. . . .

AXEL: You *do,* do you? . . . At any rate, since Gerda and I don't get enough to eat in this house, Gerda and I intend to keep house for ourselves.

THE MOTHER: And what about me, then?

AXEL: You are as big as a barrel—you don't need very much. . . . You ought to lose a little weight for the sake of your health—as we have had to do. . . . But now, Gerda, will you step outside for a moment, and in the meantime we'll get a fire going here in the stove. . . .

(GERDA *goes out.*)

THE MOTHER (*trembling with rage*): There is wood in the stove.

AXEL: No, there is not—there are a few sticks, but now you are going to bring in some logs. I want you to fill the stove full!

THE MOTHER (*tarries*): You want me to burn up my money!

AXEL: No—but you have to burn wood to get warmth! Now hurry up!

(THE MOTHER *lingers.*)

AXEL: One—two—three! *(He strikes the table with the stick.)*

THE MOTHER: I don't believe there is any wood left. . . .

AXEL: Either you are lying or you have stolen the money, because we ordered a fathom the day before yesterday.

THE MOTHER: Now I see what kind of man you are. . . .

AXEL *(seats himself in the rocking chair)*: You would have known it long ago, if your age and your experience hadn't duped me in my youth. . . . Speed it up now—go out for the wood, or I . . . *(He raises the stick.)*

(THE MOTHER *goes out and returns immediately with some wood.*)

AXEL: Now, make a real fire, and not one of those fake ones! One—two—three!

THE MOTHER: You look exactly like my husband now, sitting there in his rocking chair!

AXEL: Light the fire!

THE MOTHER *(now repressed, but still in a rage)*: I will, I will! *(Lights the fire.)*

AXEL: Now, you watch it while we go into the dining room and eat our dinner!

THE MOTHER: And what will I have for dinner?

AXEL: You get the porridge that Gerda has in the kitchen for you.

THE MOTHER: With blue skimmed milk . . .

AXEL: You had the cream—so that's only fair, isn't it?

THE MOTHER *(in a stifled voice)*: Then I am leaving. . . .

AXEL: If you try, I'll lock you in.

THE MOTHER: Then I'll jump out of the window!

AXEL: Go ahead, if you like! You ought to have done that a long time ago, and then the lives of four people might have been spared! Get the fire going now! Keep blowing on it! That's right! Now you sit here until we come back. . . . *(He gets up from the rocking chair and leaves.)*

(There is a pause. THE MOTHER *goes over and stops the rocking chair; after that she stands listening at the door; then she removes some of the logs from the stove and hides them under the chaise longue.* FREDRIK *enters. He is slightly inebriated.)*

THE MOTHER (*shrinks together*): Is that you?

FREDRIK (*seats himself in the rocking chair*): Yes.

THE MOTHER: Is anything wrong with you?

FREDRIK: Yes. I don't think I'll live much longer. . . .

THE MOTHER: You are just imagining it! —Don't keep rocking like that! . . . Look at me, I am already . . . well, I am not exactly young. . . . Still, with all the work I have to do, I go on living—and toiling and slaving for my children and my home, don't I?

FREDRIK: Ha! And a pelican giving her life blood! Zoology tells you that is a lie.

THE MOTHER: Have I ever given you reason to complain— have I ever?

FREDRIK: Listen to me, Mother! If I were absolutely sober, I would not give you a frank answer: I simply wouldn't have the strength. . . . But now I am going to tell you that I have read Father's letter, which you stole and then threw in the parlor stove. . . .

THE MOTHER: What's that you are saying? Which—what letter was that?

FREDRIK: You *have* to lie, don't you? I remember the first time you taught me to lie—I was scarcely able to talk. Do you remember?

THE MOTHER: No—I don't remember anything at all! —Stop rocking!

FREDRIK: And the first time you lied about me? I also remember that once, when I was a child, I hid under the piano—and just then a friend came to see you—and you sat and lied to her for three hours, while I had to listen to you!

THE MOTHER: That's a lie!

FREDRIK: But has it ever occurred to you why my health is so poor? I was never suckled—I had a nurse and was given a bottle. . . . And when I was a little older, she let me accompany her to her sister's—who was a prostitute! There I had to witness such secret goings-on as generally only dog owners treat children to, in the springtime and fall— out in the open air! When I told you—I was only four then—what I had seen in that house of lust and vice, you said it was a lie and beat me for it—although I had told the truth! Encouraged by your approval, this nursemaid initiated me into all kinds of secrets when I was only five years old. . . . *(He sobs.)* And then I was put on a starvation diet and had to freeze, along with Father and Gerda. Not until today did I find out that you were stealing the money that was given to you for the household and for the wood. . . . Look at me, you pelican—look at Gerda with her underdeveloped and sunken chest! How you murdered my father, you yourself know best! But driving a person to despair is a crime that the law does not punish. . . . How you have brought my sister to the brink of the grave, only you are aware of—but now she knows it, too!

THE MOTHER: Stop rocking! What is it that she knows?

FREDRIK: You know very well—but I can't say it! *(He sobs.)* It's terrible to have to say all this—but I must say it! I have a feeling that, as soon as I sober up, I'll shoot myself! . . . That is why I keep on drinking. . . . I don't dare sober up. . . .

THE MOTHER: Lie some more, why don't you?

FREDRIK: Once, when Father was angry, he said that you were one great fraud of nature—that, as a child, you learned to lie before you could speak and that you always neglected your duties for the sake of having a good time. And I remember the time when Gerda was sick and lay hovering between life and death, and you took off for the opera in the evening. . . . I can still hear your words: "Life is hard enough without making it too unbearable!" And I think of the summer you went to Paris with Father and spent three months there enjoying yourself, and spending so much money that Father got into debt! That summer Sister and I had to stay in the city, shut in with two servant girls in this apartment. . . . In your and Father's bedroom a fireman squatted with the chambermaid, and they slept in your bed. . . .

THE MOTHER: Why didn't you tell me all this before?

FREDRIK: Evidently you have forgotten that I did, and that you gave me a beating because I was gossiping, or lying—and you took me to task for both—for whenever you heard a word of truth you called it a lie!

THE MOTHER *(stalks around the room like a trapped wild beast)*: Never in my life have I heard a son talk like this to his mother!

FREDRIK: I admit it is a little unusual and quite contrary to nature. . . . I know it is—but for once it had to be said! You went about as if you were asleep, and nothing could wake you; therefore, nothing could change you, either. . . . Father used to say that, even if you were put on the torture rack, you would never acknowledge an error or confess that you had been lying.

THE MOTHER: Father! And do you think *he* didn't have any faults?

FREDRIK: He had some very great faults—but not as far as his relations with his wife and children were concerned! But there are some secrets in your marriage that I have long suspected but never dared to delve into. These are the secrets Father took with him to the grave—some of them, that is!

THE MOTHER: Have you had your say now?

FREDRIK: And now I am going to have a few more drinks. . . . I know I am never going to graduate; I place no faith in laws. Laws seem to be written by thieves and murderers for the purpose of acquitting the culprit. A truthful, trustworthy person is not acceptable as a witness; but two false witnesses are considered competent and have the power to condemn a man! At eleven-thirty my case is won—but half an hour later I have lost it: the wrong word, a mistake in spelling, a missing marginal notation is sufficient to send me innocent to prison. If I am compassionate toward a scoundrel, he takes revenge on me by suing me for slander or libel. My contempt for life, for humanity, for society, and for myself is so great that I don't think it worth the struggle to live. . . . (*He gets up and moves toward the door.*)

THE MOTHER: Don't leave me!

FREDRIK: Are you afraid to be in the dark?

THE MOTHER: My nerves are on edge!

FREDRIK: The two go together!

THE MOTHER: And that chair drives me mad! Those rockers always reminded me of two chopping-knives when he sat there in that chair . . . and hacked away at my heart. . . .

FREDRIK: You don't mean to say you have a heart? (*He starts to leave.*)

THE MOTHER: Don't go! I don't dare stay here—Axel is a scoundrel!

FREDRIK: I thought the same—until just now! Now I think

he has merely been a victim of your criminal inclinations. . . . Yes—it was he, because he was young, who was seduced!

THE MOTHER: You must have been out in bad company!

FREDRIK: Bad company, yes! I have never been in anything but bad company!

THE MOTHER: Don't leave me!

FREDRIK: Are you beginning to wake up!

THE MOTHER: Yes—now I am waking—as from a long, long sleep! It is horrible! Why couldn't someone have awakened me before?

FREDRIK: No one did—because no one could, I suppose! And, as long as no one could, I suppose you were not conscious of what you were doing!

THE MOTHER: Say those words again!

FREDRIK: I presume that you couldn't help being the way you were. . . .

THE MOTHER (*kisses his hand slavishly*): Speak to me some more!

FREDRIK: I haven't the strength any longer. . . . Yes, there is one thing I would like to ask of you: Don't remain here! It will only make things worse.

THE MOTHER: You are right! I shall go—out. . . .

FREDRIK: Poor Mama!

THE MOTHER: Do you feel compassion for me?

FREDRIK (*sobs*): Of course I do! How often haven't I said, "She is so mean that she is to be pitied!"

THE MOTHER: Thank you for saying that! Now go, Fredrik!

FREDRIK: Is there no way out of this?

THE MOTHER: No—it's the only way!

FREDRIK: Yes—it's the only way! It's the only way out!

(*There is a silence.* THE MOTHER *is alone. She stands for a long time with her arms folded across her chest. Then she walks over to the window and opens it. She looks out, then steps backward into the room and is about to jump when three knocks at the door, rear, cause her to change her mind.*)

THE MOTHER: Who is there? What was that? (*She closes the window.*) Come in!

(*The doors, rear, open.*)

Is anybody there?

(FREDRIK is heard sobbing hysterically, convulsively, inside.)

It is he—down in the tobacco patch! Isn't he really dead? What am I to do? Where am I to go?

(She hides behind the bureau-desk. Suddenly a gust of wind blows through the room, as before, and sheets of paper fly hither and thither.)

Close the window, Fredrik!

(A flowerpot is blown down.)

Close the window! I am freezing to death, and the fire is dying in the stove!

(She turns on all the electric lights and closes the doors, which open again a second later. The rocking chair starts to rock from the draft. She walks in circles around the room and finally throws herself, face down, on the chaise longue, burying her face in the pillows.)

(The curtain falls for a fleeting moment.)

o o o

SCENE FIVE

"Il me disait" is heard from outside. THE MOTHER is seen in the same position as before, her head buried in the pillows. GERDA enters with a bowl of porridge on a tray, which she puts down. Then she extinguishes all the electric lights but one.

THE MOTHER *(suddenly seems to awaken; rises)*: Don't put out the lights!

GERDA: Yes, we have to save.

THE MOTHER: Are you back so soon?

GERDA: Yes, he didn't think it was amusing when you were not with us.

THE MOTHER *(her eyes gleaming with vanity)*: You see!

GERDA: Here is your supper. . . .

THE MOTHER: I am not hungry.

GERDA: Oh, yes, you are—but you don't like porridge!

THE MOTHER: Yes, occasionally I do.

GERDA: No, you don't. However, it's not for your hunger but for your malicious smile every time you tormented us with oatmeal porridge. . . . You reveled in our misery— and you fed the same porridge to your hunting dog!

THE MOTHER: I can't stand skimmed milk—it gives me the shivers!

GERDA: After you skimmed off the cream for your morning coffee! What's sauce for the goose, and so on! *(She puts the porridge on a small table.)* Now let me see you eat!

THE MOTHER: I can't!

GERDA *(reaches down and pulls out the logs from under the chaise longue)*: If you don't, I'll tell Axel you have been stealing wood!

THE MOTHER: Axel . . . he missed my company, didn't he? He wouldn't harm me. . . . Do you remember how he danced with me at your wedding? . . . To the tune of *"Il me disait"!* Do you hear it? (*She hums along with the second reprise, which is now being played.*)

GERDA: It would be a little more discreet of you not to remind me of your outrageous behavior. . . .

THE MOTHER: And I had verses dedicated to me, too, and the nicest flowers were the ones I received!

GERDA: Keep quiet!

THE MOTHER: Would you like me to recite the verses for you? I know them by heart. . . . "In Ginnistan . . ." "Ginnistan" is a Persian word for the garden of paradise where lovely *peri* live, breathing fragrant perfumes. . . . The *peri* are elves or fairies so created that the longer they live, the younger they grow. . . .

GERDA: God in heaven, are you laboring under the delusion that you are a *peri*? . . .

THE MOTHER: Certainly, don't the verses say so? . . . Yes, and Uncle Victor has asked me to marry him. . . . What would you say if I should . . . ?

GERDA: Poor Mama! You are still walking in your sleep, as the rest of us have been doing, but will you never wake up? Don't you know that people are laughing at you? Don't you realize that Axel has only scorn for you?

THE MOTHER: Scorn—for me? I think he is always more polite to me than to you. . . .

GERDA: Even when he raised his stick and threatened you?

THE MOTHER: Threatened me? It was you he threatened, my dear child!

GERDA: Mother, have you lost your mind?

THE MOTHER: Didn't he miss my company this evening? Didn't he? We always find so many things to talk about; he is the only one who really understands me—and you are nothing but a child. . . .

GERDA (*takes her by the shoulders and shakes her*): In God's name, wake up, Mother!

THE MOTHER: You are not grown up yet, but I am your mother and I have fed you with my blood. . . .

GERDA: You never did—you put a nursing bottle with nipple of rubber in my mouth; when I was a little older I had to steal food from the cupboard—but there woul be nothing to eat except stale rye bread, and I would eat that with some mustard on it; when it burned my throat, I would cool it with a swallow of vinegar. . . . The bread-basket and the cruet stand—that was my cupboard. . . .

THE MOTHER: Oh, so you were already stealing when you were a child! You certainly were a nice one—and you are not even ashamed to tell about it! To think that I have sacrificed myself for such children!

GERDA (*crying*): I could forgive you everything . . . but that you ruined my life, *that* I can never forgive. . . . And—yes, he was my life—because it was only when I met him that I began to live!

THE MOTHER: How can I help it that he preferred me to you? Perhaps he found me—how shall I say?—more entrancing, more charming. . . . Yes, he had better taste than your father. . . . *He* never knew how to appreciate me—not until he found that he had rivals. . . .

(There is a pounding at the door: three separate knocks.)

Who is that pounding on the door?

GERDA: I won't let you say anything bad about Father! I am afraid my life won't last long enough for me to atone for all the misery I have caused him—but I shall make you suffer for it—you who egged me on against him! Do you remember how—when I was a tiny little child—you taught me to speak malicious, sarcastic words that I didn't even comprehend? He was understanding enough not to punish me for those arrows, for he realized all too well who had bent the bow! Do you remember when you taught me to lie to him, saying that I needed some new books for school, and how you and I divided the money after we had deceived him? Do you? How shall I ever be able to forget all these things? Is there no potion strong enough to still one's memory without snuffing out life? I only wish I had the strength to go away from it all—but I, like Fredrik, am helpless. . . . We are weak and vacillating victims—your victims—you hardened woman, who haven't the courage to suffer for your own crimes!

THE MOTHER: Do you know what kind of childhood *I* had? Can you imagine what my home was like—what evil things I learned there? It seems to be something we inherit—something that originates far back in the family—but where, from whom? From our original parents, we were told in children's books; and that seems to fit. . . . And so, don't put the blame on me—then I won't put the blame on my parents—who in turn could cast the blame onto their parents, and so on, without end! Besides, it is the same in all families. . . . The only difference is that not all outsiders are made aware of it. . . .

GERDA: If that is so, I don't care to live. . . . But if I must, I want to pass through this miserable life without being able to see or hear . . . and with a hope that a better life may follow. . . .

THE MOTHER: You are so overwrought, my dear. . . . When you have children, you will have other things to think about. . . .

GERDA: I won't have any children. . . .

THE MOTHER: How do you know?

GERDA: The doctor told me.

THE MOTHER: He is mistaken. . . .

GERDA: Another lie! I am barren, abortive, just as Fredrik is, and that is why I don't care to live. . . .

THE MOTHER: You talk nonsense!

GERDA: If it were possible for me to do something evil, which I have an urge to do, you would not be alive! Why is it so hard for me to do something mean and despicable? Whenever I raise my hand against you, I strike a blow against myself!

(*The music comes to an abrupt end.* FREDRIK *is heard sobbing hysterically inside.*)

THE MOTHER: Now he has been drinking again!

GERDA: Poor Fredrik, yes . . . what is he to do? . . .

FREDRIK (*enters. He is in a state of semi-inebriation.*): I think —I think it's . . . There seems to be smoke in the kitchen!

THE MOTHER: What are you saying?

FREDRIK: I think— I . . . I think—it's burning. . . .

THE MOTHER: Burning! What are you saying?

FREDRIK: Yes . . . I think—I think it's burning!

THE MOTHER (*rushes over and opens the doors in the rear and is met by a fiery red glare*): Fire! How will we get out? . . . I don't want to burn! . . . I don't want to burn! (*She runs wildly hither and thither.*)

GERDA *(embracing her brother)*: Fredrik! Try to get out! There is a fire! Let us get out!

FREDRIK: I haven't the strength!

GERDA: Get out! You must!

FREDRIK: Where? How? . . . No—I don't care. . . .

THE MOTHER: I'd rather jump out—out the window. . . . *(She flings the balcony door open and plunges to the pavement below.)*

GERDA: Oh! God in heaven help us!

FREDRIK: It was the only way out for her!

GERDA: You started the fire!

FREDRIK: Yes—what else was there to do? There was no other way out! Was there? . . .

GERDA: No! . . . Everything had to burn—or we would never have gotten out of this! Hold me in your arms, Fredrik! Hold me tight, tight, brother dear! . . . I am so happy now—happier than I have ever been! . . . It is getting brighter. . . . Poor Mama—who was so mean and selfish. . . .

FREDRIK: My dear sister! . . . Poor Mama! . . . Do you feel how warm it is now—how warm and comforting? Now I am no longer freezing. . . . Can you hear it crackling in there? The fire is consuming all that's decrepit—all that is stale and decayed—all that is foul and ugly and mean. . . .

GERDA: Hold me tight, brother dear. . . . We shan't burn— we'll merely suffocate from the smoke—don't you feel the fragrant odor—it's the palms that are burning—and Father's wreath—his laurel wreath—now the linen closet is burning—you can smell the lavender. . . . And now—the roses. . . . My little brother, don't be afraid—don't be afraid—it will soon be over. . . . You must not weaken— you must stand up straight, my dear, dear brother. . . . Poor Mama—she was so mean! Hold me tighter—hug me tight, as Father used to say! . . . This reminds me of Christmas Eve, when we had dinner in the kitchen—the only day we got enough to eat, as Father used to say. . . . Do you smell the fragrance—it's the buffet that is burning now—with the tea and coffee—and the spices, the cinnamon, and the cloves. . . .

FREDRIK *(in tragic ecstasy)*: Has summer come? The clover is blossoming—the summer vacation has begun. . . . Do you remember when we went down to the pier to look at the white steamers and to salute them when they had been freshly painted and lay waiting for us? Then Father was really happy—then he really lived! he said—and we no longer had to worry about compositions and examinations! That's the way life should always be, he said—and I think it was he who was the pelican, for he went without things for our sake—his trousers were always unpressed, and the velvet collar on his overcoat was threadbare, while we were dressed like children of the nobility. . . . Gerda, hurry up, Gerda, the bell on the steamer just struck— Mama is sitting in the forward saloon—no, no—she is not coming with us, poor Mama—she is not with us. . . . Can she have been left ashore? . . . Where is she? I don't see her. . . . We can't enjoy ourselves without Mama. . . . There she comes now! . . . Now our long summer vacation is starting! . . .

(There is a silence. The doors in the rear open, and the red glare is strongly visible. FREDRIK *and* GERDA *fall to the floor.)*

CURTAIN